More Praise for *A Banker's Journey*

"Edmond Safra was truly unique, founding four banks on three continents—all of them successful. To start Republic National Bank of New York and grow it into a thriving institution in one of the world's most competitive markets was an extraordinary achievement, and he repeated this success again and again around the world. He was the rare combination of conservative banker and brilliant, thoughtful risk-taker. Edmond cared deeply for his staff and his clients, and, perhaps above all, he changed the lives of millions of people through the help he gave to schools, hospitals, and other causes. He was inspirational and an example to us all, and I am delighted that his story is finally being told."

—SIR JOHN BOND, Group Chairman
HSBC Holdings (1998–2006)

"Upon meeting Edmond Safra for the first time fifty years ago, I was immediately struck by his complete and total dedication to the safety and security of his bank's depositors and also by his deep and sincere admiration of America as a land of opportunity. Although many consider him to have been the greatest banker of the twentieth century, he never lost his sense of modesty nor his belief that success must be built upon trustworthiness and compassion. This is a book that must be read."

—ARTHUR LEVITT JR., Chairman of the Securities
and Exchange Commission (1993–2001)

"Commercial banking was Edmond's heritage and his consuming passion. At an age when most of us were thinking about what college we'd like to enter, he was sent out pretty much on his own to explore business opportunities in both Europe and America. He built his banks, made his money, and, not so incidentally, established his name the old-fashioned way. But when it came to a decision, Edmond could match any modern entrepreneur. Through it all, Edmond was strongly motivated by a more personal responsibility that couldn't be counted in numbers."

—PAUL VOLCKER, Chair of the Federal Reserve (1979–1987)

A BANKER'S JOURNEY

—————————— HOW ——————————

EDMOND J. SAFRA

BUILT A GLOBAL FINANCIAL EMPIRE

DANIEL GROSS

RADIUS BOOK GROUP

New York

Radius Book Group
A Division of Diversion Publishing Corp.
New York, NY
www.RadiusBookGroup.com

For more information, email info@radiusbookgroup.com.

First edition: August 2022
Hardcover ISBN: 978-1-63576-785-8
eBook ISBN: 978-1-63576-789-6

Manufactured in the United States of America

1 3 5 7 9 10 8 6 4 2

Cover design by Jen Huppert
Interior design by Neuwirth & Associates, Inc.

Radius Book Group and the Radius Book Group colophon
are registered trademarks of Radius Book Group,
a Division of Diversion Publishing Corp.

For the remarkable, resilient, and vibrant
Jewish communities of Syria and Lebanon

CONTENTS

1

A Banker's Journey

On Thursday, November 13, 1947, Edmond Safra made his way to Lod field, the small airport a few miles from the sands of Tel Aviv in Mandatory Palestine. The fifteen-year-old Beirut native had made the 130-mile journey over land from his hometown. The only flight serving his destination, Milan, directly from Beirut left on Saturday. And Edmond Safra, an observant Jew, didn't travel on Shabbat.

At the airport, a onetime British military base on the outskirts of a thriving Jewish metropolis, Safra and his twenty-year-old chaperone, Jacques Tawil, checked in for the KLM flight to Amsterdam, which stopped in Rome.

Safra and Tawil were two of the millions of people in motion in Europe and the Mediterranean basin in the years after World War II. Refugees and exiles, businesspeople seeking opportunity, hopeful emigrants, soldiers of occupying armies, and returning prisoners of war—all were uprooted, seeking stability and a place in a world in which the old order had been uponded.

The plane took flight over the white city of Tel Aviv, the burgeoning home to the ingathering of refugees from Europe. As it carved a route to the north and west, Safra could see in the distance the plains of Aleppo, his father's birthplace. Closer, the corniche of Beirut, the Safra family's increasingly tenuous home, carved a crescent into the

Mediterranean. The propeller plane chugged over the displaced persons camps of Cyprus, from which hundreds of European Jews had, four months earlier, made a desperate, unsuccessful attempt to emigrate to Israel on a ship named the *Exodus*.

A few hours later, the plane touched down in Rome. With connecting flights to Milan cancelled due to the thick shroud of autumn fog, Safra and Tawil were obliged to continue their journey by bus, finally arriving in Milan just before sundown on Friday. Thus began, in cinematic fashion, the opening scene of the dramatic career of Edmond Safra.

Poor, broken, and not yet able to stand on its own two feet, Italy may not have seemed like a place where an established, cosmopolitan, third-generation Jewish banker like Jacob Safra might want to send his teenage son to put down stakes. Two years after the end of the war, the pall of fascism hung over Italy and Europe. Many Italian cities remained strewn with rubble. In Milan, Edmond Safra could have strolled by the central train station, from whose infamous Platform 21 many thousands of Jews had been deported to death camps just three years earlier.

But everything is relative. In 1947, shattered Western Europe was rebuilding under the protection and occupation of the United States. Meanwhile, the Levant, comparatively stable during the war, was enduring a wave of disruption from the unwinding of the British Empire and French colonial adventure. The earthquakes that would cleave the three territories that tugged on the Safra family's collective heart—Syria, Lebanon, and Palestine—into hostile countries were already beginning. Within a decade, they would render Beirut, the seat of the family business, uninhabitable for the Safras.

Thirty years earlier, Jacob Safra, Edmond's father, had left his native Aleppo for the relative safety of Beirut as the collapse of the Ottoman Empire rattled the region's foundations. Now, Jacob Safra dispatched his second-born son—just two years past the age of Bar Mitzvah—to Milan to set up a gold trading and foreign exchange business. And, more importantly, to act as a scout who could establish a beachhead for the family and its enterprise on more stable ground.

Upon arrival in Rome, Edmond Safra presented his official papers, which told only part of the story of who he was. His identity was both clear and multifaceted. He was a son and brother. A Safra. An apprentice banker. A Jew. A Beiruti and Lebanese national. A Halabi (as natives of Aleppo called themselves).

The tangible possessions the boy carried were unimpressive. A briefcase and clothes, and a few gold coins. But he carried with him intangible baggage—including both assets and burdens. These included introductions to connections his father's bank, Banque J.E. Safra, had built. An appreciation of tragedy: Edmond's mother had died in childbirth when he was ten, and he had lost a sister when he was five. A sense of responsibility and duty, not just to his father, but to his eight siblings, his community, and his fellow Jews. A heritage, a set of values, and an ethic that had been explicitly taught by his parents, embedded in his DNA, and absorbed through osmosis. Perhaps most importantly, his possessions included his mind, his heart, and bountiful common sense.

The long journey from Beirut to Milan marked an inauspicious and humble beginning for the business career of a man whom James Wolfensohn, the former president of the World Bank, would deem to be the greatest banker of his generation.[1] Over the next fifty-two years, in a career unrivaled in the second half of the 20th century, Edmond Safra carved an arc like a brilliant meteor in the dark night sky. Milan and Monaco, where his life tragically ended in 1999, were separated by just 190 miles. But in an exceptional half century, Safra traveled immense distances—geographically, financially, socially, and intellectually. He built and endowed institutions and left a lasting impression in the many places he called home. His life story is a dramatic one, with overtones of both Horatio Alger and Shakespeare—remarkable repeated success visited by conspiracies of hostile forces, family conflict, a debilitating illness, and ultimately, a premature death.

When the two main banks Edmond built, Republic and Safra Republic Holdings, were sold to HSBC, they brought a price of $10 billion. And upon Edmond's death on December 3, 1999, his estate was valued at more than $3 billion. But the value he created in his lifetime, and far beyond, in providing jobs, protecting wealth, providing credit, enabling trade, and bringing dignity and hope through philanthropy, can't be measured in dollars and cents. The way Edmond Safra built his fortune was unique and instructive. But so, too, was the way he behaved in doing so, what his work meant to others, what he did with the power and resources he amassed, and the humility of his ultimate goal: to create greater dignity in the world.

Edmond Jacob Safra was born on August 6, 1932, in Aley, a summer mountain resort outside Beirut. Weeks before, Franklin Delano Roosevelt had been nominated by the Democratic party as a candidate for US president, and the Nazi party under the leadership of Adolf Hitler had won the biggest share of seats in the German parliament.

Precocious, restless, and perhaps foreordained to set out for Italy (Edmond had stowed away on a family trip to Trieste at the age of five), the teenager, after arriving in Milan, embarked upon an improvisational, peripatetic career. In the ensuing five decades, he was involved with an astonishing array of activities—real estate, factories, shipping, financing films, bartering industrial goods in Eastern Europe, investing in art. But it was banking that captured his heart and allowed his talents to flourish. Edmond Safra's art was banking, and the world was his canvas. "Edmond took a checkbook out of his own pocket and said, 'I'm going to start a bank,' and did it four times, and every one of them was a success," John Bond, the longtime CEO of HSBC, noted. "And he was about to launch another financial institution the day he died."[2]

The banks he founded on three continents grew into massive endeavors, thriving in a tumultuous era of consolidation, systemic failures, and rolling crises. Republic, the New York–based startup founded in 1966, grew to become the eleventh-largest bank in the United States, and yielded its public investors a compounded annual return of 23 percent. Trade Development Bank (TDB), founded in Geneva in the 1950s, similarly notched a 23 percent compounded annual return when it was sold for more than $500 million in 1982. Safra Republic Holdings, the Luxembourg-headquartered parent company of private banks that Edmond created in 1988, grew into a titan with $21 billion in assets in its eleven-year life span. And Banco Safra, which Edmond's brothers

Moïse and Joseph would ultimately take over and run, remains one of the largest financial institutions in Brazil.

Edmond Safra was an avatar of globalization and financial intermediation before the terms became part of the lingua franca. He was born and raised in the cosmopolitan hothouse of Beirut, in a world of trade and financial networks that stretched to the east and west. And he thrived by negotiating the fault lines of global trade, working the seams in between crumbling empires, dawning powers, and shifting regulatory regimes. From a young age, he was instinctively aware of the possibility of loss. But his response was to stride confidently and be undaunted by barriers. Edmond Safra was not an imposing man personally, with a stocky build and cherubic face framed by thick eyebrows. Prematurely bald, he had a grandfatherly mien as a middle-aged man. In person, he was engaging and quick to laugh, with inquisitive eyes and a watchful manner. He often seemed to be taking things in—and he was. But as a businessman, he was a swashbuckling campaigner, in the mold of Errol Flynn, whose films he financed as a very young man. Wherever he alit, Edmond Safra always went directly to the center of the action. Throughout his career, he took repeated leaps of faith, and encouraged others to take the leap alongside him.

In a whirlwind period after landing in Milan, the teenager conducted gold trades between Europe, the Middle East, and Hong Kong—to which he dispatched his older brother-in-law. When Beirut became untenable for Jews in the 1950s, Edmond, then in his early twenties, engineered the family's move to Brazil, one of the few countries that would grant the Safras visas. There, in a closed economy, he reinvented himself as an enthusiastic importer-exporter and trader—trading dry goods, chemicals, coffee, and industrial machinery. Continually traveling back to Europe, he founded a private bank, TDB, in Geneva in 1959. In 1965, Safra came to the US and, uncowed by giant competitors like Citibank and Chase, founded a *retail* bank in the heart of Manhattan. Republic Bank was a new bank—nearly a century old, as the slogan put it. The startup reeled in depositors by offering free television sets and appliances, sold shares to the public, and quickly grew into one of the largest US banks. Republic acquired savings banks in the New York area and started new units in Florida and California. Through the years, Edmond Safra's entities opened representative offices, branches, and subsidiaries from Hong Kong to the Caribbean and South America. By the 1990s, he was managing a multibillion-dollar enterprise with 7,000 employees in two dozen offices on four continents. Even as he expanded, he clung fiercely to the places that mattered most to him. Edmond could never bring himself to sell BCN, the tiny bank in Beirut that his father had founded and that survived through the worst of Lebanon's civil wars.

Fluent in six languages, Edmond Safra in his lifetime lived in Lebanon, Italy, Switzerland, France, Brazil, the United States, Monaco, and England, and was a regular visitor to dozens more countries. One of his gifts was the ability to operate simultaneously in different contexts. He had an eye for spotting arbitrage opportunities. Blessed with a mind like a steel trap for detail and the processing power to connect the dots, Safra could intuit inflation from the price of a pastrami sandwich and gauge the impact on asset prices in Tokyo of an announcement in Washington about the gold standard.

In banking, rapid expansion in size is often a prelude to disaster. But the Safra banks avoided the traps that ensnared many other institutions because Edmond had a vision of banking that diverged sharply from the form of banking practiced by MBAs and corporate executives with their buzzwords, organizational charts, and five-year plans. This vision was dictated in large measure by the things he carried with him when he got off that plane in Rome. "The book on banking was written 6,000 years ago," he said. Safra's institutions typically were not powerhouses in investment banking, advising, proprietary trading, stock picking, or any of the other trends that the faddish industry latched onto.

Edmond Safra grew up in a time and place when states could take away everything, armies rolled across borders, and civil wars tore society apart; when communities that had been comfortable and part of the establishment could be expelled; when hyperinflation, technological change, and consolidation repeatedly wiped out wealth. And so to him, the first and primary duty of banks was to protect assets. "The duty of a banker is to safeguard what customers have entrusted to him," he told the *Financial Times* in a rare interview. "He is a confidant, sometimes a friend. He is the custodian of people's secrets. And our clients show their trust by confiding money to us. We invest it prudently, because it is not our money." That's a simplification. But as Edmond Safra liked to say, banking was "a simple, stupid business."

A company or a government might not honor its commitment. But a Safra would. Having grown up in a world without deposit insurance, strong central banks, or a system of prudential regulation, he believed—and acted as if—he, and not shareholders or governments, was responsible for the safety of the deposits. Some of the extraordinary episodes in his career were moments in which he acted according to his own personal code, whether it was instructing his bank in New York to provide funds to a depositor from Beirut who showed up without documentation, or personally assuming $700 million in potential liabilities due to a criminal fraud by an investment adviser with links to Republic in the late 1990s. "It was more important [to him] to do things right and not make money than to do something wrong and make a lot of money," Maurice Levy, the CEO of ad agency Publicis, said.[3]

And so he took great personal care in placing deposits in income-producing assets. Safra's banks lent both carefully and shrewdly, on reputation and personal relationship, and, wherever possible, on guarantees. He used his global connections to marry the savings of middle-class New Yorkers, lawyers in Beirut, or merchants in France to central banks in Asia or South America, to banks, government agencies, or loans guaranteed by the World Bank. As a result, the Safra banks rarely suffered credit losses. On the rare occasions on which he permitted himself to boast, it was about the banks' pristine balance sheets.

Edmond Safra's banks participated in activities that didn't require excessive extension of credit to others—but that were essential to the functioning of the global economy. The Safra banks were big players in trade finance such as factoring and discounting notes, in the vital but low-margin business of moving banknotes around the world, and in a niche business his family had been active in for generations: gold.

He managed to avoid many of the pitfalls that befell so many others in banking and finance, in part because his birthright wasn't simply a family business, but an operating code and system. The seeds he carried could thrive in the Alpine soil of Switzerland, the hurly-burly of New York's retail banking world, or the protected hothouse of Brazil. Safra's banks never needed a bailout from any government. At the heart of this creed lay a sense of personal and reciprocal responsibility between a banker and a customer. Whether you were borrowing or lending, it wasn't just money and a signature on a piece of paper or a set of assets that were at issue. It was your name and your reputation, and that of your family—your parents, siblings, and children. Edmond Safra always felt a banker needed to be beyond reproach. He was a stickler for formal, discreet, and attentive customer service, and insisted on exactitude and professionalism from his employees. There was a right way for a banker to dress (blue Italian suits), to relate to customers (with great courtesy, regardless of the size of their account), and to behave (a banker would never be seen in a casino). Edmond Safra paid remarkable attention to detail—the furniture in the banks, the design of ashtrays and business cards, the food in the cafeteria. And yet he didn't let tradition hamper progress; the banks continually embraced new ways of doing business, whether it was innovations of marketing, or deploying communications technology and computer systems to get a leg up.

Everywhere he went, and in every business in which he participated, Edmond Safra was supported by a latticework of family relationships, kinship networks, and community support. Whether he was starting a private bank in Geneva or a retail bank in New York, he could tap into the loyal base of depositors among Sephardic Jews—particularly Syrian and Lebanese—as potential customers. He had an instant network of contacts, borrowers, and counterparties in a dozen-odd financial capitals. And he made a practice of hiring relatives, in-laws, friends, and people he "knew" because someone in his extended family had a connection to them.

Comfortable in the councils of power, palaces, and corporate headquarters, Safra prized his membership in the community of Lebanese and Syrian Jews above all. Wherever he lived or traveled, there was a synagogue where he could be at home, and, as time went on, wel-comed as a hero: in Europe and South America, in the Middle East and New York, and in Israel. Indeed, among the Sephardic diaspora, Edmond was regarded as a source of protection—a *moallem*, in Arabic, which can translate into *leader* or *teacher*. The Jewish communities of Beirut and Aleppo had formal organizations, officials, and leadership. When they dissolved and began to reconstitute themselves in South America, Europe, and the United States, Edmond Safra often stepped in to provide guidance and support. In the Sephardic world, there were no Jewish aristocrats like those who had risen in Europe in the nineteenth century. But Edmond was regarded as a natural leader— "our crown," said one community member after his death.

At a young age, Edmond Safra embraced the role of paterfamilias. With his elderly father ailing after having moved to Brazil in the 1950s, Edmond took responsibility for the education and apprentice-ship of his younger brothers, setting them up in school in England and in business in Brazil. "Effectively, I was brought up by you, Edmond," his youngest brother, Joseph, said in 1997. "You are for me my father, my dear brother, my teacher."[4] This sense of familial responsibility extended to the broader community of Lebanese and Syrian Jews. Time and again, when people fled to Brazil, the United States, or Israel, Edmond provided jobs as well as financial and moral support—like an angel from the sky, as one rabbi who left Lebanon in 1977 put it. He used his influence to protect a Jewish cemetery in Egypt, to retrieve Torah scrolls from Beirut, and to purchase airplane tickets for the last Jews held hostage in Syria in the 1990s.

Charity was part of the rhythm of life, whether it was making a donation for the honor of being called to the Torah on a Saturday morning service or sending funds to the charity associated with the Torah sage Rabbi Meir Baal HaNess. "If I don't give, who will?" he said. Edmond made his first recorded donation in 1948 to the Ecole Normale Israélite Orientale, part of the Alliance Israélite Universelle in Paris.

For Edmond, there was always an explicit connection between success in business and charity. Time and again, he personally backed efforts to create new community institutions for Sephardic Jews—in Brazil, Switzerland, New York, and many points in between. His sense of charity was intensely personal, but evolved as he grew older into something more institutional. Donations were always given in the name of the family, in honor of his parents. He endowed the first chair in Sephardic Jewish history at Harvard in the 1970s, and helped found ISEF, an organization that funds higher education scholarships for Sephardic Jews in Israel. The names of Edmond's parents, Jacob and Esther Safra, appear in prayer books in synagogues around the world, on yeshivas, and on a public square in Jerusalem. Edmond's charitable efforts found their ultimate expression in the creation of the foundation that bears his name, which was endowed with the proceeds of the sales of two of his banks in 1999. With the guidance of his wife and partner, Lily Safra, the foundation Edmond created and endowed has, for more than two decades, assisted hundreds of organizations in over forty countries around the world, in areas that Edmond prioritized during his life: education, medical care, and Jewish religious life, as well as social welfare and humanitarian relief.

Although giving was at the core of Edmond Safra's Jewish ethos, it was not a substitute for it. Rather, Judaism for Edmond Safra was a force that dictated the rhythm of life—putting on tefillin for daily morning prayers, observing his parents' memorials, leading the Passover Seder—and the way he conducted himself as a businessman and human. A globe-trotting billionaire, he remained a child of Aleppo's Jewish quarter and Beirut's Wadi Abu Jamil neighborhood. While he was coolly rational in business, Safra was a superstitious man. In a tailor-made pocket inside his suit jacket—invariably a blue three-piece suit, such as his father had worn—he carried a blue eye amulet, to ward off evil. In both the Muslim and Jewish cultures of the Middle East and North Africa, the number five carries a particular meaning. And so he might have carried a Hamsa, a piece of jewelry or charm in the shape of a hand (*Hamsa* means five in Arabic). He made sure his telephone extensions ended in 555 and that his license plate number was EJS-555. He once held out to sign one of the largest deals he conducted until the eighteenth of the month, believing the date to be auspicious. While the practices of Sephardic Jews often struck outsiders, including Ashkenazi Jews, as exotic, this mindset was both natural to Edmond and perfectly in keeping with the large and influential Jewish culture of the Middle East, North Africa, and Israel.

There was one vital area in which Edmond departed from the traditions of his community. He came from a world in which people traditionally married young, and married closely within their own circles—often within their own families, and in arranged marriages. But Edmond ultimately chose another path, and it made all the difference. A bachelor deep into adulthood, at age forty-three Safra married Lily Monteverde, a Brazilian-born widow whose parents had emigrated from Europe. Blonde, Ashkenazi, fluent in six languages, Lily possessed refinement, worldliness, and a sense of independence. They formed a strong bond and an enduring love. Edmond doted on her children, and eventually her grandchildren, as if they were his own. And she opened his eyes to a broader social world, a deeper understanding of art, culture, and education. In their twenty-five years together, Lily would be the love of his life, his rudder and keel, and, as he grew older and was stricken with illness, his solace and caregiver. In the years since his death, she became the carrier and guardian of his legacy.

Edmond and Lily owned beautiful homes in Geneva, London, Paris, New York, Monaco, and the French Riviera—the latter, La Léopolda, being a former property of the king of Belgium. With their combined eye for quality and value, they amassed a world-class collection of paintings and sculpture—works by Miró, Picasso, Modigliani—and were discerning collectors of furniture, watches, and carpets. Edmond forged personal relationships with Yitzhak Rabin and Yitzhak Shamir, Henry Kissinger and Margaret Thatcher, Robert Kennedy and the Reagans. He occupied rarefied air, attending state dinners at the White House, doing business with the Rothschilds, and hosting glittering receptions at the National Gallery of Art. Yet he was just at home in a small synagogue in Rhodes or Brooklyn, at delis in London or New York, and in the homes of childhood friends from Beirut. He had a capacity for dealing with people from a remarkable array of backgrounds, despite the cultural and political barriers that had been set up: middle-class New Yorkers, Saudi sheikhs, central bankers in Asia or South Africa, CEOs in Brazil. Edmond Safra didn't see personal differences as barriers. And he regarded the other barriers life would throw up as obstacles rather than walls.

Just as he was destined for a career in banking, Edmond Safra was in some ways destined to be misunderstood by contemporaries, rivals, critics, the press, and historians. Even though his banks were publicly held, providing quarterly detailed reports on their activities and precisely how they made money, Edmond was regarded as a secretive outsider. He kept no diary. He didn't sit for long interviews, engage in detailed correspondence, or ever appear on television. His preferred modes of communication were the telephone and talking in person. He ran public companies, but was a private man—a private banker at heart. Edmond's reticence, combined with his origins, accent, and modus operandi, seemed to lay the foundation for rumors and conspiracy theories.

Edmond had much in common with the titans of finance: drive, ambition, an eye for numbers, a fantastic memory. But there was also an essential humility to the man, born of his upbringing and heritage. In Edmond Safra's world, you left the earth not with possessions, but with attributes and relationships: your good name, the *shem tov*, your family, your reputation and your legacy. Because he regarded business as a highly personal endeavor, he took attacks on his reputation severely. He had a calm demeanor—unless his integrity was challenged. This made the episode for which he got the most publicity in his lifetime all the more galling.

In the years after he sold Trade Development Bank to American Express, a falling-out with the acquiring company led to a bizarre turn of events that remains difficult to account for even decades after the fact. American Express executives helped orchestrate a seedy campaign to insinuate that Safra was involved with drug trafficking and money laundering. This effort exacted an enormous personal toll, because it was an attack on his life's work and good name. It's noteworthy that when American Express offered a public apology, in what the *Washington Post* called "an extraordinary act of corporate contrition," Safra didn't ask for punitive damages—he forced the company to make $8 million in charitable donations to the International Red Cross, the university hospital of Geneva (Hôpital Cantonal), United Way of America, and the Anti-Defamation League of B'nai B'rith.[5]

Edmond Safra was a man for whom every business was by definition a family business. A fourth-generation banker, he grandly set a goal "to build a bank to last a thousand years." In a patriarchal worldview, the business was the life's work for the individual, his brothers, his sons, and his nephews. But having married later in life, he didn't have children of his own to groom and mold. As large as his enterprise grew, he still viewed himself as a link in a larger chain. Jacob Safra had taught him to judge a man's creditworthiness by looking him in the eye. "I speak to my father every day," Edmond said in 1997. "I ask his advice. And when I don't approve a deal, this is what I tell myself: My father would not have done this."

In the decades after the family settled in Brazil, his brothers Elie, Moïse and Joseph had pursued their own paths—often parallel—in banking and investment. Over the years, however, the relationships frayed, and they were unable to reach an agreement on how Edmond's banks could remain under the management of Safra family members. This challenge became more pronounced in the late 1990s as Edmond was stricken with a devastating degenerative disease. Parkinson's is one of the most unforgiving ailments. As the 1990s went on and the disease took a toll on his expansive sense of possibility, he recognized that it would be difficult to maintain his pace. "Please, *chérie*, never let me lose my dignity," he told Lily. And so in 1999, at the age of sixty-six, he embarked on an effort to settle his affairs.

When Republic, which by the mid-1990s was the eleventh-largest bank in the US, was sold along with Safra Republic Holdings to HSBC in May 1999 for nearly $10 billion, it solidified and monetized Edmond Safra's fortune. But rather than viewing it as a capstone of a brilliant career, Safra saw it as a moment of sadness. In his mind, banks were not built to be sold to international conglomerates.

They were meant to be run by families for generations. "You see, I've sold my children," he told a longtime friend when she offered congratulations.

While ailing and weakening, Safra still had a clear mind, and indeed he had already established new investment companies and a new charitable foundation over which he would preside. But in December 1999, he died in his apartment in Monaco after a member of the household staff set a fire, hoping to be seen as a hero in coming to the rescue. A few days before the twentieth century came to a close, so too did one of the great chapters in banking history. There would be—and could be—no heir to the Safra banking business, no successor, and no imitator.

Inevitably, the circumstances of Edmond's death inspired scurrilous rumors and innuendo that have continued to circulate for years. The American Express affair, memorialized in the best-selling book *Vendetta,* and Edmond's death in Monaco are tales that have been told and retold. Left untold, until now, has been the more compelling story of his life. What many people know about Edmond Safra is how his reputation was attacked, and how he died. How he lived is less well-known.

What follows is the story of the life and legacy of a sui generis entrepreneur, banker, and individual.

And it starts in Aleppo.

2

Aleppo

(1860–1920)

"I think God made sure I was born in a specific place, [and] that I became a banker because my father was himself a banker,"[6] Edmond Safra told a colleague in the 1990s. As a child, he imbibed the tales of his forebears, who were traders and money changers. Thanks to the explicit and implicit example set by his father, Jacob, who had learned from his uncles, Edmond knew that honesty, hard work, and reputation were the keys to success. His parents taught him the twin disciplines of banking and charity—making money and giving it away. And he absorbed the values of a close-knit family and Jewish community. A profession, a network of connections, a code of ethics, a sense of responsibility to a community (and, seemingly, his hairline)—these were all important attributes and characteristics Edmond Safra inherited from his father. And while Edmond Safra wouldn't have his own biological children whom he could name after his father and mother, as is commonly done among Syrian Jews, he would view the businesses and enterprises he created, and the institutions he endowed, as manifestations of the family's legacy.

To understand Edmond Safra's life and career, to grasp what drove him, we first have to understand the world of his father and mother. And that was the world of Aleppo, which now lies in ruins and no longer has a Jewish community. Although poor in natural resources, Aleppo was rich in talent and human capital, and was blessed with a geographic location that served it well until the twentieth century. It was in Aleppo, the third-largest city in the Ottoman Empire, that the Safras lived, for unknown numbers of generations. There they worked and prospered, started their business in finance, and, in the late nineteenth century, emerged into the modern world.

Edmond was born near Beirut in 1932, a dozen years after his father had relocated to the Lebanese capital. But Aleppo played an outsized influence in Edmond's life—through the networks and worldviews formed there, the languages he spoke, and his fierce loyalty and enduring connections to family and colleagues in Brazil, Geneva, and New York who traced their origins to Aleppo, or Halab, as it is known in Arabic. A century after their forebears left the city, people continue to identify themselves not as Syrians but as Halabis.

History and custom, especially a reliance on oral tradition, make it difficult to reconstruct Jewish genealogy in the Middle East. In the Ottoman Empire, each religious community maintained its own register of key life events, and many Jewish records were destroyed in the nineteenth and twentieth centuries. What survives is often incomplete and difficult-to-parse lists of (male) births, weddings, and deaths from the 1850s to the 1920s.[7]

In the absence of solid documentation, a certain amount of mythology seeps into every family's history. The story of Rav Safra, a 4th century figure, has links to Edmond Safra that are either remarkably foreshadowing or eerily coincidental. A scholar and wine merchant in Babylon, Rav Safra visited business associates in Caesarea, in Palestine, where he was involved in importing goods. Jewish texts described him as a man "known for scrupulous honesty in business." Rav Safra was so pious, the story goes, that when a client wanted to negotiate a deal, Safra, absorbed in prayer, didn't say a word. Interpreting the silence as a hard no, the client doubled the price, slapped his money on the table, and walked out. Later, Safra tracked down the man and refunded the difference, since the price wasn't a fair one.[8]

No evidence links Rav Safra of ancient Babylon to the Safras of Aleppo. But contemporaries in nineteenth-century Aleppo would have been able to intuit a lot about a person's history and trade just by knowing their first and last names. Among Jews in the region, firstborn sons were named after their paternal grandfathers, while younger sons were often named after uncles. Last names were frequently linked to trades and professions, which were also handed down from generation to generation. Common names for Jews in Syria included Dabbah (slaughterer) and Haddad (blacksmith).

Jews had been in and around Aleppo since the time of the Second Temple. Aleppo was known to its Jewish residents as Aram Tzova, a city first referred to in the Book of Genesis. In the Book of Samuel, we learn that Joab, David's general, conquered Aram Tzova. Lore holds that he laid the foundations for the Great Synagogue of Aleppo. One of the longest-serving houses of worship in history, the Great Synagogue contains a stone plaque dated to 241 CE, and was probably built after the fifth century CE. Destroyed during Tamerlane's subjugation of Aleppo in 1400, it was reconstructed in 1418. The nearby village of Tedef Al-Yahud housed a shrine to the biblical prophet Ezra. The Great Synagogue housed the ninth-century Aleppo Codex, the oldest surviving manuscript of the Torah, prophets, and writings including vocalization and cantillation signs, which native Halabis regarded as "the most precious possession of Jewry." (A portion of the Aleppo Codex was smuggled out in 1947 and ultimately found its way to Israel.[9])

In the early 1500s, many Spanish Jews who fled the Inquisition settled in Aleppo, assimilating into the community. The city grew into prominence during the Ottoman Empire, which, at Suleiman the Magnificent's death in 1566, encompassed the Arabian Peninsula in the south, the Balkans in the north, Iraq in the east and North Africa in the west. Ottoman rulers afforded their Jewish subjects the *dhimmi* status that had originally been assigned to Christians by the seventh-century Pact of Umar. If they paid a tax and deferred to the superiority of Islam, they could worship freely—"second-class citizens—but citizens," as the historian Bernard Lewis put it.[10]

Though not on a major waterway or coast, Aleppo nonetheless occupied an important location at one end of the Silk Road, allowing it to function as a link between Central Asia, India, the Far East, and

Europe. For centuries, caravans crossing from east to west would stop in Aleppo, carrying loads of Persian silk, Syrian cotton, agricultural products, and gold. "Her husband's to Aleppo gone," the First Witch notes in Act I of *Macbeth*. As time went on, the city emerged as a vital node of connection between three great empires: Ottoman, British, and Hapsburg. In 1580, when Queen Elizabeth sealed a pact with Sultan Murad III—the so-called capitulations treaties—that gave European countries trading rights and its subjects exemptions from taxes in the Ottoman Empire, the first British consul took up residence in Aleppo. The Levant Company, a London-based trading company founded in 1581, planted its headquarters there. Trade grew to include sending silk and cotton cloth, soap, and olive oil to Europe and importing finished goods in turn.

In the eighteenth century, European Jews, especially those from Livorno in Italy, followed the commercial path to Aleppo. "They came to be called Francos, often adopting the surname for themselves, and dominated local commerce and international trade by using the Capitulation rights derived from their home countries," historian Stanford Shaw notes. Rafael de Picciotto (1742–1827), a Livornese Jew, became the Austrian consul based in Aleppo, and other members of his family and his descendants represented European powers in the city through the nineteenth century and became part of the community.[11]

Aleppo in the mid-nineteenth century was the third-largest city in the Ottoman Empire, after Istanbul and Cairo, with a population of 100,000 in 1860.[12] But in the second half of the nineteenth century, a series of revolutions and transformations roiled the global economy, and the Aleppo region in particular. In the short term, the combination of these forces would open up new opportunities, but in the long term, the pressures unleashed would cause Aleppo to be left behind, and would ultimately conspire to pull—and push—Jews out of the city. A vital diaspora of Halabis would take shape in Beirut and Europe, in the Far East and South America, and in the United States. The Safras would ultimately count themselves among the exiles—and plug into these networks to great effect.

The first transformation came with the Industrial Revolution, which left the makers of handmade linens and textiles of the Middle East unable to compete with the output of the mills of Manchester. The shift helped reverse the flow of trade from the Middle East, and began to attract a small number of Aleppan Jews to move to England. The opening of the Suez Canal in 1869 largely ended the caravan trade. But as steam power replaced wind as a means of propulsion, and the distance necessary to travel between the Far East and Europe shortened, the flow of goods between Asia, Europe, and the Middle East grew by leaps and bounds. Freight traffic, once scattered among many small Mediterranean harbors, migrated to large ports like Alexandria and Beirut, which emerged as rival centers of financial and commercial gravity.[13]

Though railroads began to be built across the region to connect commercial centers, no train would reach Aleppo until the twentieth century. The emergence of the telegraph as a communications technology—especially throughout the British Empire—further knit the world together. The result of these developments was a quantum leap in the volume and velocity of trade. Family businesses that specialized in finance and trade suddenly found they had a much greater ability to do more business around the world. In Europe, the Rothschilds and Warburgs sent family members to establish beachheads in cities far from their German bases. In the nineteenth century, the Sassoon family, known as the "Rothschilds of the East," branched out from Baghdad to Bombay, and then followed the British Empire into Malaya, China, Hong Kong, and England. Another Baghdadi Jewish merchant family, the Kadoories, expanded from Baghdad to India and China, as well as Egypt.

As the world became connected by wire and steel rail, it was also increasingly linked by overlapping and intersecting personal and familial networks. Many of them were forged by Jews who enjoyed a higher level of trust among coreligionists and could seal further bonds through marriage. Given the existing connections between Aleppo and Livorno, it was not uncommon for Aleppan merchants to move to Italy, and a Sephardic community grew in Milan, the financial capital of northern Italy.[14]

Social and educational revolutions followed the Industrial Revolution. Increasingly freed from geographic limitations in the second half of the nineteenth century, Jews in Aleppo also found themselves liberated from some of the social and cultural restrictions that had stifled their development. In February 1856, when Sultan Abdülmecid I granted all non-Muslims full legal equality, the special tax was cancelled.[15]

At the same time, newly empowered and emancipated Jews in Europe acted to improve the lot of their coreligionists throughout North Africa and the Middle East. In 1860, well-off French Jews formed the Alliance Israélite Universelle (AIU). Feeling a sense of duty to relieve poverty and advance education, they aimed to establish a network of European-style independent middle and high schools, with instruction in French on modern subjects. The first AIU institutions were in Damascus and Baghdad, and the AIU, backed by German-Jewish philanthropist Baron Maurice de Hirsch, would go on to operate over 100 facilities for men and—crucially—women in most Ottoman cities in the 1860s and 1870s. In 1869, the AIU established a school for boys in Aleppo; a girls' school opened in 1889. Literacy levels in Aleppo's Jewish community were higher than anywhere else in the Syrian province.[16]

In effect, the AIU gave Jews in the Middle East further entrée into a far wider European world. It established new networks by putting local leaders in contact with the Ashkenazi Jews who founded and supported the Alliance schools. It made French the second language for the Jews of North Africa and the Middle East, which enabled them to move seamlessly between their homes and much of Europe. "An AIU teacher thus reported to Paris later in the century that out of some 300,000 Jews then in the Empire, as many as 100,000 knew French and only 1,000 understood Turkish," Stanford Shaw noted. The overlap influenced the way they dressed, the names they gave their children, and their companies.[17]

To live in Aleppo in the late nineteenth century, then, was to live in multiple worlds at the same time. Businesspeople would correspond and conduct commerce in multiple languages, and in countries throughout Europe and Asia, riding the waves of the latest technology as they plugged into expanding commercial and social networks. At the same time, their personal lives remained contained in a relatively small, even closed, circle, and intimately connected to the past. Businesses were run with family members. Jews tended to live in the same neighborhood and socialize almost exclusively with one another. Rabbis received great deference, and life revolved around Jewish observance and holidays. Marriages were generally arranged, often between cousins.

It was into this world that the Safras first emerged on paper. On March 29, 1858, Edmond's great-grandfather, Yaacov Safra, married Garaz Hacohen in Aleppo.[18] There is little documentation surrounding the life and work of Yaacov and his son, Elie, Edmond's grandfather. In its promotional literature, Republic National Bank of New York liked to claim that the Safras were "an old established family of bankers and gold traders in Aleppo who financed the camel caravans of the Silk Road" and had outposts in the Far East, Istanbul, and Alexandria. Along with other Jewish moneychangers, the Safras operated at the nexus of trade between Europe and Asia. All the trade that coursed through the region needed lubrication—financing and liquidity, letters of credit, gold, the exchange of currency. In the absence of an integrated banking system, this work was carried out by individuals. A modern financial system was being born in England and the US in the late nineteenth century, but such coordination was relatively primitive in the Middle East.

The Safras bought coins from the Ottoman central bank and sold them in Aleppo at a premium. They financed international trade in and out of the city, supplying loans and letters of credit so merchants could trade goods such as silk, spices, fruit, nuts, textiles, and soap between the Middle East, the Far East, and Europe.[19] And they traded gold (in Arabic, *Safra* translated as yellow or gold). The fact that two rabbis presided at the wedding of Yaacov and Garaz—one of them, Ezra Attie, was a scion of an important Aleppo rabbinic dynasty— suggests that the family already had significant status.

Yaacov and Garaz had four sons, Ezra (the eldest), Joseph, David, and Eliyahu (or Elie in French). In the 1880s, those sons institutionalized their trade by establishing a money-changing concern, which they endowed with a French name: Safra Frères & Cie. The four sons in turn married and began to have children. Elie married Sabbout Husni, and their first son (after two daughters) was born on December 19, 1889. As the tradition held, he was named after Elie's father, Yaacov—Jacob, in French. As was also common, the parents recorded his official birth date as 1891, as part of an effort to put off being drafted into the Ottoman army.[20]

Elie Safra died when Jacob was an infant. As was common, Elie's brothers took responsibility for the upbringing and livelihood of their nephew. While the duty of the father—or the uncles, in this case—was to make sure that the family's sons had a place in the world, among brothers, it was the responsibility of the eldest to make sure that the younger siblings found their place.

Ezra Safra took Jacob under his wing. After Elie's death, Ezra and his two brothers concentrated on gold trading and established new lines of business. They traded on personal connections to other Sephardim across Europe and Asia, and linked up with Muslim and Christian merchants throughout the Ottoman Empire, Iran, and Central Asia.[21]

From a young age, Jacob Safra was aware of who he was, how he fit in, and what he was destined to be. Virtually all businesses in his part of the world were, by definition, family businesses. They ran on a culture of honor and trust based on personal relationships and verbal understanding, not contracts or credit checks. This is one of the reasons there is so little documentation of these generations of Safras. The trust that enabled the system to work was based in part on one's conduct and bearing, and in large part on one's name. Businesses were meant to be retained in the family, which is one of the reasons it was common for men to marry their first cousins. (Women were generally prohibited from inheriting property.)

Even as a boy, Jacob Safra was keenly aware of his responsibilities to his family and community. Joseph Sutton, a historian of the Aleppo diaspora who was born there in 1907, noted: "Class and rank were based on religious preeminence and wealth, i.e., on scholarliness, and outstanding generosity and devotion to religious institutions, support of the corps of indigent rabbis, orphanages, and care for the large numbers of the poor. In addition, Aleppan Jewry took into consideration the family respectability and kinship—*adamiyeh* and *ayleh*—over several uninterrupted generations."[22]

Aleppo was a city of 24 quarters, which were essentially self-contained villages. The 1900 census showed a population of about 108,000, of which 70 percent were Muslims, 24 percent Christians, and about 7 percent Jews—some 7,306, to be precise. Most of the Jewish population lived in the Bahsita Quarter in the northwest portion of the Old City, where the Great Synagogue was. Some middle-class and upper-income Jews lived outside the walls in Jamiliya and the al-Sabil and al-Saghi neighborhoods built at the end of the nineteenth century. Jacob's home lacked running water, electricity, and a telephone.

As the child of a wealthy family, Jacob probably attended the local school of the Alliance Israélite Universelle, which was in the Jamiliya neighborhood. He knew his way around the souks, where many of Safra Frères' clients maintained stalls or operations, and around the center of town. The Bab al-Faraj, the "gate of deliverance," stood at the city's open central square, home to the post office, the telegraph building, Baron's Hotel, and the Orosdi-Back department store, a chain started by two Austro-Hungarian Jews that was known as the "Harrods of the East."

The clock tower, one of Aleppo's highest structures, showed both European and Oriental time, which neatly highlighted the complexities of life in the region. In Jacob Safra's world, things others might have seen as contradictions were normal. Two systems, modes of belief, and ways of looking at the world coexisted. The Safras lived in the Middle East and spoke Arabic at home, but conducted business in French. They maintained a family business as members lived in distant cities. They traded and maintained commercial relationships with people in Europe, India, and Asia, but married cousins. They embraced the modern world while holding fast to ancient traditions. They modernized and embraced opportunity and education without abandoning what they believed or who they were. They were comfortable in the world but identified most strongly with their local community.

As he approached the age of Bar Mitzvah, Jacob learned more about the informal councils—consisting of rabbis and lay leaders—that collected funds and distributed them to schools, charities, orphanages, and associations that facilitated the marriage of poor young men and women without dowries. After working at the office on weekends and holidays as a boy, Jacob formally entered the family firm at 14, the beginning of a lengthy apprenticeship.

The sands continued to shift as Jacob Safra was growing into his role and place. Not much had changed in Aleppo itself during most of the Ottoman period. But in the 1900s and 1910s, a series of forces conspired to upset existing arrangements and set people into motion. But while the influence of Aleppo as a city may have been declining, the groundwork was being laid for the influence of Aleppans to increase.

In the wake of the 1908 Young Turk Revolution, as reform groups strove to centralize power and modernize the state, the Ottoman Empire ended the practice of exempting minorities from military service. Aleppan Jews thus joined the legions of people from the Middle East and Europe who were in motion. Some went to Manchester, England, where they got involved in the textiles industry. Others made their way to the Far East. Those with the least to lose, or perhaps nothing to lose, went the farthest. A trickle of Aleppan Jews boarded steamships in the 1890s for New York and Brazil, France and Mexico City. Others stayed in the region but flocked to Beirut or Cairo or Alexandria, joining tens of thousands of fellow Syrians who found opportunity in the lively port cities. The trickle grew into a stronger flow in the early decades of the twentieth century. Everywhere they went, they formed small communities, often bringing rabbis from Aleppo to lead them. In Jerusalem, a Halabi rabbi, Ezra Attie, ran the Porat Yosef yeshiva, the leading Sephardic rabbinic institution, which was built in the Old City. Like pushpins filling in a map of the world, the Aleppo diaspora began to take shape.

Some Aleppans had the comparative luxury of thinking more strategically about their relocation. One tried-and-true method of diversifying and increasing influence was to send family members to establish operations in more dynamic cities. With this in mind, the principals of Safra Frères began to disperse themselves while remaining a single business entity. With Ezra staying in Aleppo, the other brothers migrated to nodes of greater opportunity within the Ottoman Empire. David went to Istanbul, and Joseph set up shop in Alexandria. In 1913, twenty-four-year-old Jacob went to Beirut.

Beirut proved to be something of a false haven. When World War I started, the Ottoman Empire allied with the Germans, and residents of the region found themselves subjects of a power that was engaged in a long and furious war against France, Italy, and England. Food shortages became widespread as the Ottoman authorities requisitioned supplies, and an Allied blockade inhibited trade and transportation. It was estimated that 500,000 people died in the Syrian province during the war.[23]

Beyond widespread death and destruction, World War I brought an end to the fragile political order that had governed Aleppo and the larger region. As the Ottoman Empire collapsed and was replaced by separate new regimes, the scaffolding that had maintained peace and a measure of prosperity for generations also collapsed, and the assumptions on which Safra Frères, and so many other businesses in the region, relied were no longer operative. When the Ottoman Empire came apart, Britain and France essentially divided the Middle East between them. A League of Nations mandate assigned Palestine, Jordan and Iraq to Britain, and Syria and Lebanon to France.[24]

This new geography was challenging for Safra Frères. Previously, it had maintained outposts in four Ottoman cities, which could trade freely with one another. Now, the operations were governed by Turkey (Istanbul), England (Alexandria), and France (Aleppo and Beirut), and Turkey was eager to enact new trade barriers against its former possessions. Suddenly, the arrangement of organizing a family business with branches in Aleppo, Istanbul, and Alexandria made less sense.

The end of the war and the dissolution of the Ottoman Empire also unleashed dangerous nationalist sentiments throughout the region. After the Armenian genocide in Turkey, thousands of Armenian Christians flocked to Aleppo as refugees, subtly changing the demographic balance. The arrival of British and French colonial rule inspired incipient nationalist movements in Syria, Lebanon, and elsewhere. And the Balfour Declaration, the British government's 1917 announcement that it favored the creation of a Jewish homeland in Palestine, inflamed anti-Jewish sentiment. If the factors leading to the economic decline of Aleppo had materialized over a series of decades, these social and political impulses materialized seemingly overnight after the end of World War I.

For the first time in living memory, Aleppo faced sectarian strife. In an age of scarce resources, Muslims who resented the presence of Armenian Christian refugees from Anatolia in February 1919 attacked refugee camps in Aleppo, killing 48 Armenians. The following winter, the American consul in Aleppo concluded that the city was "primed to explode."[25] It was now clear that Aleppo, which had housed the Safra family for so long, would no longer be a safe place for the next generation. They, too, would have to join the growing Aleppan diaspora. So Ezra Safra, the eldest of the Safra Frères, summoned his family to a meeting. There, the Safra brothers and their nephew, Jacob, decided to dissolve the family business and seek out their own fortunes.

Jacob wouldn't be embarking on his next step alone. In 1918, he married Esther Safra, his first cousin, the daughter of his uncle Joseph. Having worked and lived in Beirut, he and Esther decided to return. The city on the Mediterranean was about 230 miles southwest of Aleppo, but in some ways, the distance separating Aleppo and Beirut was vast. More dynamic and less provincial, and situated on the Mediterranean coast, Beirut had a far more European feel than Aleppo, and it was the political capital of Lebanon. It was home to many different ethnic and religious groups, who generally coexisted peacefully. But Beirut lacked Aleppo's strong and cohesive Jewish community. Most of the Jews in Beirut at the end of the Ottoman

Empire were fairly recent immigrants; the Jewish population of the city increased from 908 in 1900 to 3,431 in 1912. The infrastructure that defined the Safras' life in Aleppo—synagogue, charitable organizations, local networks in which they had been known for generations, and a well-established family business—didn't yet exist in Beirut. Nevertheless, the young couple would set about building a new life and establishing a new legacy for the family name in the city.

3

Beirut

(1920-1947)

The Safra family's sojourn in Beirut lasted 32 years, from 1920 to 1952, and Edmond left the city in 1947. But the connection would endure and prove enormously influential. Beirut was the place in which Jacob Safra emerged as a force in business and communal affairs, where his many children were born, and where his wife died. Beirut is where Edmond Safra, starting at a remarkably young age, absorbed the knowledge and developed the mentality that would carry him into the world. Throughout his life, Edmond Safra clung to Beirut—to the people who hailed from there, to his father's bank, to the *idea* of the city—long after it seemed economically rational or safe to do so.

Beirut was already a large city when Jacob Safra had first begun working there in 1913, with a population of 200,000. By the time he established himself in 1920, it was in the midst of a transformation. In September 1920, French High Commissioner General Henri Gouraud proclaimed the creation of the state of Greater Lebanon. From the language spoken in government offices to the names of streets, in its ambitious urban renewal projects and its orientation toward the Mediterranean and Europe, Beirut quickly began to assume the mien of a modern French city. While Aleppo was struggling to grow its way out of the nineteenth century, Beirut, the political and commercial capital of Lebanon, home to a thriving port and seven universities, emphatically embraced the twentieth century, with "drinking water, gas street-lighting, trams, postal and telegraphic services, schools, hospitals, as well as printing and publishing houses."[26] More self-consciously European than any other city in the Middle East, except perhaps Alexandria, Beirut was a place where different religious groups lived comfortably in a clearly defined entente. While most of the major cities of the Ottoman world were predominantly Muslim, Beirut was home to a large and influential Christian population. French poet Alphonse de Lamartine dubbed Lebanon "the Switzerland of the Levant"—not just because of its snowcapped mountains but because of the capital city's sense of coexistence and comparative neutrality, all lubricated by deals and commerce.

Beirut's Jewish community lacked the long and storied history of Aleppo's, but in 1920, it was much better situated and poised for growth. The Alliance established a primary school for boys in Beirut in 1869 and a primary school for girls in 1878. In the late nineteenth century, Jews began to move into the Wadi Abu Jamil neighborhood, near the Ottoman government buildings. As the community prospered, fed by a continuing influx of Jews from Damascus, Aleppo, and elsewhere, the predominantly Jewish mountain summer resorts of Aley and Bamdoun began to take shape, complete with their own synagogues. In Beirut, Jews were not simply tolerated, they were accepted and encouraged. The period between 1920 and the 1940s was something of a golden age for Beirut's Jewish community. Jacob and Esther Safra, who arrived just when it was modernizing and building institutions, quickly assumed a leading role.

In Beirut, Jacob founded the grandly named Banque Jacob E. Safra in 1920. It was in fact a more modest affair, "a counting house by the harbor," in the evocative description provided by a contemporary, Ezra Zilkha. (The Zilkhas' bank, established in Baghdad in the nineteenth century, had opened a branch in Beirut in 1904, and participated in loans with Jacob Safra and sold gold on his behalf in Baghdad.) Banque Jacob E. Safra, which lacked a banking license, was a source of liquidity for farmers who bought and sold agricultural products and merchants who traded textiles with Manchester. From its base on Rue Allenby, near many other businesses, Jacob discounted notes—a form of short-term debt—offered credit, and evolved to offering savings accounts.[27] Like Safra Frères, though, it became best known for trading precious metals. In Beirut, where gold traded freely, Jacob could buy gold coins and ship them to Aleppo, Iraq, Saudi Arabia, Kuwait, and Dubai. Demand was strong throughout the chain from jewelers and merchants. From the Persian Gulf, merchants could move the gold into restricted markets like India. Amid the volatile currency markets of the 1920s and 1930s, he also exchanged currencies for merchants involved in international trade.[28]

Jacob possessed many of the physical and professional attributes that would later appear in Edmond. With a hairline that receded swiftly and early, Jacob may have looked older than his years. Unerringly discreet, and always wearing a blue suit, he had a talent for converting multiple currencies almost instantaneously. Having suffered significant losses and dislocation as a youth—orphaned as a very young child and forced to move from his hometown—Jacob was mindful of loss as well as gain. "Always take the sure thing," he would counsel his sons.

The documentary evidence surrounding his business is remarkably slim, in large part because Jacob was known for rarely writing anything down. The knowledge Jacob Safra needed about his counterparties and customers didn't reside on a balance sheet or a ledger; it was in his head and before his eyes. Business was often conducted verbally, underwritten by personal reputation. He could turn to his uncles in Egypt, Syria, and Turkey for credit, and forged links with Jewish European banks such as Mocatta & Goldsmid and N.M. Rothschild in London.[29]

And he maintained intensive ties with other Aleppans. Many prominent Aleppo businessmen had moved to Beirut or other cities after the fall of the Ottoman Empire, among them the Picciottos, the Nehmads, and the Dweks. Jacob circulated easily among the coffeehouses, souks, and shops of Beirut, sealing deals with a handshake. Because there was no deposit insurance and comparatively few banking regulations, character and caution on both sides of every transaction were vital. Financing was not a matter of assuming risk, but managing it.

Jacob and Esther took their relationship to the rapidly evolving Beirut community seriously. As late as 1918, according to a contemporary report, there was "no Hospital, no Home for the Aged, no Orphanage, no soup kitchen, no Institution for clothing the poor" for the local Jewish community, and no proper synagogue.[30] But that began to change under the French mandate. In 1926 the French created a new constitutional republic in Lebanon—a democratic system in which freedom of religion and equality were enshrined into law, and the diverse communities, such as Shiite and Sunni Muslim, Druze, Maronite Catholic, Chaldean, Jewish, and others, were empowered to oversee marriage, education, and other matters. Under the leadership of Joseph David Farhi, a Damascus-born textile merchant who served as the community's president, the Jewish governing body, the Conseil Communal, grew and expanded. It had an elected president, more than a dozen officers, and discrete committees for education, health, burial society, poverty relief, and the provision of breakfast for needy children. The initiatives were formally funded through the *aricha* (*the arrangement* in Hebrew), a tax on the wealth of adult Jewish males. The notion behind the *aricha* was that charity was, in a way, compulsory. In a community of 4,000 or 5,000, it was well known who was well off, and who wasn't.

Jewish institutions began to flourish. In 1921, a Jewish newspaper, *'Al-'alam 'al-Isra'ili*, was founded. On August 25, 1926, the community marked the dedication of Magen Avraham, its central synagogue. The imposing structure, with vaulted windows and a cavernous interior, was funded by Moïse Abraham Sassoon, a wealthy merchant of Syrian extraction who lived in Calcutta, in memory of his father. It stood in stark contrast to the much smaller ramshackle synagogues that dotted the neighborhood. Magen Avraham would occupy a prominent place in Beirut, and in the Safras' life.[31]

Jacob and Esther had quickly put down roots in the city. Elie, the first-born, arrived in 1922. Next came Paulette in 1923, and Eveline in 1924. And they began to construct a life that revolved around a small area: their gracious two-story apartment at 26 Rue Georges Picot, the Alliance school on the same street, and the newly built synagogue, on Wadi Abu Jamil, around the corner; the Banque on Rue Allenby, less than a kilometer away; and a summer house in Aley, fourteen kilometers up the mountains.

Alongside the Atties, Elias, Farhis, Saadias, and Hararis, the Safras were among the key families in the community. At a time when Jews had the option of assimilating more aggressively, Jacob held tightly to his religion. Contemporaries remember him as a constant presence in the synagogues in Aley and Beirut. A major donor to the thriving Beirut Alliance school, where he also served on the school committee, he financed a *beit midrash*, a hall where men studied Talmud. "His generosity for the communal needs knew no limits," one contemporary put it. The practice in synagogues was to auction off honors such as having an aliyah for the Torah reading, and Jacob was known for bidding the highest. But he did not give indiscriminately. A frustrated school administrator would later write to the AIU in Paris complaining that Jacob was "tight with money."[32]

As might be expected, there is less known or documented about Esther Safra. "She was known for her good heart," recalled Emile Saadia, a neighbor and contemporary of both Edmond and Jacob. From 1922 until her death in 1943, Esther gave birth to nine children, assumed responsibility for their care and upbringing, and ran a bustling household. She was also heavily involved in the interconnected web of Jewish charities that functioned as a communal safety net. Malbishe Aroumim gave out clothes and provided wedding dresses and dowries for poor young women so they could get married. There was a food bank on the grounds of Magen Avraham. Another organization, Matane Ba-seter ("gifts in secret"), provided financial assistance. Esther—referred to as "the mother of the poor"—would give coins and food to people who came to the Safra home, and then direct them to Jacob's office for further assistance.[33]

It was into this world of expectations, rituals, and responsibilities that Edmond Jacob Safra was born on August 6, 1932, in a 30-bed hospital in Aley—the event itself a departure from tradition. Edmond would be followed by three sisters and two brothers: Arlette in 1933, Moïse in 1934, Huguette in 1936, Gaby in 1937, and finally, Joseph, in 1938.[34]

Jacob had grown up in one sense quite secure, and in another, in a world of loss and danger. In comparison, Edmond enjoyed an early childhood that was in many ways idyllic and privileged. The family had access to the private beach near the fancy St. George Hotel. In the summer they would repair to Aley, a Druze village built into the steep hills, often shrouded in fog. There, Edmond and his siblings had free run of the hills, watched movies in town or went to Baroudi for ice cream. The summer haven would remain a touchstone for Edmond, calling to mind leisure and ease. Later in life, when he acquired a boat that would become a beloved summer refuge, he named it *Aley*.[35]

Simply by virtue of who he was, where he lived, and what he did, Edmond learned from a young age what it meant to be part of the leadership of a community. He was aware that he was better off and had a responsibility to help others. Absorbing Arabic in the home, on the street, and in the market; French at school and in commerce; and Hebrew in the synagogue, he learned to interject expressions of the three languages into his casual speech. The multiple identities he was born with were relatively easy to combine. Being Jewish in Beirut in the 1930s carried little stigma—quite the opposite. The city essentially shut down for major Jewish holidays. Representatives of the government and Muslim and Christian communities would flock to Magen Avraham for a community-wide reception every Passover. When Maronite patriarch Monsignor Antoine Arida visited the Jewish community in April 1937, Wadi Abu Jamil was festooned with Lebanese and French flags and palm branches, and five-year-old Edmond was likely among the children from the youth groups who lined the street leading to Magen Avraham.[36]

The expressions of goodwill were more than lip service. When outside agitators like the Palestinian nationalist Mufti Haj Amin Husseini stirred up trouble in the 1930s, and the occasional anti-Jewish riots broke out, civic authorities protected the Jewish community. Jews tended to ally with the Kata'ib party, the mostly Maronite paramilitary-style youth organization partially inspired by the movements of Franco in Spain and Mussolini in Italy. A photo from this era shows Jacob Safra and other community leaders, including Rabbi Benzion Lichtman, with Kata'ib party leader Pierre Gemayel.[37]

Edmond was precocious, mischievous, and possessed of a firm sense of his own mind. In late 1937, Jacob and Esther thought they had left Edmond at home with his younger siblings when they got on a boat headed for Trieste. They were going to Vienna, a center for polio research, to seek treatment for Paulette's debilitating polio. Their itinerary also included Venice, Milan, where Jacob had business contacts, and Carlsbad, a spa town in western Bohemia. When they were several hours out to sea, a five-year-old stowaway jumped out of a cupboard. It was Edmond, desperate not to be left behind. When the boat arrived in Trieste, Jacob rushed to get his son a passport.

It is impossible to say whether Edmond and his family witnessed any signs of the rising anti-Semitism throughout Europe. But they took in the sights. A photo survives of Esther, Elie, Huguette, and Edmond, in pantaloons, posing amid flocks of pigeons roosting on their arms and shoulders. Sadly, the search for a cure for Paulette proved futile. She was already having difficulty breathing, and the doctors in Vienna couldn't reverse her decline. Paulette died that year.

It's likely that Edmond started attending the Alliance school after the Jewish holidays in the fall of 1938, when he was six years old. Located on Rue Georges Picot, near the family's apartment, the Alliance was a thriving institution. In 1935, under the directorship of Emile Penso, the school had 673 students, with boys and girls in separate buildings. In 1936, it opened a preschool with an auditorium for 250 people. Since his older brother and sister had graduated, Edmond often was walked to the Alliance by the family's handyman and housekeeper, Shehadeh Hallac. (Fifty years later, Edmond was thrilled to discover that his new aide, Jimmy Hallac, was Shehadeh's grandson.) [38]

The Alliance took itself, and its mission as a modernizing influence, seriously. Many of the teachers were supplied by the Ecole Normale Israélite Orientale in Paris. Most students learned some Hebrew, and studied Arabic and English. But the majority of the instruction was in French. The goal was to prepare students for the *Brevet élémentaire*, the official examination that generally marked the transition from formal schooling to work. Edmond and his fellow students learned the history, geography, literature, and politics of France, in addition to physics and math.[39]

Among the faculty, the nearly universal verdict was that young Edmond was not a model student. Well-liked and talkative, he was described by contemporaries and classmates as "*un boute-en-train*" (the center of attention) and a "*grand blagueur*" (a joker) who rarely got into trouble because of the status he and his siblings enjoyed. "Our families were well off, and I believe, at the Alliance, the professors gave us special treatment," Maurizio Dwek, a longtime friend, recalled. Edmond was occasionally singled out for special treatment. Albert Zeitoune, a classmate, was told by the teacher to sit in the back row of the class with Edmond and tutor him in math, and a beloved teacher, Joe Robert, went easy on him. These kindnesses were not forgotten. In a pattern that would repeat itself time and again throughout Edmond's life, years later, after Joe Robert had fled Beirut and needed work, he found a job in Edmond's bank in Brazil. Albert Zeitoune became one of Edmond's most trusted employees.[40]

However, some of the demanding teachers had little patience for students who didn't toe the line, even if they were Safras. The Hebrew teacher smacked Edmond on the fingers with his baton, and the director of the school many times rapped his knuckles. And Edmond earned something of a reputation among teachers and parents who confused his lack of interest in his studies for a lack of ambition. Years later, when Joseph, Edmond's youngest brother, was acting up in class, the teacher, Madame Tarrab, interjected: "Joseph, you're going to end up a cart driver like your brother."[41]

At the same time, some of his teachers saw Edmond's native intelligence as an immense asset. One of his Alliance schoolteachers, Monsieur Abraham, once chided Edmond's classmates, "If one day Edmond sets his mind on doing something, he will be the best, better than all of you." Outside school, Edmond continually proved himself to be clever and ambitious. In the summer of 1940, he convinced his father's driver to let him sell rides to passing businessmen—charging by the weight of the passenger.[42]

Boys began to apprentice in their family's business as soon as they were able—in Edmond's case, at around eight or nine years old. After school, during school holidays, and during the summer break, which began in the second week of June and extended through the Jewish holidays in the fall, Edmond went to the office and trailed Jacob on his rounds. At the souk, Jacob would dispatch his son to assess the clients' inventory. Did they have the same number of bolts of cloth they had told Jacob they had? Was the man's family well dressed? These things mattered because the only way to lend in Beirut in the 1930s was based on character. Jacob always told his sons they should find out how many times a week a prospective client showered. "If we have to go and ask him to pay us back the money we will have to kiss his ass, and I want to be sure it is clean."[43]

Jacob sensed there was something special about his second son. "A visitor to the Safra household in 1940 was captivated with the precocious, eight-year-old Edmond, who was full of chatter about banking, gold, and the long walks he and his father took into the souks," the journalist Bryan Burrough reported. "When I'm walking with Edmond," Jacob told the visitor, a newlywed bride from Aden, "I don't have to speak. There is an electricity between us. He understands what I'm thinking, and I understand what he's thinking." And while he may have had difficulty with authority figures in school, Edmond at this young age formed a fierce, reverential devotion to his father that would last his whole life. Years later, his relative Albert Nasser met Edmond in New York and suggested that he stop working so hard because, after all, he couldn't take it with him. The response: "Albert, I am not working for Edmond Safra. I am working for Jacob Safra, my father."[44]

Edmond learned important lessons from his mother about charity. It was important to bid generously on aliyahs and serve on the communal council, as Jacob did. But young Edmond also accompanied Esther as she carried out the mitzvah of *bikur cholim*—visiting the poor and the sick. And he learned that a vital part of tzedakah was to listen to those seeking help, encourage them in their lives, and work to protect their dignity.

Ritual played an important role in the rhythm of the Safras' lives. Every Shabbat, they attended synagogue at Magen Avraham, or at the Ohel Yaacov synagogue in Aley. On Shavuot, when it was a practice for men to stay up all night studying Torah, Jacob would invite scores of people to his apartment. The Safra boys received additional religious training, and Jacob often brought rabbis to tutor Edmond.[45]

This was a world in which children followed the paths set out for them with little question. And for the Safra children, this meant marriage at a relatively young age, often in an arranged match to someone who was either from Aleppo or who traced his or her roots there. On January 5, 1940, Eveline, Edmond's older sister, then fifteen, was wedded to Rahmo Nasser, a distinguished surgeon from Aleppo, many years her senior, who practiced in both Beirut and Aleppo. They may have been living in Beirut, but the Safras were still Halabis. And they, and their fellow Aleppans, would cling to that sense of identity for decades to come, on every continent. "There is no Jewish community in the diaspora that resembles Aleppo in the closeness of its members," observed Yigal Arnon, Edmond's lawyer in Israel later in life. "It's like they are one big clan. To this day, they are all closely connected."[46]

Whereas Jacob, a native Aleppan, had adapted to his new home, Edmond was a natural product of Beirut: bustling, confident, open, polymathic. The old commercial center, where they lived and worked, was oriented around wide boulevards: Rue Allenby (where the bank was) and Rue Foch, and Rue Weygand, running along the water itself. The waterfront Corniche, complete with palm trees, resembled Nice's Promenade des Anglais. Nearby, however, were the warrens of souks and shops. It was not uncommon for someone to drive a small flock of sheep across the tram tracks on Rue Georges Picot. People may have stuck to their own kind when it came to marriage, but Beirut was tolerant and accepting of differences. Edmond had a deep sense of belonging to a multiethnic, multireligion Lebanese culture. Beirut was a place, as Philip Mansel described it, where people put "deals before ideals." Albert Hourani, the Lebanese historian, summed it up as follows: "To be Levantine is to inhabit two worlds, without really being a part of either." Edmond and his fellow Beiruti Jews managed this without cognitive dissonance. [47]

The cordiality evident in Beirut was even more distinctive given what was going on in Europe in the 1930s. In Germany, the home of the Enlightenment, a country where Jews had long since been emancipated, fascism was taking root, spreading its insidious hate and prejudice throughout the continent, and wreaking havoc on the national aspirations of its neighbors. As Germany's armies rolled east and west throughout the European land mass, the machinery of genocide followed. But Lebanon and its Jews were spared the worst. In June 1940, after Germany defeated France, the Vichy regime took control of Lebanon and Syria. Vichy troops occupied Beirut, a major supply center, and jailed members of several Lebanese communities, including many Jews. In June 1941, the Allies launched Operation Explorer. When the Free French and Allied troops took back Beirut and Damascus, they lifted the anti-Jewish restrictions that had been put in place. The occupying territories scheduled elections for 1943, which were supposed to lead to Lebanese independence. But Beirut remained under Allied occupation for the remainder of the war.

Amid the tumult, Jacob Safra was a leader to whom many in the community turned, not simply because he had resources and power, but because he was accessible and he embraced his role as a guarantor of dignity. Individuals who needed a scholarship, a job, a loan, a discount on a note, would turn first to Jacob rather than another Jewish banker in town. Meir Ashkenazi, who grew up in Beirut, remembers that during the war, his father worked for a pharmaceutical company that had copied a drug produced by a German company. Authorities closed the factory and took the employees to jail on a Friday. When the man's wife went to Jacob to ask him to sign a bond to get him out of jail, Jacob got in his car, went to see the judge, and signed the guarantee so the man could be home by Shabbat. [48]

The Safras avoided the communal misfortune that befell so many Jews in the region during the war, but they were not immune from personal tragedy. Esther Safra was in continually fragile health, one of the consequences of giving birth to nine children over an 18-year period. She became pregnant again in 1942, and in February began to endure a difficult labor and went to a hospital in Beirut. On February 14, 1943, despite the efforts of her doctor, a French professor of medicine, both Esther and her unborn child died.

Esther's death was a hammer blow to the family, including young Edmond, and to the community. In a sign of respect for the family's status, all the students from Edmond's class at the Alliance came to the cemetery and to the Safra house for shiva.

Edmond, just entering adolescence, had already endured the death of an older sister, and now his mother—personal losses that would be a factor in what would become an endemic pessimism. Although to many he met, Edmond may have seemed a joker with few cares and a willingness to take risks, he was already learning to fear the worst and to plan for it. It's likely these devastating early personal losses enabled him to accept the inevitable financial set-backs that would occur in business, and to keep them in perspective. And just as he would spend his adult life, in effect, working for his father, Edmond would shoulder the burden of carrying out his mother's good works. "My mother told me that one day she would not be there, and that I would be the one who would take care of the others," he said. As a young man and adult, Edmond was also reluctant to form close relationships and was in no rush to start his own family, perhaps because of concerns over potential abandonment and loss.[49]

In many families, it would have been common for an older sister or a sister-in-law to step in. Elie, the oldest sibling, married Yvette Dabbah in 1943. Born in 1927, she was too young to be a surrogate mother for the younger Safras. Eveline, the eldest daughter and a mother to a newborn daughter, moved from her home in Aleppo back to the family's apartment in Beirut to care for her younger siblings. Urged by Eveline to marry again, Jacob reluctantly began to seek a new partner. Not everybody was on board with the plan. When Jacob began dating a young woman in Aley, Edmond enlisted his brothers and sisters to rig water buckets atop the front door. After a few drench-ings, the woman lost interest in Jacob.[50]

Edmond also began to act out in school. In June 1943, Edmond passed both the French and Lebanese *Certificat d'études* given at the end of elementary school. But when school started again, Edmond began to skip class. He received special dispensation for being the son of a prominent supporter of the Alliance. But Edmond was a generally difficult presence at school. And finally, in September 1945, after he clashed with a teacher, Madame Alalou, the administration indicated that it might be best if he pursued other options.[51]

So Jacob enrolled Edmond at St. Joseph d'Antoura, a boarding school about twenty kilometers outside Beirut run by the Lazarist order of the Catholic Church—which Elie had also attended. Founded in 1651, St. Joseph was the oldest French school in the Middle East and was a popular destination for the children of the Lebanese elite, as well as for Christians, Jews, and Muslims from around the region, including Iraq and Egypt. To meet the school's requirement of fluency in three languages, Edmond studied more English (and possibly some Italian), which would prove invaluable for his future. He was clearly on a more constructive academic path. But in Beirut, he had the run of town and enjoyed being a part of his father's business world and part of a large clan.

At St. Joseph, he also formed a lifelong friendship with a fellow Jewish student, Maurice Mann. (Mann's parents were not always enthusiastic about the influence that the undistinguished student was having on their son. Maury's mother once insulted him in Arabic: "How are you going to be a man if you hang out with Edmond Safra?"[52]) Edmond vented his frustrations in letters to his older sister, Eveline, and she, in turn, prodded Jacob to let Edmond come back to Beirut. Upon his return to the Alliance, the drama continued. Edmond failed the *Brevet élémentaire* on his first attempt. But with the help of his friend Albert Zeitoune, who tutored him in math, and his teachers, Messieurs Robert and Levy and Madame Tarrab, Edmond succeeded in passing the test in the spring of 1947.[53]

The end of formal schooling surely came as a relief to Edmond, and to his teachers. And he was poised to start working full-time with his father. But as Edmond and his family were managing the turbulence of his teen years, the environment in Beirut and the region was changing rapidly. Lebanon and its Jewish population remained protected from the devastation and violence that had ravaged so much of Europe and the Mediterranean basin. But the end of the war set into motion the forces that would first boost the Jewish population of Beirut, and then push all of them to leave. Slowly, then all at once, these forces would shake the foundations on which the Banque Jacob E. Safra and the Safra family's comfortable life in Beirut rested.

In 1943, Lebanon was granted its independence and emerged as a democracy. The new Lebanese president, Bechara el-Khoury, a Maronite Christian whose family had close links to the Safras, brokered a deal that apportioned parliament and government posts among religious and ethnic groups according to the 1932 census, on a six-to-five Christian–Muslim proportional basis. The presidency went to the Maronites, the premiership to the Sunnis, and the speaker of the house to the Shia. Jews shared a minority seat in parliament with smaller Christian groups—Latin Catholics, Syrian Jacobites, Syrian Catholics, Nestorians, and Chaldeans.

In Lebanon, underneath the apparent sectarian harmony, there were ancient rifts among factions who disagreed about how power should be shared in the country's future. With the weakened European powers France and England ceding their mandates, new nations—and new nationalisms—took shape in Iraq, Syria, Egypt, Jordan, and Palestine between 1945 and 1948. Lebanon's diversity would ultimately prove to be a particular problem. Among Sunni Muslims, there was a yearning to become part of a larger, pan-Arab state (non-Muslim minorities would enjoy protections as they did under the Ottomans). Maronite Christians, for their part, saw Lebanon as a European nation.[54]

The rise of nationalist sentiment was further complicated and aggravated by developments just to the south of Lebanon—in Palestine. In the aftermath of World War II, displaced people were on the move throughout the region. These included thousands of Jews, survivors of the Holocaust, who were making their way to Palestine to join the growing settlements and provide more momentum for the push for a Jewish state. Publicly and officially, the Conseil Communal in Beirut was not overtly Zionistic. But community members were moved by the plight of their coreligionists. During and after the war, youth organizations such as Maccabi and B'nai Zion helped Jews move underground from Europe and Turkey across the border to Palestine at the frontier at Naqoura, and small numbers of Lebanese Jews began to join the Jewish self-defense forces in Palestine.

The competing nationalisms created a toxic mix. While Beirut remained safe, in November 1945, about a dozen Jews were killed in anti-Jewish riots in Tripoli. In 1946, foreign forces withdrew from both Lebanon and Syria, leaving nationalist impulses to flourish in their wake. In April 1946, Syria declared its independence. That year, as riots broke out, Jews began to be fired from government jobs. As security deteriorated, some 6,000 Jews fled from Syria to Lebanon.

Jacob Safra had already witnessed and survived the breakup of one empire—by leaving Aleppo for Beirut. Now, twenty-seven years later, he was grappling with the end of the European colonial presence in the Middle East. In the spring of 1947, as Edmond was preparing for his exams, talks were starting at the United Nations to partition Palestine into two states—one for Jews and one for Arabs. Suddenly the future for Jews in Beirut looked very uncertain.

Jacob had some key decisions to make about his future. Where would it be best for his children and grandchildren to grow up? How could he ensure the survival of his bank, and his assets, given the inevitable turbulence? Jacob had no desire to leave Beirut. But it was clear that, as he and his uncles had found before, it was now both prudent and necessary to seek out climates that were more hospitable to business, and to shift part of the family's wealth outside Lebanon. But where? And how?

The Safras had resources and connections, but not so many that exceptions would be made for them. As the situation in the Middle East became more challenging, small numbers of Aleppans and Beiruti Jews, motivated in part by fear and in part by opportunity, migrated to places where they could get visas. They went to Iran; to Italy; to the Philippines, Hong Kong, and Japan; to all parts of South and Central America; and to Mexico. The United States, already home to thousands of Aleppan Jews, had essentially shut the door on immigration from Syria and Lebanon.[55] As for London, the historic financial center of Europe remained a shadow of its prewar self. The London gold market had yet to reopen. Amsterdam, spared many of the ravages of heavy bombing, presented a significant language barrier. That left Milan.[56]

Among Europe's commercial capitals, Milan was the most appealing. Milan and, more broadly, Italy's industrial north, were largely untouched by the military campaigns of 1944 and 1945. By late 1947, its textile and automotive industries were back online. Trade finance and convertible currencies were in high demand. Milan was a center of jewelry production, and hence a key trading post for gold. Perhaps most important, it was comparatively easy for people in Beirut to obtain Italian visas.

Jacob Safra could scarcely pack up his children and go to Milan himself. The natural choice would have been to send Elie. At 25, he was already married. He and Yvette would soon be expecting their first child. And it was assumed that Elie, who had been schooled at the Alliance, at Antoura, and at the Banque Jacob E. Safra, and who had already shown promise as a gold trader, would ultimately take over the family firm. But there were compelling reasons for Jacob to overlook tradition and instead consider his precocious second son, Edmond.[57]

Although Edmond had not been conducting business on his own, there was a general sense that the indifferent student was a business prodigy. His intelligence, acumen, and intense interest in business and banking affairs were evident to all, as was his independent spirit. If he was relatively uninterested in chemistry and language studies, Edmond was eager to learn about the world at large. At the age of twelve or thirteen, he would pump visitors from abroad for information about the world and pester officers at Banque Jacob E. Safra for information on how to calculate discount rates and trade gold. Jacob and Edmond already had a unique relationship and understanding, and Edmond was ready to launch his career.[58]

There were other reasons for Jacob to consider sending his head-strong son to Milan in 1947. Widowed since Esther's death in 1943, Jacob was now engaged to Marie Douek. Born in Aleppo in 1911, and the daughter and granddaughter of prominent rabbis, "Tante Marie" was a charming, vivacious woman in her thirties who didn't have children of her own. She got along well with Jacob's children—save Edmond, who selfishly and understandably resisted anyone who would take the place of his mother. Meanwhile, Edmond had himself fallen in love with an Alliance school classmate of whom Jacob disapproved.

Sending Edmond to Milan would thus solve several problems for Jacob. And so in the fall of 1947, Jacob summoned Edmond and gave him the news. This time he wouldn't have to stow away to go to Italy, for he was being sent to Milan to build a gold trading and foreign exchange operation.

To ask a fifteen-year-old boy to leave the safety and security of his family and the only home he had ever known, to carry the hopes and expectations of the family on his shoulders, was a significant decision. And for a man steeped in tradition and obligation, elevating the second son over the first was both unorthodox and emotionally difficult. The decision would have significant ramifications for the family.

On one level, the move—and the conflict it would set up with his brother Elie—made Edmond uncomfortable. It placed a set of bur-dens on his shoulders that he would carry with him for the rest of his life. But Edmond was also motivated by a strong sense of duty, and a deep self-confidence. He was ready, and he wouldn't be going on his own. Jacques Tawil, a twenty-year-old clerk in Jacob's bank, had already entered the family's circle of trust. Jacob had been Jacques's *sandak*—the person who has the honor of holding the baby during the *brit milah*. And once in Milan, Edmond and Jacques would have a small Syrian and Lebanese community to plug into. As important, there would be financial resources waiting for them. Jacob had transferred a substantial amount of gold to a Rome bank, to be relied upon for capital and as an emergency nest egg for the family—one source suggests Jacob had transferred a total of $5 million into Italian banks. He also established a $1 million credit line with Banca Commerciale Italiana, a bank with Jewish origins, on which Edmond could draw.[59]

When the partition of Palestine was formally announced on November 29, 1947, roughly 2,000 people turned out to celebrate at Magen Avraham in Beirut. But this time, Edmond wasn't part of the crowd. Three weeks earlier, he and Jacques Tawil had driven across the border separating Lebanon and Palestine. After staying in Tel Aviv for two nights, they boarded a KLM flight for Rome.

4

Coming of Age in Europe

(1947–1954)

The trip to Milan, a distance of about 1,500 miles that should have taken several hours by plane, was something of an odyssey. Since the weekly direct flight from Beirut to Milan left on a Saturday, when they didn't travel, Edmond and Jacques Tawil trundled their way to Lod by car. From there, they caught the weekly KLM flight to Amsterdam, which made it to Rome in six hours. Their plans to catch a connecting flight to Milan were stymied when a thick sheet of fog caused flights to be cancelled, so they eventually caught a bus to Milan, a 360-mile journey that took an excruciating seventeen hours. Having difficulty finding the apartment Jacob had set up, they checked into a hotel.[60]

A fog hovered over Europe, too. Milan then, as now, was Italy's financial, textile, and industrial capital and occupied an important role in what was left of the European economy. The war had ended thirty months before, but large swaths of the continent had been laid to waste by bombing campaigns and mechanized assaults. Cities large and small were strewn with rubble. More than 36 million people had been killed. Hundreds of thousands of desperate people were in motion, homeless and stateless, in search of safe havens and new homes. Italy was dotted with displaced persons camps.

Edmond Safra and Jacques Tawil were neither refugees nor immigrants. Odd as it may have seemed to a stranger, the two, aged fifteen and twenty, with little experience and not much Italian between them, were traveling businesspeople. Like so many others, they showed up with very few possessions. But unlike so many of those sojourning in Italy, they had significant capital waiting for them, along with a network of connections, and a somewhat vague charge: "To see if we could make business," Tawil said.

The two young men were acutely aware that they had arrived in a new and somewhat alien culture. From the moment of their arrival, Safra and Tawil engaged in constant improvisation. Cancelling the lease on the apartment, they settled into the hotel. The duo subsisted on room service until Tawil perfected the challenging task of twirling spaghetti in public. Edmond couldn't register a business—or rent office space—until he received a resident visa, so to create the impression that he was something more than a fifteen-year-old in a hotel room, he hired a secretary to type noisily in the background when he was on the phone.[61]

As Edmond would do time and again wherever he landed, he went straight to the middle of the action. Wearing what would become his trademark suit—navy blue—he hung out in the lobby of Milan's grandest hotel, the Principe di Savoia, which had served as Nazi headquarters during the war and was now a gathering place for businesspeople, including other Syrian and Lebanese Jews. His briefcase was filled not with contracts, but with newspapers and pistachio nuts—a staple of his diet. Edmond was mortified when one day, the undistinguished contents spilled onto the floor of the art deco lobby.[62]

Tawil's role was somewhere between chaperone and colleague. "I was like his tutor, you know," he later recalled. And he coached his charge to keep his ears open and speak only when necessary. Before an interview with the Milan police about his immigration status, Tawil told him, "Just answer the question that the policeman asks you. Don't make any suggestions. You're not there to be helpful. If the policeman asks you, 'Did you enter this building through the window?' the answer is 'No.' Don't say, 'I came through the door.' The answer is 'No,' because that is the answer to the question that he asked."[63]

When Edmond and Tawil arrived, a clutch of Syrian-Jewish families were already in Milan, and a stream of others were passing through. "In Milan, we knew about four, five, or six families from Beirut or Aleppo: Nehmad, Matalon, Stambouli," Tawil recalled. In the Syrian diaspora, a community could be found among a small group, most of whom were related or connected through marriage or business. It was typical for families to have seven or eight children. One person might thus have dozens of first cousins, and connections to hundreds of others who were related by marriage. Among those in Milan was Nessim Dwek. Nessim, who wasn't related to Edmond's stepmother, was one of seven brothers in a family that specialized in the global textile trade. He had often joined Jacob for coffee in Beirut. In Milan, Edmond and Jacques Tawil would join the Dweks for dinners on Friday or Sunday night, or for the traditional Saturday midday lunch. Nessim Dwek would become something of a surrogate father to Edmond. After Dwek's death, Edmond would place pictures of him in the bank's offices.[64]

Despite the initial language and cultural barriers Milan presented, it was a hospitable place. And Edmond showed an instinctive gift for blending in. Edmond had a talent for finding mentors, guides, and peers among men ten and twenty years older than he was. In Milan, he found easy entrée into the larger circle of Italian-Jewish businessmen who had their own important familial connections. Umberto Treves, scion of a distinguished Lombardy Jewish family, was a well-known local stockbroker. His father, a banker, had been deported to a Nazi death camp by German troops in 1943, and he was related by marriage to Camillo de Benedetti, a cousin of Italian industrialist Carlo de Benedetti. Treves introduced Edmond to Milanese businessmen. Perhaps as important, he taught Edmond to dress like a local; for the rest of his life, Edmond would buy his shirts only from Corbella Milano and his shoes from Morandi.[65]

The business got off to a slow start. In the first few months, Edmond and Tawil managed to complete just a few small currency deals. Their status as outsiders, however, did grant them an edge in dealing in precious metals, and especially in gold.[66]

Valued as a currency, a store of value, and a material for jewelry; significant as a monetary base; and in constant demand for religious and social purposes, gold was, in effect, an indestructible global currency. And with hard borders separating countries, European integration a far-off dream, Soviet expansion fueling uncertainty throughout Europe, and revolutions brewing in the Middle East and Asia, stable currencies were few and far between. "Whenever there is distrust in currencies, people always come to gold," noted Edward "Jock" Mocatta, of London gold dealers Mocatta and Goldsmid.[67]

In Europe in 1947 there wasn't much of a market for trading gold. First, the price was essentially fixed. At the Bretton Woods conference in 1944, the International Monetary Fund pegged most global currencies to the US dollar, the most stable currency, and set the value of gold at $35 per ounce. Moreover, gold was scarce. At the time, 75 percent of the world's monetary gold and half the gold mined in history rested in vaults in the United States, safe from the world's convulsions. But there were exceptions. In Lebanon, for example, gold continued to trade freely. Regulations allowed gold in Europe that could be used for jewelry, for example, so-called "manufactured gold," to sell at a premium of $3 or more per ounce. Edmond Safra was uniquely situated to mine the seams of the global economy and its fracturing empires for profits in the precious metal trade. And the biggest supply of gold in Europe was right next door.[68]

During the war, neutral Switzerland emerged as a kind of safe-deposit box for the Nazis' personal wealth, much of it held in gold; Switzerland also sold munitions and other supplies to Germany during the war, again for gold. By 1945, Swiss banks like Union de Banques Suisses (UBS) and Swiss Bank Corporation (SBC, or Société de Banque Suisse) between them had the gold equivalent of 1.6 billion Swiss francs ($18.25 billion in 2021 US dollars). "Buying gold in Switzerland," wrote Timothy Green, a historian of the postwar gold market, "was like going to the baker to buy bread." So Edmond and Jacques Tawil made their way to Zurich.[69]

It is hard to imagine an environment more different from Beirut than Zurich. Beirut was sunny, oriented to the sea, characterized by easy sociability and Mediterranean informality. By contrast, German-speaking Zurich sat in an isolated, landlocked region, surrounded by mountains, housing inward-looking, intensely private banks and large institutions. Still, Edmond strode into the new city with a confidence that wasn't always warranted. Although he was proving to be a linguistic savant, his German was barely rudimentary. He entered what he was sure was a mortgage bank (*hypothek*) only to find his interlocutor dumbfounded when he asked about a loan; it was an *apotheke*, a pharmacy. Still, he spoke the language that was most easily understood in Zurich: commerce. Edmond opened a line of credit with UBS. Francophone Geneva was more to Edmond's liking and would in time become one of the family's bases.[70]

Edmond and his father, who were in touch by telephone and telegraph, quickly found arbitrage opportunities. The Maria Theresa thaler was an Austrian silver coin stamped with the face of Empress Maria Theresa, the mid-eighteenth-century Hapsburg. In an early and overlooked example of financial globalization, the Maria Theresa thaler was commonly used throughout Europe, the Middle East, and Africa through the 1950s, often as an official currency. But Edmond knew that in the Arab world, coins featuring a woman's likeness traded at a small discount to their full value in Europe. So Jacob Safra used his network to buy Maria Theresa thalers in the Middle East and shipped them to Europe, where they could be swapped on a one-for-one basis with coins bearing Emperor Franz Josef's image. This was a trade essentially without risk—the type of sure thing the Safras loved. But it could succeed only if you had the infrastructure to work in multiple contexts simultaneously. Edmond worked with Bulgarian brokers—forwarding agents—in Milan to track down Franz Josef thalers in London, Paris, and Brussels.[71]

Greater profits could be made shipping gold in larger quantities from the places where its price was fixed (namely, Europe) to areas where it was freely traded, and to places where people angling to clandestinely import gold into closed markets might pay a hefty premium. In the postwar years, demand for gold was constant in the Middle East, India, and the Far East. In China, a civil war had started in 1948. Britain, which still controlled Hong Kong, had banned gold imports. But British traders in Hong Kong could move gold to nearby Macao, controlled by Portugal, where Chinese smugglers would pay a high price for it, turn it into powder that could be concealed in peanut shells, and move it back into Hong Kong or into China. Gold that sold for $38 an ounce in Europe could command $55 an ounce in Shanghai or Beijing.[72]

The Safras, along with others in their circle, already had a well-established way to get gold from Beirut to Kuwait (to be sold into India and points beyond). First, as legend had it, they used camel caravans; later, the gold traveled overland by train through Baghdad. After the war, gold importers in Beirut brought gold from Europe by plane, often in 12.5 kilogram ingots, moved it through customs, repackaged it in their own boxes, and shipped it via air to Kuwait or Dubai. The Safras were also known quantities to the London-based firms that played an important role in the European gold trade. In time, a group of Aleppo Jewish businessmen in Europe, including Jacques Douek, Tante Marie's brother, formed a shipping consortium to handle the movement. The volume of gold moving through Beirut soared from 335 kilograms in 1946 to 12,500 kilograms in 1947 and peaked at 89,000 kilograms (about 100 tons) in 1951. By the early 1950s, noted historian Kirsten Schulze, about "30 percent of the private international gold trade went through Beirut."[73]

But to carry out this trade at scale, the Safras needed a trusted person at the far end of the trade. And while a handful of Syrian Jews were active in the Far East at the time, none was sufficiently close to be taken into confidence. Edmond was in Milan. Elie, his older brother, was working in Europe, married and about to have his first child. So they turned to an unlikely person: Rahmo Nasser, Eveline's husband.

It was rare for families to bring sons- and brothers-in-law into the business. And Rahmo Nasser seemed to be settled in life. He had studied medicine at the University of Lyon and was chief surgeon of the American Hospital in Beirut for many years. He was the father of two children, Camille and Ezequiel, Jacob's first grandchildren and Edmond's first niece and nephew, and in 1947 was preparing to open his own surgery clinic in Aleppo. But on November 30, 1947, just two weeks after Edmond had arrived in Milan and the day after the UN General Assembly voted to create the State of Israel, mobs rampaged through Aleppo, destroying Jewish businesses and setting fire to synagogues, including the Great Synagogue. The Jewish presence in Aram Tzova, which had lasted more than two millennia, was suddenly tenuous. Rahmo abandoned his plans to return his family to Aleppo, and he and Eveline decided to stay permanently with Jacob on Rue Georges Picot. By the end of that tumultuous year, half of the 30,000 Jews in Syria had left.[74]

Although he had no experience in gold trading or conducting financial affairs of any sort, Rahmo was shrewd and meticulous. Most important, he was family. Rahmo agreed to Jacob Safra's suggestion that he move to Hong Kong and share fifty-fifty in the returns he expected to make. On May 14, 1948, the day Israel formally proclaimed its independence, Nasser set off on the arduous and lonely journey to Hong Kong, leaving his wife and children behind.[75] In Hong Kong, where housing was scarce, he stayed with a cousin.[76]

Entering the gold trade was like playing chess on an international board. While Jacques Tawil stayed in Zurich, Edmond went to Amsterdam, a historical financial market that had reopened while the London gold market was closed (it would remain so until 1954). There, Edmond bought $1 million worth of gold (about $14 million in 2021 US dollars) from the Rothschilds. As Edmond traveled, he continually bumped into people he knew, or people who knew of him and members of his family. Ezekiel Schouela, a Syrian from Aleppo who had moved first to Egypt and then to Milan, was in the Amsterdam waiting room of the Central Bank of the Netherlands in 1948 when he saw a young man announce himself to the receptionist as Edmond Safra. "Are you by any chance related to Jacob Safra?" The young man said, "Yes, he's my father." Schouela asked, "What are you doing here?" He said, "I'm buying gold for my father."[77]

Next, it was on to Paris in April 1948 in search of more gold. Instead of staying for a few weeks, as he had in Zurich and Amsterdam,

Edmond sojourned in Paris for several months. Paris proved to be an appealing and vibrant base. The Marshall Plan, enacted in 1948, began to funnel aid to France and other European countries. Here, as in Milan, Edmond headed for the center of the business world and the financial establishment—on the Right Bank.

The French government was dialing back its sales of gold at the same time that demand was rising from the private sector. Edmond quickly saw that despite the limitations on trading, gold in Paris commanded a higher price than it did in Zurich or Amsterdam, which presented an opportunity to bring in gold from Zurich and elsewhere. Moving gold in and around Europe, Edmond realized, could be as profitable as shipping it from Europe to the Far East.[78]

Given his fluency in the language, and the long-standing presence of many French banks in Beirut, Edmond found Paris a congenial place. Emile Saadia, a law professor turned banker from Beirut, was at the headquarters of his company, BCNI, on the Boulevard des Italiens. "I found Edmond Safra from Milan at the bank, to see people and make contacts," he recalled, and vouched for him. As in Milan, a group of Syrian and Lebanese Jews, peers and elders, were studying or setting up businesses—or, in the case of Maury Mann, Edmond's roommate from boarding school at Antoura, spending their inheritance in the red-light district of Pigalle.

Edmond and Mann shared a room in the Grand Hotel near the major French and foreign banks. The Café de la Paix, on the hotel's ground floor, attracted the city's financial elite. There was a seamlessness between business and social life, and Edmond's extended group of friends functioned as a surrogate family. Nessim Dwek had arrived from Milan, and Cyril Dwek, his son, was in boarding school in Paris. Edmond's other Paris-based friends included Leon Aslan Sassoon, nicknamed "Sir Philip," after Sir Philip Sassoon, the aristocratic scion of a Sephardic banking dynasty. Without formal homes or offices, they spent their work and free time in restaurants, cafés, and commercial and bank offices. Nearby was the Cercle Haussmann, a casino in Place de la Madeleine that was popular with Lebanese. While hardly abstemious, Edmond had a sense of self-control and self-possession, even as a teenager. He didn't enjoy gambling, and would have a drink or two, but never drank to excess.[79]

Paris housed the headquarters of the AIU as well as the Ecole Normale Israélite Orientale (ENIO), its training academy. Like a fraternity with chapters in many cities, the institution connected its alumni in a kinship network, giving them not just a working knowledge of the French language, but a common background and a sense of solidarity. So when Edmond needed a work permit in order to do business in Paris, he showed up at the ENIO, where a family friend from Beirut, Isaac Obersi, was studying, and asked "if he could get the Alliance to help him with some papers." When the administration assisted Safra and the papers came through, Edmond responded in two ways that were characteristic of his approach to business. He took Obersi and another teenage friend to a posh nightclub—"we might as well have been wearing short trousers," Obersi recalled. And in a recognition of his (and Jacob's) belief in the link between success in business and the obligations of charity, Edmond asked if there was anything the school needed, and offered to buy the commercial refrigerator the administration indicated would be very welcome. The administration, unsure whether to take this young man seriously, called the Alliance in Beirut and asked if Edmond Safra was for real. The answer came back in the affirmative. (In 2011, the Alliance renamed its training academy the Centre Alliance Edmond J. Safra.)[80]

This wasn't the only charitable effort that peers and associates noticed. One night late in 1948, according to Mann, Edmond took the new overcoat he had bought that day and draped it over a homeless man. (Mann jokingly pleaded with him: "Edmond, ya habibi, give him my coat, and give your coat to me.")

As a teenager, Edmond simultaneously occupied a world of carefree adolescents like Mann and the serious world of adults. In 1948, Rahmo Nasser sent a telegram to Edmond asking him to host Panama's ambassador in Hong Kong, who was about to visit Paris. Lacking his own driver's license, Edmond tapped Mann to be his driver, bought a Buick, and traveled with the ambassador to the South of France—Cannes, Monte Carlo, and Nice. While driving the new car, the boys were pulled over by police, and Mann, who had been drinking, was tossed into prison for a week.[81]

Mann exasperated Edmond no end. When Edmond gave him money to make a donation to the Jewish Agency at the Israeli Embassy in Paris in 1948, Mann lost it gambling. At the end of the year, having squandered much of his inheritance and no small part of Edmond's goodwill, Mann moved to Israel. But the two remained in touch. When Mann faced financial difficulty later in life, Safra provided him with a monthly allowance.[82]

Edmond's first visit to the South of France evidently made an impression. He would return time and again to the region in the summer, and it would become one of his home bases. As for the ambassador, the contact would come in handy decades later when Safra was looking to establish a representative bank office in Panama City and sought passports for Syrian Jewish refugees.

Edmond's sojourn in Paris was coming to an end. As gold prices in Europe harmonized, Edmond returned to Milan in late 1948, and Tawil went back to Beirut. Safra set himself up at 3 Via Giuseppe Mazzini, a stone's throw from the Duomo, and frequented the Oratorio Sefardita Orientale, on Via Guastalla. In 1949, likely through connections in Beirut, he recruited several Arab sheikhs as clients for Jacob's bank. Among the transactions he engineered was a $25 million deal to ship gold from Saudi Arabia to Greece.[83]

Gold and precious metals were moving in all directions, and Edmond, still a teenager, had his own ideas about how to profit from the flow. He would buy bags of gold with all kinds of coins: Swiss Vreneli, Turkish lira, French Napoleons, British gold sovereigns. He'd send some of them to Lebanon, where Turkish gold coins were in demand, and send the British coins to the Far East. Samy Cohn, a former Israeli Air Force officer who had a commodity trading operation in Europe, recalls meeting Edmond in 1947 or 1948 at a lunch in Milan with a group of older men. The conversation centered on Hungarian gold coins. "Now, he was a trader because there was a special . . . cunning where he could smell a business at a mile away," Cohn recalled. When market conditions shifted, Edmond would melt coins down into ingots.[84]

To do this work, however, Edmond needed an export license, so he went to the Italian Ministry of Finance and rolled out what he would dub "the Buongiorno Technique":

> You just have to show up in person. You don't know anyone. You say "Buongiorno" to the doorman or the porter. He says "Buongiorno" and you leave. The next day, you come back, you say "Buongiorno." Maybe you meet the coffee lady. You say "Buongiorno," she says "Buongiorno," and you leave. The third day, you come back. You see an assistant to the minister, you say "Buongiorno." I guarantee that after four days of Buongiornos, you get to see the minister himself.

It worked. Edmond quickly obtained the export license.[85] In Paris, he employed a variation on this theme: "the Mattress Technique." He showed up at the office of Wilfrid Baumgartner, the governor of the Banque de France. "You have to put your mattress down in front of the minister's door and be prepared to sleep on it." No matter that Baumgartner was thirty years older and a graduate of the Paris Institute of Political Studies, they formed a friendship that lasted until Baumgartner's death in 1978.

As he traveled around, Edmond showed a preternatural ability to meet people, to form mutually beneficial relationships and friendships and file them away in his powerful memory. In Geneva, he met Victor Smaga, an Alexandria-born auditor who was working for Jewish organizations and had known Edmond's cousin Edgar Safra in Egypt. "I remember very well that he was sixteen, and still wearing shorts," recalled Smaga, who would become a lifelong friend. A kid in short pants, Edmond also presented himself as an equal, casually suggesting business terms to those twice his age. In Milan, he met Rahmo Sassoon, an Aleppo-born trader who had moved to Japan and who specialized in finance and importing and exporting. When Sassoon came to Milan in 1949 to meet a Syrian woman to marry, Edmond asked Sassoon, who was old enough to be his father, to set up contacts with his associates in Shanghai, Japan, and Bangkok, agreeing to split the commissions.

And Edmond was always aware of who was on the other side of the trades, even if there was no direct connection. Albert Hattena, a Syrian Jew who left Cairo in 1948 for Hong Kong, worked in the commodity and precious metals trade. As part of his work, he regularly mailed records of the shipments to an office in Milan that turned out to be Edmond's. When they met years later, Hattena recalled, "he knew my name, and he told me once that he was impressed from the way I was giving him the *compte-rendu*, the full accounting."[86]

Edmond didn't regard doing business as "work." Even as he operated under immense financial and familial pressure, photos taken in this era show him to be at ease. For Edmond, business was an intensely social activity. Friends, family, clients, counterparts—they were all part of the same large circle. Business could be conducted in an office, on the phone, in a café, or in the home, during the day or at night, during the workweek or on holiday. "Making money was very important to him. For him, it was sheer pleasure," Rahmo Nasser said.[87]

Edmond's equanimity was even more impressive given how the stakes were growing. He wasn't simply trying to make money; he was striving to carry on Jacob's work and help provide for an extended and growing family whose needs were growing more complex.

Until 1947, the Safra family rested on two solid foundations—Aleppo and Beirut. By 1949 and 1950, Milan was starting to replace Aleppo as a base, and the situation in Beirut was growing more perilous. At the same time, the family's life was getting more complicated.

In Beirut, the Safras still enjoyed the haven of Rue Georges Picot, the Alliance, Magen Avraham, Aley, and the bank. The Beirut Jewish community, of which the Safras were an anchor, was protected. Edmond always had one foot back home. One childhood friend recalls going into Jacob's bank in the late 1940s and Jacob telling him to discount the note with Edmond, even though the interest rate Edmond offered was a half point higher. One night in Beirut, a singer at a nightclub owned by his friend, Jean-Prosper Gay-Para, became ill. Edmond summoned a doctor, paid for her bill—and then signed up the physician as a client.[88]

But in 1949 and 1950, slowly, and then all at once, the pillars that upheld Edmond's view of how the family would function, and what its place was in Beirut, would start to crumble. The first pillar to fall was the unity of the family. Edmond's relationship with his older brother, Elie, the firstborn son who was ten years Edmond's senior, had been problematic from the moment he left for Europe. In 1948, Elie and Yvette welcomed their first child, a son, Jacqui, named after Jacob. In typical birth-order scenarios, the oldest child conforms to parental wishes and it is the middle children who rebel. But in the Safras' case it was the opposite. Elie was in Milan and Switzerland, and the brothers cooperated on a handful of deals for gold coins.[89] Ambitious and independent minded, Elie was not pleased that Jacob had backed his younger brother with a significant sum of capital. "Elie was also intelligent, but sometimes had fixed ideas," Rahmo Nasser recalled. In 1949, believing gold would rise, Elie established a large position, only to suffer a loss when the price of gold collapsed. Edmond, for his part, had hedged his exposure. In the fall of 1949, Elie fell out with his father, and, at the age of twenty-seven, asked for his inheritance—precipitating a sort of family divorce. On October 21, Jacob bought Elie out of the family firm for $300,000, in recognition "of all my efforts and the business I have handled on my father's behalf until this day, both in Beirut and in Europe." Elie moved to Geneva, where he would remain within the family's loose orbit for the remainder of his life. The split only served to reemphasize for Edmond that the business he was conducting, and the capital he managed and made, was for the family at large.[90]

Meanwhile, the establishment of Israel, and the ensuing arrival of large numbers of Palestinian refugees, began to unsettle the fragile entente that had made Lebanon's multiconfessional society work. And Beirut's Jews, the "tightrope walkers," as the community's historian, Gabrielle Elia, would describe them, were being buffeted by increasingly powerful winds. As the Syrian government turned against its Jewish population—all Jewish government employees were fired by May 1948 and anti-Jewish riots raged unchecked—Beirut's Jewish community swelled with new arrivals, making

Lebanon the only Arab country whose Jewish population rose after 1948. There were occasional flare-ups, including an explosion in the Jewish quarter in 1948 that injured eleven. But order was restored in March 1949, when Israel and Lebanon signed an armistice agreement. Army guards watched over the entrance to the Jewish quarter, but life went on as usual. Each morning, Jacob went to work at the bank on Rue Allenby, and Edmond's younger siblings made the short walk to the Alliance school.

On January 22, 1950, early in the morning, a powerful time bomb that had initially been set to go off at 8:00 a.m., rocked the Alliance school in Beirut, killing Madame Esther Penso, the head of the girls' school. Two weeks later, Eveline decided it was time to go. She, her children, and her brother-in-law, Albert Buri Nasser, boarded a boat bound for Genoa, and joined Edmond in Milan. [91]

Eveline and Edmond had always enjoyed a special rapport, which had only strengthened since the death of their mother. In a matter of months, Eveline was reunited with her husband in Milan. The opportunities to arbitrage gold in the Far East were declining. In mid-1950, China closed its borders and Britain began confiscating gold shipments to Hong Kong. In July 1950 the Korean War broke out. A few days after the war started, Rahmo was on a ship headed for the safety of Italy. After staying for several months in Milan, Rahmo and Eveline left for Bogota, Colombia, where one of Rahmo's cousins lived in the country's small Syrian community. Edmond was alone again in Milan. More significantly, the Safra family had established an outpost in South America, which was soon to become a haven for the entire family. [92]

Jacob loved Beirut, where he was an important member of the establishment. In the spring of 1950, he was still serving on the Community Council. Bechara el-Khoury, a friend of the family, was the president. For the sake of maintaining stability, Maronite allies urged Jacob not to leave—arguing that other Jews would take a cue from his actions. Mindful of the growing threats, prominent Maronites would warn Jacob to stay away from the Jewish quarter on particular evenings. On April 27, 1951, the Jewish community held its usual Passover celebration, with notables from the Muslim and Christian communities among the 3,000 attending. On June 10, 1951, the community celebrated the twenty-fifth anniversary of Magen Avraham synagogue; that fall, Joseph Safra, the youngest of Jacob's eight surviving children, celebrated his Bar Mitzvah.

But Beirut was growing increasingly inhospitable to even the best-connected members of the community. In early 1952, the Safras' elegant apartment on Rue Georges Picot was ransacked. That was the last straw for Jacob. "He thought we needed a more stable place far from wars," Edmond recalled. And so with great ambivalence, and a belief that the departure was only temporary, Jacob began to make plans to leave Beirut and join Edmond in Milan—even if it meant breaking up the family to a degree. Assets were transferred into Italian banks. Moïse, then eighteen, moved to Milan to work with Edmond. Arlette Safra got married.[93] Fourteen-year-old Joseph enrolled at Whittingehame College, a Jewish boarding school in Brighton, England. With aspirations of being the "Jewish Eton," Whittingehame attracted in these years scores of Sephardic students, including some of Joseph's friends from Beirut.

In late 1952, Jacob and Marie, and his daughters Gaby and Huguette joined Edmond and Moïse in Milan. Jacob left behind thirty-two years of work and memories, and the bank bearing his name. Still believing in the future of Lebanon, and unwilling to fold up his life's work, Jacob left Banque Jacob E. Safra in the capable hands of its managers.

With his family joining him, Edmond, now twenty years old, continued to pursue options for arbitrage. The Far East had effectively shut down as a destination for gold. So he turned his attention to India, where gold had always had immense religious and social significance. Converting the weight of gold bars from kilograms to tolas, he sent gold through Kuwait.[94] He also engaged in a more complicated arrangement. In Hong Kong, traders could arbitrage the difference between the postwar dollar/Sterling exchange rates in London and Hong Kong. They bought metals or woven cotton products in London at the official dollar/Sterling exchange rate in London—ostensibly to be sent to Hong Kong. But once the ships passed Singapore, they

continued on to the United States, and sold their wares at the unofficial dollar/Sterling exchange rate that prevailed in Hong Kong.[95]
Edmond bought platinum in London or Amsterdam at the official
dollar/Sterling exchange rate and shipped it to Kuwait alongside his
gold bars—and then sold the platinum at the prevailing unofficial
dollar/Sterling rate in Kuwait.

In his first few years in Europe, Edmond didn't do much classic
banking, that is, using the family balance sheet to extend credit to
others. But in 1952, he began to tap into the extended networks of
Sephardic Jews and Alliance connections to put capital at risk in a
famously challenging business: motion pictures. Edmond
Cohen-Tenoudji, an Algeria-born film producer and distributor, and
a board member of the AIU, owned the French distribution rights to
a film titled *La Fille du Regiment* (*The Daughter of the Regiment*). Edmond
Safra teamed up with Cohen-Tenoudji and other investors, including
his associate Leon Sassoon and Raffaele Pinto of Posa Films, to bring
the film to market. But *The Daughter of the Regiment* was a flop. "You're
lucky to have found a few outlets to limit your losses," Pinto told
Edmond, who took a $50,000 loss. "Many in the film industry started
with millions and lost it all to their last shirt." A year later, Edmond
provided financing to the swashbuckling actor Errol Flynn, who was
attempting a quixotic comeback by making an ambitious version of
William Tell. Flynn plowed $500,000 of his own cash into the produc-
tion, and Edmond lent him and the production company, Pakal Film,
the rest of the budget at 10 percent interest.[96] But Flynn ran out of
money a few months into production in Courmayeur, an Alpine village where he had built an extravagant set. The film was never completed. Thus ended Edmond's adventures in filmmaking. (His nephew,
Jacqui, Elie's son, would become a successful film producer.)[97]

This must have been a disorienting period for Jacob Safra. Now
sixty-three, and perhaps starting to feel the effects of a series of ill-
nesses, he was leaving behind the Franco-Levantine world he had
known his entire life. And with Beirut, for now, in the rearview mirror,
it fell to young Edmond to craft a long-term strategy for the family
and its businesses. Should they try to put down deeper roots and settle

in Italy? Or should they look elsewhere for opportunities? Increasingly, the conversation in the cafés and synagogues of Europe revolved around the possibilities of South America.

In the years before World War II, Syrian and Lebanese Jews had joined, in small numbers, the larger wave of Jewish emigration to South America. In 1947, the Argentinian Jewish community numbered 250,000. Many South American countries freely offered resident visas to Syrian and Lebanese Jews.

Rahmo Nasser and Eveline had settled in Bogota in 1951, where Rahmo traded precious metals. But Nasser quickly began to seek a more hospitable home, and traveled around South America in 1951 and 1952.[98] In May 1952, Rahmo and Eveline's third child was born and was named after the maternal grandfather—Jacob or Jacky. In the summer, Jacob sent Edmond to Bogota to meet the newest member of the family. On August 4, 1952, Edmond arrived by plane to New York, making his first visit to the Western hemisphere and to the United States, and then traveled to Colombia. Edmond didn't record his first impressions of the region. But it's likely he returned brimming with information from Rahmo about South America, and in particular, about Brazil.

During these years, Safra's extended family seemed to be increasingly setting its sights on South America. Two cousins from the Alexandria branch were on their way to the region: Jose Safra to Uruguay, and Elliot, the future husband of Edmond's sister Gaby, to Argentina.[99]

Edmond's interest was piqued. After several years of successful business experience, he had developed and displayed an ability that can't be taught. He knew how to find opportunities; figure out the mechanics, logistics, and human relations to bring these opportunities to fruition; and then to pull back or move on, without excessive sentimentality, when things were no longer working; and finally to start the cycle again. So he began to think that perhaps Milan was played out as a base, at least for now. Many of the attributes that had made it appealing in 1947 were no longer as salient in 1952 and 1953. The stimulus from the Marshall Plan was waning, and growth was slowing.

There was no longer much of a need to be close to Beirut now that the family had left. With the London gold market poised to reopen on March 22, 1954, larger traders would enter the market and the potential for intra-Europe gold arbitrage was set to decline.

So on March 29, 1954, Edmond boarded a plane bound for South America. Upon arrival in Rio, he checked into the Hotel Serrador. Later that week, his brother-in-law Rahmo Nasser joined him.[100]

5

A New Base in Brazil

(1954–1959)

L ike Beirut, Rio de Janeiro was a cosmopolitan city lying between the sea and dramatic mountains. Rapidly growing Brazil, with a Mediterranean climate and easygoing culture, was, like Lebanon, something of a dichotomy. Synonymous with good times—Carnival and the bossa nova set the tempo for life—Brazil had been an accommodating and welcoming place for immigrants from Europe and the Middle East. It was at once hospitable to Jews and hospitable to those hostile to them. Many former Nazis had found a safe haven in Brazil, for example. But the 50,000 Jews in Brazil, most of them Ashkenazi, lived in dignity and peace. Oswaldo Aranha, a Brazilian, headed the UN General Assembly when the partition of Israel and Palestine was approved. There were Syrians there too, mostly from Damascus, but a few from Aleppo. One Syrian Jewish family, the Chouekes had come a generation prior and thrived in real estate and business, and they encouraged others to join them. [101]

With a population of 63 million people, Brazil nonetheless had a relatively small and porous elite, Late to embrace modern manufacturing, in the 1950s it was in the throes of industrialization. All this made it fertile ground for people with capital, international connections, expertise in manufacturing, and business savvy. The Safras came to Brazil in a methodical, well-planned manner. Jacob Safra, who arrived in the summer of 1954, was a wealthy man, leaving behind a functioning bank in Beirut and something resembling a family office in Milan. In September 1954, Eveline, Rahmo, and their children arrived in São Paulo.[102] The family had access to a small cadre of professionals who formed a circle of confidence and support. Nessim Dwek, longtime mentor to Edmond, had arrived in Brazil earlier in 1954. Then there were the four Khafif brothers. From Aleppo and Beirut, they had initially dispersed to Italy. Menahem Khafif, who had worked for the Safras in Milan, came to Brazil in 1954 to continue his work. Upon finishing his studies at the London School of Economics in 1954, Moïse Khafif was offered a position in Brazil by Edmond, and arrived in 1955.

In this era, most of those who left Beirut went to settle somewhere else on a permanent basis. The phrase *j'ai quitté* peppered the conversation, correspondence, and memories of the Jews of the Middle East. But Edmond Safra wasn't necessarily quitting Beirut, or Milan, or Europe out of fear. Rather, he was seeking a place where he could settle his aging father and younger siblings in comfort, gain citizenship, and establish a new base for conducting business. Brazil became yet another canvas on which Edmond could practice his art.

In swapping Beirut for Brazil as their home base, the Safras exchanged one set of strictures and tensions for another. Although Brazil was an open society for immigrants, the economy was closed in many ways. It would be difficult, if not impossible, for Jacob and Edmond Safra to continue their freewheeling financial dealings based on personal knowledge and trust. Few people would seek out the Safras to discount notes in Rio or São Paulo. Only Brazilian citizens could own banks, so a formal financing operation would have to wait. And the government monopolized gold trading. Brazil had its own fragile social entente, based not on ethnicity, but on left-right political cleavage and class. In the summer of 1954, just as Edmond arrived, high inflation and violence in the streets led elected President Getulio Vargas, himself a former dictator, to resign and kill himself.

As he had done in Europe seven years earlier, Edmond headed for the center of the action. He rented an apartment near the beach, in the Leme section of Avenida Atlantica, and began to pick up

Portuguese through osmosis, and by listening to the radio. While not relinquishing his vision of conducting international banking operations through his family network, Edmond swiftly pivoted in order to reinvent himself as an importer-exporter who could feed the growth of Brazil's young industrial economy. In the 1950s, Brazil was pursuing an "import substitution" policy that encouraged domestic manufacturers and discouraged imports. That meant that mills and factories in Brazil had a need for raw materials and machinery that Brazil could not produce. At the same time, Brazil produced commodities such as coffee and cotton that, under the right circumstances, could find profitable markets overseas.

Almost immediately upon arrival, in July 1954, Edmond created a private partnership called Algobras Industria e Comércio de Algodão Limitada, and, still only twenty-one years old, set up shop on Avenida Rio Branco, Rio's main commercial street. Edmond supplied 90 percent of the firm's starting capital; Rahmo Nasser's brother Ezra was one of the minority investors. As its name implied (algodão is Portuguese for cotton) the goal was to export cotton. A subsidiary based in São Paulo, dubbed Brascoton, defined itself as an importer-exporter. In September, Algobras morphed into a publicly traded company, Expansão Commercial Sul Americana SA (ECSA), with Edmond as general manager.[103]

Then, Edmond headed back to Europe to tie up loose ends and open new accounts. In the fall of 1955, he was back in Milan at the residence/office at Piazza Missori, seeing off the family's goods. On November 2, 1955, eighteen parcels of the personal effects of the Safras were stowed aboard the SS Athina, which left Genoa for Santos in Brazil. On November 24, 1955, Edmond left Milan for Brazil.[104]

Upon arrival, he immediately began to work through networks and contacts in Europe. Machines and chemicals, in short supply in Brazil, were in surplus in West Germany, Hungary, and Yugoslavia, whose governments were in need of hard currencies. Despite the Cold War barriers, businessmen from Lebanon and Europe could freely travel to Eastern Europe and meet with key government officials. Edmond and his network of contacts were already skilled at arranging cross-border transactions in gold, from the Far East through Europe. And he was in constant touch with commercial-minded people who had businesses in shipping, textiles, and electronics. So in short order, ECSA became a voracious acquirer of goods. "[We] had to go and find out what the material was good for," recalled one of his employees in São Paulo. "It was crazy, but [Safra] bought them at a very cheap price and it was convenient for him to take the risk and bring it here." In August 1955, Edmond created a new trading company, Safra SA Importação e Comércio. Imports involved a complex set of foreign currency auctions, in which goods were ranked in five categories; auctions were held in multiple cities at once. That enabled a shrewd operator with offices in multiple cities to arbitrage between exchange rates for every category of goods. With offices in both Rio and São Paulo, Edmond was able to take advantage of these market inefficiencies.[105]

In Brazil, changes were afoot. With the planning for the creation of a new capital far to the north in Brasilia, the center of economic gravity was shifting to São Paulo, the industrial and financial capital of Brazil. A booming city, São Paulo marked its quadricentennial in 1956 with the opening of Oscar Niemeyer's huge green park, Ibirapuera. It was the economic engine of a forward-looking region in which manufacturing had displaced agriculture as a driving force. Between 1945 and 1960, Brazil's manufacturing sector expanded by nearly 10 percent every year.[106] Textile and pulp and paper mills popped up in the region, and attracted workers from abroad. Edmond moved his family into a duplex apartment at 810 Avenida Paulista, an elegant boulevard on which high-rise apartment buildings were displacing mansions in the commercial and cultural heart of São Paulo. They took office space at first on the seventh floor of a building overlooking the Praça da República, and later at Rua Libero Badaro 93.

As he was building institutions in Brazil, Edmond was also putting down roots in Geneva. In February 1956, he formally closed his Milan office and sent Leon Aslan Sassoon (aka Sir Philip) to Geneva. "I am always occupied with Edmond's affairs," Sassoon wrote a colleague. He took up residence in the Hotel des Familles on the bustling Rue de Lausanne, where Edmond would also stay. (His telegraph address was: SIRPHILIP-GENEVE.) In October 1956, Edmond established Sudafin Société Financière et Commerciale SA in a small office on Rue du Stand with capital of 500,000 Swiss francs. Sudafin was a sister company to the Brazilian operations and the Beirut branch—an unregulated financing firm specializing in international trade and financial transactions that served as a vehicle for Edmond's ideas and ambitions. Profits were plowed back into the firm, and its capital would grow to 2.5 million Swiss francs by 1959.[107]

The account books and correspondence of Sudafin and ECSA in those early years reveal a dizzying array of goods traded and moved around the world. Aside from such Safra staples as precious metals, there were commodities like titanium oxide, paraffin, aluminum, and tin. There were bulky industrial machines such as agricultural harvesters, and specialized needles from Germany bound for textile mills. He bartered with a Hungarian trade company for Swiss watches, and traded staples including oats and frozen shrimp, which was sent from Hong Kong to the US. Edmond had no qualms about walking into markets that others deemed to be risky and opaque, clearing foreign exchange trades between the Bank of Hungary and financial counterparts in India or Denmark.[108] Safra and his colleagues also engaged in "switch operations," taking advantage of the differential value of European currencies against the dollar. They would ship merchandise to Hungary and Yugoslavia as ports of transit and sell them into England and Brazil. And like experienced Middle Eastern businesspeople, the Safras and their cadre were skilled at bartering—which Brazil permitted for certain goods under bilateral treaties with several European countries, especially in Eastern Europe. For example, from the many afternoons he had spent in the cafés and coffeehouses of the continent, Edmond knew that Italians loved smoother Arabica coffee beans while the French preferred more bitter Robusta.[109]

Edmond was able to conduct such a large volume of business because he relied on a key group of employees—all of whom were Jews who traced their ancestry to Syria. When Menahem Khafif died in a car accident in 1956, Moïse Khafif was in Yugoslavia and Hungary securing merchandise to import. He returned and took on his brother

Menahem's role. Rolando Laniado, who had left Egypt for Italy as a teen and arrived in São Paulo in 1953, started to work for Edmond at the age of eighteen in the chemical and metal import company. In 1958, Umberto Treves arrived from Milan to join the crew.

In each instance, Edmond asked a person to take a leap of faith in his enterprise, and to embrace a new professional role in a strange setting. Treves, for example, spoke no Portuguese. But Edmond inspired his employees by expressing a preternatural confidence in their abilities. Laniado went to the port of Santos every day for eighteen months to taste the coffee that Edmond was trading. "Why am I going to taste coffee? I don't know anything from Adam," Laniado told him.

"Don't worry about it," Edmond responded. "You go there and you're going to see, it's easy." If they invested their time and effort, he would have their back, especially in times of need.[110]

In Brazil, or in Geneva, a strong sense of solidarity with the broader Aleppan and Beiruti community prevailed. Wherever they found a new base, the Safras and their friends acclimated, but didn't assimilate—not with the local culture, and not even with the local Jewish community. Amid all the focus on moving goods around the world, one shipment sent by Edmond from Europe to Brazil was particularly valued. In the spring of 1956, the *SS Provence* left Genoa bound for Santos with precious cargo directed to Gaby Safra in São Paulo: glassware, a refrigerator, and several staples of Syrian cooking that were unavailable in Brazil, including sixteen pallets of pistachios, one kilogram of the spice mix za'atar, one package of pomegranate juice, and five kilos of pine nuts.[111]

Jacob Safra was ailing, and Edmond, still in his twenties, was cast into the role of paterfamilias. He used accounts at the Banque pour le Commerce Suisse-Israélien, an Ashkenazi Jewish bank in Geneva, to pay Joseph's Whittingehame College school bills (142.4 British pounds) in June 1956. After Joseph finished in 1957, Edmond wrote to the University of Pennsylvania, where Cyril Dwek (Nessim's son) was a student: "My father, the Chairman of Banque Jacob SAFRA of Beyrouth (Lebanon), is anxious to have my brother take banking courses," Edmond wrote. "Would it be possible that he could attend your School for the next two years—which is the maximum of time he can spare?" The dean at Wharton said it wasn't possible,[112] so Joseph returned to Brazil and worked for the family companies before pursuing training in the United States several years later. Moïse Safra, who had finished his schooling, was helping Edmond set up businesses in Brazil for the textile mills. And Edmond found himself continuing to sort out the needs of his older brother's family, while hoping that Elie would continue to remain involved with the Safras' interests.[113]

Edmond assumed another role that Jacob had relinquished upon leaving Beirut—as a leader of the virtual community. In São Paulo, and in Geneva, and in every other city where small groups of Syrian and Lebanese Jews moved, there was nothing like the councils, committees, Alliance schools, and synagogues that had provided a thick web of mutual assistance and solidarity in Beirut. Sephardic immigration from Lebanon and Syria to Brazil had started in the 1920s. São Paulo counted only about thirty Jewish families from Aleppo in the 1920s. In 1950, there were about 26,000 Jews in São Paulo state, a small minority of them Sephardic; many of them resided in the Bom Retiro and Higienopolis neighborhoods. In 1929, Jews from Greece and Turkey established a synagogue on Rua Abolição, which, though Sephardic, followed rites that were different from those of the Syrians and Lebanese. Slowly in the 1950s, in small and then larger groups, people trickled out of Lebanon and Syria, and, after the 1956 Suez crisis, from Egypt. Many of them were French-speaking graduates of Alliance schools who knew—or knew of—the Safra family. Without institutions of their own, and often impoverished because they had to leave everything behind or because the government had confiscated their assets, they turned to one another for help. Edmond was happy to take people under his wing, providing short-term financing and helping them move assets and find employment. [114]

In 1956, Rolando Laniado recalls, Laniado's mother and uncle, who had cancer, and who had just fled Egypt, were in Geneva. Edmond put a chauffeur at their disposal and looked after them. When a distant cousin, the daughter of Garaz Mizrahi (Jacob's aunt), lost an eye and was hospitalized in Argentina, and was facing a 20,000 peso ($500) hospital bill, it was the twenty-four-year-old Edmond who naturally assumed the responsibility to pay it.[115]

Charity remained both a personal and an institutional commitment. Edmond, like Jacob before him, had a particular reverence for Rabbi Meir Baal HaNess, a Roman-era Talmudic scholar whose grave in Tiberias became a shrine for both Ashkenazi and Sephardic Jews, and whose name was imbued with mystical powers of protection. A charity associated with his name supplied meals for Shabbat and holidays, cared for widows and orphans, and provided emergency medical and financial aid. A yeshiva (religious seminary) bearing his name was built in Tiberias. Since traveling via Tel Aviv back in 1947, Edmond had never visited Israel, largely because it was impossible for a Lebanese national to do so. But in the summer of 1956, he made his first recorded donation to the charities of Rabbi Meir Baal HaNess, following the lifelong example of his father. The following year he donated 200 Swiss francs to help a Sephardic synagogue in Tel Aviv. In the 1950s, Safra became a regular supporter of Porat Yosef, a prominent Sephardic rabbinical school in Jerusalem with strong Aleppo ties, and established a relationship with Ozar Hatorah. An institution similar to the Alliance, Ozar Hatorah was founded by Syrian families to offer education to children throughout the Middle East, North Africa, and, later, Europe. [116]

Although he was often abroad, Edmond made efforts to put down roots in Brazil. Exhibiting yet again the confidence to seek out the establishment and make friends in high places, he expanded his circle to include pillars of Brazil's media industry (Roberto Marinho, director of the Globo media group; Adolpho Bloch, director of Bloch Editores SA), legal establishment (Francisco Roberto Brandão Campos Andrade, a lawyer), policy elite (Roberto de Oliveira Campos, head of the Banco Nacional de Desenvolvimento Econômico e Social [BNDES]), and financial establishment (banker Walter Moreira Salles). Beyond friendship, Edmond offered these men options to invest alongside him and to serve on the boards of his companies. Edmond's prominence in Brazil was all the more impressive given that he was only typically there between April and June, the period overlapping with Passover and Shavuot.

Succeeding in business in Brazil required constant adjustment, especially after the Brazilian government abolished its complex currency auction system in 1957. Edmond's modus operandi had been to invest in arbitrage opportunities—taking ownership of currencies, gold, metals, and industrial goods and products for only as long as needed to turn a profit. But in Brazil, he began to invest in more permanent structures and operating businesses. Along with Nessim Dwek, Edmond and Moïse invested in a struggling cotton mill and imported modern machinery so that it could profitably export yarn to Eastern Europe. The mill would later operate under the name Sacaria Paulista, making jute bags for the transport of coffee beans. Safra tapped into funds from Brazil's development bank to finance the construction of a paper mill, which operated in partnership with Champion, an American company.[117]

He also found value in the vehicles that carried commerce. In 1958, Edmond and Joe Michaan, a New York-based entrepreneur of Aleppan heritage who would be a partner in many endeavors, teamed up to buy a half dozen World War II–era "Liberty" cargo ships. They loaded up the boats with railroad equipment and any other metal they could find and sent the ships and their cargo to be scrapped in Italy.

Edmond also branched out into real estate, which was not a natural investment for him, particularly in Brazil, plagued as it was by high inflation. In the late 1950s, the Dweks and Edmond teamed up to establish a company called IMOFINA, established to invest in commercial and residential properties in France. In this period, Edmond also financed properties in and around major cities, including apartments in Milan and Paris and commercial buildings in West Berlin.[118]

Edmond finally received his Brazilian citizenship on January 31, 1958, and soon had a Brazilian passport (#307478). In his passport photo, the twenty-seven-year-old financial entrepreneur presents an optimistic visage: a slight smile, his thin handsome face framed by large eyebrows. Edmond had reason to be optimistic. His business was thriving in Brazil. ECSA, his publicly traded company, quickly grew into a significant enterprise and was consistently profitable starting in 1957. In 1960, ECSA would notch a profit of 7.7 million cruzeiros ($817,000 in 2021 US dollars). "It was very easy to make money in Brazil in those days, but Edmond found it easier than most," Moïse Khafif said. In tandem, both ECSA and Safra SA migrated toward Safra's natural businesses, providing credit and trading in gold and foreign exchange. Armed with his newly acquired Brazilian nationality, Edmond was able now to turn Safra SA into Safra SA Financiamentos e Investimentos, which provided trade finance to Brazilian manufacturers. It was this entity that, over time, would evolve into Banco Safra. [119]

Brazil was indeed proving to be a hospitable home. The family had been reconstituted, to a degree. On Friday night, they would meet at Jacob's for Shabbat dinner, and on Saturday afternoon, after synagogue, they would meet at Eveline and Rahmo's for lunch. Edmond would often stay with his father, or with his sister, making a point of bringing gifts to his nephews and nieces from Europe, once dragging an electric train set through customs for his nephew Jacques Nasser. [120]

Over time, the Aleppans and Beirutis who trickled into São Paulo essentially took over the Rua Abolição Sephardic synagogue. In 1958, at Edmond's suggestion, they began to discuss expanding it in their own image. Rahmo Shayo and Rahmo Nasser convened about two dozen men on a Sunday in the presence of Isaac Dayan, a rabbi from Aleppo, and tallied up commitments for about half the total expected investment, with the understanding that Edmond would provide the rest. The vision slowly expanded to include a synagogue, Talmud Torah school, and reception hall. In the fall of 1959, Edmond wrote Isaac Shalom in New York to inform him, among other pieces of news, that he was "still anxiously looking forward to receiving the construction project of the São Paulo synagogue." [121]

Jacob Safra's illness and state of mind weighed on the family. He was moody and forgetful, and generally in low spirits. In 1957 and 1958, he saw doctors in Milan, Geneva, Mexico, and New York, who disagreed about his diagnosis. Some suggested a brain tumor, while others thought he suffered from arteriosclerosis. In 1958, when Eveline and Moïse took Jacob to consult with the head of neurology at Mt.

Sinai Hospital in New York, Edmond met him there, staying at the Sherry-Netherland.[122]

For Edmond, who was something of a nomad, it wasn't a big deal to pop over to New York for a few days. In 1957 and 1958, he still maintained a base in Milan, where he occasionally attended synagogue, and bought clothes for himself and his father. In July and August, he would steal away to Juan-les-Pins in the South of France, often to the Hotel Provençal. Edmond enjoyed waterskiing and gadding about the Mediterranean in a motorboat. But he was not a particularly good vacationer. He would spend much of his time on the phone, or arranging to use it. At the time, he'd have to go to the hotel, wait a half hour to get through to Brazil, or make an appointment to connect with New York.

Edmond was also in Beirut quite frequently. Homesick for Lebanese food, which was hard to come by in Europe and South America, he'd go directly from the Beirut International Airport to Al-Ajami, an iconic Lebanese restaurant that had opened in 1920 near the office of the Banque Jacob E. Safra, before checking into the St. George Hotel. He would sometimes stay at the Palm Beach, because he was friends with its proprietor, Jean-Prosper Gay-Para. Beirut, despite the continual tensions, was a convivial place for Edmond to do business, socialize, and recruit workers. And he needed to be there to ensure the health of his father's bank. (One story holds that when Edmond caught wind that there would be a run on the bank in the 1950s, he borrowed $1 million from Banque Zilkha, obtained mountains of small Lebanese bills from the Central Bank, and piled them atop tables in the reception area. When the people waiting in line saw that the first several people emerged with their deposits and testified to the availability of cash, the run dissipated and Edmond quickly returned the funds to the Zilkha bank.)[123]

Still, the bank was thriving. At the end of 1957, it had capital of about 1.6 million Lebanese pounds and a balance sheet of about 43.7 million Lebanese pounds.[124] Lebanon's economy was booming, even amid the instability caused by the influx of hundreds of thousands of Palestinian refugees. The Trans-Arabian pipeline, which Standard

Oil built to deliver crude from the Saudi Arabian oil fields through Syria to the Mediterranean coast at Sidon, was completed in 1950. Lebanon in 1956 passed a new bank secrecy law, which made it more appealing as a destination for deposits. The only Arab capital where the press was free, Beirut maintained an environment that was welcoming to businesspeople and companies from around the world. While Jews were emptying out of North Africa in the 1950s, lured from Morocco by the Israeli government, or pushed out of Egypt by President Gamal Abdel Nasser, the Jewish community in Beirut, despite the Safras' departure, persevered in relative peace. In 1956, the community still numbered more than 5,000, and five Alliance schools in Lebanon operated with a combined 1,443 pupils.[125]

But living and working in Beirut meant walking a tightrope. The summer of 1958 was a time of great ferment in the Arab world. Egypt and Syria had united to form the United Arab Republic. In Lebanon, where the National Pact still maintained a fragile truce between ethnicities, nationalist impulses began to engineer a coup of sorts against President Camille Chamoun in mid-July. On July 14, Bastille Day, officers in Baghdad engineered the overthrow and assassination of King Faisal II. The same day, Chamoun appealed to the US to intervene to preserve the status quo in Lebanon. And on July 15, 1958, Marines started to land in Beirut.

On July 14, 1958, Edmond happened to also be in Beirut. Amid fireworks and gunfire, Emile Saadia, a well-known banker and economics professor, drove down from his home in Aley in his Peugeot to meet Edmond at the St. George.[126] Undeterred by the turmoil, Edmond wanted to talk about business: he had plans to transform Banque Jacob E. Safra into a joint stock company and bank, and to turn Sudafin in Geneva into a formal Swiss bank—both of which could act in cooperation with his operations in Brazil. And he wanted Saadia's help.

Others in Beirut were far less sanguine about the future. The week after that meeting, Jacques Douek, a brother of Edmond's stepmother who had worked for banks in Beirut, wrote to Edmond to seek his counsel. "We are living the last two months [and] a half in a full civil war, of firings and explosions and blowing of cannons. The situation is untenable, especially for those in charge of a family with kids of young age." With the family hiding in a hotel, "the future looks somber." Many Beiruti Jews were looking to leave. "Do you think I can fend for myself in Brazil? Or do you think Argentina would be better? Or can you make another suggestion?" he wrote. Edmond responded a few weeks later, noting that he would be back in Beirut in the fall. "We can discuss this affair in person and look at the different solutions."[127]

Within a matter of months, Douek moved to Geneva to work with Edmond. Others were making plans. An article in the Lebanese newspaper *Filastin* in September 1959 reported that thirty-two Jewish businessmen were liquidating their affairs in Beirut and moving to Brazil. Chief Rabbi Ben Zion Lichtman left for Israel in 1959. He was replaced as chief rabbi by Chahoud Chrem in 1960.[128]

There had remained a certain informality to the operations of Banque Jacob E. Safra, but the updating of the laws, the growing sophistication of the global financial system, and Edmond's ambitions made him realize that he needed to adapt. What's more, while its employee and client base remained predominantly Jewish, the country's changing demographics and political realities suggested that a shift in strategy was needed. In 1959, he hired chartered accountants Russell & Co. to compile an official balance sheet and prepared the applications and paperwork necessary to transform the family enterprise into a joint stock company, to be named Banque de Crédit National (BCN). To run it, Edmond needed a professional. And he found the perfect candidate in Henry Krayem. Born in Damascus, Krayem had worked for the Central Bank of Syria until 1948, when he was fired along with all the other Jewish employees, and then moved to Beirut, where he worked at the Zilkha bank.[129] In June 1959, Edmond offered him the job with the title of directeur-adjoint and a five-year contract.[130]

In August 1959, a letter from Beirut announced that Mr. Assaf, of the Ministry of National Economy, had agreed to the application to change the name of the institution to the Banque de Crédit National. On August 8, Jacques Ades, a longtime Safra employee, told Edmond that they had liquidated the old bank balance sheet and established a new one, and that construction on the offices at Allenby Street was continuing. A new strong room and set of safe-deposit boxes were installed, along with telephones.[131]

By 1959, Edmond, still just twenty-seven, stood at the nexus of a far-flung group of modernizing entities with bases in three countries. He still operated in a generally informal and direct manner, keeping an eye on dozens of transactions, checking in with hundreds of clients and counterparts, looking after his brothers and father, supporting charities and communities in need around the world, and trading for his own account. He did so by spending an enormous amount of time on the telephone, on the telex, and in personal conversation. "Good evening here Edmond Safra," began the start of a burst of telexes between Edmond and William Feingold, an importer in New York, haggling over the amount of coffee (result: 50,000 bags) and the price (result: $42.50 per bag) to be bought in Paraguay, its quality insured by Moïse, and sent to Feingold's firm in New York, Schwabach & Company.[132]

Edmond carried it all off with great aplomb. But he had a growing sense that his operations had to be even more integrated and more professional. Given the scope of his enterprises and ambitions, decisions could no longer simply be made over coffee, or based on instinct and personal knowledge. And they couldn't all be made by Edmond. In May 1960, BCN in Beirut set up a formal credit committee, composed of George Rabbath, Henry Krayem, Selim Shehebar, Elie Tawil, and Jacques Ades, to discuss applications, and clients who were late in paying. The balance sheet of BCN was published and shared with counterparts and clients, so they could have a greater sense of comfort—beyond the fact that they were dealing with a Safra. And its employees had to be comfortable operating in multiple contexts. In May 1960, Edmond wrote to George Rabbath after hearing that a new employee of the Beirut bank didn't speak Arabic. "We have a need, for the bank, of people who speak at least two languages, French and Arabic, if not English," Edmond wrote. "I beg you, dear Monsieur Rabbath, to not interpret the contents of this letter as a reproach, but simply a recommendation made in the interest solely of the future development of la Banque de Crédit National."[133]

This was a long way from Jacob judging creditworthiness based on how many bolts of cotton a merchant had in his stall, or knowing who someone's father was. Edmond deemed that the modernizing of the bank and the impositions of a more formal mode of doing business were essential not just for survival, but for the growth of the Safra family enterprises. For as he was standing up BCN, Edmond was working on his next important project: creating a banking operation in one of the most formal business environments of them all.

6

The Rockefeller of Geneva

(1960–1964)

E dmond had been a very regular visitor to Geneva since 1948. The same forces that had pushed his family to Brazil and that bolstered Beirut's prosperity made the City of Calvin a compelling place to build a bank in 1960. The world's wealthy—Saudi oil sheiks and Italian industrialists, South Americans worried about inflation and political instability, French-Algerian merchants concerned about unrest—were anxious to protect their assets. Thanks to Switzerland's political neutrality, strict banking secrecy regime, and rock-solid stability, Geneva attracted a great deal of "flight capital."

Many of those seeking safety in the late 1950s and early 1960s were in Edmond Safra's orbit. As Jews continued to stream out of the Middle East—from Lebanon, from Egypt and Morocco; some with a great deal, some with nothing—there were comparatively few places that they trusted. The Jewish banks in Europe were very small, and they catered largely to Ashkenazis. Existing giants like Union Bank of Switzerland didn't warmly welcome textile merchants from Cairo.

Since its founding in September 1956, a month after the Suez crisis, Edmond's firm Sudafin had grown at its office on Rue du Stand, fortified by profits from his trading activities and the assets of a few clients who had opened accounts. To ensure its integration into the local scene, Edmond recruited politically connected Swiss board members: François Lugeon, an honorary consul to Brazil and coffee importer who had done business with ECSA; attorney and parliament member Marcel Guinand; and François Boissier, the son of a Red Cross administrator who had worked in Lebanon and Syria in the 1920s. As more people sought to entrust their assets to Edmond, he began to take the necessary steps to turn Sudafin into a bank. First, he recruited trusted associates from Beirut. Jacques Douek arrived in February 1959, as well as his chaperone from the Milan days, Jacques Tawil. On April 21, 1960, Safra was granted a Swiss banking license, and Sudafin was transformed into Banque pour le Développement Commercial, or Trade Development Bank (TDB). [134]

Setting up shop in the historical fief of the world's private bankers was an audacious move for a twenty-seven-year-old Lebanese Jew with a Brazilian passport. Aware that—once again—he was an outsider, he brought in a senior local to help. Swiss banks were controlled by a federal commission that delegated supervision to private assurance and accounting firms such as Ofor. Roger Junod, an Ofor employee, advised Safra on the intricacies of the law and ultimately joined TDB as an early full-time employee. Junod told Edmond he couldn't make him any money, but he could help TDB navigate the strict Swiss banking rules and regulations. The two could not have been more different: Junod thrived on order and rules, and Edmond seemed perfectly comfortable amid chaos. "I was horrified," Junod recalled. "I saw openings of accounts with a postcard sent from overseas, signed 'kisses.'" When Junod noted such processes were significantly out of order, Edmond initially turned white, and then empowered Junod to do his work. By the end of the year, Junod had created the particular documentation in line with Swiss expectations and a clear list of assets, totaling about 37 million francs (about $8.5 million). And by February 1961, Edmond was sending Leon Aslan Sassoon packets of the new forms necessary to open accounts.[135]

Edmond predictably turned to the Aleppo diaspora to attract capital, suggesting people invest in increments as small as $5,000. Early shareholders included associates and relatives like David Braka, Albert Manila Nasser, and members of the Dwek family. They in turn tapped into their network of Syrian and Lebanese friends in France, England, and Canada. At the same time, Edmond asked this group to become customers. Eli Douer, a Beiruti who had moved to Brazil in 1956 and was in the textile business, told Edmond he wanted account number one, while his brother took the auspicious number five.[136] Edmond offered these people the same compelling proposition he offered in Beirut and São Paulo. But now the Safra name and reputation were married to the full suite of Swiss banking services, including deposits, securities, gold and commodities, property management, commercial and documentary credit, and exchange.

Edmond presided over a family of businesses that was itself a family business. TDB and Safra SA were separate entities, but these sister companies, as Edmond called them, worked out of the same offices in Brazil. When Junod signed a three-year contract with TDB, it was countersigned by Joseph Safra in Brazil. Moïse Safra worked closely with TDB, bringing in new corporate borrowing clients from Brazil. TDB made loans, then syndicated them, selling participations to Rahmo Nasser, among others.[137] TDB was thus a multinational firm of sorts from the day it was founded. And Edmond set about expanding its footprint. In 1960, he sent one of the Khafif brothers, Moïse, to Buenos Aires to open TDB's Argentina office. It was natural for TDB to open an office in Rio, where the Safras knew many wealthy potential clients. Those who signed up there included Alfredo "Freddy" Monteverde, who owned a major electronics and appliance chain, Ponto Frio. Among the new employees in São Paulo was Raymond Maggar, who had fled Alexandria for Brazil, and who was a nineteen-year-old trainee making $200 a month at a tobacco company in 1961 when Edmond asked to meet him. When Edmond asked him what it would take to join TDB, Maggar blurted out "$600." Edmond agreed, and Maggar joined the next month.[138]

TDB's headquarters in Geneva moved to offices on the fifth floor of a building on Rue Chantepoulet, on the other side of the lake from the main banking area. It was an unorthodox operation in many ways. Emile Saadia, whom Edmond had first approached about joining him in 1958, arrived in March 1962, after finally getting his work permit.

He found a dozen or so people working in cubicles. "When I got there, there were people who didn't know what credit documents were," he recalled. The Swiss staff sat cheek by jowl with the crowd from Beirut and Aleppo, and customers, clients, and supplicants continually came and went. Alexis Gregory, a young American Express executive, came to the office expecting to see the "Rockefeller of Geneva." Instead, "there was a crowd, everybody gabbing in Portuguese, Arabic, French. It was like the souk." And in the back was a little office where Edmond sat.[139]

Edmond was constantly on the move in search of growth. In the fall of 1961 he was already raising more capital for TDB, which would expand its financial capacity substantially. "We have now gathered participants representing at least twice the total amount of the increase, which is sw. frs. 12.5 million," he wrote to a friend that year, offering him and a partner the opportunity to invest nearly 1 million francs. In January 1962, TDB's capital was formally raised from 7.5 million to 26 million Swiss francs, nearly quadrupling.[140]

TDB, which had a representative bureau in Milan, in the summer of 1962 opened a full office in Chiasso, in the Italian-speaking Ticino region of Switzerland. To staff it, Edmond hired Sem Almaleh, a Bulgaria-born chemistry student whose father knew Edmond. At its helm, he placed a new recruit, Albert Benezra. Benezra was something of an outsider, even among this collection of outsiders. Born in Aleppo, he was a business teacher who had worked in Iran and moved to Milan. There, he worked for the Nehmads, Aleppans with financial and commercial interests who were distantly related to the Safras. Not part of the Beirut community, Benezra was cut from a different cloth—obstreperous, tough, and ambitious. He quickly gained the confidence of Edmond. Then Edmond called Moussi Douek, who was finishing his final exams at the University of Geneva. "Fill up your car, and don't worry about the results. You're going to Chiasso." There, Douek reported to what one employee described as a not very impressive office "on the second floor of an old apartment building" across from the train station.[141]

Edmond tried to inculcate his expanding crew of client-facing employees with a sense of how they should treat customers. This stemmed from his innate ability to empathize with people's need for dignity and security. As Jeff Keil, a longtime Safra associate, later described it, Edmond had an "inviolate principle, which is that a banker exists to protect his depositors' funds." Safra customers had to know that they could leave the money with him, and he would personally scour the globe for safe short-term interest-paying time deposits, or participations in discounting of bonds. He took a personal and direct interest in even small amounts. "To place $5,000, I suggest about $3,000 in a fixed deposit that the Banque pour le Développement Commercial has in Greece," he wrote a client in Milan in 1961. "For the rest, I've reserved for you a participation in a new affair in Brazil we expect to conclude." To another, he offered deposits in a Japanese bank and bonds from Mexico's electric authority. [142]

But TDB wasn't simply involved in transactions. Being a client at a Safra bank was like being a member of a club, or part of a very large extended family. Clients were people in motion, and often under duress, many of them struggling to find purchase in new areas. If you were a TDB client, your banker might pick you up at the airport, set up a ski vacation in Switzerland, or help your child enroll in school. Many clients also needed assistance getting work permits, or obtaining the documents necessary to establish residence or citizenship in new lands. With his extensive connections in Beirut, Europe, the US, and South America, Edmond was often able to help. In August 1962, he was trying to retrieve Eveline and Rahmo's official marriage license from Beirut, which had to be presented to the Brazilian consulate in Beirut, presumably to enable their application for citizenship.

People with assets and cash could find interest anywhere, or discretion in many places. But they could find Edmond Safra in only one place. "If the market was 6 percent on a $2 million deposit, you gave 5.75 percent. [The client] wouldn't shout; he wouldn't take his account to Manufacturers Hanover. But he expected you to be there for him whenever he wanted you, and you were," said Raymond Maggar. Even junior bankers knew they could introduce any client to the head of the bank. "[They sat] with Edmond for five minutes [and] they were in heaven," Rolando Laniado said.[143]

Beyond dispensing financial advice, Edmond was happy to act as a sort of one-man employment agent and life coach. When friend Simon Alouan was thinking of leaving Lebanon in 1960, Edmond told him to go to Brazil, and that he would come for him when he was next there. Alouan arrived in November 1960 and found work. Sure enough, the next April, Edmond arrived and hired him to help open a TDB office in Rio, even though Alouan didn't speak Portuguese.[144]

Edmond also assumed the role of chief marketing officer for his banks. At the outset, he told Roger Junod that in Switzerland, he'd be competing against an army of institutions that had been there for 150 or 200 years. So he had to do what Union de Banques Suisses, Credit Suisse, and la Société de Banque Suisse wouldn't deign to do: market aggressively throughout Europe. This wasn't a burden for Edmond, though. He loved finding clients himself. For years, he had been filing people and relationships away in his steel-trap memory. On the phone, and in letters, he'd cajole friends and colleagues in his huge network on four continents, offering inducements and commissions, leaping at any opportunity to help them open an account with TDB or BCN—with essentially no downtime.

He campaigned in a good-natured and almost martial manner—tromping off to Antwerp to see Ashkenazi diamond merchants, repeatedly going to Paris in the winter of 1961–1962 to meet with anxious French-Algerians who were fretting about their future. TDB opened a branch in Paris, which was run by René de Picciotto, a member of another far-flung Beirut financial family. At times it seemed as though no point on the map was too distant. A Mr. Choueke of Paris was trying to sign up a Muslim grandee in Senegal who had a big account at a rival bank. "I hope that you will do everything possible to win the new client and to give him the best treatment," Edmond wrote Henry Krayem in Beirut in March 1962. In the same letter, he noted that Nessim Dwek, while in Zurich, ran into a man named Albert Bawabe, who banked with a rival Sephardic financial institution, Mirelis, in Geneva. "Bawabe promised Nessim that he'd transfer his account to us."[145]

While freewheeling, Safra remained insistent that things be held to a certain standard, including the uniform of his profession: most days he would be dressed in one of his twenty navy blue suits and a conservative tie. Once, when boarding a plane, Raymond Maggar brought a conversation with a potential client to a close when he turned right into the economy section while his interlocutor remained in first class. This angered Edmond. "Look, you're Mr. TDB. And you've got to act like Mr. TDB. You've got to be accepted. You've got to be one of them. So you fly first class. You mix with them as Mr. TDB, because otherwise you're always going to be the other guy in the back." Edmond occasionally stayed in character to the point of comedy. In February 1962, when the World Ski Championships were held in Chamonix, near Geneva, he told Moussi Douek to round up the crew, rent a house, and support the team. He invited the team and the Lebanese ski federation to lunch. While everyone else skied, Edmond showed up on the slopes in a suit and tie.[146]

He also demonstrated to colleagues how to treat people who could bring no financial benefit to the firm. An old woman was sitting in the Beirut bank on an intensely hot day for what seemed to be a long time. Edmond asked his staff what she was waiting for. An employee told him that she was a poor woman who came from time to time to receive donations. Edmond sat with her, apologized for the wait, and pulled a wad of bills from his pocket. "God bless you, you're the son of your mother," she responded. Edmond personally saw her out, and gave the director who had let her sit there a good telling off for making her wait.[147]

There was also a less conventional point to Edmond's campaign for more and more deposits. For most banks, deposits were a base from which to make mortgages, or business and consumer loans. This was explicitly not the goal of TDB, or BCN, or the growing Safra financing business in Brazil. That was too risky. He wanted to build not an empire, but a large bank in the image of his father. He would always tell people that his philosophy, derived directly from Jacob, was to "Make a dollar a day, but every day, make a dollar."[148] And so he sought the types of risks he could manage carefully. The bank would trade gold and currencies for its own account and facilitate the trades of others. There was trade finance, including letters of credit to individuals and companies—except instead of Lebanese sheep farmers and textile importers, the credit was now extended to multi-national manufacturers. Among the clients in TDB's inaugural year were a Colombian steel company, which borrowed $50,000, and ITATI SA Comercial y Financiera in Buenos Aires, which borrowed $100,000 and offered shares as collateral. TDB provided financing to industrial companies like Mercedes-Benz, which was importing cars into Brazil, and the Brazilian division of Cummins Diesel, which borrowed $1 million. Edmond always sought out situations in which another party might guarantee all or part of the transaction. In 1962, a $10 million loan to a Japanese company was effectively guaranteed by the Bank of Tokyo.[149]

This may have been the age of the "organization man" and the creation of vast corporate bureaucracies, but Edmond's banks were remarkably flat and nonbureaucratic. He managed less through organizational charts and more through direct communications and giving people belief in the efficacy of their own judgment. Simon Alouan, an early employee, remembers that when he'd propose something, Edmond would respond: "Are you sure of yourself?" If the answer was yes, Edmond would respond in Arabic: "*Allah maak*." ("May God be with you.")

Though content to let trusted lieutenants manage affairs, Edmond also wanted to be in constant contact. For that reason, he was obsessed with communications technology. When Moïse Khafif opened the TDB office in Buenos Aires in 1962, Edmond instructed him to put in a telex line to Geneva: "It will give us advantage over the *casas de cambio* in handling/settling currency (deutschmarks, francs, liras)." "He'd sleep with a telephone in his hand" was how Roger Junod put it. When he was renovating a new apartment in Geneva at 14 Rue Crespin, to which he moved in 1964, Edmond told the contractors to make sure it had Louis XVI furnishings—and several telephone lines. His secretary knew the number of every public telephone booth on the route between Rue Crespin and the TDB office on Rue Chantepoulet. That way, Edmond would never be out of range—even if he was walking home.[150]

His attention to detail wasn't limited to telephones. Edmond fretted over the size of the bathrooms in the office in Geneva (he wanted them to be sufficiently small to stop people from feeling comfortable reading the newspaper there during the day). In April 1962, he wrote to Joseph, who was in the US, to go buy 1,000 Parker pens—"500 black and 500 of different colors, for example: gray, red, green, blue, etc."—that he could engrave with TDB's name, in French for Geneva and in Italian for Chiasso.[151]

It was a miracle that he could stay on top of as many activities as he did in an era before mobile communications, for he was always on the move. A reconstruction of his movements in 1962 shows that in January he was traveling between Geneva, Paris, and Beirut. In February, he went to Chamonix for the ski championships and then again to Paris for a few days. He returned to Paris from Geneva in both March and April. On April 15, he went to São Paulo, so he could arrive in time for the first Passover Seder, then went to Rio (April 29 to May 1), Buenos Aires (May 6 to May 16), back to São Paulo, and then off to New York (June 4 to June 10), and then to Montreal (June 10 to June 11) before returning to Geneva. He spent the summer bouncing between Milan, Chiasso, Geneva, and the South of France. And in the fall, it was off to Beirut.

In all of this there was a seamlessness between Edmond's life and work. In Europe in the early 1950s, time in the office rolled into evenings spent in bars, nightclubs, and casinos with friends and colleagues. The discussions continued at the homes of his now older friends with their children. In Geneva, he was frequently at Jacques Douek's house, where he'd debate economics and politics with Moussi. He'd often call Jacques's wife asking if he could bring clients over, and she'd cook Syrian food. In his Rue Crespin apartment, Battista, his valet, cook, and chauffeur, would prepare a simple plate of spaghetti for him when he came home late. On the weekend, he would go to Albert Manila Nasser's house outside Geneva, where he'd play cards, chat with friends, and eat Syrian food. "Give him pita and cheese and watermelon—*khebza, wa-jebna, wa-bettikha,* in Arabic—and he would take it forever," Nasser said.[152]

The need to be connected to his roots as an Aleppan/Beiruti Jew was elemental. Aleppan Jews were known for being religiously observant while avoiding fanaticism. Edmond followed Jewish rituals faithfully. If he came to the office early in Geneva, he'd sequester himself in his office for an hour to put on his tefillin and pray, if he hadn't already done so at home, which was his usual daily practice. Every year around the time of his mother Esther Safra's death, he'd call Mourad Mamieh, a friend in Beirut, and ask him to take ten people and a rabbi, and go to the cemetery to pray at her grave. He had a firm belief that religious devotion made a difference in life, often repeating the phrase *"Alef emunah, Beit berakhah."* The first two letters of the Hebrew alphabet represented *emunah* (belief) and *berakhah* (blessing), in that order. One followed from the other. [153]

Edmond's attachments to superstitions common among Aleppo Jews was a source of some bemusement to his colleagues. But for people who grew up in Beirut in the 1930s and 1940s, the concepts of luck and the evil eye were very real. He carried white and blue stones and other small objects in his pockets as talismans—"gris-gris," as his niece called them. Amid a discussion of business, to ward off bad luck, one person might utter the word *Hamsa* (the number five in Arabic), and the others would respond: *Hamsa.* When he was able to choose his telephone numbers, at the office or at home, he would ask for the maximum number of fives to be included.

Edmond Safra viewed his institutions and role as helping to keep the culture of Aleppo and Beirut alive. On more than one occasion, he wrote to an associate at the bank in Beirut with instructions to send pistachio nuts and *ka'ak* (sesame cookies) by air, as a present to friends in Geneva.[154] More significantly, he forged relationships with other leaders of the Syrian diaspora, among them Isaac Shalom in New York. Edmond sent money to Shalom to take to Israel for the charities of Rabbi Meir Baal HaNess, and to coordinate aid to help the dwindling number of Syrian Jews who were still in Damascus and Aleppo. When Jacob Laniado, a wealthy Cairo businessman of Aleppan extraction who had an account at TDB, died without survivors, he designated Edmond as the executor of his estate, along with Ezekiel Schouela, whom Edmond had first met in Amsterdam in the 1940s. Together, they managed donations to the construction of a hospital in Israel. The Schouela family had relocated to Canada and was building a substantial business there. They recruited Edmond as an investor in the Golden Mile Shopping Centre in Toronto.[155]

Cool-eyed rationality and superstition, piety and modernity, respect for tradition and a tendency to rebel—these were among the many contradictions Edmond Safra embodied and handled with equanimity. There were more that became apparent in these years. The prodigious donor to causes in Israel was unable to be associated publicly with the Jewish state. "Edmond can't engage in correspondence with people living in Israel," Jacques Douek wrote to an official in Israel who was asking about the Laniado legacy. When pitched an investment in Israel the same year, Edmond responded: "For political reasons mainly, I am not in a position to accept a participation in this investment."[156]

Edmond had a busy social life, although much of it was connected to his business. He was a member of the Bowling Club of Geneva, belonged to the Club Nautique in Beirut, and was angling to join Le Club, the high-end social club, in New York in 1963. He developed a taste for the finer things, especially cars. His personal fleet in these years included a Fiat 1200 Spyder Convertible, a massive Chrysler Imperial, and a Bentley S2 Saloon. From 1960, he owned an Italian-built Riva boat and spent a small fortune on mooring in and around Juan-les-Pins. He would frequently lend the boat to friends and business associates like Jean-Prosper Gay-Para or William Feingold, with whom he traded coffee. But he also relished rubbing shoulders with an earthier crowd in Beirut. While in Beirut, he once asked a friend, Mourad Mamieh, to find the man who used to bring Jacob's shawarma lunch every day. His name was Nahmou, and he ran a tiny shop that sold crayons and other goods. When Nahmou responded that he was too busy, Edmond cracked up. "Find him, I'll give him money."[157]

Yet the garrulous social person, who loved talking politics with friends and family, was also somewhat lonely and typically found himself alone at the end of the day. It was rare for people in Edmond's milieu to be single as they entered their thirties. Edmond certainly did not lack for female companions wherever he went. And the testimony of a half dozen contemporaries suggests that he had come close to getting married in the early 1960s. On his visits to Beirut, he was courting Tania Beyda, the worldly daughter of a cultured Aleppan family involved in finance. But the difference between the two—in age, in political worldviews (many teenagers in that milieu in Beirut were left-wing), and in aspirations—were too vast. Edmond wasn't quite ready to settle down, and the young girl wasn't prepared to marry an international banker twelve years her senior. [158]

Edmond continually embraced new modes of doing business. In 1962 and 1963, he began to tap into mass media to market the products and services of his finance companies in Brazil and Switzerland. In Brazil, Safra SA ran newspaper advertisements for "*letras de câmbios Safra*" (Safra letters of exchange), which offered absolute security, liquidity at any moment, and protection against inflation. Ads in *Time* magazine offered customers of TDB the ability to open accounts in other currencies. Another TDB ad in English featured a man in lederhosen responding quickly to a call: "We answer fast!"

On December 5, 1962, TDB was formally accepted into the Association of Swiss Bankers. And Edmond was busy forging personal and professional ties to large institutions in a new frontier: the United States. But what he consistently relished were growing signs of the acceptance of the family and its enterprise within the international banking establishment. To develop Joseph's career, Edmond set him up with an internship in 1961 at Bear Stearns, in New York, under the tutelage of John Slade, a German-Jewish banker whom Edmond had met. Next, Edmond thought it would be good for his brother to "follow a full training course with the Bank of America New York." Joseph rotated through the San Francisco headquarters in 1962 and returned to Brazil.[159]

In the spring of 1963, TDB established credit lines with two American WASP redoubts: Bank of America and Chase Manhattan, the bank chaired by David Rockefeller. When the United Nations opened an account with TDB in 1963, he wrote exuberantly to several colleagues. He told Joe Michaan, "I am sure that you will be equally pleased by this news, which shows the ever growing importance and prestige of our bank." A photo of Edmond appeared in the April 1963 issue of the British magazine *The Banker*: "Edmond J. Safra: Vice President and Managing Director, Trade Development Bank, Geneva and Chiasso, Switzerland."[160]

It was all working. By the end of 1963, TDB had assets and liabilities of 218 million Swiss francs, up 50 percent from 144 million at the end of 1962. Safra had progressed from the scrawled "bilans" and notebooks of the late 1950s to reams of printouts that listed the securities, accounts, and participations in minute detail. In 1965, TDB moved to larger offices at 16 Place de la Fusterie. It was now a substantial institution, with assets having more than doubled in three years, to 372 million Swiss francs. TDB reported profits of 5.6 million Swiss francs (equivalent to $8.3 million in 2021 US dollars).[161]

And it was all run by Edmond Safra. Although Jacob's name appeared on key documents and he occupied ceremonial roles, his declining health left him unable to participate in the family's business affairs. He simply wasn't well enough to fully engage. His mental state continued to deteriorate, and he developed a large hernia in 1960. Jacob's condition weighed on Edmond, in part because he felt guilty about having moved him to Brazil, where Jacob had been transformed from a recognized leader of the community to what seemed like a mere exile. In May 1960, Edmond wrote Isaac Shalom in New York, sending $4,000 to "acquire a third room at the Yeshiva Rabbi Meir Baal HaNess, as I would like to devote the same, together with the two already booked, to the creation of either a Midrash or else a drawing room in my father's name." He also asked if Shalom, on his next trip to Israel in June, could organize prayers for healing for Jacob at the yeshiva.[162]

The family took steps to make Jacob feel comfortable, and to maintain his dignity. The laying of the cornerstone of the new Sephardic synagogue in São Paulo on December 19, 1961, which would ultimately be named *"Ohel Yaacov"* ("Tent of Jacob") in his honor, must have given him pleasure. Even seemingly trivial items held rejuvenating potential. In February 1961, Edmond thanked Rosette Mamieh, in Beirut, "for sending me the shirt with the cotton swabs of Jojoba oil for my dear father." That summer, he wrote to Dr. Bender at Mt. Sinai Hospital in New York, who had seen Jacob in 1958, asking about the efficacy of "a medicine and a treatment for absentminded-ness for elderly people" he had heard about. Bender replied that it was "of no value," but sent him the anti-anxiety medication Elavil.[163]

While Edmond remained the obvious heir apparent to Jacob and had control of the many interlocking family companies, it was clear to him that he and two of his brothers were still partners—equal partners—in the family firm. Moïse and Joseph owned shares in the Brazilian entities that Edmond had set up. In 1962, Joseph received 10 million cruzeiros each of TDB and Banque de Crédit National shares. Edmond also set up some of his investment vehicles in the name of his sister Eveline. [164]

However, mindful that he couldn't manage everything, and of the need to avoid conflicts of interest, Edmond began to cede more oper-ational and legal control of the Brazilian financing operations to Joseph and Moïse. A profile of Grupo Safra, the family's Brazil hold-ings in 1963, included the cotton mill and jute bag manufacturer Sacaria Paulista, the import-export business ECSA, and Safra SA Credito Financiamento e Investimentos, with capital and reserves of 455 million cruzeiros. The leadership listed Jacob Safra as president, Moïse Safra as director general, and Joseph Safra as finance director—with no mention of Edmond.

In late 1963, Cyril Dwek wrote Edmond Rabbath, a lawyer in Beirut, expressing surprise that Safra SA Credito Financiamento e Investimentos had been put on a blacklist by the office in Syria that maintained a boycott of companies that did business in Israel. "We have never had any contact with Israel either directly or indirectly," he wrote. "Our business is conducted mostly with the Arab colony in Brazil, whom we constantly endeavor to serve at the best of our ability."[165]

Considering the turmoil affecting the Middle East, the decade after the Safras left Beirut was a generally happy one. The family was grow-ing, thriving, and largely intact. But in the spring of 1963, the Safras suffered a devastating blow. After a second hernia operation, Jacob got an infection and ultimately died of pneumonia on May 28, at the age of seventy-four. Edmond observed shiva, and he was intent on not shaving for the first thirty days after the death, as was custom. At the same time, he was cognizant that an international banker couldn't present himself to clients with stubble on his face. And this seemingly small conflict between religious and business duties clearly weighed on Edmond. A few weeks after Jacob's death Rahmo Nasser telexed Edmond. Rahmo had consulted with four different rabbis in Brazil, Sephardic and Ashkenazi alike, who agreed that it was permissible for Edmond to shave after fifteen days—in part because Jacob had died on the eve of Shavuot. Moreover, one rabbi said he could shave in less than fifteen days if he had to meet important people. "In conclusion you can shave."[166]

Jacob's passing was marked on three continents. TDB took out a death notice in the *Journal de Genève*. Sunday morning, June 23, a memorial service was held in São Paulo. In Beirut, the Community Council organized a service on June 27—to mark the end of the traditional thirty-day mourning period—at 6:30 in the evening, which Edmond attended. It summoned the pomp and circumstance that had become de rigueur for this still-confident but diminishing community. Community president Dr. Joseph Attie spoke, choirs of children from the Alliance and the Talmud Torah sang, Rabbi Yaakov Attie chanted psalms, and Chahoud Chrem, who was to be the last chief rabbi, offered the traditional prayers. Around Rosh Hashanah, employees of Safra SA surprised Joseph, Moïse, and other family members by presenting them a bronze bust of Jacob, which was installed in the lobby of the São Paulo office.[167]

Jacob's loss weighed heavily on Edmond, inspiring an uncharacteristically intimate and personal exchange with Rahmo Nasser. Edmond thanked him for his support "during the days of anguish that we are going through."[168]

"I consider myself for you a big brother, and nothing that touches you will be indifferent to me," Rahmo responded. "As you know, dear Edmond, one of our grand preoccupations, for Evelyn [sic] and me is to see you and your brothers to settle down. There are certainly in the world other things than business; to have a hearth, an agreeable wife, children and to raise them, and other satisfactions no less great. And I hope that you take it seriously."[169]

But if Edmond was married to anything, it was his bank, and many employees noted, not wholly in jest, that they were married to him. And while he was quick to trust associates on a personal or professional basis—especially if they came from the community—he was slower to trust on an intimate level. One friend recalls him saying as a young man that if he got married, he'd "need a television set to see what she's doing; I'd have to watch her."

It's also possible that Edmond's life was saturated with a remarkable multiplicity of daunting roles: he was head of the family, responsible for his older and younger brothers and large extended clan; running three institutions; tending the legacy of his father; looking out for the interests of clients and Sephardic Jews around the world. The rhythm of his life, the constant travels in Europe, Brazil, and, increasingly, New York, and the hundreds of transactions and relationships he managed daily must have been exhausting. Perhaps there simply wasn't room in his life at that time for a single relationship to monopolize his attention. Perhaps he had simply not yet met the right person.

In any case, Edmond Safra was in no way ready to settle down, or slow down. By 1964, ten years after leaving Milan for Brazil, he presided over a network of loosely affiliated but coherent and increasingly well-capitalized companies that were part of the regulated international banking system. He had established himself as a leader in his industry, and in the communities in which he alit. But he believed there were still bigger worlds to conquer. For all their appeal and dynamism, Beirut, Geneva, and São Paulo were in some ways provincial. The global economy, with its manifold connections, was growing, and needed the lubrication of finance and credit. The Safra empire was conspicuously absent from a wealthy, vital financial capital—one with a large Sephardic community, one that embraced immigrants, and one that was suffused with an entrepreneurial energy that Edmond found irresistible. In 1963, he was already talking to associates about building a bank in New York.

7

Coming to America

(1964–1968)

A t the age of thirty-one, Edmond Safra was already moving among elite global banking circles. "This is to express my sincere thanks for the kind welcome you gave me in London on Wednesday last," he wrote to Edmund de Rothschild on March 2, 1964. "It was very nice meeting you."[170] Although the Safras' banks in Geneva and Beirut were small by the standards of the global industry, Edmond knew, by virtue of his patrimony and his experience of nearly two decades, that he belonged, and that he shouldn't fear competing with them directly. So in 1964, having established a safe beachhead in Brazil for the family, and still mourning the death of his father, Edmond set his sights on simultaneously staking claims in the two most important financial capitals in the world: New York and London.

It's unclear when he made his first visit to London, a city in which the Safras had commercial contacts going back generations. But since his first visit in New York in 1952, Edmond had been a frequent visitor to America's largest city. Over the years, he had built up business and personal relationships with fellow members of the Syrian diaspora like Joe Michaan, with financial counterparts, and with correspondents at banks, including Bear Stearns, Bank of America, and Manufacturers Hanover.

In the early and mid-1960s, though based in Geneva, Safra was often in Brazil in April, around Passover. He would spend chunks of time in the South of France or in the Mediterranean in the late summer, and rove between Beirut, Paris, and other European cities in which he had business in the months between. New York was to become a more frequent destination. When he stopped in New York, often on his way from Europe to South America, he would usually stay at a hotel in midtown—the Sherry-Netherland, the Regency, or the Plaza. Edmond was in New York in May and again in June 1964. Amid the skyscrapers and banking giants, he was plotting to plant a sapling. The appeal was obvious. New York was the largest single consumer and financial market in the world's largest economy. The US offered a unique combination to financial entrepreneurs like Edmond—a massive and prosperous middle class eager to establish banking accounts and to borrow money, and a large and growing cadre of companies seeking global connections. They were all wrapped in a regulated banking system in which the government insured deposits, and the central bank, the Federal Reserve, carefully oversaw the banking system. New York boasted a large community of Syrian Jews among whom Edmond would feel welcome, and a business and commercial culture that, while vastly different from Beirut, Geneva, or Brazil, suited his ambition and personality. And whereas Europe and the Middle East were still mired in ancient rivalries and modes of doing business, New York—home to that year's futuristic World's Fair, thrusting skyline, and a pulsing commercial bustle, and historically open to newcomers—very much seemed like the future.

For Edmond, the US also offered a different type of opportunity—protection from the sectarian violence that could disrupt life in Beirut, protection from the inflation and political instability that wreaked havoc in Brazil, and the potential for immense growth. "New York is for the big boys," Edmond had told his New York–based friend David Braka earlier, explaining why he wasn't quite ready to set up shop there. In 1964, he was ready.

Edmond, aware that he was an outsider again, found established locals to help him negotiate the regulatory and financial culture, just as he had in Brazil and in Switzerland. Chief among these guides was lawyer Herman Cooper, a veteran of the financial and legal scene who provided entrée into New York's financial establishment. The easiest method a foreigner could use to gain a bank charter in the US would have been to purchase a bank that was already operating. "I have looked into the possibilities of acquiring an existing bank rather than setting up a new one," attorney Donald Schnable wrote to Edmond in May 1964. Safra and his colleagues had some contact with the Hebrew Immigrant Aid Society, a nonprofit group, which had a dormant bank. But it didn't make sense.[171]

The natural next step was to seek a charter from the State of New York. But Seymour Scheer, who was New York's acting superintendent of banks in April and May 1964, was apparently taken aback by the young man with an indeterminate accent who had the audacity to open a bank in the financial capital. Opening the window in his office, Scheer gestured and told Edmond: "Do you see all those banks? What makes you think you can compete with those banks?" In any event, the answer from Scheer appeared to be no. Still, Schnable was optimistic that when Scheer's successor came in, "whatever difficulties you have encountered may be overcome."[172]

Rather than wait, Edmond plunged ahead. While driving through midtown in a car with Herman Cooper, he noticed several banks with unfamiliar names. Cooper pointed out that these were all comparatively new banks with federal charters. James Saxon, who had been appointed comptroller of the currency, whose office regulated federally chartered banks, had taken a more liberal approach to bank formation. In 1963 and 1964, he had approved charters for more than 300 banks. So in July 1964, Edmond went to Washington to see Saxon, who was more encouraging. When they met, Saxon asked what the bank would be called, and Edmond replied, "I have always liked the name 'Republic.'" Safra would later say that he chose the name "Republic National Bank of New York" because it was "the most American name I could think up."[173]

Encouraged by the meeting, Edmond immediately began to search for a building that would serve not just as a place of business but, ultimately, as a home. As usual, he went right to the middle of the action. The story goes that Edmond was shopping for a hat and bought

a building. The Knox Hat Company occupied a lovely ten-story
Beaux Arts structure, built in 1902, on the corner of Fifth Avenue
and Fortieth Street, across from Bryant Park. Designed by John
Duncan, the architect who had also conceived Grant's Tomb, it would
not have looked out of place in Geneva or Paris. On June 9, 1964,
broker George S. Kaufman of Kaufman Realty wrote to Edmond
with good news. Edmond had authorized him to pay up to $1 million
for the building, but Kaufman was able to get it for $925,000 plus
brokerage commissions. Edmond closed on the building in the summer of 1964.[174]

Throughout his working life, Edmond relished acting as a leader
of campaigns. The army he assembled to launch Republic was a
mix of New Yorkers—Jews, Catholics, and WASPs, and Sephardic
allies from far and wide. When Marty Mertz, an accountant at Peat,
Marwick, Mitchell & Co., was assigned to work with a new client,
he went to Joe Michaan's midtown office, where Edmond had set
up shop. "I'm opening a bank," Edmond told him. "You are going
to do the work. We have to file the application!"[175] Mertz adapted
an application previously used for Citibank and set things in motion.
In the spring and summer of 1964, lawyers and accountants and
bankers toiled in the midtown offices of Manufacturers Hanover,
which had thrown its institutional support behind the effort. On
July 2, they formally submitted an application to organize a national
bank—albeit one that would have a fundamentally different model
than its all-American peers. This new institution "expects to gen-
erate approximately 80% of its deposits from abroad as well as from
US firms engaged in foreign business and foreign firms similarly
engaged in domestic business." And it would work through the
"interlocking financial network provided by the Trade Development
Bank, Geneva, its affiliates and associates."[176]

The Office of the Comptroller of the Currency granted preliminary
approval in the fall of 1964. With a home, a charter, and a name, the
bank needed a CEO. Of course, Edmond intended to run Republic,
but because he was not a US citizen, they would need a local professional to head the bank. They turned to Peter White, who ran

Manufacturers Hanover's metropolitan New York division, and was nearing retirement.[177]

Now to raise the capital Republic needed. Edmond had settled on the idea of raising $10 million by selling shares at $20 each (about $88 million in 2021 dollars). This was at once a small amount of money, and a significant sum—the largest amount of capital for a startup bank in the US at the time. But it wouldn't be a particularly heavy lift given Edmond's network. TDB would own a controlling stake, contributing $4 million (BCN added $80,000). By the summer of 1965, individuals who had long been associated with Safra enterprises had invested as well: Jacques Tawil ($20,000), Moïse Khafif ($200,000), and Jacques Douek ($220,000), for example, and much smaller amounts came from TDB employees like Roger Junod and Edmond's assistant Claudine Favre. By the time he left Geneva for New York on July 23, 1965, Edmond carried in his hand the list of subscribers. At the last minute, Joe Michaan told Edmond he wanted to invest $1 million in the new enterprise, so the subscription was bumped up to $11 million, leaving TDB with a 36 percent stake.[178]

If there were restrictions on his ability to operate in the US, Edmond nonetheless appreciated the opportunities it offered, and he appreciated the idea that anybody could apply for a license and expect to have it examined objectively. "What a fair country," he would later tell colleague Jeff Keil. "What an open, big country it is—that welcomes competition and only requires you to be honest." Edmond referred to it as "the big blue sky of America." This was a long way from putting a mattress down in front of the door of a minister's office or showing up to say Buongiorno.[179]

At the same time, elements of the reception in New York angered Edmond—especially the press. On July 1, 1965, the *New York Times* printed a seemingly innocuous article about a new bank charter bid in New York that identified some of the key players, and suggested, per Herman Cooper's comments, that it would "tie in with a group of banks abroad" in Switzerland, Germany, and Latin America.[180] Edmond, livid, lit into Cooper in a lengthy telegram on July 5, 1965, which he sent from a hotel in Lisbon, where he was working on a real estate transaction. It is worth quoting at length because of the passion on display: "times article in hands we protest energically [sic] much surprised at your declaration that no formal relationship exists between new bank and trade development which completely incorrect stop such declaration gives impression you attempt deny trade development paternity in republic bank which creates very bad impression and prejudices our reputation stop shocked your acting despite our understanding article would be prepared by you stop. . . . in future no spokesman allowed without consulting me fullstop." Cooper responded, noting that he couldn't control the press. Moreover, he continued, given the recent negative publicity surrounding Swiss banks and the reporter's appetite for a sensational story, Cooper had felt it was important to avoid pointing out the identification between TDB and Republic—which Edmond took as an insult to his family's pride and dignity.[181]

Even as he was setting up an entirely new bank in one of the largest consumer markets in the world, Edmond maintained an exacting attention to detail throughout his growing empire—believing that the image his institutions presented to the public was paramount. When a client from Istanbul, a Mr. Shaho, who had about $200,000 on deposit with BCN in Beirut, sent an associate to make a payment, the man was apparently treated poorly by an employee in Beirut, so Shaho sent him to open an account at Zilkha's bank. This was a setback Edmond couldn't abide. "You know, as I do," Edmond wrote Henry Krayem on October 14, 1965, "the importance attached to the manner in which we receive clients, and I beg you to give instructions to our employees at the cashier's desk and at reception so that this doesn't happen again." A week later, he wrote to Joseph in Brazil asking him to send 15,000 wooden bases for calendars they could give to clients, some for Geneva and some for New York—although he wanted to discuss the price before ordering.[182]

This concern over details and aesthetics carried over to the new enterprise in New York. While the executives were organizing the paperwork and regulatory filings, workmen were busy carrying out more than $2 million in construction to outfit the interior of 452 Fifth Avenue in grand style. Working at the direction of Ernest Bonanny, a French-born principal at the architectural firm Kahn & Jacobs who had designed the interior of the Plaza Hotel, they installed an 8.5-ton vault door, a safe-deposit room with 500 boxes, and a massive banking hall framed by three chandeliers copied from French palaces, each containing 4,200 prisms and beads. The European feeling continued through the upper floors, which featured offices for the loan department, offices for top executives, dining facilities, and, on the ninth floor, an apartment for Edmond. Throughout, the same wood paneling used in TDB Geneva graced the walls, and the floors were filled with Louis XVI furniture.[183]

On August 16, 1965, Republic sent the stockholders list to the Office of the Comptroller of the Currency, which approved the bank's corporate existence two weeks later. On Wednesday, September 29, 1965, the day after Rosh Hashanah, the beginning of the new year on the Jewish calendar, the organizers of Republic met at the Sky Club on the fifty-sixth floor of the Pan Am Building. At 12:15 on November 15, 1965, the board of directors convened at 40 Wall Street, just around the corner from the New York Stock Exchange. Among those present were labor lawyer Ted Kheel, William MacMillen, Joe Michaan, Peter White, and Edmond Safra. Peter White was named president, at a $50,000 annual salary, and Edmond was named honorary chairman.[184]

On the morning of Monday, January 24, 1966, Robert F. Kennedy came to cut the ribbon and formally open the building. A photo captures Kennedy talking to reporters holding microphones in his face, while Edmond, smiling broadly, stands to the side with his arms crossed. Here, the former attorney general, current US senator, and possible future president had come to bless the inauguration of Edmond Safra's new business. While it started with more initial capital than any other commercial bank in US history, "Republic National, of course, will be a pygmy among New York City's banking giants," the *Times* noted. By comparison, Chase had $15.3 billion in assets in 1965. "We're off and running," Peter White said. "We're budgeted for $25 million in deposits for the first year, but I think we'll do better than that."[185]

Although the Safra modus operandi had, for nearly a century, relied on personal relationships, discretion, and familial connections, Edmond quickly embraced the American way of doing things as well. In New York, the enthusiastic, even boisterous, marketing and promotion of financial services, which was entirely frowned on in Beirut or Geneva, was commonplace. And Edmond understood intuitively how to reach the mass market. Republic's single branch, smack in the middle of midtown, two blocks from Grand Central Station, was designed to welcome and wow the public. The day it opened, Republic ran a splashy ad in the *New York Times* and other publications: "Today! A New Bank." Customers who opened an account with $25 or more could get a thirteen-piece decorated ovenware set, or a three-piece heavy stainless steel mixing bowl set. The combination of the location, the awe-inducing premises—here a middle-class American could bank like a European aristocrat—and the incentives worked. The first day, 1,200 accounts were opened; on February 4, just nine days later, the 10,000th account was opened. The foot traffic was such that accountants from Peat Marwick were brought in to act as tellers. By June 30, 1966, Republic had garnered $32.1 million in deposits, far surpassing the goal for the entire first year.[186]

But what to do with those deposits? Edmond was happy to assume the liability of taking deposits from people he didn't know, in large part because the Federal Deposit Insurance Corporation in 1966 began insuring accounts up to $15,000. But when it came to building assets for the bank, Edmond wasn't willing to extend mortgages or consumer credit to thousands of individual New Yorkers. Rather, the theory was that he would do here what he had done in the many countries in which he had already conducted business: use the deposits to make low-risk loans to companies or government agencies abroad, or to other banks; to find low-risk arbitrage opportunities; to scour his own large network and connections to put the money to work in places and in ways that Chase and Citi wouldn't.

There was a complicating factor, though. The US government in the 1960s was growing increasingly concerned about the balance of trade—America was running a rising trade deficit—and was seeking to rein in the activities of banks. On March 5, 1965, a voluntary Foreign Credit Restraint Program was promulgated, under which banks committed to cap the foreign direct investments they made. (A new hard limit would be installed in 1968.) New banks were prohibited from lending more than $450,000 overseas, which was obviously problematic for Republic. Edmond didn't want to lend to home buyers on Long Island; he wanted to place his funds in overseas deposits and loans.

After Republic's lawyers engaged regulators, Republic was able to work out a compromise. Republic was effectively an importer of capital, via the subscriptions it had raised and the deposits it was collecting from overseas. It suggested, and the government agreed, that it wouldn't place more funds overseas than it derived from abroad—which staked the upper limit at something closer to $8 million. The money was already being put to work in 1966, earning interest from banks in London and Japan, discounting $976,000 in promissory notes from Argentine financial institutions, and lending $761,000 to Banco Nacional Hipotecario Urbano y de Obras Públicas in Mexico. By the end of 1966, Republic had $33 million in loans and was boasting of how it had "efficiently integrated its manifold services with the Safra network of associated banks and financial houses in Europe, South America, and the Middle East."[187]

Republic was an American bank, to be sure. But it was clear who was in charge. The key staff in Republic's early years were all people with Beirut connections. Joshua Yedid, Edmond's childhood friend from Beirut, was in charge of trading. Cyril Dwek, Nessim's son, was in charge of lending. Moïse Khafif was summoned from South America to New York in 1967 and helped spearhead the drive for deposits. And, of course, Edmond was truly running the show. Leon Gell, a banker brought in from Chicago to serve as vice president, resigned after just three months because he realized he would not be part of the tight-knit decision-making team. As Moïse Khafif bluntly told CEO Peter White: "We put you here because we have to show the public that we have an American who is a banker."[188]

To a degree, Edmond's patrimony and past, which were an immense source of pride to him, were also a challenge, and for reasons that remain unknown, Edmond was worried about how he was being perceived in the US. He became aware that there was damaging misinformation about him circulating in documents that had stemmed from investigations in Italy in the 1950s. And in June 1966, he wrote a lengthy letter to Michael Picini, an official at the US Embassy in Rome, in which he uncharacteristically shared personal information: his life story, the relationship of the brothers (Elie was still receiving a subsidy "to enable him to live"), and references including officials such as Walter Moreira Salles, the former Brazilian minister of finance, and Pierre Edde, the former Lebanese minister of finance. "I have never been arrested, indicted, convicted or charged . . . with any crime in any place in the world . . . I have never in my life engaged in any act contrary to law." He mentioned the high principles of morality "which always prevail in my family." Accordingly, he asked Picini "if you could make the most complete investigation, sparing no effort or method to reach the truth. I believe this is the only way I could see my position cleared for ever." He continued: "I have nothing more precious than my honor and my name and I am ready to devote all my time and efforts to their defense. I am sure that in the tradition of democracy of your great country you, as a United States official, will grant me justice and discourage any further attempt to [damage] my reputation."[189]

While the regulators were putting a crimp on his bank's activities—who could be the CEO and the owners, how much it could lend—Edmond embraced the bumpers and safety they provided in the US. The channels in the US were both formal and transparent. The dangers of an environment where regulation was more lax—or nonexistent—were evident in Beirut that fall. Intra Bank, founded in the 1950s by Yousef Beidas, an aggressive Palestinian entrepreneur, had grown rapidly and attracted thousands of depositors from around the Middle East. Its holdings included Middle East Airlines and real estate around the world, including the Phoenicia Hotel in Beirut and an office building at 680 Fifth Avenue in New York. By the fall of 1966, Intra accounted for 15 percent of the country's bank deposits. So when Intra stopped payments on October 14, 1966, a financial crisis ensued. The Lebanese authorities, waking from their slumber, ordered all banks in Beirut to close, including BCN. Edmond flew enough money to Beirut to pay every depositor and was eager to reopen his doors—not wanting to show weakness or create burdens for his customers. But he felt that if he defied the authorities, the Jews of Beirut would suffer a backlash.[190]

Beirut remained an important part of Edmond's increasingly complex and intermingled business and social life. In April 1966, when he was visiting the city, he went with Jack and Doris Waage of Manufacturers Hanover, and Henry Krayem and his wife, to a show at the Casino du Liban. The same year, while in Beirut, he met with Rabbi Chahoud Chrem and agreed to send hundreds of prayer books to Magen Avraham synagogue in Beirut, as well as supplies to Rabbi Youseff Shasho, who was still faithfully shepherding the remaining families in Aleppo, including several hundred high holiday prayer books and thirty sets of tefillin.[191]

As the Safra empire grew to encompass TDB in Geneva, Banco Safra in Brazil, and now Republic in New York, BCN remained an important node. Selim Kindy, a Beirut-based businessman, opened an account at Republic in 1967. He would bring cash to BCN, which would then place it in a pouch bound for New York and credit it to his account at Republic the next day. Mahmoud Shakarchi, the Beirut-based money changer and trader who was a great friend to Jacob and Edmond Safra, opened accounts at Republic and encouraged others dealing with him in dollars to clear trades through Republic. In 1968, thanks to Shakarchi's influence, Abdul Aziz and Ali Al Yousif Al-Muzaini, key financial intermediaries in Kuwait who had traded gold with Jacob, opened an account with Republic. Edmond thanked Shakarchi: "May I add that we all here value highly your assistance and the fact that you are sparing no efforts to strengthen our old friendship and mutually rewarding relationship," he wrote.[192]

Edmond held fiercely to his Beirut connections even as they continued to disperse, and in some instances, die out. In late 1966, when Gilbert Tarrab, the son of Madame Fortunee Tarrab, Edmond's teacher at the Alliance, wrote his first novel, *Les Desabuses de Beirut*, Edmond bought 100 copies. In June 1966, Nessim Dwek, who had been a surrogate father figure to Edmond, died at the age of fifty-five. Edmond, in turn, assumed a somewhat paternal attitude toward Nessim's son, Cyril. The following year, in July, Jacob's second wife, Marie Douek, died in Geneva after a long and painful illness, at the age of fifty-six.[193]

The deaths at a young age, the strong connections he always felt, and the rare meetings he found in his travels made Edmond a sentimentalist about his old connections. Joe Cayre, a businessman of Aleppan extraction in New York who became a good friend in the 1960s, said that Edmond would frequently make comments like, "I saw so-and-so's father when I was in Milan ten years ago. How's he doing? Could you arrange a lunch for us?" When lawyer Charles-André Junod told Edmond he was marrying his assistant at the university, whose family name was Arueste, Edmond asked, "Is your future father-in-law Henri?" Gleeful, he summoned Albert Benezra, telling him that Arueste, who worked for the Nehmads, was the person with whom he had done his first deal in Milan. "I bought, I don't know, some kilos of gold against pounds sterling." Edmond's Syrio-Lebanese identity was expressed in who he socialized with, and in how he ate. When businessman Rahmo Sassoon came from Japan to visit Edmond in the 1960s, Edmond would "serve fasoulia [white beans] and caviar at the same time." And when the first Lebanese restaurants began to open in London in the late 1960s, Edmond would make a beeline for them upon arrival. [194]

Lebanese food wasn't the only attraction of London. If Republic was Edmond's new baby, demanding significant attention, TDB was the rapidly growing teenager. By the 1960s, London, having finally dusted itself off from the wartime damages and ended its rationing, was reassuming its role as the leading banking center of Europe and a locus of capital markets activity. The parent of Republic, resting on a solid base, was starting to expand and grow in Europe. In 1965, Edmond sent Raymond Maggar to set up a representative office of TDB in London. By 1967, when TDB's balance sheet was a substantial 533 million francs,[195] it would have representative offices in Paris, Milan, Buenos Aires, and Rio de Janeiro.

Edmond had been doing business in London for years, trading gold with Mocatta & Goldsmid and the Rothschilds. But here, too, there were opportunities to take in deposits and to lend to businesses. As was his practice, he set up an office at 21 Aldermanbury, smack in the middle of the City of London. It would receive authorization to operate as a bank in 1968. Unlike Republic, this was explicitly not to be a consumer business. It was there to provide services to businesses and to other banks. For example, the London unit began to offer to ship banknotes in foreign currencies back to their home destinations and take a very small margin. In time, this would emerge as a significant low-risk arbitrage business for the Safra family of banks.

The term in French for affiliated companies is *filiales,* which implies a family relationship. And regardless of the name on the business card—TDB, BCN, Republic, Banco Safra—or the business model pursued, this term was very appropriate for the Safra family of banks. In June 1966, Edmond's assistant wrote to Moïse in Brazil, asking him to send portraits of Jacob Safra to Geneva and New York, where they would occupy prominent positions.[196]

Brazil in the 1960s remained not just a haven for the family, but the center of operations for important family businesses and a hub for the larger South American region. In November 1965, Moïse was naturalized as a Brazilian citizen, at the age of thirty-one.[197] In 1969, Joseph married Vicky Serfati, whose family had immigrated to Brazil from Greece. The financing and industrial businesses Edmond established continued to thrive, and he increasingly left their operations in the hands of his younger brothers. And Brazil remained an important source of clients for the network. In the fall of 1966, Joseph Safra wrote to Jacques Douek at TDB in Geneva, asking a favor: "A good friend of ours, Mr. Monteverde, who is a good client of ours, wants to spend time in Switzerland for the winter. Could you rent for him a chalet in Saint Moritz, a minimum of three rooms, from 12/15 through the next 3/15?" Mr. Monteverde was Alfredo Monteverde (born Greenberg), a Romanian immigrant to Brazil and owner of the highly successful retail chain Ponto Frio. He would likely have been traveling with his wife, Lily, whom he had married the year before.[198]

Edmond was still a bachelor, without children of his own. But his older siblings' children were coming of age, and Edmond took steps to ensure the next generation would find their way into the family business. In 1966, he was speaking with Ezy Nasser, the eldest son of Rahmo and Eveline, in São Paulo. Ezy was trying to figure out what to do after graduating from college. "Look," Edmond told him, "do you want to stay in São Paulo, or do you want to be able to meet David Rockefeller?" So in 1967, Ezy came to New York to work as Edmond's assistant. Despite the distance between Elie and the other brothers, Edmond hired Jacqui Safra, Elie's oldest son, in 1968 to work on foreign exchange. [199]

Edmond trained his younger relatives in much the same way Jacob had trained him, by sending them to Europe in search of low-risk financial intermediation opportunities. The Safra interests in Brazil had pioneered the business of clearing between the Central Bank of Brazil and Communist-dominated Eastern European countries, swapping coffee for industrial merchandise. Edmond would call Ezy from Geneva and dispatch the twenty-two-year-old to Belgrade, or the Soviet Central Bank, to discount clearing operations. Ernest Sasson, who left Beirut in June 1966 and started as an assistant to Emile Saadia in Geneva, was sent on his first assignment to Czechoslovakia, and then to East Germany and Poland. Twenty years earlier, a teenage Edmond had trekked through the postwar capitals of Western Europe in search of gold. Now, he was dispatching the next generation of young Sephardic men to the grim limestone finance ministries and central banks behind the Iron Curtain, earning a discount on the movement of Brazilian coffee beans, gold, textiles, and industrial supplies.[200]

Edmond's expanding operations defied his ability to impose order. Republic was somewhat chaotic in the early years, as it grew with great speed and without formal functions. Fred Bogart, the son-in-law of David Braka, Edmond's longtime friend, was offered a job at the bank in 1966. He wanted $200 a week, and Edmond offered him $100. A year later, he came back and Edmond said, "We'll split it in the middle: $135." When Bogart joined in March 1967, working on collecting federal funds, he sat with a group of four people on the cavernous fourth floor. "At that time everybody did seventeen jobs," he said. There was, of course, no organizational chart. [201]

Still, Edmond remained meticulous, even obsessive about certain details. Showing people around Republic, he was furious that an employee, Fred Kattenberg, had a cigarette burn on his desk already. "You give a slob a beautiful desk, and look what he does to it." Edmond would fire off notes to Cyril Dwek about the status of a loan, or about purchasing from M. Possollo in Lisbon items for the ninth-floor residence, like an Empire banquette, or a Louis XVI bed and armchair. But his method of keeping on top of operations wasn't to matrix out responsibilities and read weekly reports. Rather, he would hold court in the evening in his apartment at the top of Republic. He'd summon Joshua Yedid, Cyril Dwek, and a variety of others, sit behind his desk while enjoying a drink, and talk through the day's operations.[202]

This method was a challenge. Because he wasn't a citizen, Edmond was restricted in how much time he could spend in the US each year. He would generally come twice, often for three months at a time. And so as the empire grew and expanded, the telephone became an even more important instrument for Edmond than it had been before. He would call employees around the world through the business day, at night, on Sundays. (He was mindful of colleagues' interest in observing Shabbat.) He did so in part because he wanted to keep up with events, and in part because he enjoyed the constant connection with others. Sem Almaleh, who worked for TDB in Geneva and Chiasso, recalled that Edmond would call on the weekend. "What's new?"

"Edmond," he would respond. "It's Sunday. Nothing is new." But, Almaleh remembered, "you could be on the phone with him for an hour and a half about what this person and that person were doing." If he couldn't reach someone, he'd call Jacques Tawil, and ask him to find that person, and then reach out to four or five other people with the same message—and the unfortunate recipient would be bombarded with several calls.[203]

The traffic wasn't one-way. As much as Edmond relished reaching out to individuals, he was also someone whom others would not hesitate to seek out. Still in his early thirties, Edmond was already known as the person to see for Jewish organizations. In 1965 or 1966, Clement Soffer, then twenty-one, secretary of the Egyptian Jewish congregation that was aiming to build a new synagogue in Brooklyn, came to ask Edmond for a $100,000 loan. Edmond said he'd supply the cash, but told him: "I want your guarantee also that this will be repaid." Soffer protested, noting that he was barely out of his teens. "It's not the guarantee, it's the principle," Edmond told him. When the leaders of the São Paulo Jewish community came to New York to ask Edmond for a large donation to build the Hebraica de São Paulo, he told them he would lend them the money at a very low interest rate. When they responded that they didn't have the funds to pay back the loan, Safra told them that they'd just have to pay the interest—but that he wanted them to commit to that small portion immediately. Then he told his secretary to write a check for the remainder.[204]

Edmond continued to live in Geneva, now at 56 Rue de Moillebeau, a location that offered faster access to the airport. But in 1968, he spent only sixty-eight days there. As he still lacked his own personal nuclear family, his life remained very much invested in the bank. In the case of Republic in New York, the bank literally was his home. In 1966, when his associate Rolando Laniado came to visit from Brazil, they went out to dinner. "I haven't gotten out of the bank this week," Edmond told him. The senior executives, many of whom were distantly related, were a sort of family for him. To Maurice Benezra, Albert's son, growing up in Geneva in the 1960s, he was "Uncle Edmond," who gave him a TDB stock certificate for his Bar Mitzvah and once showed up with eighteen birds in two cages as a present. The identification between his self-image and that of his business enterprises was intense. On more than one occasion, Edmond said: "My banks are my children."[205]

Gregarious, with hundreds of contacts and a large number of relatives, Edmond was constantly on the move, and never alone for the Jewish holidays. Friends and associates would continually cycle through various cities where he was. And he would travel with them. When Simon Alouan was spending a few months in Kenya in 1968, Edmond traveled to Nairobi, where the two were guests of one of their lawyers, an eccentric man. Edmond took a brief safari, enduring a white-knuckled trip on a small plane and close encounters with an elephant. He had a more personal interaction with wildlife at the lawyer's house, where the pet chimpanzee, Sam, was treated like a member of the family. At one point, the chimp jumped up on Edmond's lap and started to caress his face. After dinner, as they walked in the garden, the chimp held his hand, causing the usually easy-going Edmond quite a bit of discomfort.[206]

It wasn't all work. Edmond never lacked for the company of women, when he wanted it. He belonged to social clubs in New York and London. In May 1968, for example, he was at the opening weekend of his friend Jean-Prosper Gay-Para's fabulous new hotel in Saint-Tropez, the Byblos. In the late 1960s, Edmond had a girlfriend for about three years, a French woman named Nicole Gotteland. Not much is known about her, but records show that starting in the summer of 1966, they frequently traveled around Europe together, to the South of France, to Athens (from where Edmond chartered yachts in the summers of 1966 and 1967), and to Beirut.

With each visit to Beirut, Edmond would find fewer members of the old community still there. The Six-Day War in the summer of 1967, which permanently altered the geopolitical landscape in the Middle East, destabilized Lebanon further. Amid the tumult, BCN continued to function as before, moving large quantities of gold from Mocatta & Goldsmid in London to the Middle East—some 800 kilos in November 1967 in several different transactions. That fall, BCN was functioning as a channel for aid flowing from Geneva to Jews in Damascus. But slowly, the remaining tightrope walkers began to leave. On July 2, 1968, Joseph Moadeb, a lawyer who had worked on real estate with the Safras, wrote to say that he was planning to liquidate. "I'm hesitating between Canada and Brazil. I'm asking for your advice, which I'd greatly appreciate." Among those coming out were the Cohen family, including their daughter, Chella. Born in 1951, she moved with her family to Brazil in 1968 and married Moïse Safra in 1969. [207]

Edmond continually fielded requests for aid from Beiruti Jews. Selim Chehebar, a longtime associate of the family, wrote in December 1967 that he was deep in debt due to expenses related to his daughter's wedding. "I know you have a good heart and that you help everybody.

What do you say to me, who has been at your service for 45 years?" For Chehebar, and many others fleeing Lebanon and Egypt in the late 1960s, the Safra family banks—especially Republic—were a refuge. Edmond found a place in New York for Chehebar, who left Lebanon when he was 65 and barely spoke English, in the loan department, discounting notes. Abraham Shamma, who worked for Jacob Safra around the house on Rue Georges Picot, was offered work in the mailroom. When Joe Robert, one of Edmond's patient teachers at the Alliance school, left Beirut for Brazil, he was given a job. Nathan Hasson worked at BCN until 1966, along with Michael Elia. Elia was offered a job in Brazil, and Hasson fled to Canada. In April 1968, Henry Krayem called Hasson from Beirut and told him to go to New York. He showed up at the bank and was ushered into the penthouse. Edmond, who was standing there in his bathrobe, along with Joshua Yedid, Moïse Khafif, and Ezy Nasser, handed Hasson two $100 bills so he could get a hotel room and told him to show up for work the next Monday in the loan processing department. Victor and Albert Hattena, brothers from Cairo, joined Republic in the late 1960s. "When people came from Lebanon or Syria, they'd say, go to Victor Hattena's department, because he can train employees."[208]

By 1968, Edmond, now in his mid-thirties, had assumed greater responsibility for his community and had successfully planted roots in American soil. By virtually any measure, he had met and exceeded the expectations of his family, community, and colleagues. The international family of banks that he had envisioned was now up and running, although Republic's growth had stalled after the quick start. Edmond had traveled a great distance in his twenty years in business, and he had arrived in the crucial new capitals of New York and London. But to a degree, Edmond had yet to fully establish himself in either of those capitals. And while he was wealthy and extremely busy, he was far from satisfied—professionally or personally. The coming years would usher in a period of growth on both fronts.

8

Growing in Public

(1969–1972)

Republic was unique, and people didn't always know what to make of it. It had an unlikely mix of European refinement, Middle Eastern personal banking, and American hustle. "A new bank—nearly a century old" was its slogan. (It had been developed by the same public relations firm that worked for Irving Trust, which Edmond had known in Beirut.) Republic was certainly the only bank in Midtown that held a small party when it put a large silver mezuzah on the front door. Most banks prohibited multiple family members from working in the same place at the same time, as it might make it easier to embezzle. But at Republic, "you would look at the directory and see the same names, five of some, seven of another," recalled Greg Donald, who joined the bank in 1972. When Republic published stock certificates, they contained the face of Jacob Safra. The logo of the bank was that of Edmond's global group—a stylized shield bearing the letters BJS (representing "Banque Jacob Safra") superimposed over each other, which had been designed by a Beirut printer for a coin produced by BCN.[209]

Unlike many of Safra's other endeavors, Republic wasn't a huge success from the outset. The bank lost money in its first few years, in part due to the lavish spending on the building. After the fast start, deposits in 1968 stood at only $72 million, and Republic earned a relatively meager $454,000 in profits. One investor, concerned about the investment, asked for his $1 million back.

Part of the challenge had to do with the competition. Unlike the Jews of Beirut or businessmen fleeing Egypt for Brazil, New York consumers had legions of choices among banks. And part of it was because Edmond, steeped in the practices of Aleppo and Beirut, was suspicious and skeptical of borrowers he didn't know. The American way of lending—to strangers, based on a formula, without a personal guarantee—was completely alien to him. Every time there was a loss, Fred Bogart recalled, Edmond would ask, "Did you look the guy in the eye? Did you sit across from him? How do you lend money to a guy if you don't know all that?" For large banks, losses were simply a part of doing business. For Edmond, each setback was something akin to a personal wound, and it was the principle of accepting losses that was as important as the material outcome. George Wendler, a Republic executive, recalls discussing a problem loan on which Republic had a maximum exposure of $20 million for four consecutive nights. "You know, George," Edmond told him, "I can afford to lose $20 million. I just will not like it." And he would move quickly to stop small losses before they snowballed into larger ones. When his nephew Jacqui Safra was down on some currency trades and told Edmond they would come back, Edmond responded: "Do not worry. I sold you out. You're starting over."[210]

As quick as he could be to extend assistance to someone in trouble, Edmond Safra was perpetually suspicious that people might be trying to take advantage of him. In 1968, the venerable Penn Central railroad merged with the New York Central. The story, told by many, was that senior executives came to Republic to seek a loan that year. Of course, Safra was flattered by the prospect of doing business with this storied company. But he wasn't interested. "Why did Central Railroad come to Republic?" he wondered aloud, rather than any of the dozens of other establishments. Sure enough, in 1970, the railroad went bust in spectacular fashion, in what was the largest bankruptcy in history at the time.[211]

Given its overhead, Republic needed scale in order to pursue profits—more deposits that it could invest in foreign financing and arbitrage opportunities, especially in the Eurodollar market, which paid higher interest rates. But here Edmond was hamstrung in part by regulations. Due to regulations, banks couldn't appeal to customers by offering better interest rates on deposits. The small premiums, like pots and pans, had worked in the early years—but the Federal Reserve's Regulation Q forbade banks from paying out premiums above a small amount to customers. However, in classic Safra fashion, a senior employee found a seam in the regulations, and Edmond had the foresight to mine it with alacrity. In late 1968, Morris Hirsch, a veteran banker who was a senior executive at Republic, realized the regulations were essentially silent on what banks could offer a third party to refer a customer to them. So what would happen if Republic appealed to New Yorkers to bring their friends, relatives, and neighbors in to open, say, a $10,000 time savings account—and rewarded the referrer not with a $20 toaster, but with a $400 television?

Thus was born a highly successful consumer banking campaign, one that would put Republic on the map. "Bring in your friends and take out a free TV!" blared Republic newspaper ads in early 1969. The appeal set off a frenzy among savvy New Yorkers. By the time the bank opened at 9:00 a.m., there was a line of customers stretching down Fortieth Street to Sixth Avenue. The police set up barricades to contain the crowds. Inside, staffers would usher new customers to upper floors in groups of ten, seating them amid the lavish antique furnishings to open accounts. The referrer would then receive a certificate and make his or her way to a ground-level space Republic had rented on Thirty-Ninth Street to hand out the TVs. Edmond would receive a daily report on the traffic. One woman, Ida Schwartz, referred people who opened twenty-five accounts, and gave televisions to all her grandchildren. (She would often call Republic Bank and ask why a particular set wasn't working.)

The impact on Republic was transformative. At one point, Republic was among the largest distributors of RCA color televisions in America. Deposits, which had grown only slowly in the previous few years, began to boom, soaring 43 percent to $103 million in 1969, and more than doubling, to $239 million, in 1970. [212]

The deposits would be deployed not into mortgages and credit cards, but into businesses that Edmond had long worked in. With larger sums at his disposal, he could use his intuition and interest in trading to build new lines of operations—many of which were generally shunned by other New York banks. First among these was precious metals. In Europe and the Middle East, the Safra banks had always done a significant business in gold. But in the US, circumstances surrounding silver, which, unlike gold, traded freely, made the less-precious metal an attractive option. Albert Hattena, who joined Republic in August 1969, was put in charge of silver. Edmond would call three or four times a day from Europe, and depending on the price in New York, place orders to buy or sell. Republic also opened a depository, which meant it could earn fees from the storage of the metal. As the market price of silver appreciated in the late 1960s, the silver content of US coins began to exceed their face value. Repeating what he had done in Europe with gold coins, Edmond mined the discrepancy for value. In 1970, the Federal Reserve told Republic it could count "currency and coin" at the bullion value for the purposes of banking reserves on hand rather than reserves at the central bank, which were non-interest-bearing. So Hattena went and bought all the silver coins he could, certified the market value of the silver embedded in them as reserves, and then sold the equivalent amount of silver bullion forward—thus locking in significant income on the value of the silver.[213]

BCN in Beirut through 1967 and 1968 was moving large quantities of gold from London to the Middle East. But the US was to offer both a new hub and a significant series of opportunities. The price of gold remained fixed through the 1960s at $35 an ounce, and it wasn't widely traded. Such trade as existed was for jewelers. But speculation on gold rose outside the US, and Europeans flush with dollars from exports to the US began to purchase gold in large quantities at the fixed price from the US Federal Reserve. In an attempt to halt the flow, in March 1968, the US announced it would no longer buy or sell gold in commercial transactions and encouraged private banks to take out gold licenses to meet industrial demand. Amid rising volatility in the currency markets, the London Gold Pool, the mechanism through which the price of gold was pegged at $35, collapsed, and gold began to trade freely. Republic was among the first US banks to take out a gold license. And it quickly established a gold department in New York. Mimicking the trade it conducted with silver, Republic would buy gold at the current spot price and sell it for future delivery at a higher market price. So long as such differences between current and future prices persisted, Republic could lock in significant profits without taking any risks. The bank also set up a licensed gold depository, which meant it could earn money storing gold for others just as it previously had with silver.

Cautious to lend, Edmond was bold on pushing personally into new frontiers. In April 1969, he traveled to Japan, meeting with financial and industrial companies on behalf of his Brazilian operations, and laying the groundwork for a deal in which Japanese companies Marubeni and Teijin would establish a joint venture in Brazil with Grupo Safra to make polyester in 1972.[214]

He also met people who could provide supplies. In July 1969, he penned a lengthy letter to Peter M.S. Yagi in Osaka about 3,000 ashtrays. "We in principle are prepared to place such an order with you, but we would like to know whether the backside of the ashtrays could be fitted with suede, as per our sample, or at least an imitation of this material, rather than the vinyl leather mentioned in your offer," he wrote. In addition, Safra wanted them to "be adorned with a golden rim of approx . . . ½ cm thick on the upper edge."[215]

Expanding on his preference for the furniture and other accoutrements of European aristocrats, he began to purchase fine art. In the late 1960s, he had acquired a painting by Chaim Soutine, *Woman with Umbrella*. "I hope you will enjoy the Soutine," London art dealer Andras Kalman wrote Edmond on June 18, 1968. "I have a beautiful small landscape by Renoir. Could we show this to you?"[216] (Edmond passed on the Renoir.)

He also continued, perhaps subconsciously, to mimic the philanthropic actions of the small coterie of Jewish European aristocrats. He was a stalwart financial supporter of the Communauté Israélite de Genève, giving 10,000 Swiss francs annually. But he also had a soft spot for small Jewish communities that lacked resources, such as the Egyptians in Brooklyn. In 1968, when the tiny Jewish community in Madrid was planning to build the first new synagogue in the country since the 1490s, Edmond tasked Eveline's brother-in-law, Albert Buri Nasser, to provide the funds. It was ultimately named Beth Yaacov, after Jacob Safra. The same year, in 1968, he donated 5,000 prayer books to the synagogue in Milan, in remembrance of his father, and pledged $10,000 to fund the dining room at the Magen David Yeshiva in Brooklyn. When he met Safra in 1970, Rabbi Abraham Hecht, an Ashkenazi Chabad rabbi who was the longtime spiritual leader of Shaarei Zion, the Syrian synagogue in Brooklyn, identified him as "the counterpart of Baron Rothschild in the Sephardic world."[217]

The outward professions of faith—putting on tefillin for his daily morning prayers, keeping the Book of Psalms in his office, the mezuzahs in the bank—weren't simply rituals or rote. For Edmond, Jewish teachings and traditions informed both business and charitable efforts, and his speech was often peppered with references from the Bible and Talmud. If Jacques Tawil pointed out someone making a lot of money, Edmond would say, *"Hebel habalim amar Kohelet"* ("Vanity of vanities, Kohelet said"), the first line of the Book of Ecclesiastes, referring to the fleeting nature of wealth.[218]

In one significant area, however, Edmond continued to diverge from the path expected of men in his milieu: getting married. In the world of Beirut and the Aleppo diaspora, the usual—and expected—practice was that men, once they were established professionally in their late twenties or early thirties, would marry a woman from the community. Typically, she would be someone five or ten or fifteen years the man's junior, and someone the family knew. (In prior generations, it had often been a cousin, as was the case with Jacob and Esther Safra.)

But Edmond wasn't interested. His relationships with women seemed generally to have been a matter of companionship or convenience. As he continued to build his empire, trotting between four countries, seeking someone to share his life with, or even to build his own nuclear family with, wasn't a priority. But although Edmond always maintained that he was simply too busy, the truth of the matter was that he would have had a difficult time finding someone suitable among the Aleppo diaspora. In the culture of the Sephardic communities, women generally were not offered broad horizons or educated beyond high school, or taught to be worldly and ambitious. Their role was usually to make a home and have children. As Edmond became more cosmopolitan himself, and as his businesses became more global, the likelihood of him settling down with a girl from this tradition decreased. He needed someone he knew wasn't only after his money, someone who could hold her own with him, and someone who was his social and intellectual equal.

He would finally find that person in the summer of 1969. Lily Monteverde had the kind of background and dramatic life to which mythology would attach. But the facts themselves were of sufficient interest. She was the child of Jewish immigrants to South America—Wolf Watkins, an engineer of Czech and British origins who had prospered in Brazil and Uruguay, and Anita Noudelman, whose family fled pogroms in Odessa for the safety of Brazil. Born in Porto Alegre and educated in Rio, Lily married young—to Mario Cohen, an Italian-Jewish stockings manufacturer who lived in Montevideo, Uruguay. They had three children—Claudio, Eduardo, and Adriana. Lily and Mario divorced in 1964, and the following year she married Alfredo "Freddy" Monteverde, the proprietor of the Ponto Frio appliance store chain. In August 1969, Monteverde, who suffered from bipolar disorder, ended his life, leaving Lily as a young widowed mother with substantial resources and a complex familial and financial situation.

After Freddy died, Lily relocated to England, where her older children attended school. (Carlos Monteverde, Freddy's ten-year-old adopted son, joined her.) To a degree, she was already in Edmond's world. She had attended Joseph Safra's wedding in Brazil, and they knew many of the same people. Perhaps more significantly, Freddy Monteverde had been an important client of the Safra banks.

In 1969, Lily made what she thought would be a quick business trip to Switzerland to check in with advisers at S.G. Warburg in Zurich, and at TDB in Geneva. The plan was to meet her advisers in Zurich in the morning, go to Geneva for lunch, and then return the same night to London. But the complexity of her affairs, and the frailties of communication networks, played a providential role. As Edmond examined her situation, he realized there were issues he needed to discuss with attorneys in Rio. They drove to lunch at a restaurant across the border in France, placed a call, and waited for it to come through. When Lily was summoned to the phone, "I felt that Edmond was looking at my legs," she recalled. Since the parties couldn't agree to a mutually agreeable conclusion on the phone, Edmond suggested she stay in Geneva for a few days. With only a day's worth of clothing packed, Lily went into the boutique operated by Anita Smaga, wife of Victor Smaga, an old friend of Edmond's. The next day, Lily and Edmond kept talking.[219]

And they found they had a great deal to talk about. Unlike many of the other women he had met, Lily was on Edmond's wavelength. Like Edmond, she was fluent in several languages, among them Portuguese, English, and French. They both loved collecting. In fact, Lily had a huge head start on Edmond, having acquired an art collection that included paintings by Klee, Picasso, and Van Gogh. She had the resources to rent her own apartment in London, or yacht in the Mediterranean.

In Lily Monteverde, Edmond had found an equal—in stature, in wealth, in ambition, in independence, and in fortitude. Aware that this was a potentially different situation, he became more self-conscious. At the same time, she seemed to kindle a degree of interest and happiness that friends had not seen in him before. When he was getting ready to see Lily at the Hotel President Wilson in Geneva, Edmond would spend ninety minutes in front of the mirror, "moving his two hairs from one side to the other," Simon Alouan recalled. He'd check to see that his shirt and suit were nicely pressed.

Lily had not only her own resources, but her own schedule. This was someone whose life he would have to adapt to, not the other way around. Edmond would visit Lily frequently in London, where she lived at the Dorchester Hotel and ultimately bought a flat, and gingerly began to step into a sort of father figure role for her children. In the summer of 1970, Edmond and Lily cruised on the Mediterranean in a yacht that Lily had rented. But Edmond decided he urgently needed to get back to New York, and the boat was far from their ultimate destination, Capri. So he urged the captain to take the boat ashore amid turbulent seas, while he and the other passengers tied themselves to their deck chairs. Lily also purchased a farmhouse in the South of France, in Vallauris, to which Edmond became a frequent visitor.

But their romance was not without drama. Even if he was clearly smitten, Edmond was also accustomed to not being tied down. In the summer of 1971, Lily was expecting Edmond for dinner in London on a Friday evening—he was coming to town for a meeting of the board of Globex, Freddy Monteverde's company, of which they were both members. But Edmond never showed up. Lily thought it was likely that Edmond was dating a second woman in London. So she called the woman's home, posing as a TDB employee who was alerting Edmond to an emergency at the bank. When he picked up the phone, Lily told him: "Thank you. I was waiting for dinner. Forget me." At the Globex board meeting, fellow directors were shocked when Lily dramatically ripped up the letters Edmond had written to her and tossed them at Edmond. Edmond was devastated. For several months, according to one friend, "he had no will to do anything. He lost interest in most of [what] he used to love, even business."

On an impulse, and to make Edmond jealous, Lily married Samuel Bendahan, a London-based businessman of Moroccan extraction, in Acapulco, Mexico. Less than two months after the marriage, Lily left Bendahan, triggering a series of acrimonious legal actions. When she got in touch with Edmond, he suggested that instead of returning to London, she go with Simon Alouan to a place nobody would think of: the King Frederik Hotel in Copenhagen. Edmond came to meet her. "It was moving to see them, hand in hand, like two high school students," Alouan recalled. Edmond was so happy he didn't bother calling the bank. They determined to rebuild their relationship and move forward together—but doing so would have to wait until Lily could receive a divorce.[220]

While Edmond was encountering obstacles in his personal relationships, he was notching new triumphs in business. He had twin goals for Republic: increase deposits and increase capital. The television giveaway campaign was taking care of the first. Raising capital for the bank, which would help solidify Republic's standing and improve its strength, would be a greater challenge. Thus far in his career, Edmond had raised capital for his institutions in the Old World way: from friends and family. A major participant in financial markets, Edmond had not been active in capital markets, which require the sale of shares or bonds to strangers. In 1970, Republic had only $16.7 million in capital. Now he was trying to sell $10 million in new capital notes—again, essentially on his own. Having managed to sell only $700,000, he was open to new ideas.

This quest brought him into contact with a group of ambitious, self-made financiers who would prove influential to Republic's growth. The Wall Street brokerage world was largely divided between old-line WASP firms, like Morgan Stanley, and old-line German-Jewish firms, like Goldman Sachs, which traced their origins to the nineteenth century. After World War II, a new generation of brokers, many of whom didn't have access to these networks, began to forge their own way. Among them was the firm Cogan, Berlind, Weill, and Levitt. In 1971, Jeff Keil and Peter Cohen, two young bankers at Cogan Berlind, went to see Edmond. They suggested that their firm could underwrite Republic's offering, essentially buying the whole thing and selling it in pieces to their clients. When they invited Edmond over for lunch, they were debating what to serve. They didn't want to put on airs, but they also didn't want Edmond to think they weren't classy. In the end, they decided to go with their usual fare: pastrami sandwiches. This was fortuitous, since Edmond loved Jewish deli and found the formality surrounding business lunches oppressive. "You know," he told them, "I don't like to waste a lot of time on lunch. In Europe, people lose two hours, they eat their lunch, they drink their wine." Besides, he was miffed that a competitor, also a Jewish bank, had invited him for breakfast and served bacon.[221]

If Edmond was impressed with Keil and Cohen's down-home style, his counterparts were often bemused by his aristocratic ways. When Keil flew with Edmond to the West Coast to see investors, he was surprised that Edmond's valet, Francisco Pereira, accompanied him, going back to the economy section while Edmond and Keil sat in first class. No sooner had they sat down then Pereira came up with a beautiful leather case, extracted crystal glasses, opened a bottle of mineral water, and poured it out. The stewardess, agape, asked: "Who are you?" Edmond responded, "Oh, I'm just a businessman."[222]

While Edmond continued to mostly eschew the organization charts and five-year pro formas typical of Fortune 500 companies, he was willing to engage in long-term thinking when it came to raising capital. Keil had prepared an idea for expanding the bank's capital to $250 million over a five-year period. When Edmond saw it, he told Keil he was thinking of the exact same number. Why? "It's how much Irving Trust has," Edmond said. "If you have that much capital, the bank can be run by idiots." Republic would achieve that $250 million goal in three years and eight months.[223]

In October 1971, Republic issued a rights offering, which it followed with a $15 million convertible debenture offering in March 1972. Republic's capital raising brought ambitious young Wall Streeters into the bank's orbit, including an aggressive trader who had made his way from Hungary to London and New York and was working at Arnhold and S. Bleichroeder, itself a Jewish firm from Germany. "As you know we have taken a substantial position in Republic National Bank and have developed a great deal of interest in the bank," George Soros wrote in a telex to bank management in 1972, "We received formal invitation this morning to be a member of your underwriting group for capital note issue." Soros asked that, while being a late addition, they be put down for $350,000.[224]

As Edmond's companies were assuming more public roles and gaining greater prominence, so too was Edmond emerging as more of a public figure. In the early part of his career, in deference to the sensitivities in the Middle East, Edmond had avoided any overt or public identification with Israel. That was beginning to change. During the 1948 war for independence, Porat Yosef, the yeshiva across from the Western Wall with strong ties to the Aleppo community, had been left in ruins by Jordanian forces. After the 1967 Six-Day War, as Israel took possession of the Old City of Jerusalem, a group of Aleppo families—among them the Ades, Laniados, Gindis, Shaloms, and Safras—shouldered the financial responsibility for restoring Porat Yosef to its former glory.[225]

And he continued to take a personal interest in the plight of his community in Beirut. In September 1971, Albert Elia, head of the Community Council in Beirut, disappeared. Elia had been assisting the dwindling core of Jews in Syria who were eager to leave, and he was kidnapped by Syrian agents and hustled over the border to Damascus. Edmond reportedly tried to pay a ransom in an unsuccessful attempt to free Elia, who was killed in 1972. Vicky Mamieh, a friend from Beirut, in December 1971 wrote Edmond to thank him for having sent her 2,000 pounds: "My sister Tamam was at the cemetery earlier on the anniversary of your mother's death and asked God to protect you at every instant." Along with her thanks, she sent a package of pistachios. In the summer of 1971, Rabbi Chahoud Chrem of Magen Avraham wrote Edmond to remind him "of your good habit of participating at the Temple in the diverse donations for the philanthropic works of our temple, and to reserve certain aliyot in the memory of your father and your mother." People also sought Edmond out as a kind of secular authority. When Freddy Salem, the son-in-law of community leader Joseph Moadeb, and a 1960s BCN employee, had a dispute over money with his four brothers, they all agreed to go to Edmond to arbitrate. "People trusted that he would come up with the just solution," Salem recalled.[226]

Amid his whirlwind life—tending to the needs of Jews in Lebanon, negotiating his complex relationship with Lily, managing the affairs of three banks and a host of business interests around the world— Edmond remained the same shrewd trader he had always been. For him, the world continually presented opportunities for low-risk arbitrage to those with capital, ambition, and the ability to act quickly. An illustrative case came in the summer of 1971. Amid continuing challenges, the US dollar was losing value against other global currencies. Foreigners, as they lost faith in the US—which was waging an unsuccessful war in Vietnam, struggling with inflation, and dealing with an unfavorable balance of trade—continued to demand the ability to trade their dollars for a more stable asset: gold. The Nixon administration came to believe that abandoning the official peg of the dollar to gold—the gold standard—would make sense. On the evening of August 15, 1971, a Sunday, Nixon gave a speech in which he said that the US would, effective immediately, halt the convertibility of the dollar into gold, and that foreign governments could no longer swap dollars for gold.

Edmond, who was in his apartment above the bank having dinner with Rafael Kassin and Ezy Nasser, heard Nixon's speech and immediately grasped the subtext. Despite Nixon's protestations to the contrary, this move would hasten the devaluation of the dollar. The clear and obvious play was to buy yen and sell dollars. And at that time, the markets in Japan, which was ten hours ahead of New York, were already open. Edmond called Jo Romano, who ran the bank's administrative operations. "Call the foreign exchange people. Get cots. Get food. We are trading!" He gathered his team and went down a few floors to the telex room, because it was difficult to get open phone lines to Tokyo, and operated the telex himself. Within a flurry of twenty minutes or so, the markets had adjusted, but Republic had racked up millions in profits.[227]

The public was not always privy to the details of Edmond's maneuvers. But people were increasingly learning about—and participating in—Republic's growth and expansion. On January 12, 1972, Republic's common shares had listed for trading on the American Stock Exchange, and on July 14, 1972, Republic's shares were listed on the London Exchange. The twin campaigns to increase capital and increase deposits were yielding significant results. Total assets soared from $75.2 million in 1967 to $411.7 million in 1971, and deposits catapulted to $348 million. They would nearly double again in 1972, to $643 million, representing a tenfold increase in five years. The bank, which had eked out a small profit in 1968, earned $28 million in 1971. A healthy chunk of its earnings came from sources other than credit—owning municipal bonds, trading gold and silver, foreign currency operations. Its loan-to-deposit ratio in 1972 was around 40 percent, and the lion's share of loans were made to banks and governments in Europe and South America. "In six years we haven't written off a loan," said Morris Hirsch.[228]

By 1972, Edmond had built not just a base in New York, or a node in the network of family institutions, but a powerful new engine of growth. In the space of several years, Republic had assumed its role as a public entity. And to a small degree, Edmond had done the same. Approaching his fortieth birthday, he had forged important new relationships, and had positioned himself, his family, and his financial institutions for future growth.

9

Leaps of Faith

(1972–1975)

As much personal and professional growth as Edmond had experienced in the previous five years, there was more to come. And it would come in leaps and bounds, a result of several uncharacteristic and, ultimately, life-changing moves.

From the time of Safra Frères, the Safras had sought growth organically—establishing new institutions, bringing a new generation into the business, and adding nodes to their global network. This was a labor-intensive and slower form of growth than, for example, pursuing mergers and acquisitions. In 1972 in the US, there were well over 12,000 banks. And through shrewd marketing, Republic, with its single branch, had managed to grow into the 200th largest—among the top 2 percent in size. But as it was enjoying the fruits of the television incentive, Republic was also taking steps to increase its footprint by pursuing the acquisition of Kings Lafayette.

Kings Lafayette, a classic savings bank, had eighteen branches in Brooklyn and Queens and roughly $204 million in deposits, about as much as Republic. Edmond began to buy shares in the bank in 1970, with an eye toward a potential acquisition. But he wasn't the only interested party. In November 1971, Ted Silbert, the chairman of Standard Prudential, which controlled Sterling National Bank, was talking to Kings Lafayette about a potential merger. And although Edmond thought he had positioned a credit line from another bank to fund the $32 million purchase price, he and investment banker Jeff Keil learned the same bank was also backing Silbert. When Keil complained that it wasn't fair, Edmond told him not to be so naive. "You know, you're raised in a rich country, and so for you what is fair or not fair is very important," he said. Safra continued: "Where I come from, life isn't fair."[229]

Here, however, was another campaign to spearhead. The strategy for gaining control was to acquire as many shares as he could, quietly, on the open market with his own money, and then to offer a public tender for a slug of the shares he didn't own, thus giving him the majority. The trick was to do so without calling attention to the offer. Keil knew there were a few buildings on Court Street in downtown Brooklyn where lawyers had offices. He thought many of them either had Kings Lafayette shares or represented clients who did. Keil decided to take the elevator to the top floor and work his way down, introducing himself and offering to buy shares on behalf of Safra. Every night, Keil would report to Edmond on his haul—900 shares, 1,000 shares, 2,000 shares. To Edmond, it was reminiscent of his modus operandi at the central banks and finance ministries in Europe. He called it "knocking doors." As he later put it, Edmond bought the shares with his own money because he was "much more liquid than the banks."[230]

Kings Lafayette was involved in the hurly-burly of New York politics and had strong ties to the Brooklyn Democratic Party. In 1971, it was in the news because eight men, including several reputed Mafia members, had been arrested on charges of illegally obtaining loans from the bank. Eager to avoid controversy, Edmond paused his pursuit. But, by the summer of 1972, with Kings having been cleared of any charges, and Edmond having already spent $12.5 million to buy 44 percent of the shares, he was prepared to make a tender offer.[231] Here he enjoyed an advantage over his rival. A bank seeking to purchase a large chunk of shares had to notify the Federal Reserve and wait ninety days before acting. Edmond, acting in his own capacity, was under no such obligation. In early August 1972, Standard Prudential filed a tender for 51 percent of the Kings Lafayette shares at $40 a share. Two weeks later Edmond announced his own tender offer at the same price, and started buying immediately. On August 24, Edmond announced he had acquired all 189,678 shares of Kings Lafayette tendered under his cash offer, bringing his total holdings to 68 percent of the 786,028 shares outstanding.

Edmond was always portrayed in the press as a kind of mysterious interloper. "A foreign banker invades Brooklyn," read the *Business Week* headline on August 17, 1972. It referred to him as "a respected but little-known Lebanese-born Sephardic Jew who is a Brazilian citizen but lives in Geneva." But he took it all in stride. "I'm now competing with the big boys in their own country," he told the *New York Times*. "I must say the Americans have been more than fair to me. Doing business in America is beautiful."[232]

At the same time, Edmond and his colleagues were working on a transaction that would represent another quantum leap for the growing family of banks—and for the Safra family. TDB was the majority shareholder of Republic. Pursuing an entirely different business model than Republic, TDB in just eleven years had expanded rapidly, garnering some $1 billion in deposits. With total consolidated assets of $1.5 billion, TDB was solidly profitable, earning $10.2 million in 1971. Whereas Republic was provincial, with a single branch, TDB was global. It was well-represented in Europe, with offices in London, Chiasso, and Paris; and in South America, with offices in Panama, São Paulo, and Buenos Aires. In 1972, it opened two new representative offices, one in Frankfurt, and the other in Caracas, Venezuela.[233]

In Latin America, TDB leveraged the Safras' presence in Brazil on a continent-wide basis. In every major capital in South America, it could open an office to take deposits from Sephardic businesspeople, and then use the office as a launch pad to make contacts in large corporations and the types of government agencies to which TDB preferred to lend. With its links in the US through Republic, TDB could match borrowers with investors. In 1971, TDB was arranging a 40 million Swiss franc loan to Venezuela. The following year, it helped underwrite $35 million in fifteen-year bonds for the Federal Republic of Brazil.

The bank was also expanding in Europe. In 1972, TDB acquired Paris-based Banque de Dépôts et de Crédit, and transformed it into TDB (France). Edmond quickly realized this new unit could make use of a treaty that gave French investment in Brazil preferential treatment. When TDB decided to lend $30 million to Locomotive and Machine Works, which was fixing the railway that ran up the Corcovado mountain in Rio, on whose summit stood the giant *Cristo Redentor* statue, TDB saved 2 percent annually on the interest income.[234]

TDB remained, at root, a Swiss bank—private, and quiet. But the anonymity wouldn't last for long, because in 1972 Edmond was preparing to take TDB public as a means of raising capital. First, he established a holding company for TDB in Luxembourg. Though part of the European Common Market, Luxembourg was a preferred home for multinationals because it taxed institutions' capital, not their revenues. In June 1972 almost all shareholders in TDB Geneva traded their shares for shares in TDB Holdings SA Luxembourg. Then, that company prepared to raise capital in London. TDB planned to sell 16 percent of its capital, which would leave Edmond with 64 percent of the shares and others with 20 percent. "Safra Comes to London," the *Economist* reported in September 1972. "This is the first time that a non-British company has chosen to go public on the London market." Why London? The quotation will "help to bridge the credibility gap for what, to many of the new stockholders, will be a hitherto almost unknown banking group," the *Economist* concluded.[235]

The offering was a big deal, in part because it meant sharing information more broadly. By nature and profession, Edmond was reserved, and also somewhat paranoid. To keep competitors and enemies on the back foot, he didn't like to show his cards publicly. When he was setting up shop in Luxembourg, he told Minos Zombanakis at Manufacturers Hanover to "try to keep away from the Ashkenazis. They'll kill me." When the British lawyers asked him to fill out a curriculum vitae in connection with the offering, which was usual practice, Edmond balked.[236]

In the end, Manufacturers Hanover and a classic Ashkenazi bank, N.M. Rothschild, led TDB's offering of 2.5 million shares, raising

$41.25 million (or 16.8 million British pounds, equal to $275 million in 2021 dollars). What the *Guardian* referred to as the London Stock Exchange's "most exotic, new company flotation" was in fact the largest new issue in the exchange's storied history. It left TDB with a market capitalization of $255 million—and put Edmond in rarefied air. At the opening of Republic six years earlier, he had been content to remain in the shadows. Now, "one of the least known major bankers in the world," as the *Wall Street Journal* dubbed him, was front and center at this moment of arrival—as a player on the international financial scene. [237]

Proud of his legacy and accomplishments, Edmond appeared at a news conference announcing the offering. In an interview, he discussed his career, and added that he felt like a resident of the "Pan American World Airways round-the-world flight, which I'm always on." And he seemed to relish the recognition. "I remember as a boy we used to deal with the Rothschilds," Safra told Edmund de Rothschild as papers were signed for the giant underwriting. At a meeting, Jacob Rothschild turned to Edmond to say: "We knew your father, we knew your grandfather, and we knew your great-grandfather."[238]

Edmond also sat for an interview with the *New York Times*, which dubbed him a "collector of banks," and peeled back some of the mystery surrounding his persona. "He likes to collect watches and banks, dons blue jeans on Sundays when in New York to go bicycle riding in Central Park and keeps a fully staffed 100-foot yacht—named Aley, after the hillside village near Beirut where he was born—anchored at Cannes," the *Times* reported. He told the paper of record that he wasn't interested in money "because I've always had it" and conceded the flotation would boost his net worth by $150 million. Edmond offered up aphorisms handed down from Jacob Safra: "You should never take a loan you can't afford to have in default." "A bank is a virgin and it must always keep its virginity," and "Bankers should keep straight and lend carefully—no dirty gimmicks."[239]

At the airport in London after the offering, Edmond turned to his friend Simon Alouan, and said, "You know, Simon, we are a very rich family." The offering brought further attention to the family's operations. The Brazilian magazine *Exame* in November 1972 ran a cover story about "the fabulous Safra brothers," complete with pencil drawings of Edmond, Moïse, and Joseph. Images included a depiction of Joseph showing an atlas and pointing out the family's operations. Inside, it included photos of the three brothers standing with a bust of Jacob.[240]

The more the operations grew, and the more the public knew about those operations, the more important it was for Edmond to maintain his image and reputation. He continued to use the same Japanese silk for shirts that his father had used, made by the same Milanese shirt maker, Corbella, and to purchase his suits from Rovello. He told Jeff Keil that the difference between a well-dressed and not well-dressed man was $30,000 per year—and then gave him the name of his tailor in Milan. The sense of honor, propriety, and dignity in conducting business was a point he hammered home—in public and in private. Roberto Faldini, who trained at Republic and worked at Banco Safra in Brazil, was on the receiving end of one such lesson. In the early 1970s, the US Export-Import Bank had granted a $3 million line of credit—run through Banco Safra but guaranteed by Republic and TDB—to a Brazilian company. When the first payment was due, six months later, on June 30, the client paid the money to Banco Safra. But the authorization from the Brazilian Central Bank to remit the funds to the US Export-Import Bank didn't come through until July 1. Joseph Safra angrily called Faldini and sent him to New York to explain to Edmond why the payment was a day late in arriving. Faldini, twenty-one at the time, went to 452 Fifth Avenue and received a tongue lashing. "Roberto, I know your family very well," Edmond told him. "But what happened is not admissible in our bank. We have a bank with a tradition of 100 years, and we do not admit one day delay even if you give any explanation." Next time, he should call Joseph or Edmond. "I will pay from my pocket," Edmond said, "but we will never be delayed one day."[241]

That said, when it came to how he was treated, Edmond was sometimes more indulgent. When he was told that Jeffrey, who chauffeured

TDB's Jaguar in London, had been reassigned because he was blind in one eye and had poor vision in the other one, Edmond joked, "They gave me a chauffeur who couldn't see." And when Edmond learned the chauffeur had been transferred to signature verification, he cracked up: "Can you imagine choosing someone who cannot see to be checking the signature?" Thereafter, anytime he encountered an absurd situation, he would say: "Signature verification!"[242]

Things seemed to be progressing in his personal life as well. In August 1972, Samuel Bendahan agreed to a legal separation from Lily Monteverde. Three months later, Lily flew to Las Vegas, with her eldest son, Claudio, eager to obtain a quick divorce. Edmond visited several times. One would have been hard-pressed to find a more unlikely place for Lily Monteverde and Edmond Safra to continue their courtship than the booming, tacky casino haven in the desert of the southwestern United States, but Edmond willingly added this new stop to his lengthening itinerary.

On February 6, 1973, a Nevada court granted Lily a divorce. Edmond and Lily began to live as a couple, even though they were not yet married. Lily's house in Vallauris, France, became Edmond's main summer destination. In 1974, when London art dealer Mark Kelman sent Edmond's assistant an invoice for *Dual Form*, a six-foot bronze sculpture by Dame Barbara Hepworth, he wrote, "Please send my best regards to Mr. and Mrs. Safra."[243]

The combination of the public offering of TDB and the acquisition of Kings Lafayette kicked Edmond's operations into a higher gear. This was now a small empire with around 600 employees in more than a dozen offices. Armed with more capital and a broader base of deposits, Edmond and his colleagues could invest in the resources that would enable them to paint on an even larger global canvas—and work together in new ways. Republic and TDB set up teams of Jews, Muslims, and Christians working out of New York and London to open accounts in Saudi Arabia and Kuwait. Now it could lend in larger chunks and help organize syndicates for bigger borrowers. In the summer of 1973, Republic announced a $50 million loan to the Philippines, and TDB opened a revolving credit line for the Central

Bank of the Philippines. In March 1974, Republic was helping to arrange a loan to the government of Bolivia and had participated in one to the government of Senegal. No place was off-limits. In late 1973, Safra dispatched Joshua Yedid and David Mizrahi to Turkey and Iran, accompanied by Edmond's old friend Mahmoud Shakarchi, to prospect for business. "I am happy to see that this relation of friendship that was first made between my late father and your goodselves is getting stronger and stronger with the passing of days," Edmond wrote.[244]

TDB itself operated through nearly twenty subsidiaries, many of them based in South America. In Mexico, TDB set up Sudafina Mexico, enlisting a local businessman of Syrian heritage, Joseph Chowaiki, to run it, and sending the ever-reliable Umberto Treves to oversee operations. Its main business was discounting notes, making short-term credit available to manufacturers and importers, taking collateral, and charging effective interest rates of around 13 percent—for example, doling out $182,750 in March and getting paid $200,000 in December.[245] Argentina had emerged as a vital center in its own right. Albert Buri Nasser, Rahmo's brother, had moved to Buenos Aires in 1969 with Moïse Khafif, and they would stay there until the 1976 coup. Mayer Attie, a friend from Beirut, was the director of TDB's Buenos Aires offices. Raimundo Shayo, a cousin, lived there as well. On his trips through South America, Edmond would often visit Buenos Aires and spend Shabbat with Shayo, Nasser, and Khafif.[246]

As it became a larger, more far-flung operation, Edmond still maintained his attention to detail—knowing how much interest one client paid on a previous loan, approving dozens of transactions daily, putting in personal trades for gold and silver. But he recognized that his approach wasn't sustainable. The more Republic and TDB wanted to expand, the more they would need to have a more traditional organization. For his closest aides, however, he still looked very much to the family circle and his men of confidence. In 1973, when his nephew Ezy Nasser was ready to move on, for example, Edmond hired as his replacement Eli Krayem, Henry's son, who had studied at Cambridge and who began working part-time as Edmond's assistant while pursuing an MBA degree at Columbia University.

Over the years, as Edmond became more secure in his business and public image, he began to identify more closely with Israel—although he had yet to travel there. In 1973, he donated to an emergency campaign from the Keren Hayesod development agency after the Yom Kippur War. The same year, Rabbi Yaakov Attie, who had finally left Beirut in 1969, asked Edmond for help building a synagogue for the small community of Lebanese Jews assembling in Bat Yam, just south of Tel Aviv. Edmond called him on the eve of Passover, asked him to send the plans, and sent an assistant to investigate. Construction began later that year. In 1974, Rabbi Yehuda Ades, of the revered Aleppo rabbinic family, invited Edmond to the opening of Yeshivat Kol Ya'akov, named in memory of Jacob Safra, which Edmond had funded, in the Bayit Vegan neighborhood of Jerusalem. Beyond the religious needs of Sephardic Jews in Israel, Edmond began to invest in initiatives aimed at improving the socioeconomic status of the disadvantaged Sephardic communities there. He agreed in 1973 to support the Iraqi Jews Scholarship Fund at $5,000 a year—foreshadowing the major scholarship effort he would soon make for the larger Sephardic community.[247]

After the TDB offering, London would become an increasingly important place for Edmond. Lily had an apartment there, and it was a base for her children. The relationship with the Rothschilds, who had underwritten TDB, continued to deepen. In 1974, Edmond agreed to join the board of Poliarco, an investment vehicle run by Jacob Rothschild that invested in fine art.[248] More significantly, given the presence of corporations, small businessmen, and property investors, London was a key source of demand for TDB's credit. The bank seemed to have a monopoly among customers in the carpet business, and TDB became an active lender on property. Edmond became good friends with Jack Dellal, a Sephardic businessman and real estate investor. TDB's modus operandi was more conservative than that of the local lenders, as it would extend credit against only 70 percent of the value.

In 1974, a real estate crash in England caused several investment banks to go under. The property crash and the aftereffects of the oil embargo punished capital markets in Europe severely, and TDB's shares, which had gone public at $16, fell to $2; in the US, Republic's stock fell by nearly three-quarters. But here, again, Edmond's careful and contrary approach proved its utility. Because his banks lent primarily to governments and agencies, rather than individuals, their credit losses were kept low. TDB wound up taking possession of some 1,800 apartments in London as borrowers defaulted, but Edmond gave Raymond Maggar carte blanche to deal with them quickly.[249] Seeking a safe haven for their capital, depositors put more cash into both TDB and Republic. As interest rates spiked, Edmond found he could lend at higher rates to other banks. Profits at TDB and Republic rose 30 percent in 1973, and assets and deposits continued to rise.

In the meantime, Edmond continued to find ways to profit from the movement of money around the world—ways few others would have conceived of or would have been able to execute. In 1973 and 1974, for example, he found large profits in one of the oldest Safra businesses: gold. After President Nixon took the US off the gold standard in 1971, the price began to increase, and pressure mounted to make it legal for American individuals and institutions to hold and trade gold. Congress eventually passed a law legalizing the formal trade of gold as of December 31, 1974.

Republic, one of the few banks to take out a gold license in the late 1960s, was perfectly situated to reap profits from small wrinkles in the market. Regulations had always permitted the import of gold coins with numismatic value—i.e., coins that collectors would be interested in, owing to their rarity or provenance. In practice, this meant that foreign gold coins minted before 1933, when the US first abolished the gold trade, could be imported into the US freely. With the price of gold bullion rising, Edmond and his colleagues recognized an opportunity. There were millions of older gold coins circulating in Europe as currency, and Americans would pay a premium to the face value in order to get their hands on this hedge against inflation.

And so Edmond mounted a global campaign to acquire gold coins. In London, he would purchase bucketloads of English sovereigns, quarter-ounce gold coins that dated back to the 1890s and were imprinted with an image of Queen Victoria, at face value, and send them to New York, where they could be sold at a 5 percent premium. Realizing that Mexico in 1959 had minted gold pesos stamped with the year 1915, Edmond dispatched Cyril Dwek to Mexico City to work out deals with the Mexican Central Bank, in which Republic would send gold bars (which it couldn't sell freely in the US) in exchange for gold coins. Austria continued to mint the old Austro-Hungarian Empire one-ounce gold coins, and Republic and TDB bought them at a 3 percent premium from the government, selling them in the US for a 10 percent markup. Knowing that Hungary was part of the same empire, Edmond went to Budapest, where he had been conducting business for twenty years, bought gold coins at a 3 percent premium, and brought them to the US.[250]

Republic was notching profits of several million dollars per quarter on gold operations alone, which caught the attention of Wall Street. Manufacturers Hanover, eager to learn about the gold business, asked Edmond if it could send some people over to train and observe. Naturally wary, Edmond set up a separate room where the Manufacturers Hanover staff could "observe." They left after a few weeks. "They thought that I was a schmuck, that I would teach them how to get my business away," he told Minos Zombanakis.[251]

The genius of the gold coin gambit was that it didn't require speculation, or long-term holdings, or the extension of credit. Rather, it involved arbitrage—moving money, or a currency, from a place where it had one value to a second place where it had a higher value. This mentality led Republic and TDB to build a second distinctive global business in banknotes.

Initially, TDB in the 1960s provided service to other banks by taking all the foreign currencies off their hands at once and repatriating them in exchange for a small fee. This tied in nicely with the company's foreign exchange business. After the 1973 oil embargo, another prospect emerged. Cash-rich states in the Middle East would pay foreign workers on their mammoth infrastructure projects in dollars, which the workers would send to the Philippines and Korea. Countries in which tourism was growing also found they had a need to move banknotes. This was a business with very thin margins but very little competition. For people who understood how globalization worked, and who understood the logistics surrounding the movement of gold— air cargo, insurance, security—banknotes presented a low-risk opportunity. Republic and TDB became the leading transporter of banknotes in the world. "With the banknotes, we could have $300 million in airplanes at any one time," recalled TDB executive Moïse Tawil.

Edmond's personal enthusiasm for the work was infectious. "Safra describes himself as a 'priest of my work' but there is nothing priest-like in his energy and enthusiasm, which radiates from him," *Finance* magazine noted in January 1973.[252] But given the scope of activities— opening offices in Mexico and considering expanding to the Far East; managing the integration of Kings Lafayette; overseeing the construction of two buildings in Geneva for TDB, one at 2 Place du Lac to house the general management, the foreign exchange operations, and the equity group, and one at 96/98 Rue du Rhône, due to be completed by the end of 1974, to house other departments—it was clear that Edmond needed greater assistance. "In 1973 we plan to step up the recruitment and training of executive staff with a view to bringing new blood into our group's management team," Edmond wrote in the 1972 TDB report.[253]

For the first time, Edmond, who had eschewed management and organizational charts, was embracing formal corporate practices. The acquisition of Kings Lafayette, with its extensive branch network and consumer business, necessitated a new approach. In May 1973, a formal integration committee was set up to work out the postmerger organization. In October 1973, Republic and Kings signed an agreement to combine as subsidiaries of Republic New York Corporation. In the newly merged company, two Kings Lafayette executives were given responsibility for administration, while the core Republic crew of Morris Hirsch, Joshua Yedid, and Cyril Dwek maintained the other senior posts.

Throughout the operations, a mix of formality and informality applied. Bruce Littman, a veteran banker, interviewed for a job at TDB in 1974 with Albert Benezra, who was always referred to as "Mr. Benezra," never "Albert." But Edmond never stood on ceremony. "Edmond's business was baronial, like he was in the middle and everybody had a different relationship with him," Littman recalled. "If he wanted me to do something, he would call me and ask me to do it." In a highly apt metaphor, Littman compared TDB and Republic to an orchestra with a lot of soloists, and Edmond as the conductor. When Edouard Schouela, a financier from Canada with whom Edmond had invested in real estate, came to dinner in Geneva, he noted that the phone didn't stop ringing—with people around the world calling Edmond for decisions, advice, and approval of transactions. Edmond remained generally hostile to organizational charts and didn't respect them, because they didn't comport with the way he thought business should work. Soon after joining Republic in 1973, Jeff Keil presented Edmond with a classic organizational chart for the bank that looked like a pyramid. Edmond turned it upside down. "This is really how it works," he told Keil. "The people at the top are really working for the other people to help them do a good job."[254]

And he remained very much the patriarch of a multigenerational family. In February 1974, he wrote a letter to Harvard Business School to support the application of his nephew, Jacques Nasser—Eveline and Rahmo's second son. It is worth quoting at length because it provides, in Edmond's voice, the clearest articulation of his view of the businesses he ran. "As a member of our family, he will necessarily be involved in the international banking, finance, and industrial activities in which we are extensively engaged," Edmond wrote. "The writer is managing director of Trade Development Bank in Geneva, which controls a number of banking institutions abroad, as well as the Republic Bank of New York. Members of our family also engage in extensive banking, financial, and industrial enterprises in South America, particularly in Brazil, of which country Jacques is a resident-citizen. . . . Our institutional objective is to encourage the best possible education and training of promising young men like

Jacques in anticipation of their subsequent employment by us in a responsible managerial post."[255]

But there were only a certain number of Safra children, in-laws, cousins, and old friends from Beirut and Aleppo, and veterans from Geneva. If the banks were to live up to their full potential, Edmond realized he would have to engage outsiders more frequently. Soon after, TDB did what was standard practice for Fortune 500 companies but unheard of for a Safra enterprise: it hired a management consultant. TDB engaged Booz Allen & Hamilton, which had done some consulting for the Republic–Kings Lafayette merger, to conduct a study. "This study will have two principal objectives," Edmond wrote in a memo to staff. "First, to assure ourselves that the structure of our work and the direction is the right one; and second, to establish the points where it will be possible to improve." The consultants would also enable them to benchmark the banks against Chase, Dresdner, and other banks.[256]

A memo in the summer of 1974 laid out the new management committee of TDB, which was very much like the old one. Edmond was at the top, and discrete areas of responsibility were parceled out to Albert Benezra (treasury, precious metals, exchange), Emile Saadia (banking relations, Far East, general economy), Roger Junod (balance sheets), Jacques Douek (clients and credits), and Ernest Sasson (client development).[257] But there were to be newcomers.

In the summer of 1975, Safra was wooing Rodney Leach, an Oxford graduate who had been a key lieutenant at Rothschild for twelve years. In handwritten letters, Leach laid out his vision—and concerns. He would be happy to come aboard as a senior leader, defining policies, dealing with other banks, enabling the bank to maintain success and "have the management depth to survive and the reputation to stand high in international financial circles whatever happens to you (God forbid!) personally." But he would need to be given the real and apparent authority to do these things. "It would therefore be essential for you to make it clear that my authority throughout the group would be second only to yours, and to support this by the appropriate title or titles." In January 1975, Leach hired on as a general manager of TDB in Geneva, and he joined both the board and executive committee.[258]

Even as he delegated and outsourced more, Edmond continued to revel in the details of his operations. None was too small to escape his eyes. People knew Edmond was coming to Republic's headquarters in New York when they saw Louis, the maintenance man, polishing the brass in the lobby. He was closely involved in the construction and design of the new facilities on Rue du Rhône in Geneva, down to the prospect of erecting a floating map in a circular staircase.[259]

And Republic still maintained its quirky, unique culture—whether it was the boss living on the top floor of the building, Arabic being spoken on the banking floor, or its subtle but fierce self-identification as a Jewish bank. After his father died, Victor Hattena would start leaving work briefly to attend prayer services and fulfill the obligation to recite the Kaddish in his father's memory. So management began to carve out a space in the headquarters where employees could gather for a minyan (the group of ten men required for a communal prayer service). Although the chef in the cafeteria bought kosher meat, he would occasionally mix it with milk products, so the more observant Jewish staff members would bring their own food, as mixing meat and dairy is forbidden. One day, Edmond noticed Victor Hattena eating just yogurt and cottage cheese. "What are you eating?" Edmond asked. When he learned of the issue, he ordered the dining room to be kept strictly kosher in keeping with Orthodox requirements.[260]

His perspective was growing ever more global, but Safra continued to relate to people on an individual basis. When Marty Mertz met his sister and brother-in-law in Geneva in 1975, he called Edmond to say hello out of respect. Edmond insisted they have dinner, and when Mertz showed up at the apartment, Edmond went to the garage to get the car. "This is Switzerland," he said. "My chauffeur is at his summer home for the weekend."[261]

And while he was rubbing shoulders with the Rothschilds and arranging loans for central banks in the Philippines and Russia, Edmond kept in touch with his oldest friends who were living much humbler lives, like Maury Mann, who was struggling to make it in Israel. "With me, it is so, as always. It is very difficult with seven children," Mann wrote in the summer of 1975, asking for $500 to help pay for his daughter Rachel's wedding and buy her a washing machine. Edmond agreed.[262]

Now in his forties, Edmond was growing more comfortable in his own skin, and in the spotlight. To be sure, his concern over personal and communal security remained acute, to the point where TDB in the spring of 1975 developed kidnap/ransom notification procedures and guidelines.[263] But at the same time, Edmond was increasingly secure in talking about his philosophy and operations to the broader public. He told *Forbes* that while TDB had $105 million of precious metals on its books, "those figures about the gold we are carrying don't exist for me." Why? "They were wiped off the books the day we bought that gold, for in that moment, that very second, we also sold ahead." He told the magazine he could have made $20 million in gold in the previous year, "but I chose to make, maybe, $8 million." Pointing to the portrait of Jacob hanging behind him, he continued: "That's what my father always taught me: Take the sure thing."[264]

For Edmond, Jacob's lessons and the legacy of Beirut remained top of mind. In one of the more remarkable aspects of the Safra story, Jacob's bank persisted in Beirut even as the postwar sectarian entente continued to crumble and the Jewish community continued to decline. The original Safra bank was now a tiny speck in Edmond's empire, with a balance sheet of 36.6 million Lebanese pounds in 1974. But in all the documents that listed the now-vast holdings of the Safra empire, Banque de Crédit National on Rue Allenby, formerly Banque Jacob E. Safra, occupied pride of place. The 1974 document showing its balance sheet refers to it as "Anciennement Banque Safra," and as number thirty-six on the Lebanon list of banks. Edmond was still listed as president and director general, with Henry Krayem as member and director general. Other officers included Dr. Edmond Rabbath, George Rabbath, and Abdulkader Noueri. A story goes that a Lebanese man came to Republic in New York and told an official that he had done business with BCN in Beirut. He said he had left $50,000 in deposit but had had to flee the country quickly during the civil war and didn't have any documentation. Ernest Ginsberg took the man's name and went to Edmond. "I remember the family," Edmond said. "Give him his $50,000."[265]

In April 1975, when Palestinian gunmen tried to assassinate Pierre Gemayel, the Maronite leader, as he was leaving church, violence erupted, and Lebanon's fifteen-year civil war commenced. In June, some 30,000 Syrian troops invaded. And yet many of the institutions and people fearlessly held on. Although he had left nearly thirty years before, Edmond remained a vital and concerned son of Beirut. In December 1975, the Rev. Lee Poole, director of development for North America for Beirut University College, asked Republic to renew its gift so it could keep the college open. "We expect to lose almost one half of our students (and subsequently the tuition income) and most of our gift income from Lebanon," he wrote.[266] A week later, Mourad Mamieh, a stalwart of the Jewish community, wrote Edmond from Beirut. "By a miracle we are alive. But the bombs are blowing up in our quarter—for a month we were under fire, for days without electricity, without telephone, without medicine, without money." One of Mamieh's brothers had died. "After the Calvary we are going through, I have decided to go to rejoin my brother Moïse to assure for the future and the security of our family. I pray, my dear Edmond, that you take my letter into consideration and that you respond to me as is well known with your help. I can't go on any longer."[267]

The trauma in Beirut was a rare point of pain for Edmond Safra in 1975. His banks had powered through the financial crisis that engulfed the world in the wake of the Yom Kippur War and the oil embargo. Republic, a kernel of an idea just ten years prior, had grown to become the seventy-fifth largest bank in the US, with more than $1.2 billion in deposits. His global network of affiliated banks now included offices in well over a dozen countries. His brothers were safe, secure, and thriving in Brazil, and Edmond was able to deploy his profits to benefit Jewish communities from Beirut to Buenos Aires. It even seemed as if the final piece in the puzzle was about to fall into place. With the London Court of Appeals dismissing the final legal actions that had been filed against Lily Monteverde and Trade Development Bank, she and Edmond were free to move forward into the next chapter of their lives.

10

Investing in Institutions

(1976–1980)

E ven as the head of a growing family and a now-large family of banks, Edmond Safra by 1976 was accustomed to leading a somewhat solitary, unsettled, and improvisational life. That would begin to change. While valuing and maintaining his independence, Edmond, now in his early forties, began to anchor his personal life and philanthropy on more secure footing and also took steps to institutionalize his businesses.

The first item on the agenda was—finally—investing in the institution of marriage. When word began to spread in early 1976 through the Safra network that Edmond and Lily had become engaged, most of those close to him were thrilled.[268] Yet because of the role he occupied, and the nature of the Safra family business, many people felt entitled to weigh in on his decisions, including this one. Some family members—particularly his brothers Joseph and Moïse—fretted that Edmond was diverging from the norms in the Aleppo-Beirut community. Lily wasn't Sephardic, and she already had her own children. Given their age, it was likely that Edmond and Lily would not have their own children, so there would be no heirs to carry on the family business. They went so far as to call Edmond's friends in an attempt to dissuade him. For Edmond, none of these objections were an issue. For years, he had fended off suggestions that he find a young Syrian match. His horizons had broadened in keeping with his peripatetic business, which he had long believed was inconsistent with being the parent of his own children.[269]

As the wedding date of June 14 approached, Edmond and Lily's far-flung universes converged in Geneva. The guest list of 250 featured many of Edmond's siblings, friends, and colleagues from Beirut, Brazil, the South of France, New York, and Israel—bankers and merchants, nightclub owners and rabbis. A small group—a dozen or so—went with the couple for the civil wedding at the City Hall in Eaux-Vives, a picture-book building with clock tower and turrets a few minutes' walk down the Rue du Rhône from TDB's headquarters. Rabbi Ovadia Yosef, the Sephardic chief rabbi of Israel, came from Jerusalem to conduct the religious ceremony, which was held a short distance away, at Geneva's four-year-old Sephardic synagogue, Hekhal Haness. Built in a concrete and steel brutalist style, it had none of the colorful or historical aesthetic of Beirut or Brazil. But the stark interior, lit by skylight, was enlivened by scores of lily-of-the-valley flowers.

Edmond and Lily knew that, to a degree, their relationship would defy convention. For one thing, they regarded each other as equal partners. At the civil wedding, when the official read a sentence from the civil code specifying that the husband is the head of the marital union and chooses the common dwelling, Lily looked at Edmond and broke out laughing. With an eye for detail; an outgoing personality; and broad interests in art, fashion, and culture, Lily relished hosting events and expanding their already large social circle. For Edmond, Lily was someone with whom he could let down his guard and indulge his softer, romantic side, and talk about things other than business. He delighted in buying jewelry for her and sending her dozens of yellow roses on her birthday. "He was sweet, clever, very funny. He was a totally different man in his private life than in his banking life, *totally different*," Lily recalled.[270] Lily moved into Edmond's apartment at 56 Rue de Moillebeau and that year acquired a 60 percent stake in the large, ten-story block nestled on a hilly street in Geneva. And he moved into her country home, Mas Notre Dame, the farmhouse on a winding road in Vallauris in the hills above Golfe-Juan. Together, they would create new homes—in Paris, New York, London, and the South of France—and fill them with the art and furniture they collected.

Edmond found the rhythm of his life changed. On the wedding day, Edmond was already fretting about the prospect of being away for two weeks. A week or so after the ceremony, Marty Mertz, a KPMG partner who would become a Republic director, was in the restaurant at the Plaza Athénée hotel in Paris, and he was surprised to see Lily walk in. "He went back to work," she said. When in New York, Edmond continued to hold his séances after work on the top floor of Republic's offices, and in Geneva, the evening meetings at TDB with the "happy few"—Jacques Tawil, Albert Benezra, Emile Saadia, and Roger Junod—continued. But for the first time, he had someone waiting for him at home. "Around 9:00 p.m.—thank God—Lily would be on the line, yelling at him, because he had to go home," Junod recalled.[271]

Edmond liked to tell friends that in the Syrian community there were no aristocrats. But by virtue of their success, the Safras by the mid-1970s ranked among the world's most prominent Jewish banking dynasties. On November 19, 1976, Edmond was in London, meeting with Jacob Rothschild about Poliarco, the art investing vehicle of which Edmond was a director. He strengthened relationships with the Rothschilds through professional and personal relationships and community affairs. The Rothschild bank, which had helped take TDB public in 1972, participated in a $100 million loan TDB arranged to the Philippines in 1976. In December of that year, Edmond responded to an appeal from Edmund de Rothschild, contributing $10,000 for the Central British Fund for Jewish Relief and Rehabilitation, writing that he hoped that his "contribution will help in our efforts to further the well-being of the Syrian Community in particular, and of all our people throughout the world."[272]

With Lily, he now had greater incentive and desire to participate in the social opportunities on offer. The following December, Edmund de Rothschild invited Edmond and Lily to a concert in Westminster Abbey, in aid of the Queen's Silver Jubilee Appeal and the Council of Christians and Jews.[273] In the past, he might have wavered at attending such events; no longer. Edmond also traveled down the road that wound along Lac Leman to the village of Blonay, to visit Sir Sigmund Warburg, the seventy-five-year-old scion of the Warburg banking family. "I was particularly pleased to be given the privilege to meet you and to proceed to an exchange of views of the greatest interest," Edmond wrote to Warburg in 1977. "I would like, if you see no objection, to refer to you from time to time and benefit of your great experience."[274]

Edmond was also increasingly on an equal footing with the American banking elite. In June 1977, David Rockefeller, the grandson of John D. Rockefeller and the chief executive officer of Chase Manhattan Bank, wrote to Edmond: "If you're going to World Bank and IMF, we'd be pleased if you and your wife could join us at a small luncheon."[275] Rockefeller was referring to the annual meetings of the two major global financial institutions. Held in Washington, except for every third year when they took place in another country, these events were a key gathering place for the global financial elite. The world's most important banks therefore competed to hold receptions and events that drew hundreds of central bank governors, ministers, and executives. ("Properly planned, the IMF meetings can be as valuable as a round-the-world trip," Rodney Leach, who joined as director of TDB Holding Group in 1976, would write to Albert Benezra in 1978. "Priorities for us are presumably Brazil, Philippines, Mexico, South Africa, and Venezuela.") Starting in 1977, Republic began throwing parties at the meetings. With Lily's involvement and attention to detail, Republic's lavishly catered events in grand and exclusive venues like the National Gallery of Art became an institution that would ultimately attract more than 5,000 people. Here, Edmond was in his element, standing in receiving lines for hours, greeting contacts from every continent in one of the half dozen languages he spoke.[276]

Indeed, the intensely private banker was growing increasingly comfortable assuming a public role. "I'm a big believer that in the banking industry we have to behave and we have to be watched, because we are dealing with the money of the public," he told *Finance* magazine in May 1977, in an article titled "A Conversation with Edmond Safra." Regulation, he argued, stopped banks from lending too much. And it was only proper that authorities supervise banks closely, "because after all, it's not our money. It's the public's money."[277]

In keeping with the evolving view of his banks as institutions, as opposed to simply businesses, Edmond leaned more heavily on the assistance of a rising cadre of professional managers. From his base in London, which was becoming an ever more important hub in global financial markets, Leach, Edmond's number two, in effect, with oversight responsibility for both Republic and TDB, began to attempt to impose order and bring the banks up to what he viewed as the London standard. Republic was increasingly expanding its global lending business, as TDB stayed focused on deals. Leach noted, "There is thus a growing danger of divergence of business style, and of individual traffic accidents, to the point where the bank's [TDB's] image could suffer." He said it raised the question of whether the banks should merge. At TDB, Leach convened a new committee of senior executives to meet monthly and tackle issues small ("We discussed the need to ensure adequate control of luncheon expenses in both buildings") and large, such as the harmonization of titles and codes of conduct across different offices. After devoting considerable effort in London to getting management figures in order, Leach wrote in the summer of 1977, "They have now reached a stage where we are not completely ashamed of them."[278]

Edmond was also increasingly taking conscious steps to professionalize. As he continued to find places for people from Wadi Abu Jamil and the Alliance Israélite Universelle schools, he also began to recruit at INSEAD and from rival banks. In 1977, at Edmond's suggestion, Republic, TDB, and Banco Safra began to organize two-week bank management courses at Stanford University; every year twelve to sixteen participants from New York, Brazil, and Geneva would travel to Palo Alto for intensive coursework.[279]

And yet TDB and Republic still maintained the mien of a family operation. Many of the senior executives jokingly referred to Republic as "the candy store," because it seemed to be run like a small family business. Virtually anyone who had left Beirut or Aleppo would be given an entry-level job at Republic and allowed to rise or fall based on their ability. A distant relative of Edmond's who worked in the mailroom would open and read the mail. Edmond still didn't respect organizational charts—he would call a bank manager or a lower-level loan officer if he wanted information—and many junior people enjoyed a direct connection to the boss. At Republic, recalled long-time executive Fred Bogart, "assistant vice presidents had a lot more power than executive vice presidents because they had that rapport with Edmond, which was outside the structural framework of the bank."[280]

And existing relationships among the large network of contacts built on the Aleppo diaspora endured. In June 1977, Cesar Sassoon, whose Japan-based family had been a trading partner for decades, wrote from Tokyo to Edmond: "I wish to inform you that I have sent you by air parcel post 35 meters of Fuji-Kanebo silk 5500 as a present from Maurice Lebovich and myself. I hope you will enjoy making some shirts with this material."[281] In the 1960s and 1970s, Edmond's companies began to work more formally with institutions in Asia, striking a joint venture with a Japanese company for a textile plant in Brazil or lending to the Philippines Central Bank. And so it made sense for TDB and Republic to expand their physical footprint. "Our group is already powerfully implanted in Europe, North America, and Latin America," Rodney Leach wrote in the fall of 1977. "The next and final step must be the Far East."[282] That fall, Edmond and Lily traveled to Asia. In Hong Kong, they met Sir Lawrence Kadoorie, the scion of the prominent Sephardic merchant dynasty. In Tokyo, they inaugurated the representative office of Republic, visited contacts at the Bank of Japan, and saw old friends, including Shinzo Ohya of Teijin, the Japanese fabric-maker with which Safra's companies in Brazil had done business. When Ohya's wife, Masako, admired Lily's Yves Saint Laurent cape, she took it off and gave it to her.[283]

Edmond and Lily returned to Geneva through India and Iran, where they stayed for a week, ostensibly as tourists. Iran, even in the later years of the Shah's regime, had all the factors that made it an appealing place for TDB to conduct business. The farthest eastern point of the Alliance school network, Tehran was an important regional financial hub, home to Jewish businessmen who were active importers and exporters. Joseph Shalam, a second cousin of Edmond's born in Egypt who had moved to Geneva, managed Iran accounts during the 1960s and 1970s. TDB had a strong relationship with Hassan Ali Mehran, governor of the Central Bank of Iran, which borrowed from TDB. Shortly, Iran would also become, like Lebanon, Egypt, and Morocco, a source of flight capital. When the Shah was overthrown in early 1979, Iranians—Jews, especially, but also non-Jews—fled to Milan, Switzerland, New York, and California. Isaac Obersi, who had first met Edmond at the Alliance in Paris in the 1940s and had moved to Tehran after leaving Beirut, fled Iran in May 1979. Arriving in Geneva, he was hired by TDB and posted to Chiasso to recruit new clients amid the Persian diaspora.[284]

Still concerned about the sensitivities of Muslim clients in the Middle East, Edmond continued to avoid doing business explicitly in Israel. In 1976, when he went to a private dinner with former defense minister Moshe Dayan, he took pains to make sure that the news wouldn't get out. But the tectonic plates were shifting in the Middle East in ways that would create more stability and openness. In November 1977, Egyptian president Anwar el-Sadat became the first Arab leader to address the Israeli Knesset, and negotiations on what would become the Camp David Accords were underway. In the fall of 1978, Joseph Gross, a lawyer in Israel, wrote to Albert Benezra at TDB noting that he had met with Oded Messer, the supervisor of banks in Israel. Messer had said that if the Safras started a bank in Israel they could keep the ownership a secret so long as they told the Bank of Israel the names of the shareholders.[285]

While not yet ready for formal and open business ties in Israel, Edmond was more willing to establish open philanthropic ties. His prolific giving to Jewish communities remained intensely personal and often informal—donations to synagogues and yeshivas from France to Australia, $500 each fall to pay for a cantor for the High

Holiday services at the tiny synagogue on Rhodes, funding the construction of a mikveh in Brooklyn.

But he was now seeking to institutionalize so that he could aid organizations in Israel on a larger scale. In 1975, he created the Fondation Terris (a play on the name of his mother, "Teira," the Lebanese-Arabic form of "Esther"), pledging $1 million to support the construction and maintenance of Sephardic synagogues and religious institutions in Israel. The work would be overseen by a committee in Israel that included Chief Rabbi Ovadia Yosef and two government representatives. Edmond closely followed the progress, reviewing plans and critiquing the cost or construction of the synagogue he was building for his rabbi from Beirut, Rabbi Yaakov Attie, who had settled in Bat Yam. "The price of IL 6 m is too high, and the cost of $500,000 would be more appropriate," he wrote. In 1977, he made further significant contributions to the Porat Yosef yeshiva overlooking the Western Wall. [286]

But Edmond soon came to understand that the needs of what was now the largest community of Sephardic Jews in the world extended far beyond places of worship. As successful as they had become in New York, Brazil, and in small communities in Europe, the masses of Jews who had fled Yemen, Syria, Iraq, Morocco, and Egypt were generally suffering in Israel. Shunted to development towns, excluded from the political mainstream, and treated largely as second-class citizens, they faced prejudice and low expectations. Barely 6 percent of Sephardic Jews in Israel attended college, and many were pushed into vocational schools. Nina Weiner, who was born in Egypt and trained as a psychologist, knew Edmond because her husband, Walter, was Edmond's lawyer and would later become president and chairman of the board of Republic. [287] In 1976, while visiting Edmond and Lily in Vallauris, she was describing how Sephardic children wouldn't have the opportunity to integrate fully into Israeli society unless they were able to achieve the higher levels of education of which they were capable. Edmond responded, "Well, let's try and do something to help them." Thus the International Sephardic Education Foundation, which became known as ISEF, was born. On June 2, 1977, Edmond convened a dozen or so friends from the community at his office at Republic in New York, including Joe Cayre and David Braka. On the spot, they raised $200,000. And each year, he would contribute and hold fundraising events at the bank. A year later, Safra wrote with pride to his Geneva neighbor Nessim Gaon that 400 students in six Israeli universities had already received scholarships.[288]

As gratifying as it was for him to make an impact in Israel, Edmond was increasingly powerless to help the Jewish community to which he felt the most intense and personal connection. In the months after the brutal Lebanese Civil War broke out in late 1975, Beirut was rendered unrecognizable. Allenby Street, home to BCN and many other banks, became a no-man's-land. The old Jewish neighborhood, Wadi Abu Jamil, was subject to constant shelling and warfare. The main synagogue was damaged, hundreds of homes were destroyed, and nearly 200 Jews were among the thousands of casualties. Those who could, left. TDB and Edmond acted as a safety net for the dwindling community. After the 1967 war, many Jews in Beirut had opened accounts at TDB.[289] As Jews left—by 1976 only about 500 were left in Lebanon—Palestinian refugees moved into Wadi Abu Jamil, and Jewish community life ground to a halt. Chief Rabbi Chrem and his family were evacuated in 1978. Through it all, Edmond kept BCN open. Henry Krayem, BCN's longtime director, moved to Belgium, but continued to travel back to Beirut. The bank moved from Allenby Street and rented premises on Riad el-Solh, near the Lebanese parliament building.

Edmond personally supported the increasingly desperate people who steadfastly remained in Beirut. He sent a 500 Lebanese pound monthly stipend to old friend Mourad Mamieh. In September 1977, when Rabbi Ishac Hadid, his house in Wadi Abu Jamil having been destroyed, fled and resurfaced in Bat Yam, Edmond sent him $500. "I consider you like an angel from the sky to help me with my situation in this new country," Hadid wrote. In May 1977, Selim Moghrabi Chaya, the head of the community, wrote that the religious school had closed and the Community Council had effectively run out of money. "Knowing the sympathy and the spirit of justice with which you consider the big problems of our fellow Jews for their security, I'm writing you in the hopes that this will find a favorable response and we can educate the children."[290]

The Beirut in which Jacob Safra had thrived, and which Edmond held as a touchstone deep into adulthood, no longer existed. The once-frequent trips to the lighthearted capital on the Mediterranean, the stays at the St. George Hotel and visits to favorite restaurants and nightclubs, had long since ceased to be part of Edmond's schedule. He could no longer indulge his habit of having pastries and pistachios sent from Beirut to Geneva or New York. The squalor and danger of life in Beirut contrasted ever more sharply with the quiet order of Geneva, where Edmond now spent most of his time, and with the positive energy of New York.

Even though Edmond typically spent only a few months each year in New York, he began to put down deeper roots there. In the summer of 1978, he and Lily purchased an apartment at 820 Fifth Avenue, on the corner of Sixty-Third Street, overlooking Central Park. New York had other qualities to recommend it to Edmond. The brash capitalist energy that pulsed through the streets had long exerted a gravitational pull. The city had a very large Syrian Jewish community in Brooklyn, where he could feel at home. He loved New York deli food, which he occasionally even had delivered to him in Geneva. And it was his portal to the United States, where even the most exclusive institutions and systems were welcoming.

In 1975, at Minos Zombanakis's request, Edmond made a $1,500 donation to the Harvard-Radcliffe Collegium Musicum, sponsoring the singing group's tour of Europe. In 1976 and 1977, the man who had only graduated high school was being wooed by senior administrators at the country's oldest and most prestigious university to support its Jewish Studies program. Edmond quickly settled on the idea of endowing a chair in Jewish history, with an emphasis on Sephardic history. In the fall of 1978, Professor Yosef Hayim Yerushalmi was named Harvard's first Jacob E. Safra Professor of Jewish History and Sephardic Civilization. "What a marvelous idea, and what a marvelous tribute to your father," Senator Daniel Patrick Moynihan wrote to

Edmond. Yerushalmi's inaugural lecture, given on February 26, 1979, at Boylston Hall, was, fittingly enough, about how Sephardic business-people created new patterns of international commerce.[291]

From the outset, Edmond had raved about how open the US was to people who started new businesses, and about the immense opportunities its market offered for growth. By 1977, Republic had grown to become the fifty-second-largest bank in the country. That year, the bank acquired the Kress Building, adjacent to the Knox Building on Fifth Avenue, and began to renovate it to house operations. TDB, which owned a majority of Republic, had grown to become the largest foreign-owned bank in Switzerland, and the 173rd-largest bank in the world. In 1978, the banks Edmond had founded employed 1,350 people in twenty offices.[292]

But even though banks were forbidden from operating across state lines, a banker with imagination could find opportunities. Edmond first cast his eyes to the part of the United States that had the deepest connection to South America: Miami. When the Flagship Bank of Aventura, Florida, was consolidating and selling one of its branches, Edmond's ears perked up. Jeff Keil told him he could get a license to create a new bank, and then acquire the branch. "I can have a charter of a bank for a million dollars?" he asked Keil, with disbelief. When the two visited Florida to explore the possibility, Edmond found himself in entirely new terrain. Driving on Interstate 95 from Miami, he was mystified at a billboard that blared: "Loan by phone." Keil told him that banks approved loans over the phone. "We have to open here," Edmond said. "All the competition is going to go broke." When they visited a state office in Tallahassee, Edmond marveled at a strange object in the cafeteria. "What is that? Why is it shiny?" He had never seen a tuna fish sandwich in Saran wrap.[293]

Edmond acquired the branch and the license for himself (not Republic), and Safra Bank opened for business in Miami in 1979. He sent a trusted lieutenant, Vito Portera, to run it. There were plenty of wealthy outsiders in Miami—families from Venezuela, Cuba, and Brazil, for example—whom the established banks weren't interested in servicing. Jeff Keil noted: "Foreign citizens were looked down upon in Miami. They don't speak English. All they do is deposit $40 million in the bank. It was the best opportunity yet for Safra-style banking." The plan was to take deposits and use them to conduct import-export financing and participate in the types of international loans in which Republic and TDB specialized. As for Republic, the Edge Act, a 1919 amendment to the Federal Reserve Act, permitted a New York bank to have an office in Florida that acted like an offshore bank. With this in mind, in 1978, Republic created Republic National Bank of New York International Miami, an Edge Act corporation, with capital of $25 million—housed in the same building as Safra Bank. Edmond would follow the same two-pronged approach in California—acquiring a troubled bank for his own account and then establishing a Republic Edge Act bank in Los Angeles.[294]

The banks could also link up with Banco Safra in Brazil. Under the day-to-day management of Edmond's younger brothers Moïse and Joseph, Banco Safra was thriving, earning $36 million in 1977 and $15 million in 1978. In 1978, with sixteen branches and a balance sheet of 2.13 billion cruzeiros ($130 million), it was the tenth-largest bank in Brazil.[295]

Edmond spoke with his brothers, particularly Joseph, many times a day, discussing business but also matters involving the growing number of children in the next generation. The routine remained as it had been: the Safra family, now far-flung, remained closely knit. In the fall, Edmond would typically travel to São Paulo for the Jewish High Holidays, where the extended family gathered at the house of his eldest sister, Eveline. In the summers, his brothers and sisters would often travel to the South of France with their children.[296] Elie still lived in Geneva, at 16 Parc du Château-Banquet, just over a mile from Edmond's apartment on Rue de Moillebeau. The family gathered in March 1977 for the marriage of Elie's oldest daughter, Esther, to Joseph Kattan, at the Hekhal Haness synagogue. In May 1979, they assembled again for the Paris marriage of Lily's daughter, Adriana, to Michel Elia, a Beiruti who had worked at BCN in his youth. Israel's Sephardic Chief Rabbi Ovadia

Yosef and French Chief Rabbi Jacob Kaplan officiated at the ceremony, which took place at the Pavillon d'Armenonville in the Bois
de Boulogne.[297] The famous French singer Charles Aznavour provided the entertainment.

And Edmond looked out for the welfare of the extended family in
other ways, too. When Moïse's sons, Jacob and Ezra, were attending
boarding school in Europe, Edmond's assistant Danielle Pinet would
enroll them in skiing classes at the Chaperon Rouge school in the
Swiss Alps over their winter break. His personal physician, Dr.
Edmond Sonnenblick, was on retainer for Republic and the Safra
family. In December 1977, Sonnenblick wrote Safra expressing concern about Joseph, thirty-nine, who was having heart problems. "I
think it is quite essential that your brother be operated on quite soon
if he is to survive." In the fall of 1978, Sonnenblick was tending to
Edmond's sister, Arlette, who had been hospitalized with fainting
spells and emotional stress after her husband died.[298]

As much as he was joining the establishment, Edmond continued
to carve a highly independent path in business. While connected to
the IMF and wired into the global financial system, Edmond still
pursued the model of banking he had learned from Jacob in the souks
of Beirut. He pursued low-risk opportunities, avoided crowded markets, and accepted smaller margins in exchange for greater security.
In 1978, Raymond Maggar, who ran a chunk of TDB's London operation, pushed Edmond to get back into real estate lending. "Are you
mad?" Edmond wondered. The city's financial system had been laid
low just four years before by real estate speculation. However, Edmond
invited Maggar to the South of France to discuss it further. Maggar
went to Vallauris, and he suggested lending only to developers and
companies that had survived the crisis and that already had
income-producing properties.

Rather than lending to individuals through mortgages or credit
cards, Edmond preferred to lend to institutions that could be counted
on to pay back the loans. Now he had a large international network
through which to syndicate such activity—TDB, Republic, Banco
Safra, Safra Bank in Miami. In the late 1970s, in South American

countries where the Safras had long been active—Brazil, Mexico, Venezuela, and Argentina—banks were syndicating loans to utilities, power and gas companies, municipalities, and state governments. In 1977, in fact, some 90 percent of TDB's loans were to banks and government agencies.[299]

TDB and Republic were also active in banking-related businesses that involved comparatively little risk. They specialized in the business of *à forfait*, a form of trade financing that involved selling the unsecured receivables of exporters. "We did one last year for $100 million, one signature, a German export to Russia, and we sold the paper immediately," Edmond said in 1977. The banknotes business, which involved selling physical currencies to central banks around the world and utilized the same vaults that were used for gold and silver, was another specialty. TDB, having started the banknotes business in the 1960s in London, by the late 1970s had built the third-largest banknotes business in the world, behind only Swiss Bank Corporation (SBC) and Credit Suisse, offering some 175 currencies. Republic itself started a banknotes division in 1978, with a physical inventory of over 100 currencies.[300]

While Safra continued to be risk-averse when compared with his rivals, his banks didn't remain completely aloof from trends. Responding to customers' demands for investment products, in 1979 TDB Holdings created an open-ended investment fund (similar to a mutual fund) based in Germany that could be sold by both Republic and TDB. Because Edmond was unsure what to invest in—he never liked encouraging clients to invest in the stock market because he knew that many of them were extremely risk-averse—he initially left these funds in cash, which proved a smart move when stock markets declined. And he still had ample opportunity to put his intuition as a trader to work. In December 1979, when he thought gold was going to rise, he had Republic buy large quantities. "In one month we made $40 million," Walter Weiner recalled.[301]

Despite his now presiding over a global institution, Edmond's philosophy and worldview remained rooted in the practices and the mentality of the bank on Allenby Street. Edmond felt that he—and

not a central bank, or a deposit insurance entity, or shareholders—
would be responsible for the losses if things went wrong. And for all
his sophistication, he was very much invested in the public viewing
him as the guarantor of deposits and the practitioner of a simple
form of banking. This came through in what was, for Edmond, an
extraordinary interview conducted with *Institutional Investor* magazine in May 1979. He cooperated for the cover story, penned by
Cary Reich, which appeared with the headline "The Secret World
of Edmond Safra."

"He may well be the richest and most successful banker in the
world," Reich wrote. "He is also one of the least known. Until now."
Edmond, who rubbed shoulders with Rockefellers and Rothschilds,
and who counted central banks as clients, took pains to appear as a
simple businessperson: self-deprecating, modest, speaking in idiomatic
English. "First my competition says Safra has no heart. Then they
say he has no hair. Then they say the profitability is not true," he
explained. "But I usually say, Thanks God, I would always like to
have my competition jealous of me." While people often paid him
compliments about how beautiful his office was, he added, "I say
better you should come to tell me how beautiful is my balance sheet."
Republic had $3.3 billion in assets, but Edmond presented himself as
a conduit for Jacob Safra's early-twentieth-century approach to lending. He demanded personal guarantees, for "if you see your client,
you look in his face, and if you believe he is honest you can't make
many mistakes." He didn't gamble, because "my father used to tell
me: how do you expect people to trust you if they see you gambling?"
Edmond told Reich that the stock market was a mystery, and that his
preferred method of measuring inflation was looking at deli menus.
"So when I realize that pastrami was $3 last year and now it's $4 and
that now you have to pay $4.75 for a combination sandwich, then I
realize inflation is very bad, no?" Oh, and he was personally frugal:
Edmond related that he had sold the yacht he kept in Cannes after
receiving an $800 bill for soap. (Of course, Edmond and Lily still
rented imposing yachts most summers. Relaxing and detaching from
work remained a challenge. In the cities where the boat stopped,

Edmond would reserve hotel rooms where he could sit and talk on the phone—while looking out at the boat.)

While he was at home and welcomed in the most elite institutions, whether Harvard or the IMF, Edmond expressed the lingering insecurity he felt as a perpetual outsider. In Geneva, where he had been based for more than twenty years and had just donated a sculpture by Antoine Pevsner for a public park, he didn't feel fully accepted. "Certainly, I would like to have them more friendly toward us," he told the magazine. With the experience of the Jewish communities of Aleppo and Beirut at the top of his mind, he was painfully aware that powerful forces could tear down institutions, which explained his conservatism when it came to lending and ensuring the safety of deposits. Edmond insisted on personally approving loans as small as $2 million. "I think I am delegating. But maybe unconsciously I take back the delegation." But doing so was necessary, he made clear, if his bank were to last for hundreds of years. "You have thousands of vultures who are always trying to eat you," he said. "If you're not strong, if you don't make a strong boat, they'll eat you up." The worst outcome for Edmond was "to be sometime taken short and, God forbid, have to go and beg for survival."

Other CEOs of banks in the US, content to matrix out lending decisions, secure in the knowledge that the FDIC would stand behind their deposits, and secure in their person, simply did not talk or manage this way. But fear and tentativeness were a key part of Edmond Safra's personality and way of doing business. He had always expressed the concern—the superstition, many would argue—common for people of his milieu about "avoiding the evil eye." But living in an era in which friends and colleagues had been expelled from their homes, victims of pogroms, kidnapped, or killed in wars, he had reason to be fearful. In 1978, documents circulated at TDB rolling out security protocols in case of explosive letters, kidnappings, or bombings.[302] A private detective agency in 1979 followed and questioned a man who had been behaving suspiciously near the TDB building on Place du Lac. It turned out to be a rabbi who said he had come to see Edmond about raising funds for Israel.[303]

As much as Edmond enjoyed his stability and prosperity, he was continually exposed to people close to him who were suffering the worst forms of insecurity. Not just in Beirut, but in Aleppo. Despite the vicious oppression of the Syrian nationalist regime, the power of the twenty centuries of presence exerted an intense gravitational force, keeping a dwindling Jewish community in Aram Tzova. In October 1979, a group of eight rabbis, "Les Rabins d'Alep," wrote Edmond asking him to support Chief Rabbi Yomtob Yedid, "who has spent his whole life organizing and has dozens of disciples." That summer, Edmond had sent $10,000 to support the Talmud Tora school. "We will say tehilim [psalms] for you, Eli, Moïse, Yossef, and your family," Yedid responded. Yedid, born in 1926, stayed in Aleppo into the 1980s, when he was finally able to leave for Brooklyn.[304]

Despite his expressed conservatism in lending and extending credit, Edmond continued to be aggressive when it came to expanding the core banking franchise, eager to broaden and diversify the base of deposits beyond the Jewish diaspora. When Bankers Trust (New York) was looking to get out of the retail banking industry, it put dozens of its branches up for sale. On May 27, 1980, Republic bought twelve of them, with $133 million of deposits. In August, with the sale of new common and preferred shares, Republic moved the listing of its stock from the American Stock Exchange to the more prestigious New York Stock Exchange, joining the very elite of the country's business establishment.

Edmond was able to realize another dream in 1980. Although his career had effectively been launched from the Tel Aviv airport in 1947, he had not been back to the area since—and had never formally set foot in the State of Israel. With the synagogue project in Bat Yam nearing completion, Edmond and Lily decided it was time to make their first visit. They arrived on Sunday, June 18, and checked into a hotel under an assumed name. They flew in flowers from Holland and arranged for a photographer to document the inauguration ceremony. The next night was the eve of Shavuot, which was also the *azkara* (*yahrzeit*) of Jacob Safra—the anniversary of his passing on the Hebrew calendar. As was his lifelong habit, Edmond prayed and studied through the night—this time, however, at the tomb of the revered Rabbi Meir Baal HaNess in Tiberias, along with his brothers.[305]

Edmond's life was fuller than ever—and his self-confidence, never in short supply, was growing. He had a supportive partner in Lily, whose children and sociability added new dimensions to his life. The family was thriving, and so was the family of banks. As was said about the British Empire, the sun never set on the Safra family of banks. "When I finish with New York I start wondering what's going on in Hong Kong," Edmond once said. He relished being the chairman of Republic, of TDB, and of BCN. He embraced the responsibility of being the steward of the money—and the security—of an increasingly large client base on several continents. He was the guardian, as well, of the hopes and dreams the assets represented. In some ways, however, the world was more uncertain than it had been in years. In 1979, there were revolutions in Nicaragua and Iran, the Soviet Union had invaded Afghanistan, inflation was raging, and the silver boom came to a sudden end. But Edmond believed he had constructed a ship that could withstand these storms. He told investors in early 1980, "We can confidently say that we are better placed than ever before to face whatever difficulties lie before the international banking community in the 1980s."[306]

This confidence would soon be tested.

11

Seeking Safety

(1981–1984)

As a banker, Edmond Safra had enthusiastically assumed an immense personal responsibility for the savings and well-being of tens of thousands of people: the New Yorkers attracted to Republic by the offers of free televisions, the Middle Eastern exiles who flocked to TDB, the dwindling cadre of holdouts who banked at BCN in Beirut, and new clients from Singapore to Uruguay. Edmond had managed this burden by avoiding consumer and corporate lending and instead seeking low-risk arbitrage opportunities and lending primarily to borrowers who couldn't—or wouldn't—default, such as governments and central banks. The unique approach had allowed him to create two very large banks from scratch: by 1981, TDB and Republic had more than $12 billion in assets between them.

But in the early 1980s, the unique business model turned into something of a liability. The 1980s may be remembered as go-go boom years in the US and the world. But they were roiled and disrupted by a series of busts in the domestic and global financial markets. For the first time in his seemingly charmed career, Edmond's Safra's fear and sense of responsibility overtook his tolerance for risk and ambition. The result was the ill-fated sale of one of his banks and a frustrating entanglement with American Express.

At the outset of the decade, Edmond was spending a lot of time thinking about New York real estate. In 1981, when Manufacturers

Hanover put up for sale two of its trophy office buildings in New York and London, Edmond hesitated, remarking that "the world isn't ready for a Jew" to own them. But in August of that same year, Republic struck a partnership with Salomon Brothers to purchase Manufacturers Hanover's 30-story modern skyscraper at 350 Park Avenue. Partnering with a venerable local player, Edmond paid what seemed to be a premium price for a very prominent building—at $161 million, the sale was the highest per-foot price paid for a Manhattan office building to date. But he limited his exposure: Republic put in only $3.9 million, and Salomon Brothers supplied capital as well. And he obtained financing from an unlikely member of his far-flung international network: the Kuwaiti government.[307]

At the same time, he was making another major real estate move in midtown Manhattan. Fifteen years after its founding, Republic, the upstart "television bank," had outgrown the Knox Building, the ten-story Beaux Arts jewel box that housed the bank (and, for a time, Edmond). In the late 1970s, Republic had quietly acquired adjacent properties on Fifth Avenue between 39th and 40th streets for its eventual expansion. Edmond engaged Attie & Perkins to design a modern thirty-story glass-and-steel skyscraper that would frame the Knox Building. The groundbreaking was held in January 1981, and construction began in the summer. The *New York Times* reported that the building, which would ultimately cost more than $200 million, was to be "the largest project south of 43rd Street since the Empire State Building."[308]

The new investment in New York highlighted a shift. Edmond's professional and personal lives had always revolved around different poles—Beirut, Brazil, Switzerland, London, the South of France, and New York. But now the world's center of finance exerted a greater magnetism. A schedule for 1981 shows that he spent a few days in various European countries as well as visiting Hong Kong, and took no trips to Brazil. But he was in New York from early January to mid-February, from early March to mid-April, for most of June and a chunk of July, then from September 20 through November 8. In all, that year he spent 157 days in New York, and only ninety-three in Geneva, with the rest split between Paris, London, and the South of France.[309] From a social, communal, and business perspective, New York had far more to offer Edmond and Lily than quiet Geneva. They could host leaders in social and philanthropic circles, as they did in December 1981, when they threw a party for the gala performance of *La Bohème* at the Metropolitan Opera. Or they could go to Washington and rub shoulders with cabinet members. In September 1981, Edmond and Lily invited Treasury Secretary Donald Regan and his wife to preview *The American Perspective* at the National Gallery of Art, an exhibit of 102 paintings from the collection of Joann and Julian Ganz, Jr., which Republic was sponsoring. Or he could socialize—in the usual mix of Arabic and French—with the large community of Syrian Jews who had made Brooklyn their new home.[310]

One spot that had vanished from Edmond's itinerary was his hometown, Beirut. The fragile entente between Muslims, Christians, and Jews of Edmond's childhood had long since broken down, although it remained intact at BCN. When Henry Krayem, the Jewish director who traveled back and forth from Belgium to Beirut to oversee affairs, died in 1981, he was replaced by his Christian deputy, Maurice Antoniades. In June 1982, after Israel invaded Lebanon and quickly laid siege to Beirut, a Shia Muslim employee, Ali Mortadallah, risked his life to take checks to clear each day at the central bank.[311] Amazingly, a few Jewish employees hung on. In May 1981, Selim Zeitouni, who had declined an offer from Edmond in 1956 to come work in Brazil, wrote to Edmond: "You know the situation here and it has become impossible. Everybody has left and there remain just a few families (of old people)." Zeitouni wondered if he might find work in one of Edmond's banks. "I have my passport in my pocket."[312]

Edmond retained a soft spot for BCN. In 1982, when the city was under siege, a client in Beirut put in an order through BCN to Republic to sell silver or gold bullion at a certain price. But when the market was falling and he couldn't get through to execute the order, Edmond told colleagues to just execute the transaction at the requested price. "We've done business with this guy for years, and I will give him his money."[313]

It was one thing to bail out individual depositors who had small accounts at BCN. But as far-fetched as it may have seemed, Edmond increasingly began to worry about his capacity to stand behind the deposits of his enterprises, especially because his two interlocked banks, Republic and TDB, continued to increase their exposure to international borrowers. About 70 percent of Republic's $7.3 billion in assets were outside the US, including nearly $1 billion in the UK, $1 billion in Western Europe, $514 million in Canada and Mexico, and $1.54 billion in South and Central America. Of the $2 billion in foreign loans, about $905 million were to governments and official institutions. And Republic was expanding—in London, in Singapore, in Buenos Aires, and in Los Angeles. For its part, TDB had about $5 billion in assets, and followed similar lending policies, with several hundred million dollars of loans in South America.[314]

The growth was both a blessing and a challenge. In May 1982, the board of TDB Holding (Luxembourg) noted that "the gratifying increase of deposits raises, as in all banks of the group, the problem of investment of money, of its security and productivity." It continued: "Considering the diminishing number of countries in which investments can be envisaged, we are faced with the problem of the concentration of our investments." That is to say, in pursuit of growth, the banks had placed a lot of their eggs in a few major baskets, and Edmond began to be concerned that risk was not being monitored correctly.[315]

There was a second issue. Amid higher interest rates, deregulation, and occasionally reckless practices in the global banking industry, there was simply more risk for all participants. Edmond fretted that if things started to go seriously wrong in just one or two countries, it would quickly have effects throughout the system, and banks everywhere would be jeopardized. Republic depositors were covered by FDIC insurance up to a limit of $100,000. But Edmond had no faith that the governments in any of the countries in which he operated would come to the aid of a Lebanon-born Brazilian citizen like him. What's more, TDB owned a controlling stake in Republic, and not the other way around—which meant the ultimate supervisor was in Switzerland, which didn't have deposit insurance. Although TDB was among the

In the late 1940s, while still a teenager, Edmond Safra confidently operated
in the world of adults—living out of hotels in Europe, representing his father's bank,
and striking deals for gold. (Geneva, 1948, when Edmond was 16.)

*Jacob and Esther Safra built a large family
that was a pillar of Beirut's Jewish community.*

Top: Jacob and Esther and six of their eight
children (Edmond is at the far left).
Left: In 1937, the Safras traveled to Italy
(Edmond, center, with his mother, sister
Huguette, and brother Elie).
Bottom: In Beirut, Jacob Safra (*second from
right*) met with Jewish, Muslim, and Christian
leaders, including Chief Rabbi Benzion
Lichtman (*center*) and Pierre Gemayel (*left*).

Brazil, where Edmond ultimately obtained citizenship in 1958, became the Safra family's new base of operations in the 1950s.

After leaving Beirut in 1947, Edmond spent several years living in and traveling around Europe, where he seamlessly blended work and leisure in cafés, night clubs, and the resort areas of the South of France.

In 1966, Sen. Robert F. Kennedy attended the ceremonial opening of Republic's single branch *(below)*, which occupied the ground floor of the Knox Building *(immediate left)*. Republic grew in part by offering televisions as inducements to people who referred new clients *(facing page)*. Rabbis *(above)* joined Safra to bless the 1981 groundbreaking of Republic's new modern headquarters building, which wrapped around the Knox Building.

Over thirty-three years, Edmond Safra built Republic National Bank of New York from a scrappy startup into the eleventh-largest bank in the United States.

New York Bank...
...A Worldwide Service

LONDON

SAO PAULO

BEIRUT

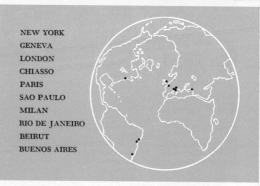

GENEVA

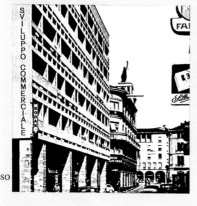

CHIASSO

NEW YORK
GENEVA
LONDON
CHIASSO
PARIS
SAO PAULO
MILAN
RIO DE JANEIRO
BEIRUT
BUENOS AIRES

Counsel
COOPER, OSTRIN, DeVARCO & ACKERMAN

Republic was a new bank with a grand old-world banking hall *(bottom right)*. From its origins, Edmond viewed Republic as a member of the family of banks he established, which had outposts in Lebanon, Brazil, and Europe's major financial capitals *(facing page)*. Edmond spent much of his professional time at the modern lakeside building in Geneva that housed the headquarters of TDB, and then Republic *(top right)*.

Edmond Safra's overlapping and intersecting worlds of business and philanthropy brought him and Lily Safra into contact with leaders in politics, business, and Jewish affairs.

De gauche à droite: Elie Wiesel, Edmond Safra et Me Marc Bonnant.

Clockwise from this page to facing page: With Elie Wiesel and lawyer Marc Bonnant in 1991, after a Swiss court ruled in his favor in a defamation case; David Rockefeller; Yitzhak and Leah Rabin; Mikhail Gorbachev; longtime Jerusalem Mayor Teddy Kollek at an event marking Edmond's donation of Einstein's manuscript of the Special Theory of Relativity to the Israel Museum; and Margaret and Dennis Thatcher.

© Sivan Farag

Edmond Safra speaks at the eighteenth anniversary celebration of the Israel Scholarship Education Foundation, an organization he helped found in 1977 to support Sephardic students' pursuit of higher education.

Edmond's support for Jewish religious life around the world was deeply personal. Here, he participated in the ceremonial completion of one of the many Torah scrolls he donated, with Lily Safra looking on.

Edmond strongly identified with his Sephardic heritage.
At top, in 1980 he inaugurated the synagogue complex he built
in Bat Yam (Israel) for Lebanese Jews who settled there, with Chief
Rabbi Ovadia Yosef and Rabbi Yaakov Attie, his rabbi
from Beirut. Above, Edmond brought his three brothers and sister
Eveline to pray for the memory of their father at the tomb of
Rabbi Meir Baal HaNess in Tiberias.

*In Lily Monteverde,
Edmond Safra met his match,
dance partner, and love.*

Top left: Edmond and Lily together at their marriage in Geneva in July 1976. *Center right:* Their civil wedding ceremony. *Below:* Together for the 1993 dedication of "Safra Plaats" at Amsterdam's Portuguese Synagogue. *Facing page:* At La Léopolda in 1998.

*In the latter years of his life, Edmond Safra took
great pleasure in the company of his grandchildren.*

largest banks in Switzerland, Edmond was not Swiss, and in a crisis, he did not imagine his bank would be high on the list to be saved. At this point TDB Holdings owned 61 percent of Republic's stock, and Edmond indirectly owned 65 percent of TDB Holdings. The weight of all these deposits ultimately rested on his shoulders. As Republic executive Dov Schlein recalled, Edmond would say: "No one will lose a penny in Republic before I lose everything I have." Edmond came to believe that it would be better if Republic owned TDB, so that the whole enterprise would be under the purview of strong regulators like the Federal Reserve and the FDIC. "Republic was FDIC, whereas TDB was still the Lebanese Jewish guy that has no backup," longtime colleague Raymond Maggar said.[316]

At a May 4, 1982, meeting in Geneva of the TDB board, discussion centered on the ever more complicated global situation. In Poland, there was unrest fueled by the labor movement. In Germany, the economic situation was worsening. In France, the socialist government was nationalizing businesses and undermining confidence. England and Argentina were engaged in a hot war over the Falkland Islands. Stresses continued to build in the financial system over the spring and summer. In May, when bond trader Drysdale Securities tanked, it saddled Chase Manhattan with a $135 million loss. In July, the Penn Square bank in Oklahoma failed, and Italy's Banco Ambrosiano, controlled by the Vatican, collapsed. In August, Mexico declared it was unable to pay the interest on its $80 billion in foreign debt. In the midst of a recession, the ratings agencies continually downgraded US banks, due to their poor capital position.[317]

Meanwhile, the balance sheets of Edmond's banks continued to grow. By the fall of 1982, the balance sheet of TDB Holdings stood at 13.67 billion Swiss francs, with 12.25 billion Swiss francs in deposits (about $6 billion). Emerging markets accounted for only a small share of assets: 3.6 percent in Mexico, 2.8 percent in Brazil, 2.8 percent in Venezuela. But even 10 percent of the total was a lot of money. Of Republic's $4.17 billion in foreign loans, $740 million was in Latin America (more than the North America total, which stood at $515 million).[318]

Edmond's personal life was thriving. He and Lily continued to spend time with their expanding family in the South of France, which now included a first grandchild, Samuel Elia, born in 1981. In early June 1982, when Diane Safra, Elie's daughter, married Oded Henin, Edmond hired Bob Azzam, a well-known Cairo-born singer, to perform at the reception at Restaurant du Parc des Eaux-Vives in Geneva. Guests included dozens of family members, as well as the author Elie Wiesel. In July 1982, Edmond's tailor from Sartoria Rovello on Via Morosoni in Milan flew to Geneva to measure him and his brother Joseph for new tuxedos.

But the joie de vivre coincided with the growing atmosphere of concern and defensiveness. At Republic, a moratorium was placed on loans, and executives embarked on an effort to reduce assets held in Latin America and to increase those in Western Europe and the Asia-Pacific region. By the end of 1982, while 70 percent of loans were still outside the US, Republic's ratio of foreign loans to assets would fall to 20.2 percent, down from 26.2 percent in 1981, and total loans outstanding would fall 14 percent to $2.5 billion. (Despite the concerns, Republic in 1982 would increase its profits to $75.2 million, up from $73.7 million in 1981.) As circumstances continued to evolve, Edmond began to consider an action that had always been unthinkable: selling one, or both, of his banks.[319]

Edmond's desire for a safe haven coincided with the ambition of a very large, aggressive blue-chip company to get into his core business. Tracing its origins to the 1850s, American Express had a storied history. It had parlayed its early businesses in delivery and traveler's checks into an international financial supermarket, with units that dealt in brokerage, travel, credit, and insurance. Among its holdings was an undistinguished global private bank—American Express International Banking Corporation—that had sixty-three commercial banking offices in thirty-five countries.

Under its chief executive officer, James Robinson III, himself the scion of a banking family, American Express was eager to expand its banking business. When the consulting firm McKinsey presented a study to American Express on private banks, TDB stood in a class by itself as an attractive target. As Robinson would later say: "We identified TDB as a jewel in the banking world. Edmond is the man who energized and built that jewel."[320]

Initial conversations started from existing connections between the two firms. Peter Cohen, a key lieutenant to Robinson, had briefly worked at Republic in the late 1970s and had a strong personal relationship with Edmond. Socializing with his friend Jeff Keil in the summer of 1982, Cohen learned of Edmond's worries about global instability and the pressure he felt to protect his clients. In September, Cohen told Robinson "there would be a remote chance that maybe we could do something with Trade Development Bank and get Edmond Safra."[321]

Economic blows kept on coming in the fall. In November, Brazil was forced to raise short-term bridge loans from US banks to cover its balance of payment deficit. The same month, Argentina introduced regulations under which authorities decided to issue bonds or promissory notes to satisfy private debt, a measure that affected some $18.3 million in Republic loans in the country.[322] In its annual report over the summer, Republic had announced it was considering a plan to amalgamate Republic New York and TDB Holdings. In the fall, when *Euromoney* asked why he was considering such a move, Edmond responded: "1—to simplify the corporate structure, therefore producing a bank with a capital over one billion US dollars; 2—in the modern age of 24-hour banking, to present a single face to our clients round the world."[323]

But the motivation had more to do with concerns over the potential for losses on the loans the banks had extended. And behind the scenes, talks about selling to American Express heated up. Keil first broached the idea to Edmond in October and found him unexpectedly receptive. On November 7, Cohen and Keil went to Paris, where they held marathon meetings with Edmond. Later that month, Robinson used the premise of the General Agreement on Tariffs and Trade meetings in Geneva as a pretext to see Edmond the week of Thanksgiving. The American Express executives, aware of Edmond's reluctance to sell, were subtly suggesting the benefits of a deal, and conversations included the prospect of American Express buying both TDB and Republic. But it was slow going. This time, Edmond was on the other side of the table—being sold to, rather than doing the selling. Deeply conflicted, Edmond nonetheless instructed his colleagues to proceed discreetly. In New York, Amex was referred to as "tiger," TDB as "copper," and, at Edmond's insistence, the entire project was dubbed "mazal tov." They met in conference rooms at Republic's law firm, Shearman and Sterling, and starting in December, groups from both parties would fly to Montreal, meeting at the Four Seasons hotel over the weekends, to avoid publicity.[324]

The momentum continued to grow, to the point that Sanford "Sandy" Weill, the energetic head of Shearson (which had been acquired by Amex in 1981), flew to Paris at the end of the year to try to close the deal. At the same time, a team led by Bob Smith, the hard-charging former GE executive who ran the Amex bank, went to Geneva to conduct due diligence. At 5:15 a.m. Paris time, on New Year's Day, they finally came to an agreement in principle. Weill called Keil and Cohen, who were together at a New Year's Eve party in East Hampton.[325] American Express would acquire Trade Development Bank and its subsidiaries. Edmond would join the board of American Express and run the international banking business. Republic was not included in the deal, for the time being.

Negotiations continued in Montreal in early January. One of the sticking points, of course, was the price. And here, the defining issue of the relationship between American Express—a blue-chip American company run by MBAs, matrixes, budgets, and spreadsheets—and Edmond Safra, the worldly but superstitious child of Wadi Abu Jamil, first came into play. American Express initially offered $350 million. Edmond's response was $555 million. That was based in part on his intuitive assessment of what the bank was worth, but also on his belief in the power of the *Hamsa*, the number five as good luck. At the Four Seasons in Montreal on the weekend of January 8–9, Robinson and Safra each assembled a group to hash it out. Peter Cohen, dubbed "little Kissinger" for the weekend, went back and forth between Safra's camp in Suite 3014 and Robinson's in Suite 2908. Edmond was getting closer to agreeing. On Sunday, January 9, Edmond flew to Brazil to see Joseph and Moïse at a family event, which included a visit to the Butanta cemetery in São Paolo where Jacob was buried. "Every time I do something, I 'talk' with him about whether it's right or wrong," he later said in an interview.[326]

The closing days were fraught and frenzied. When Edmond's friend John Gutfreund, the chairman of Salomon Brothers, which was Republic's investment banker, heard rumors of the transaction, he flew to São Paulo to talk Edmond out of it. But Edmond insisted on going forward.[327]

On Saturday, January 15, American Express sent its corporate jet to retrieve Edmond from Brazil. The next day, the American Express board met at the Helmsley Palace Hotel in Manhattan to approve the deal, and executives boarded corporate planes to Montreal.[328] The papers were ready and stacked on a table for signature. Highly profitable, with net income of $66.9 million for the year, TDB held $5.07 billion in deposits and, despite Safra's fears, had been obligated to set aside just $12.4 million for loan losses in 1982. For this pristine balance sheet, and the reputation and skill of Edmond Safra, American Express was prepared to pay a premium. Not quite $555 million, but close enough—$550 million. On Monday, at 6:30 p.m. in Geneva (12:30 p.m. in Montreal), the TDB Holdings board gathered at 2 Place du Lac. Roger Junod, Albert Benezra, and Emile Saadia approved the sale of TDB, noting that TDB Holdings would keep its shares of Republic.[329]

All that remained was for Edmond to formally sign and conclude the deal—a task he found psychologically challenging. As a trader, Edmond moved in and out of positions with alacrity. But this was far more personal. Several years before, when he had agreed to sell BCN, his emotions had gotten the better of him and he had backed out at the last minute. Secluded in his hotel room in Montreal, Edmond called people in to talk, including his brother Joseph, who had arrived from Brazil. Edmond grew increasingly agitated as the hours lengthened. Joseph, who was more confident the banks could weather the storms in Latin America, wasn't convinced selling was the right

decision. "Edmond, you don't even know these people," he said. When
he came out of one session with Edmond, he told Republic executive
Ernest Ginsberg: "Persuade Edmond not to do this deal. He will never
be happy in the American Express world." Nonetheless, just before
midnight, Edmond emerged and told Peter Cohen he had come to a
decision: "Let's sign." But he wanted to wait a little longer. With the
hour lengthening, the calendar would soon read Tuesday, January 18—
which was a positive sign on two fronts for Edmond. Eighteen is the
sum of the numeric values of the two Hebrew letters spelling the word
chai, or *life*. Further, he always preferred to conclude deals on Tuesdays.
In the Genesis story of creation over six days, on every day except
Monday, the Bible declares, ". . . and God saw that it was good." On
Tuesday, this is proclaimed not just once, but twice, and therefore
Tuesdays are considered auspicious. The deal for American Express
to acquire TDB was finally signed in Montreal at 2:12 a.m.[330]

The compensation TDB Holdings received for its stake in TDB
consisted of 2.7 million American Express shares; warrants to buy 1.7
million shares at $55, expiring in 1987; and $175 million in Swiss
franc notes issued by an affiliate. As for Republic, it would remain
independent—for now and for the foreseeable future. The morning
after Edmond agreed to sell TDB, Jim Robinson and Sandy Weill
told their Republic counterparts that they were not interested in continuing the prior conversations they had held on pursuing this second
component of the transaction.[331]

The deal had several unusual elements. First, at his request,
Edmond's lawyers had inserted what they called the "Margaret
Thatcher clause," after the British prime minister. Thatcher had come
to power having forced a general election after successfully introducing
a no-confidence vote against Prime Minister James Callaghan.
Edmond wanted a potential "out" if he felt things weren't going well.
And so, according to the clause, Edmond could ask for a formal vote
of confidence from the American Express board. If it failed—if the
company was unwilling to reaffirm its support for Edmond in that
moment—Edmond could leave. Second, while it was presumed that
Edmond would run the merged bank with Albert Benezra as his

second-in-command, American Express insisted at the last minute that Bob Smith be placed in the role of president and chief operating officer. Third, Edmond actually wasn't joining American Express on a full-time basis. As part of the deal, the parties agreed that Edmond would stay in Geneva and would serve, "as soon as he is able to do so, as Chairman of the Board and Chief Executive Officer of American Express International Banking Corp. (AEIBC)." The reason was twofold. Edmond's tax lawyers had told him to stay out of the US in 1983 to avoid paying taxes on the gains he would reap from the sale to American Express. And further, he would need to secure a waiver from the comptroller of the currency in order to become chairman of American Express bank, since he was still honorary chairman of Republic. Edmond didn't come to the press conference in New York announcing the deal.

For his part, Edmond portrayed the deal as less of a corporate transaction than a personal one. "I am delighted to be associated with Mr. Robinson and the American Express family," he noted. To antic-ipate questions from the public, American Express's public relations department drafted a Q&A for him with suggestions for how he should frame a decision many in the public might find strange.

Q: Why would someone of your stature, fame, and wealth want to be involved with AEIBC?

A: "The world is changing rapidly and international banking even more rapidly because of advanced technology, especially in communications."

Q: Do you feel sad to have your banks acquired by an American corporation?

A: "Of course. It is the same sadness one might feel at the marriage of a son or daughter. You are sad to see your child grow up and leave home. But I think you are also happy because your family has grown. If something is the right thing to do, you are never sad for long."[332]

The closing was scheduled for March 1, 1983, in Geneva. On the eve of the signing, Edmond and Lily hosted a dinner for the board at their apartment, at which everyone was presented with gold Bulgari watches. "It was a very happy moment. Edmond felt very relieved, like a heavy weight was off his shoulders," Jeff Keil recalled. Then they traveled to Paris and London, where the board met Prince Philip, and former president Gerald Ford, a member of American Express's board, gave a talk in Guildhall.[333]

Inside and outside TDB, the sale was regarded as something of a coup. American Express couldn't believe its good fortune at gaining access to the aura, skills, and connections of Edmond Safra. "You know, I've never had a billionaire report to me," James Robinson crowed to a colleague. (That was probably an exaggeration of Edmond's net worth.) Edmond was able to maximize his investment, minimize his personal exposure to troubling debt, and maintain his role and holding in Republic. For virtually any other banker, this would have been a capstone to a career. "Dear Edmond, your achievement in banking has been phenomenal and the completion of the transaction with American Express prompts me to congratulate you," Jacob Rothschild wrote on March 1, 1983. "If I look back to the days when I was working on your prospectus for going public, your progress—achieved without fuss and with the making of so many friends—has been the most exceptional of all of us who have practiced our trade."[334]

Not all were in agreement, however. TDB remained a unique institution, even as it had grown into a large international bank. Many of its depositors and customers, the members of the suitcase generation—people who always had a bag packed in case they needed to flee—felt they had a personal relationship with Edmond, not with a corporation. "We came to this bank because we knew only Edmond," Isaac Obersi summarized the sentiment expressed by some clients. "He sold the bank without asking us?" Some employees, many of whom had a familial connection with the Safras, felt anxious about the transition.[335]

And the transition was anything but smooth. The clash between old and new was evident from the beginning. Edmond was accustomed to making decisions on loans individually, based on his assessment of character. He managed informally, thinking nothing of picking up the phone in the middle of a meeting and dealing with an issue that arose in Italian, or French, or Arabic. TDB was full of headstrong, experienced, and capable executives, who were used to Edmond's unique management style and allergic to corporate hier-archies. By contrast, American Express embodied the approach of Robinson. "His style was business by the textbook, business by the numbers," wrote journalist Bryan Burrough in *Vendetta*.[336] Business at American Express was conducted via organization charts, pro-cesses, and marketing plans; its main executives spoke only English and were put off by the European and Levantine ways of their TDB counterparts. Edmond continued to work as he always did, attended by his secretary Danielle Pinet and his assistants, invariably young men of Lebanese or Aleppan heritage who would deal with everything from planning board meetings to buying floats for the swimming pool at the house in Vallauris. When American Express's head of Europe, the Middle East, and Asia, Heinz Zimmer, came to London and started to describe how things were going to change, the response was so negative that the two parties decided to stop further discussions until a master plan was developed. On April 15, 1983, just six weeks after the closing, Rodney Leach, the general manager of TDB, ten-dered his resignation to Jim Robinson. "As Edmond Safra knows, I have had misgiving about the acquisition from the start," he wrote. In Leach's mind, there were three problems: a conflict of interest with Republic, differences in management style, and frustration that work-ing parties had not yet been set up to tackle the integration. "I do not see how I shall be able to perform for [Edmond] and you up to the limit of my capabilities."[337]

On January 28, just a week after the closing, when Bob Smith proposed making a $10 million loan to Morocco, Edmond told him that in principle he was opposed to lending to Morocco due to its unstable political and economic situation—but that if Smith insisted, he would back him.[338] A new credit policy committee was created, which included Robinson, Edmond, Smith, and Albert Benezra.[339] But Benezra, who had absorbed Edmond's method of lending largely to people he knew, repeatedly denied loan requests from clients in countries with which he wasn't familiar. While Edmond and his longtime colleagues regarded TDB as Edmond's operation, American Express viewed it as one of many subsidiaries, subject to the same controls as any other. "Almost from the beginning, Robinson would not let him run American Express bank as if it were his own," Peter Cohen recalled. Edmond, Dov Schlein explained, "was not the kind of man to sit in an office in New York or elsewhere and report to American Express on a day-to-day operation."[340] At TDB, people were expected and empowered to go the extra mile for clients, no questions asked. And when Edmond asked for something to be done, it was done quickly. At American Express, the organization chart reigned, and people needed to seek permission from a host of managers to travel or call on clients.

Edmond regarded himself as one of the top executives, an equal to Robinson. He was also, after all, the largest individual shareholder of the company. To American Express, however, Edmond was one of many senior executives in one of many subsidiaries. In July 1983, American Express announced it was interested in purchasing IDS, a Minneapolis-based asset management company, in a $1 billion all-stock deal. But nobody had even bothered to tell Edmond. Furious at hearing the news from external sources, he called Peter Cohen: "What's SDI? What is this IDS? I don't know anything about it." Cohen and Robinson went to Geneva to try to explain. Although Robinson later reduced the price paid for IDS, Edmond was so angered that he circulated a letter threatening to resign. But the pattern continued: later that year, Robinson wrote Edmond a letter asking what his objectives were for the year to come, as if he were a middle manager.[341]

At Republic, when Edmond came into the building in New York it was an occurrence—there was an electricity in the air as he greeted people on his way through the lobby into the reserved elevator that went to his floor. At American Express, Edmond was treated like one of the several thousand anonymous employees. When TDB executive Michel Cartillier went with Edmond to American Express headquarters, the security guards asked Edmond for his badge. With nobody there to welcome him, he waited 20 minutes and was then shown to the office American Express had given him—a room without a window that colleague Joseph Shalam described as "like a cage." Two hours later, Edmond called Cartillier: "We're going back home!" And they returned to Republic.[342]

American Express executives may have been leery of Edmond's commitment to the enterprise in part because his waiver from the comptroller of the currency had yet to come through, and in part because he had a home at Republic, which was already a presence in many of the markets where TDB and American Express Bank operated, and which was continuing to build up its presence in Europe and Asia. Edmond was not eager to relinquish the position or his involvement with Republic. And it was easy to see why. Republic was a thriving bank in a very attractive market and had a lot of room for growth in front of it. Construction on the prominent new headquarters building was continuing. Edmond had a cadre of experienced, loyal executives who could be counted on to carry out his vision, according to his principles and values. In July 1983, Jeff Keil was promoted to president, replacing Walter Weiner, who became chief executive officer. Cyril Dwek and Joshua Yedid were named vice chairmen.

In 1982 and early 1983, Edmond saw an opportunity for Republic to enter the Canadian banking market. Led by brothers Ezekiel and Edouard, the Schouela family—Egyptian with Aleppo origins—had established themselves in Montreal, and Edmond had been investing in real estate with them since the 1950s. (Teenage Edmond had first met Ezekiel Schouela in the waiting room of the Dutch Central Bank in Amsterdam in 1948.) Republic Canada, which was 15 percent owned by the Schouelas, was inaugurated on May 24, with a celebration for the installation of the mezuzah on the doorpost at the entrance. "We are pleased to be associated with the Schouela family," Edmond wrote.[343]

At the same time, work continued to build up relationships and set up a new operating model for TDB/American Express. As Edmond waited for his waiver, the bank was run by an Office of the Chairman, consisting of Robinson, Smith, and Albert Benezra. Edmond and Lily introduced American Express executives to their lives and to their personal and professional networks—which was one of the explicit reasons American Express had purchased TDB. In the summer of 1983, Edmond and Lily hosted James Robinson and his wife in Vallauris, taking them to Le Moulin de Mougins, the famous Roger Verge restaurant that was a ten-minute drive away, and seeing them off with Framboise de Bourgogne liqueur, wines, and a golf bag. The party thrown by the American Express Bank at the IMF/World Bank meetings in the fall of 1983 attracted 1,400 guests; among those invited were Italian industrialist Gianni Agnelli, Walter Annenberg, designer Bill Blass, Princess Michael of Kent, and Andy Warhol.[344]

But actions and events within American Express continued to undermine whatever relationship was being built. In December, in a shock announcement, the company reported significant problems in its Fireman's Fund Insurance division, as premium prices eroded and claims surged. The result was a massive $242 million charge that threatened to place the company's 35-year record of earnings growth in jeopardy, causing the stock to plunge. Suddenly, the value of the American Express shares Edmond had accepted for TDB fell sharply. There was a larger issue. These sorts of things didn't happen in Edmond's banks. "When they announced that, I thought, he is going to think either they are not honorable because they knew they had a loss here and they did not tell him about it," Republic executive John Tamberlane recalled, "or he is going to think that they are incompetent."[345]

American Express may have prided itself on being a paragon of corporate management. But in Edmond's view, the CEO should know every detail about his company. The point of Edmond's long-running after-work chats was to sit around and delve into issues that were cropping up. And he would personally pepper executives with dozens of questions until he drew problems out. No one seemed to do this at American Express, and the results were disastrous. "I can't understand how this could happen," Edmond said. "Where was the management?"[346]

At American Express's offices in lower Manhattan, it was clear there was a rift. In late December, Robinson wrote a memo to the management committee outlining the four major issues for 1984: "Complete merger (get EJS on board), loan recoveries, build private banking, work with other divisions to sell American Express products." There was progress on some of these issues. Problem loans in Latin America and elsewhere were being sorted out; in fact, in 1983, the combined banks had to write off just $10.4 million in loans. The banking business was growing by doing the types of financings in which Edmond specialized, including a $205 million loan to Turkey (94 percent of which was guaranteed by the US Export-Import Bank) and a $100 million loan to the Philippines.[347]

In early 1984, when Edmond finally got approval from the US authorities, he signed a one-year employment contract and formally became chairman and chief executive officer of AEIBC.[348] But American Express viewed the short tenure of the contract as part of a larger lack of commitment. In the wake of the Fireman's Fund debacle, always eager to limit his losses, Edmond had sold—at a loss of nearly $100 million—nearly all of his American Express shares. And in early 1984, he wanted to sell off the warrants he had received as well, a move that would have required registration with the Securities and Exchange Commission and would certainly have brought negative publicity to the company.

In ways large and small, Edmond continued to feel as though his dignity and autonomy were under assault. After he circulated a memo on April 5, 1984, announcing that he was delighted to become chairman and CEO, American Express executive Charles Teicher wrote him a note. "It seems to me, however, that announcements prepared by the others but appearing over your signature should be free from basic grammatical and spelling mistakes." Teicher pointed out the misspelling of a word, the mixing of present and past tenses, and "finally, syntax, punctuation, and sometimes word choice is poor."

Eager to have the new entity continue to make the same level of charitable contributions that TDB had, Edmond wrote Jim Robinson to describe the donations made from 1980 to 1982: "As we agreed, we will continue to follow the same pattern based upon the above figures. I would appreciate your sending me your confirmation."

Robinson signed it. But later that summer, Stephen Halsey, president of the Amex Foundation, complained that these efforts "have perilously stretched the capacities of the international budget for the consolidated philanthropic programs" and complained that TDB Geneva's commitments would take up almost two-thirds of the entire budget for Europe, the Middle East, and Africa.[349]

There was also a sense of mutual recrimination arising from a fundamental disagreement over how to treat clients. American Express, as a financial supermarket, regarded all its clients as people to whom other products and services could be sold—and their contact information as an asset to be sold to other interested parties, even magazine companies. For Amex, that was the whole point of combining all the units under one roof. For Edmond, however, preserving his clients' privacy was paramount, and discretion had always been a fundamental value. In 1983 and 1984, American Express began trying to market products such as insurance and credit cards to TDB customers, with little response. They pushed account officers to add platinum credit cards to every portfolio. "But our clients preferred not to show their wealth, and they wanted green cards instead," Sem Almaleh recalled.[350] Clients in South America began to call asking why they were getting pitches to subscribe to *Time* magazine. As Bob Smith later complained to *Euromoney,* "We offered them products and Edmond said, 'I'll take them under consideration,' but nothing happened." Edmond, in response, said that he simply remembered that he had expressed opposition to selling the names of TDB depositors who also held American Express cards to outsiders. "It was my judgment that it was not in the best interests of the depositors to sell that information," he explained. In June 1984 it was decided, due to the reaction of clients, to keep TDB Geneva and American Express Zurich separate for two more years.[351]

The two sides gamely tried to move forward as a single entity. In July 1984, the bank started a new publication, *The Globe,* aimed at building a sense of community in the combined organization. It featured a joint letter from Edmond and Bob Smith, and a feature on Jacques Tawil, "the trader's trader." And in Geneva and New York, Edmond and Lily continued to socialize with the Robinsons and

Weills. But by later that year, it was clear that there was little relationship left to repair. Linda Robinson, Jim's wife and a powerful
public relations executive, tried to smooth things over. "You're
unhappy," she told Edmond, striking an understanding tone.

"Not only am I unhappy, Linda," Edmond replied, "I am dis-
gusted. I built the bank on cement and steel. But with you, I feel I'm
sitting on quicksand."[352]

American Express executives couldn't help but notice that Edmond
was tending to his own many interests, including Republic, Safra
Bank in Florida, and BCN. By the end of 1983, things were sufficiently
calm in Beirut for BCN to hold board meetings for the first time in
three years. In their new offices at Rue Riad el-Solh, attorney Anis
Daouk informed Edmond that the board had met in December 1983
to approve the accounts of 1980, 1981, and 1982. Despite the
near-impossible operating environment, the bank, whose annual
revenues were about $600,000, managed to show a loss of only about
750,000 Lebanese pounds (about $90,000). BCN also continued to
act as the representative of Republic in Lebanon, for which it received
a $30,000 annual payment. New rules and procedures were laid out
in early 1984, dictating, for example, that the opening of the safe must
be entrusted jointly to two employees, "or if the state of insecurity that
is permanent in Beirut doesn't permit, when one or the other" is
present.[353]

In May 1984, at the height of his disputes with American Express,
Edmond opened yet another new bank. Mimicking his prior move in
Florida, Edmond formed Safrabank California, a new full-service
commercial bank chartered by California, after having acquired the
physical assets of the recently liquidated West Coast Bank. Capitalized
at $6.3 million, it had offices in Beverly Hills and Encino.[354]

Convinced there was no future to the relationship with American
Express, Edmond began to negotiate to buy back TDB, and the two
sides seemed to be close. Edmond offered $450 million ($100 million
lower than the 1983 purchase price), with the caveat that American
Express keep TDB's Latin American loans. American Express countered with $500 million. While talks continued, Bob Smith at

American Express ultimately convinced Robinson to keep the bank. It was clear that American Express was highly suspicious of Edmond's motives. In the conversations, American Express executives and lawyers repeatedly expressed concern that Edmond would start his own bank and violate the noncompete agreements they had struck. Ken Bialkin, a lawyer who represented American Express and who was also a leading figure in the American Jewish community, at one point told Edmond that if he didn't adhere to the noncompete agreement, American Express might go to the Internal Revenue Service and raise questions about his tax situation.[355]

Ultimately, a deal was reached on October 22, 1984. Edmond was permitted to resign as chairman and CEO of American Express International Banking Corporation. American Express would sell him back the Geneva building (2 Place du Lac), TDB France, and the banknotes business of TDB in London. (The French authorities had, in any case, declined to allow American Express to operate a bank there, and Amex was simply not interested in the banknotes business.) Both Edmond and Joseph Safra agreed not to compete with Amex until 1988.

The parting of ways was forced and not particularly warm. "It is with great sorrow that I relinquish my direct involvement in the management of AEIBC," Edmond wrote. "I also want to express my utmost admiration for my good friend, Jim Robinson, and wish Bob Smith and Albert Benezra continued success." For their part, American Express didn't seem sad to see Safra go. "Edmond has apartments in Geneva, Paris, London, and New York, as well as two brothers in Brazil, where he spends some time," Bob Smith put it. "He prefers to have less day-to-day responsibility so he can devote time to other interests and personal affairs," Robinson said. They acknowledged the lack of chemistry. "It was worth a try," Robinson told the *Wall Street Journal*.[356]

It was in many ways a shattering experience for Edmond. He had ensured the safety of both his banks, and his depositors, but at a very high financial and personal cost. Throughout, Edmond felt that American Express was not treating him with respect. And his concerns that people wished him ill, which colleagues often chalked up to paranoia, had been validated. He walked away believing that he had done business with dishonorable people, to whom he was still tied—as he was still on the board of American Express, and many of the employees and clients for which he felt responsible remained under the American Express umbrella. He took seriously the threats made by American Express, which employed phalanxes of lawyers and public relations officers. That fall, for the first time, he engaged a well-known crisis communications firm, Kekst & Co., to be on call. And in October he requested a defensive electronic sweep of his office on the thirty-third floor of the American Express headquarters building in New York. The test, on Saturday, October 27, "failed to reveal the presence of any clandestine transmitter or listening device."[357]

The strange and frustrating episode with American Express appeared to be over. And Edmond Safra, having gone through a harrowing professional experience, was now back in a position where the fate of his fortune would depend on his own judgment and abilities. Within limits, he was free to go do what he had been doing for nearly thirty years—building banks.

12

New Beginnings

(1984–1988)

E dmond Safra's departure and divorce from American Express in October 1984 was an intensely personal and consequential move for all involved—and one that would define his life for the next several years.

From the outset of his career, depositors, clients, and employees had felt a personal connection to Edmond Safra—and he to them. In the wake of his departure from Amex, others began to leave— especially the old guard. Roger Junod, Edmond's longtime collaborator, in December 1984 submitted his resignation as administrator of TDB "because of the recent events regarding the organization of our bank, and particularly the departure of Edmond Safra."[358] François Lugeon wrote to Edmond in the fall of 1984, referring to TDB as "your baby," "There is a certain pang in the heart that I think the building in which we did your work . . . won't be the cradle of TDB anymore."[359]

American Express was both eager to be rid of Edmond and some of his loyal colleagues, and concerned about what he might do next. In 1984, when American Express first feared that Republic would open a bank in Geneva, it threatened to sue Edmond and Republic and to accuse Edmond of violations of US laws.[360] In December of that year, when veteran TDB employees Moïse and Mayer Dwek announced they were going to join Soditic, the investment bank founded by

Maurizio Dwek, they were quickly fired. The move provided occasion for a rare written sermon on management from Edmond to Jim Robinson, the CEO of American Express. The rapid firings were "symptomatic of a situation with serious implications for TDB," which they had discussed on the phone, Edmond wrote. "My concerns are now of sufficient gravity to warrant the unusual step, for me, of writing to you." Management has to maintain the loyalty and affection of its employees. "They must be assured that the Bank will maintain its unique character and identity, and the personal, confidential relationships which are at the heart of the bank's success." Firing people summarily, "while accepted in large institutions, is foreign to our small community. . . . How much better it would have been had they been handled softly and personally." Edmond also noted that a senior Amex official was "spreading the false rumor . . . that I owned a participation" in Soditic. He reminded Robinson that he had agreed to "join your Board to emphasize the positive aspects of our continuing relationship," and warned this would keep happening. "As a result of my long relationships with them, many employees and depositors identify with me. When I was attacked, they felt attacked," he wrote. "All of this was discussed between us, yet it was then ignored or forgotten. Jim, I am not sure what you can do to reverse the damage."[361]

Precisely because of that dynamic and in order to hang on to the deposits and to the officers who helped manage them, American Express deployed blunt instruments: higher salaries, new contracts with noncompete clauses, stock, perks, and the threat of lawsuits. Eli Krayem, Edmond's former assistant, remained at American Express for a year after Edmond's departure in return for a tripling of salary and signing a one-year noncompete agreement. (He would later join Republic in London to work on private banking in the Middle East.) Albert Benezra, one of the few senior TDB executives to stay on, was given a chauffeur-driven car. Benezra's decision to throw his lot in with American Express was a source of tension from which the long-standing relationship with Safra never recovered.[362]

The constant jabbing between American Express and the Safra world continued in private and in public. In the spring of 1985, Bob

Smith of American Express wrote to Walter Weiner (then CEO of Republic) to complain that in the previous six months, $24.13 million was withdrawn from TDB and transferred to Republic, mostly in Brazil. Weiner responded: "The movement of $24 million over a seven month period (which, considering press coverage, could very well have been at customers' initiative) hardly seems worth either your attention or mine." After all, the clients didn't bank with TDB or Republic. They banked with Edmond.

"I don't tell my clients to do business with me," Edmond told Minos Zombanakis. "But they were chasing me because we grew up together. They're the Jews from home, from Syria, the Jews of Beirut, the Jews of the Middle East."[363]

A month later, in what Edmond regarded as a serious breach of their mutual nondisparagement agreement, American Express executives cooperated with a *Los Angeles Times* article about what had gone wrong with the TDB acquisition. "Edmond couldn't make the cultural and mental jump from being his own boss to being part of a big organization," Jim Robinson said. Bob Smith concluded, "We learned a lot from Edmond. But I think we're a lot better off without him." Edmond, responding to written questions, called the charge "dangerously misleading" and pointed to the problems at Fireman's Fund and other issues.[364] What was really behind these efforts? Edmond was transparent about his long-term intentions. In one of his first public statements after leaving American Express, he told *Euromoney*: "I am seriously considering opening a bank in Switzerland. It is an enormous market and there is plenty of room for everybody." One Geneva banker told the *Wall Street Journal*, "Mr. Safra will replicate his old business in Europe again. You can't just sever relationships built up over 20 or 30 years."[365]

For the first time in his adult life, Edmond found that his professional responsibilities had seemingly declined. He had no role at TDB, and as part of his separation from American Express, he had agreed to refrain from opening a bank in Switzerland for nearly four years. Joseph and Moïse had established Banque Safra Luxembourg SA, and they were now largely running the day-to-day affairs of Banco

Safra in Brazil on their own. In 1981, when Banco Safra, with Edmond's blessing, opened a branch in New York, it became the first Brazilian bank to offer full banking services in the US.[366]

As for Republic, it was firmly in the hands of the experienced executive team in New York, including Walter Weiner, Jeff Keil, and Dov Schlein. Edmond had always been limited as to how much time he could spend in New York and would typically come three or four times per year, staying a few weeks each time. Of course, he was on the phone with many people at Republic on a daily basis. "Mr. Safra is the coach," Jeff Keil described it. "He can direct policy, but he can't run the plays."[367]

The plays in 1985 and 1986 involved Republic doing what TDB had done in Europe—just not in Switzerland.[368] In March 1985, Republic agreed to buy TDB France for $15 million.[369] In August, it established a new company in a nearby banking capital in the center of Europe: Republic National Bank of New York (Luxembourg). As was his usual practice, Edmond chose prime real estate, locating the office in a building on the prestigious Boulevard Royal. A ramp was constructed to enable trucks with banknotes to drive in. To staff up these operations, Republic began to hire people who had worked with TDB.[370]

Edmond's life had always revolved around different geographical poles. Over time, due to shifting business, political, and family dynamics, the gravitational pull of Beirut and Brazil had faded. Now, the South of France and his immediate family—Lily, and her children and grandchildren—became more central. Edmond was constantly moving between his homes in Geneva, New York, London, Paris, and Vallauris. The difference now was that he was able to spend much of the summer in the South of France, playing host to family and entertaining friends—while constantly talking on the phone with colleagues and clients. But here, too, in this haven, Edmond was reminded of the insecurity he had always feared. On August 6, 1985, when about forty guests were celebrating Edmond's fifty-third birthday, and despite the presence of a security guard at the entrance of the property, burglars broke into the house and stole a large amount of jewelry. The following summer, Edmond and Lily would engage four young Israelis as rotating security guards.[371]

For reasons of security, and size, the house in Vallauris was outliving its usefulness. The extended Safra clan was continuing to grow. And the desire for more space and more privacy led Edmond and Lily to a real estate transaction that would consume a great deal of their attention and would come to hold a particularly important place in their lives.

In late 1985, Edmond and Lily began looking at a property about an hour east of Vallauris, in the town of Villefranche-sur-Mer. There, in the hills just east of Nice, sat an iconic property: La Léopolda. King Leopold of Belgium had bought the land for his mistress in 1902. It was acquired in 1929 by Ogden Codman, the American neoclassical architect whose Gilded Age clients included the Rockefellers and Vanderbilts. Codman set out to build a huge villa inspired by eighteenth-century mansions like the Villa Belgioso in Milan but ran out of money during the Depression. In the 1950s, the Italian industrialist Gianni Agnelli bought the twenty-eight-room villa and hired landscape designer Russell Page to work on the ten acres of gardens. La Léopolda went through several other owners before Edmond and Lily purchased the property in 1985 and set about transforming it.[372]

With its numerous rooms, halls, terraces, and gardens, La Léopolda would provide an immense tapestry for the couple's aesthetic sense. Lily hired Italian architect Lorenzo Mongiardino to transform the first-floor reception areas and their friend, the well-known decorator Mica Ertegun, to design the second floor. For Edmond, La Léopolda was a source of wonder. In the basement, he was thrilled to find a prodigious wine cellar with bottles going back to the early part of the century. Edmond loved to watch the craftsmen at work, and would frequently take his grandson, Samuel, to check on progress. "I think he was very proud of La Léopolda," recalled Adriana Elia, Lily's daughter. "He really wanted to make that house a family home." The gardens, where workers planted hundreds of olive trees, were Edmond's domain, and he would putter around in a tracksuit and white Reebok shoes.[373]

Edmond and Lily had long been joyful and eager collectors of beautiful things—paintings, drawings, sculptures, carpets, furniture, decorative objects, watches. For Edmond, who didn't play golf or tennis or have many leisure pursuits, collecting was a passion. He loved the chase of bidding, calculating relative value, and understanding the dynamics of auctions in the same way he loved delving into markets and hunting for deals. The advent of remote bidding meant that participating in auctions was yet another activity he could do on the phone. Edmond and Lily were regulars at Christie's and Sotheby's houses on two continents, buying silverware, timepieces, paintings, and carpets. Edmond had an appreciation of the craftsmanship, the artistry, and the history of antique objects. In Paris, he and Lily would visit the Louvre des Antiquaires or furniture dealer Maurice Segoura's showroom on the Rue du Faubourg Saint-Honoré. Lily was drawn to French classical and nineteenth-century Russian art, and modern jewelry. Edmond favored exquisitely crafted mechanical clocks, furniture, and desks, in particular the work of George Bullock, a late-eighteenth-century English furniture maker. In 1987, he bid aggressively to acquire the *Mobilier Crozat* (Crozat suite), a set of chairs and sofa made for the eighteenth-century French royal financier Crozat.[374]

"I think he could see the human effort that had gone into them," said Christie's executive Charles Cator. Edmond would call Cator on Sunday mornings, as if he were a bank employee, and pick his brain about objects up for sale. Both Edmond and Lily had intimate knowledge of the objects they owned. "It could be a watch. It could be a Van Gogh," said Kenneth Cooper, a longtime Safra associate. "They could sit there and tell you the whole history of that piece, why it was important, and why it belonged exactly in that place."[375]

Even if Safra had taken his foot slightly off the gas pedal since the separation from American Express, his desk calendar from 1986 reveals the habits and routines that continued to characterize his peripatetic and busy life. He was in Rio de Janeiro from January 1 to January 16 visiting family. Traveling between Europe and the US in January and February, he and Lily had dinner with John and

Susan Gutfreund in Paris and attended a reception in London with the Prince of Wales. In March, Edmond traveled to New York, where he attended to Republic business, and then he was back in Vallauris for the eve of Passover. In late April, he returned to New York for several weeks.

In New York, as in the South of France, Edmond now alit on a more assertive and high-profile presence. Republic's new headquarters was nearing completion, its budget ultimately running to $300 million. First conceived in 1981, the thirty-story glass and steel building (with a massive vault underground) wrapped around and connected to the Beaux Arts Knox Building. Republic's headquarters now fronted nearly an entire block on Fifth Avenue. The thoroughly modern building, with a broad view of midtown Manhattan and beyond, was the bold and optimistic new flagship of the Safra family of companies. Edmond moved his personal office from the Knox Building to an aerie atop the twenty-ninth floor, which, with its thick carpets, drapes, and heavy chairs, had an opulence reminiscent of the Ottoman Empire.[376]

Edmond held fast to the rituals that had provided the rhythm of his life, which mixed religion, business, and family. On February 15, he made a note to himself to attend "synagogue for mother." On June 12, 1986, the eve of the Shavuot holiday, and the anniversary of Jacob Safra's death, he noted, "fast sunrise to 15 h," and then went to synagogue at 10:30 p.m. to study throughout the night. In late June, he relocated to Vallauris, where he spent most of July and August.

In New York, Paris, and London, Edmond and Lily circulated in overlapping and occasionally interlocking social and philanthropic circles. And they began to donate to establishment charities favored by their friends and colleagues, such as the London Philharmonic and World Wildlife Federation. But Edmond's charitable activity went far beyond showing up at galas. As always, he continued to make contributions to needy individuals and institutions in the tradition of Aleppo and Beirut. He had employees in all his main offices who were tasked with fielding requests from rabbis, institutions, and individuals around the world, and for those not approved for larger donations,

Edmond's instructions were that they were to at least receive $101, the numerical value of the Hebrew letters in the name of the angel Michael. He remained actively involved with the International Sephardic Education Foundation (ISEF), which he had helped establish, and which in 1986 distributed more than $575,000 in university scholarships.[377] Also that year, he and Lily hosted Israeli Foreign Minister Shimon Peres for a gala celebration of ISEF's tenth anniversary at the Regency Hotel in New York. And he made further efforts to support university education—particularly in subject areas that were important to him. At Harvard, Edmond created the Robert F. Kennedy Visiting Professorship in Latin American Studies as well as fellowships at a new Center for Ethics and the Professions.

The centerpiece of the fall season, one of the most important events of the year for Edmond and Lily, was the IMF and World Bank meetings. Over the years, as Republic and the Safra family of banks, grew, so, too, did their presence at the gatherings. The meetings were a subject of meticulous and careful planning, since they represented an occasion for Republic to connect with a wide range of important customers and contacts. Suites were held well in advance at the Hay Adams hotel. A fleet of cars was reserved for Edmond and Lily, the Safra brothers, and a dozen-odd executives. Republic's September 30, 1986, reception, which was held at the National Gallery of Art and which included a viewing of the Renaissance bronzes from Vienna's Kunsthistorisches Museum, was highly choreographed. The menus, decorations, and glassware were chosen by Lily and Mica Ertegun, and the main centerpiece was a chocolate model of RNB headquarters. Reception line assignments were laid out to the half hour—first Edmond, accompanied by Dov Schlein and Edouard Schouela (of the Canada branch); then Joseph, accompanied by Jeff Keil; and Moïse, accompanied by Cyril Dwek.[378] (Just three weeks earlier, Edmond and Lily had been in Washington to attend a state dinner at the White House in honor of Brazilian president Jose Sarney.)

The IMF/World Bank meetings were especially vital to Edmond because, as much as the old "television bank" continued to rely on depositors in and around New York, Republic's assets lay almost entirely outside the United States. Certainly, Republic had continued to evolve, even as it followed the well-tested Safra model of low-risk banking and protecting deposits. Whether it was discounting notes, *à forfait*, lending with IMF and Export-Import Bank guarantees, or selling gold forward, Edmond continued to focus on low-risk transactions in which a minimum of capital was put at risk. To this, Republic added a new business: factoring, which was essentially providing advances to businesses against their accounts receivable. Of $3.3 billion in Republic's domestic loans on June 30, 1986, approximately $1.4 billion was housed in the Republic factors units. By contrast, the international units accounted for about $14.9 billion in assets—loans to companies, governments, and agencies, many of them backed by international organizations like the IMF. Of the total, $3.5 billion was in Argentina, $1.7 billion in Egypt, and $2.7 billion in Venezuela.[379]

Nearly 40 years into his career, Edmond still eschewed lending money to individuals. He fretted that it was difficult to price a loan well, and that once a bank lent too much money to any individual or company, the customer would control the bank. "I will lend the wealthy money if they put a gun to my head and make me do it, but I am lending them their own money back," was how he put it.[380] That mix of mundane US deposit banking and haute international banking had created immense value for Republic's shareholders over the previous twenty years. Including reinvested dividends, holders of Republic's common shares reaped compound annual gains of more than 25 percent in the 1980s—a return that is all the more astonishing given that the bank used comparatively little leverage and avoided extending high-interest loans to risky customers.

However, this approach also hamstrung growth in a rapidly evolving marketplace. Unlike many of its peers in the American financial industry, Republic didn't react to the loosening of regulations by expanding heedlessly into new lines of business. Nor did it get caught up in the new trends, such as lending to aggressive leveraged buyouts.

In the early 1980s, Edmond had responded to the large buildup of developing market loans on his banks' books by selling TDB to American Express. But that solved only part of the problem. In July 1986, Jeff Keil noted to his Republic colleague Thomas Robards, "Republic currently faces a set of problems which it has not faced in the last ten years." Diversification was low, with exposure concentrated in a few countries. When things were going well in those areas, it was a brilliant strategy. But the fragility of such a strategy became evident when crises arose. Despite earlier efforts to reduce loans to developing countries, there was some $280 million in Mexican debt that might be problematic. More significantly, while the bank had expanded its branch presence around the world to gain more deposits, "we have not been able to identify other non-volatile lines of business outside of the ones that we have pursued for the past ten years, to generate revenue." The response would be to aggressively move bad debt off the balance sheet and raise new capital. In the fourth quarter of 1986, Republic earmarked $120 million of less-developed countries (LDC) debt for markdown and subsequent sale, far before other major banks did. (Citigroup in May 1987 would take $3 billion in reserves for its LDC debt.) The markdowns would result in a rare quarterly loss for Republic in the second quarter of 1987. To strengthen the balance sheet, Republic New York Corporation announced a public offering for 1.5 million shares.[381]

After the IMF meetings, Edmond went to Brazil for two weeks in October for the Jewish holidays, with a weekend trip to Buenos Aires. Republic New York and Banco Safra did not have cross-ownership stakes, and neither was a subsidiary of the other. But as they had done for decades, the brothers continued to work together, and Edmond regarded all the institutions as part of the larger family business. This was so even as Republic and Banco Safra found themselves operating in the same markets, such as Luxembourg or New York.

In late 1986, Banco Safra was preparing an application to receive approval from the US Federal Reserve and comptroller of the currency to operate as a nationally chartered bank. On January 1, 1987, it would change the name of its New York branch to Safra National Bank of New York.[382]

After spending several weeks in Europe, Edmond and Lily returned to New York in December, where the social season was in gear. In a busy first week of the month, they had dinner with the designer Valentino, attended a performance of the Strauss opera *Belle Epoque* with Ezra Zilkha and his wife, and hosted a black-tie dinner at their home on Friday night ("If you went to dinner on Friday night, you had to go through the prayers," Ezra Zilkha recalled). On Monday, December 8, they attended the Metropolitan Museum of Art Costume Institute gala, chaired by their close friend Estée Lauder.[383]

During the days in New York, Edmond and his colleagues were also working on an important move to diversify Republic's business. Starting in the early 1970s with Kings-Lafayette, Republic had made opportunistic efforts to increase its deposits by acquiring local banks. Williamsburgh Savings Bank, which traced its origins to 1851, had twelve branches, $2.2 billion in deposits, and an iconic headquarters of its own. The 512-foot-high copper-domed building at 1 Hanson Place in downtown Brooklyn was the borough's tallest building. In the era of deregulation, Williamsburgh boosted interest rates on deposits even as it held mostly long-term fixed assets: about $1.5 billion in mortgages. The ongoing mismatch led to an erosion of the bank's capital basis, and it was on the verge of failure. In November 1986, Jeff Keil wrote George F. Ulich, chairman of the board of Williamsburgh, to continue discussing Republic's proposal for a "constructive, friendly business combination." In late December, a transaction was announced. In what amounted to a rescue deal approved by the FDIC, Republic paid $80 million for Williamsburgh's assets, including its real estate and branches. Republic also agreed to contribute $200 million in common equity capital. When the transaction closed in March 1987, Republic's asset base rose to $18.5 billion, fueled in large part by Williamsburgh's mortgage portfolio.[384]

In the background, as he traveled, Edmond was patiently laying the groundwork for his campaign to open a new bank once his non-compete agreement expired. Opening a bank in Switzerland was a methodical and exacting bureaucratic process that would require the assembling of a new team, the construction of systems, and the foundation of an enabling "service" company. In essence, Edmond was putting the band back together, including many of those who had built TDB. Over the course of 1985 and 1986, colleagues continued to drift away from American Express. Michel Cartillier, for example, had a "Safra clause" in his contract at American Express that permitted him to quit if Edmond did, with a year's notice. In October 1985, Cartillier left, and in January 1986, Republic and Amex signed an agreement authorizing Cartillier to work immediately for Safra and Republic in exchange for a payment of 1 million Swiss francs and an extension of the time American Express had been given to vacate the Place du Lac building that Edmond had bought back from them. On February 1, 1986, Edmond announced he was leaving the American Express board. A month prior, to allay Amex's fears that Republic would quickly pursue clients in Switzerland, Safra agreed with Amex that Republic would pay TDB Amex a penalty on all deposits it took in Switzerland above a cap of $300 million.[385]

In Geneva, work continued on several fronts. In the fall of 1985, Rasmal Finance, which would conduct some of the preliminary organizational work for Edmond's new bank, was founded. Bruno Oriella, Michel Cartillier's assistant at TDB, and distinguished Geneva attorney Jean-Pierre Jacquemoud were among the directors. Rasmal began to hire from the ongoing exodus of TDB people, including Claire Favre, the former director of publicity; Claude Frossard, the director of international accounts; and Hans Hofer, head of information and organization.[386] Other former TDB-American Express employees elsewhere in the world had also been hired to new positions within the Republic empire: Eli Krayem in London, Umberto Treves in Mexico, Mayer Attie in Argentina. Several key executives were hired in Luxembourg and other offices in 1986 and 1987, with the understanding that they'd be transferred to the new bank when it opened. Among them were Jacques Tawil, who had first traveled with Edmond from Beirut to Milan in 1947, and Sem Almaleh.

None of these people were employed directly by Edmond, or in contravention of the agreement with American Express. Republic was not a party to the agreement with American Express and was transparently building up its own international business. Private banking services were still very much in demand, with London a growing center of business. When the "Big Bang" hit London in October 1986, as the London Stock Exchange implemented electronic trading and other regulations were repealed, the city became an even more attractive location. Safra's deputies jumped right in. At its landmark eighteenth-century building in Mayfair, 46 Berkeley Square, Republic's private banking team, many of whom were Arabic speakers, were expanding the company's business in the Middle East and North Africa.[387] (The bank would soon expand to a larger office in a newly purchased building in the city of London, although international private banking remained in Mayfair.)

In October 1986, after Roger Junod and Michel Cartillier submitted the necessary paperwork, the Swiss Federal Banking Commission gave approval to the formation of RENYIS, a service company that would manage Edmond's formal bank application. It set up shop at 2 Place du Lac and was capitalized with 5 million Swiss francs. In January 1987, Hofer, Frossard, and Favre transferred from Rasmal to RENYIS, along with support staff from Safra SA, among them doormen, secretaries, and receptionists. And on May 7, 1987, RENYIS officially deposited its dossier requesting a banking license in Switzerland. Edmond's application listed his and his family's holdings with pride: Republic, the banks in Florida and California, Banco Safra, and BCN.[388]

American Express viewed all these activities with alarm and waged a multipronged effort to stop Edmond and Republic. Its lawyers complained, baselessly, about the employees who had left. Republic lawyer Ernest Ginsberg wrote to Mark Ewald at Amex, "Nothing in Mr. Safra's agreement with American Express precludes this bank from soliciting or lifting your staff. This would be so even with Mr. Safra's participation. But in fact he hasn't participated in those activities because we have chosen not to include him."[389] Indeed, when colleagues would approach Edmond to talk about the progress of the bank, he would often put them off. When Cartillier traveled to Geneva to meet with Edmond in 1986 to ask about his plan, Edmond responded, "I cannot talk about it." Cartillier said: "At least I would like to know if it is a small one or a big one." Edmond replied, "A big one."

On December 3, 1986, the *Tribune de Genève* newspaper reported that a plane Edmond used, which was owned by a Republic New York company, had been chartered in May of that year by US National Security Adviser Robert McFarlane on a secret mission to Iran that became part of the Irangate affair. Never mind that the Republic company that acquired the jet hadn't even been formed until months after McFarlane used it—the retroactive guilt by association was another weapon to be used against Safra.

From the moment he stepped into the world of international finance, Edmond had fiercely protected his personal reputation—both as a matter of honor and as a principle of banking. As a Lebanese Jewish banker in Switzerland, New York, or London, as in Beirut, he knew that maintaining a personal reputation for honesty and running an operation that was beyond reproach was essential. Executives at Republic recalled a conversation after a Colombian client of UBS got into a car accident and was revealed to have suitcases full of cash. "This happens at UBS, it is page twenty. This happens in my bank, it is page one," Edmond said. "There is only one thing I own truly, that is mine: it is my name. Your job is to make sure that there is nothing in my bank that would tarnish that name."

American Express, however, was intent on stopping the new effort. In March 1987, the company filed a criminal complaint, alleging that employees like Hofer, Frossard, and Cartillier had stolen financial files and that Edmond was illegally employing former Amex/TDB personnel. After filing the complaint, American Express told the Swiss Banking Commission about it, urging the commission to refuse the banking license that Republic and Edmond had requested. This was yet another affront against Edmond's honor. "Even without seeing the complaint, Republic can confidently assert that those charges are baseless and without merit," the company responded. And "moreover, unquestionably we would not tolerate in our employ any person not of the highest moral integrity."[390] In a press release, Edmond was justifiably outraged: "This baseless complaint is the most recent underhanded tactic to which American Express has stooped in its campaign to try to intimidate, harass, and threaten my associates and me."

What was really happening? American Express, he explained, was in trouble and was losing customers. American Express, Edmond continued, knows "full well that, as a member of its Board of Directors, I raised very specific issues about the future health of its international banking operations, including the adequacy of its capital. Apparently, American Express is unable to face up to these issues and is fearful of meeting Republic in fair competition in the marketplace."[391] The reality, Edmond and his attorneys argued, was that American Express had known for several years that Republic and Edmond had planned to open a bank in Geneva, and had enabled and encouraged it—by selling the headquarters at Place du Lac and signing an agreement to allow Cartillier to work on it.[392]

Uncowed, Republic continued to execute on its plan to develop a global scale. In June 1987 its Uruguay unit was formally recognized as a bank. In July, it proposed to start a bank in Tokyo, to protect the banknotes business in Asia, and ultimately to develop trading and investment activities. Republic ultimately moved into Japan in the fall of 1987 by acquiring the Tokyo branch of Rainer National Bank. When Hersel Mehani traveled around the world to all of Republic's locations to assist in their switchover to SWIFT, the new payments system, it took three weeks. On Monday, November 16, offices in Nassau, Argentina, Montevideo, Santiago, Los Angeles, Miami, Milan, Guernsey, and Singapore all went live. That fall, Republic was ranked in *Fortune*'s 100 largest banks as the thirty-third largest in assets.[393]

The expansion, of course, exposed Republic to further risks and volatilities. Banks had weathered the emerging market debt crises earlier in the decade, and speculation was bubbling up again in global markets by the fall of 1987. Edmond, who had a sixth sense for danger, was growing concerned. In October, Bear Stearns executive Ted Serure was in Paris and had lunch with Moïse Safra on a Saturday, when Edmond called. Edmond had grown alarmed at trading he had been seeing in the markets. "If I were you, I'd go back tomorrow," Edmond told him. The market crashed on Monday, with the Dow Jones Industrial Average falling nearly 22 percent in a single day.[394]

Amid the turmoil of the 1987 crash, Republic did what it had always done: calmly pressed ahead and focused on safety. In the rapidly changing circumstances, the more conservative approach it had always followed was again a competitive advantage. An ad campaign for Republic in 1987 showed a person climbing a mountain. "Risk is an inescapable part of life," it read. "You cannot evade it, but you can avoid it by choosing a partner whose skill and commitment you can trust." Republic, "a Safra bank," "is a risk-averse institution. . . . Our fundamental principle is the protection of our customer's assets."

Work on the new Swiss bank continued, with Edmond spending much of his time in Europe.[395] Knowing they were going to open a branch in Lugano in 1988, Edmond and Michel Cartillier traveled to the Swiss city to see a building for sale. After they looked at it, Edmond suggested they walk back to the hotel, and they ended up stopping at a café and ordering a beer. Since Edmond hadn't expected to need cash that day and hadn't put any in his pocket (he normally didn't need it), the two of them laughed as Cartillier enjoyed the opportunity to lend him 100 francs.

The plan for the first three years was typically ambitious. They would open simultaneously in Geneva and Lugano. In Geneva, the headquarters at 2 Place du Lac would house management, customer service, and trading, with administrative services in a second building. In the first year, the new bank was projected to have 2,700 customers, and 6,700 by 1990.[396]

Edmond was confident because of the trust he had in his network. As Sem Almaleh recalled, when the noncompete clause approached termination, Edmond would send associates to say: "Let's start a new adventure as Republic." Isaac Obersi, who had first met Edmond in Paris in the late 1940s, recalled, "I would tell clients, 'I'm leaving American Express. I can't tell you where I'm going yet.'"[397]

From his base in Geneva and La Léopolda, Edmond worked the phones, holding court, campaigning to recruit old and new clients. Safra Republic Holdings was formally founded in March 1988. Based in Luxembourg, it was a startup bank. But unlike TDB or Republic at their outset, it was formed from several sources. The plan was for Republic New York to contribute its European operations (France, Luxembourg, Guernsey, and Gibraltar), with capital of $430 million. Edmond would commit a large sum—about $200 million—and the bank planned to raise a further substantial amount in a public offering later that fall. Ironically, Shearson, still an American Express unit, had signed on to be an underwriter for the public offering of Safra Republic. In October 1988, it would raise $490 million in a public offering. Republic New York owned 48 percent, Edmond owned 21 percent directly, and institutional investors would own 31 percent.[398]

The demand was clear and overwhelming. On March 1, 1988, Republic National Bank of New York (Suisse) SA launched in Geneva and Lugano. The building was opened at precisely one minute after midnight, the day the noncompete agreement expired, and clients lined up to open accounts at tables that had been set up in the lobby. Because many clients were eager to have the first account, managers tried to accommodate as many as possible by coming up with numbers like 01, 001, 0001. Three weeks later, the bank hosted a reception at the Intercontinental Hotel in Geneva for 1,000 guests, with people lining up long before the doors officially opened. Edmond, Joseph, and Moïse worked the room, chatting up clients, asking about their business and family. "Edmond came to talk to someone for five minutes, in a friendly way without any pretense, and they left walking backwards," François Curiel recalled. By November 1988, Safra Republic would count total assets of $3.9 billion.[399]

Lily always sought to celebrate Edmond's accomplishments. The convergence of the opening of the new bank and the completion of the renovation of La Léopolda provided an occasion for two grand parties in the summer of 1988. The first, on the evening of August 6—Edmond's birthday—attracted 300 high-society friends: Prince

Rainier of Monaco, the Aga Khan, John Gutfreund, Greek shipping magnate Stavros Niarchos, Barbara Walters, and designers Karl Lagerfeld and Valentino. The guests flocked to the terrace, which had been decorated in the style of Roman ruins, and dined on a meal prepared by the chef Roger Vergé. Guy Béart, the French singer who was a friend from Edmond's days in Beirut, performed.

But that was only half of the party. "People were calling, [asking] 'Are you going to the A party or the B party?'" Peter Cohen recalled. On Monday, August 8, a second party was held for another 300 guests—mostly professional colleagues and longtime friends from around the world, among them Joe Cayre, Stanley Chera, and Albert Manila Nasser. For the second party, set designers from the Paris Opera built a village scene on the terrace. Edmond was in his element, greeting his old friends in several languages, disappearing for a few minutes only to return and present Peter Cohen with a mezuzah he had brought from Israel. The Egyptian entertainer Bob Azzam was performing, and Edmond decided the occasion was joyous enough for him to sing, too. He took the microphone and launched into the traditional Arabic love song "Ah ya zein." "His eyes were shining," recalled Albert Nasser. At 2:00 a.m., Edmond and his old friends were still sitting by the pool, eating spaghetti.[400]

After the tribulations of the American Express years and the immense effort it took to establish a massive new bank, the parties represented something of a catharsis for Edmond, who had always made a practice of keeping his emotions in check when in public. Never content to rest on his laurels, he was at least enjoying a moment to celebrate, looking around in appreciation for his family, his friends, and his accomplishments.

Of course, given the risks in the world and the forces arrayed against his success, Edmond remained wary of calling attention to himself and his triumphs. After attending the first party, Ezra Zilkha, who had known Edmond since their youth in Beirut, posed a question: "Edmond, you and I were brought up to be afraid of the evil eye. Aren't you afraid of the evil eye?" His response: "Yes."[401]

It turned out that Edmond had good reason to fear.

13

A Cruel Year

(1988–1989)

The afterglow of the parties, the launch of Republic in Switzerland, and the late summer at La Léopolda was soon disrupted. On August 31, 1988, *Minute*, a far-right, anti-Semitic Paris newspaper, published an article about the murder of a security consultant, Glenn Souham, who had been investigating the Iran-Contra affair, and veered into alleging that Swiss bankers were laundering drug money, "especially one banker who has two villas on the Riviera and whose ties with Irangate are evident." An adjacent article identified Edmond as "Millionaire of the White Stuff," accusing him of being an associate of arms dealers and the American gangster Meyer Lansky, who had died more than five years earlier. It featured a letter, dated January 29, 1988, to Interpol from the US Embassy in Bern, noting that a Geneva-based lawyer, Willard Zucker, who was entangled financially with Iran-Contra figures, was an associate of Safra's. (Edmond had at one point engaged Zucker to form a few small companies, including one that owned an airplane he had bought in 1905, Zucker also, like tens of thousands of other people, had accounts at Republic.)

The article's thin tissue of facts leavened with innuendos and outright lies was nothing new for Edmond. Over the years, he had continually faced suspicion—because he shipped gold and moved banknotes around the world, because of his background and accent, because of his lasting connections in Lebanon, and because of his banks' unorthodox and highly successful business model. But these new accusations were as insidious as they were outlandish. He summoned an international legal team to La Léopolda, including longtime associates Walter Weiner and Charles-André Junod, and, together with Lily, they began discussing how to react.

When the article appeared, Edmond told a colleague he thought he knew who was behind it: "Son of a bitch. This is American Express." He told Peter Cohen: "This is American Express doing this to me! I smell it." Cohen, who worked for the American Express unit Shearson, told Edmond he was crazy. After all, at that moment, Shearson was preparing to raise hundreds of millions of dollars for Safra Republic in a public offering.[402]

But it did seem as though someone, or some institution, had embarked on a campaign to defame Edmond Safra. This wasn't the first article to appear that made dubious allegations. In January 1988, the Italian newsmagazine *L'Espresso* cited a 1957 report from a US law enforcement agency that seemed to claim that a man named Edmond Safra was involved in morphine trafficking. The publication retracted the article after Edmond's lawyers pointed out that it was wholly false and libelous. Just three weeks before the *Minute* article, on August 13, *La Dépêche du Midi*, a small paper in Toulouse, repeated the unfounded morphine trafficking accusations and mentioned that Latin American newspapers had published similar articles earlier in the year. Those pieces were soon located. On July 4, *Hoy*, an obscure paper in Huánuco, Peru, had published an article about drug traffickers, complete with drug routes: "Safra made his first fortune putting his bank at the disposal of drug traffickers." Five days later, on July 9, the Mexico City tabloid *Unomásuno* ran a very similar story. Clearly, there was a pattern at work among these seemingly random— and personally harmful—reports in four different countries.

And when his integrity was challenged, the normally even-tempered Edmond was stirred to anger. A family's reputation for honesty and honorable behavior was something that was built and protected over generations, and once it was lost, it would take many more generations to repair. For Edmond, anything that sullied the Safra name also sullied the memory of Jacob Safra, the larger Safra clan, and the thousands of colleagues and employees whom Safra regarded as an extended family. Not to mention his wider circle of partners and clients—and potential future partners and clients. When Walter Weiner tried to play down the significance of these articles in fringe publications, Edmond was enraged: "That's my life you're talking about."[403]

Improbable as it seemed, Edmond's instincts were right about the source of the defamation. These articles were the tip of the iceberg— the next battle in the underhanded war American Express had been fighting against Edmond since 1986. At American Express's offices in Geneva and lower Manhattan, there was lasting bitterness over Edmond's 1984 exit from TDB and his intentions to form a new bank in Geneva once the noncompete period ended. And there was a general feeling that Edmond had gotten the better of the giant corporation. In a March 1988 *Institutional Investor* article on Edmond's new venture, American Express executives expressed concern that TDB's many Sephardic customers would soon leave for the new bank. "Edmond has won in so many ways it isn't funny," one former Amex banker put it. "He essentially got [Amex] to recapitalize him and Republic." While he sold the stock, "he's gotten clear of the LDC dreck in TDB's old portfolio, bought back his headquarters and taken his pick of the staffers he really wanted back."[404]

Harry Freeman, a graduate of Harvard Law School who worked on special projects for American Express CEO Jim Robinson, was a shadowy presence at the company. In early 1987 Freeman hired Susan Cantor, a former ABC News staffer with a penchant for conspiracies, as part of the overt—and unsuccessful—campaign to convince the Swiss banking authorities not to give Edmond a license for his new bank. In early 1988, Robinson told associates that American Express would no longer try to stop Edmond from setting up his bank in Geneva. But in fact, later that year Cantor was back in Geneva peddling a dossier of misinformation on Edmond to journalists.[405] Cantor worked closely with an operative named Tony Greco, who had worked with American Express on anti-fraud campaigns over the previous decade. Greco encouraged compliant newspapers around the world to publish false allegations about Edmond. It would take a multinational team of lawyers and investigators working on three continents nearly a year to unravel the tangled web of deception. The drama, pieced together by Bryan Burrough in cinematic detail, first in *Wall Street Journal* articles in 1990 and then in the 1992 book *Vendetta: American Express and the Smearing of Edmond Safra,* was a true-crime saga.

Despite running two banks in his hands-on fashion (three, counting BCN) and looking after his family's other banks, Edmond devoted an enormous amount of time and resources getting to the bottom of the story. Every day, he was on the phone with lawyers in the US, Europe, and South America, and with his outside public relations counsel, Gershon Kekst. Safra had always viewed his business and life as a campaign in which he would enthusiastically, often joyfully, enlist colleagues—to open banks, to recruit customers, to win business. This current effort, however, was motivated by equal parts anger and fear. And the battle had many fronts.

First, he tapped into his vast network. Attorneys reached out to Iran-Contra prosecutor Lawrence Walsh and FBI agents to clear his name regarding the letter sent by the US Bern embassy to Interpol. On October 5, 1988, Walsh wrote that prosecutors had "been unable to confirm either of the allegations referred to in the January 29 letter [the Bern letter] and that the Independent Counsel's investigations of these allegations is closed."[406] Getting to the bottom of the 1957 US government report about Edmond's alleged involvement in the morphine trade took a little more digging. The Geneva police had a letter in their files dated August 21, 1957, in which an American narcotics agent in Rome, Andrew Tartaglino, had asked several agencies, including the Swiss federal police and Interpol, for information on a suspected morphine trafficker named "Edmond Y. Safra." Less than two months later, on October 9, 1957, Interpol informed the Swiss police there was no basis to continue the investigation. In fact, the chief of the Swiss Federal Police, Rudolf Wyss, wrote that Edmond had been mistaken for someone named David Safra, but the mix-up had never been communicated to the Geneva cantonal police.

Edmond's team tracked down Andrew Tartaglino in the United States, who confirmed that his letter was based on a mistake, and Maxwell Rabb, the US ambassador in Rome, wrote in his own letter that he had "asked the Drug Enforcement Administration to check into this matter. They have advised that there is no adverse information concerning Mr. Safra in their files." The letter further noted: "I have also checked the files in this embassy and there is absolutely no information concerning improper activities by Mr. Safra."[407]

Next, Safra sued to defend his honor. Attorney Georges Kiejman, acting on Edmond's behalf, filed suit against *Minute* on October 17, 1988, in Paris, even as the paper and its lead reporter, Jean Roberto, continued to publish ridiculous charges. The same month, *Minute* printed a story under the headline, "In His Villa in Beaulieu He Lives in Panic. The Millionaire Sentenced to Death." The outrageous accusation this time: Edmond had stolen $100 million from the feared Medellin cartel. On Wednesday, October 26, came another *Minute* report: "A Parisian Bank Launders Drug Money." The next week, an article splashed over two inside pages warned, "Safra had better watch out! His silence tends to give complete credence to what has only been up till now a strong presumption of the truth."

Edmond sued *Minute* for libel again, this time arguing for an immediate judgment, to which the court agreed, compelling the newspaper to print the libel judgment in its next editions. But the damage had been done. Edmond remained devastated, and told colleagues he was ever more convinced that American Express was behind it all somehow.[408]

On November 23, the first major break came. As *Minute* attorneys started to present exhibits in the Tribunal de Grande Instance de Paris, they handed over sources that the reporter, Roberto, had used. One of them was a seven-page report with bizarre connections, made-up charts, and phony information illustrating alleged criminal connections—essentially the elements of all the stories that appeared in all the papers. Another was a twenty-page article from *Life* about the American mafia. Kiejman and his colleague Olivier Laude noticed a couple of odd things about the article. First, it was dated 1967—meaning it was more than twenty years old. Second, it had printed writing across the top: "FEB 25 '88 21:25 AMEX CORP COMM * NYC." That indicated the document had been faxed from American Express.

"My eyes popped out of my head," Kiejman recalled. When looking at it more closely, Weiner noticed a second fax telltale—in this instance a British telephone number. It was traced to the American Express London legal department.[409]

But who had sent this document? And why? What were the links between the four papers in France, Peru, and Mexico? These were questions the team pursued even after December 19, when the Paris court ruled that *Minute* had libeled Edmond. Edmond was preoccupied with the efforts. Every day, he would call his nephew Ezy Nasser and his brother Joseph in Brazil, along with all of his other offices. "How are things? How are our clients? Are they leaving us?"[410] Moving in between Paris, Geneva, and La Léopolda in the fall and early winter of 1988, he acted like a quarterback for the legal campaign, even translating for lawyers from different countries during conference calls and meetings. Edmond also continued to gather intelligence from his vast network. One day in December he told his team that the boyfriend of one of the secretaries in the Paris bank had heard from a friend at *Minute* that their source for the stories on Safra was a person named Tony Greco.[411]

The name meant nothing to Edmond or anyone else at Republic. But in early January 1989, Jeff Keil at Republic spoke with Tom Sheer, a former FBI agent, who said that he might know Greco and thought he lived in Staten Island. Next, Ernest Ginsberg chimed in from New York. Ginsberg reported that a man named Victor Tirado had called Republic in Miami and said he had information on a man named Tony Greco who was working for American Express. In February, when Sheer met Tirado in Washington, D.C., Tirado told him that Greco had gone to Peru, and paid to have an article published in *Hoy*. Tirado then asked for $10,000. This wasn't quite proof. But they were on to something.[412]

In the midst of the continued assaults on their integrity, the Safras suffered an immense personal tragedy. On February 17, they received devastating news. Lily's eldest son Claudio, and his four-year-old son, Raphael, had been killed when a drunk driver in a pickup truck collided with their car while they were driving to their weekend home outside Rio. The abrupt and incomprehensible loss was that much harder to bear coming amid a period when the family was under assault. Dropping everything, Edmond and Lily traveled to Brazil to attend the funeral. The rituals of burial and shiva provided an occasion to detach, for the moment, from the troubles stemming from the negative publicity. But they were hardly a respite. For as Edmond was dedicating himself to comforting Lily and the rest of the family, his adversaries continued their shadowy work.

Greco, born in Italy, had spent time in Peru in the 1960s, moved to the US, was repeatedly jailed for criminal activities, and served as a paid FBI informant. But it wasn't clear why he would be peddling false information about Edmond Safra. And there was a sense of urgency to understand, because in the spring of 1989 more articles appeared. *Noticiero*, a Spanish-language Geneva-based newsletter, published a story saying the US Drug Enforcement Agency (DEA) was after Edmond for stealing $40 million in Irangate. Suddenly, it was also happening in Argentina. On March 1, *El Mundo*, a Buenos Aires radio program, broadcast a report saying that the DEA was warning Latin American banks against doing business with Safra. Although Edmond's lawyer got a quick retraction, several other similar reports were aired in Argentina over the weekend. Edmond, hearing the updates in New York, muttered: "Tony is working. Tony is working." For all his resources, connections, and lawyers, Edmond seemed powerless to stop the onslaught of falsehoods and continuing defamation.[413]

On March 9, when Buenos Aires tabloid *Crónica* published a short article tying Edmond and Republic to money laundering, Edmond exploded, and he decided to call Robinson directly. Robinson agreed to come to Edmond's Fifth Avenue apartment that Sunday. Although their exchanges in print and writing had generally been courtly and formal over the last several years, on this occasion Edmond didn't mince words: "I'm concerned that your people are conducting a defamation campaign against me," he snapped.

Robinson was taken aback: "I'd be dumbfounded if that were true."

Edmond responded that he had proof. "I have papers here I can't show you . . . I know everything your people are doing."[414]

For nearly four decades, Edmond Safra had been doing business with people and making decisions about who to lend money to based on personal assessments. And his instincts were finely honed. In the late 1980s, a multimillionaire surgeon and real estate investor who was a prolific foreign currency trader was doing a lot of business with Republic. In April 1989, executives at Republic realized that his position could leave the bank with a heavy exposure and flagged the account. Edmond decided he wanted to meet the investor personally.

When Edmond returned from lunch with him, he was emphatic that Republic stop doing business with the investor. "All throughout the lunch, he never looked into my eyes," Safra said. "My father told me many years ago, if someone does not look into your eyes all the time, don't trust him." He told Dov Schlein: "He's going to disintegrate, and I don't want to be around when he does." After the investor's positions were unwound, he moved his accounts to Salomon. There, between 1989 and 1991, he made thousands of currency trades, betting mostly on Swiss and Australian currencies. He ran up such huge losses that Salomon eventually sued him to recover $25 million.[415]

And now, when Robinson and Edmond shook hands as they left, Edmond looked into the eyes of his former boss, and formed an opinion. "I know Jim is lying," he told Walter Weiner.[416]

Nine days later, on March 21, Robinson called Edmond back. He said he had checked with several top executives, including Harry Freeman and Bob Smith, and they had assured him they had no idea what he was talking about. Harry Freeman told his colleagues that "as far as I know our activities are over."

In the meantime, a small battalion of private investigators were on Greco's tail, following him and retracing his movements. Hank Flynn, a former FBI agent hired by Stanley Arkin, the renowned attorney whom Edmond had retained, had been staking out Greco's house on

Staten Island. Jack Palladino and Sandra Sutherland, a husband-and-wife team from California, posed as reporters and headed to Europe. Tantalizing tidbits began to emerge. In Rome, a reporter at *L'Espresso* said the source for the anti-Safra material was an "Italo-American investigator," but didn't remember the name. On March 28, Jean Roberto of *Minute* told Palladino and Sutherland, "My source is an American," and confirmed that this source had provided him with the bizarre report *Minute*'s lawyers had handed over the previous autumn.[417]

Throughout this period, Republic's customers around the world overwhelmingly stood by the banks. Meanwhile, the misinformation continued to circulate, to be picked up by the unscrupulous, and it seemed impossible to stop. In April, Mottaz aired a report on Swiss television that seemed to implicate Republic and the Shakarchis in money laundering. Judah Elmaleh, a colleague in Geneva, called Edmond the night it aired and replayed the tape over the phone, then sent it on the Concorde so that Edmond could view it the next day.[418] In the first week of May, syndicated columnist Cody Shearer published a rehashing of the *Minute* articles in the Fort Lauderdale *Sun Sentinel*. It was quickly retracted and corrected after the threat of litigation. A Lebanese magazine, *Alkifa Alarabi*, ran an article about arms dealer Adnan Khashoggi, noting that he was friends with the Safras. "It is expected that the US Justice Department will issue a warrant to arrest these . . . partners of Khashoggi momentarily," it said. On May 5, 1989, Jean-Claude Buffle of *L'Hebdo* in Geneva essentially reprinted many of the accusations and cited the prior publications.[419]

Just as the wave of negative articles seemed to be cresting, there came another break in the case. Investigator Hank Flynn, while going through Tony Greco's garbage, found credit card receipts indicating Greco had been in Lima in late February and March. On May 7, Greco traveled to Paris and met with Sophie Hardy, a translator who had been hired by the investigators and had gotten in touch with Greco under a false name. The big break came on May 24, when investigators tailed Greco from his home in Staten Island to American Express's headquarters office in lower Manhattan, where he and a woman went to lunch at the restaurant Bouley. They followed her home to the Upper West Side and learned her name: Susan Cantor.[420]

Greco was on the company's payroll for several months, and executives knew exactly what he was doing. He had first come into the company's orbit when American Express was fighting counterfeit traveler's checks, and American Express London security chief Paul Knight put him in touch with Harry Freeman. As Bryan Burrough described in great detail in *Vendetta*, under the supervision of Cantor, and paid handsomely by American Express, Greco from 1987 to 1989 functioned as a one-man global misinformation campaign. Greco passed along a false tip to the FBI about Edmond's involvement in a $40 million letter of credit scheme to defraud banks in Austria and Switzerland—which made its way into the January 1988 Bern letter.

It was Greco who had delivered the story about the 1957 morphine trade to a reporter at *La Dépêche du Midi*. In the summer of 1988 Greco had worked with his contact Victor Tirado to place the article in *Hoy*. That August, Greco had provided Bertrand and Jean Roberto the *Life* article and the fantastical seven-page document outlining Edmond's alleged misdoings. In December 1988, he had been in Peru, asking Peruvian government press aides to deliver dossiers on Edmond's alleged criminal activities to Lima's international press, and pushing an operative to forge an Associated Press dispatch about Edmond in January 1989.[421]

Having established the explicit link between an operative with links to American Express and the disinformation campaign, Edmond and his colleagues began to turn the tables—taking actions aimed at gaining the attention of senior American Express executives. Stanley Arkin wrote a column in the *New York Law Journal* in early June, in which he said that the American business world was being undermined by "dirty tricks, reminiscent of Watergate." In a thinly veiled reference to American Express, Arkin gave a hypothetical example of a shipping company leaking a story that a competitor's boats were transporting drugs and controlled by the mafia. Such a campaign, he wrote, would constitute mail or wire fraud.[422]

In Geneva, Edmond was still heavily engaged in beating back scurrilous reports. Swiss journalist Philippe Mottaz was working on another alleged exposé, and on June 30, Edmond and Walter Weiner were working on replies to many of his questions. "For more than a year, certain members of the press, oblivious to the facts, seek to publish baseless and malicious articles about Mr. Safra and Republic National Bank of New York," they wrote. "We are at a loss to understand why."[423] Suddenly, the phone rang. It was an indignant Jim Robinson, unaware he was about to walk into a carefully laid trap.

"Hello, Edmond. My people say you're having them followed." Edmond was silent until Robinson stopped talking.

"Jim. I've got you. We've got mountains of evidence of exactly what your people have been doing. Before you hurt me again, Jim, believe me, I will hurt you far worse. I tell you, I have to protect my family, my blood!"

Robinson, stunned, beat a hasty retreat: "I think I'd better talk to my people and call you back."[424]

Robinson deputized Peter Cohen at Shearson to try to work things out and hired a former federal prosecutor, James Martin, to conduct an investigation. Stanley Arkin came to La Léopolda that weekend, entering a typical scene: several grandchildren swimming in the pool, Joseph Safra visiting from Brazil, and Sandy Weill having come for dinner. During the meal, Walter Weiner, Arkin, and Edmond shuttled back and forth from the table to the home office, where they were talking with Peter Cohen by phone. Upon his return to New York, Arkin met with Martin. And when Martin probed to see what precisely the Safra team knew, Arkin said two words that landed like a ton of bricks: "Tony Greco."[425]

That was it. Over the next few weeks, American Express lawyers met daily with Martin and Ken Bialkin. Republic could have used the incident to cause immense trouble for a blue-chip, publicly held company like American Express. But the only thing that mattered to Edmond was a public apology that would clear his name—he never asked for a penny in damages, nor any reimbursement of the estimated $4 million he had spent on lawyers and investigators while defending himself. In a single terse phone call between Edmond and Robinson, they agreed that Amex would publicly apologize and pay a total of $8 million to four charities Edmond had selected: United Way of America, the Anti-Defamation League of B'nai B'rith, the Geneva Cantonal Hospital, and the International Committee of the Red Cross.

On July 24, 1989, Robinson issued an apology worth quoting at length:

> Dear Edmond,
> Information has come to my attention that certain persons acting on behalf of American Express began an unauthorized and shameful effort to use the media to malign you and Republic National Bank of New York. I recently saw media stories which appeared in various parts of the world following this effort, and I regard them as untrue and defamatory. The entire matter saddens me personally. This effort was totally contrary to the standards of conduct of American Express as well as common standards of decency and ethics. . . . Therefore, I want to apologize to you and your organization. You have a well-deserved excellent personal and professional reputation, and you and Republic National Bank of New York are highly regarded throughout the world. Your reputation as a preeminent banker has been achieved with enormous effort over a lifetime, and so I appreciate even more how painful it must have been for you to endure these baseless attacks.[426]

The letter was released to the public on July 28, on a Friday afternoon—a classic move to avoid attention. American Express announced that it was giving only $4 million to the charities Edmond had named—half the actual number.

Thus ended one of the more bizarre and inexplicable chapters in American corporate history and a particularly painful chapter in Edmond Safra's life. The post-scandal internal investigation that American Express initiated cleared Robinson of wrongdoing. But as

Bryan Burrough pieced together the story, first for the *Wall Street Journal* in September 1990 and then for his book, other details emerged. Burrough concluded that in the summer of 1988 Cantor and Greco acted on implicit rather than explicit orders from Freeman and Robinson. Harry Freeman, who admitted to mistakes having been made, let it be known that he briefed senior executives about the operation. In the wake of the scandal, Cantor kept her job at the bank—and got a $200,000 bonus.[427]

The apology, and the attendant vindication, came almost one year to the day after the triumphant parties at La Léopolda. The year's events had scarred Edmond in a profound way. As he was under continuous siege, it was difficult for him to enjoy his family and his work. Between the barrage of assaults in the press and the overwhelming sadness from the passing of Claudio and Raphael, it had been a cruel season. And it certainly took a lot out of him. For the moment, at least, his buoyant spirit was weighed down. "I saw him in the bank after," recalled Fred Bogart. "He looked like a guy who had aged fifty years in the last two years. There was no sparkle in his eye."

For nearly a year, recalled Dov Schlein, "it completely distracted him. We were not in the banking business, we were fighting a fire."[428]

In fact, however, Edmond and Republic were still very much in the banking business.

14

Back to Work

(1989-1991)

The American Express affair took an immense personal toll on Edmond—but a remarkably muted professional one. Despite the continuing stream of bad press, customers and clients did not shy away from doing business with the Safra family of banks or entrusting their savings to them. Quite the opposite. And the precise development that American Express had aimed to forestall with its baroque campaign of intrigue—the rapid global growth of Republic—quickly came to fruition.

Sticking to its decades-old philosophy of matching cheap US deposits to safe assets around the world, Republic avoided the problems that plagued the banking industry as the go-go era of the 1980s came clattering to an end. In 1989 and 1990, the vast US financial complex was beset by carnage in the real estate industry, soured leveraged buyouts, and a collapsing junk-bond market. But Republic, despite its size, simply didn't play in those markets: loans accounted for only $6.7 billion of its $21 billion of assets in 1989. As other big banks were licking their wounds, Republic's tally of nonperforming assets stood at a mere $23 million at the end of 1989.

Edmond, the global private banker who rubbed shoulders with finance ministers and international bankers, was also intent on remaining a neighborhood banker to New York's vast middle class. No sooner did the American Express matter begin to die down than

Republic sought to gain more deposits in its own backyard. Since acquiring Williamsburgh Savings Bank in 1987, Republic had transformed the unit into a highly profitable operation with $2.6 billion in deposits. In December 1989, Williamsburgh moved to acquire a historic local rival. Manhattan Savings Bank, which traced its origins to 1860, had seventeen branches, eight of them in Manhattan, one in Queens, and eight in Westchester. In December 1989, Williamsburgh agreed to buy Manhattan Savings, and its $2.8 billion in deposits, for $200 million in stock. The move boosted Republic's deposit total to $16.8 billion, making it the twenty-sixth-largest bank in the US.[429]

Safra Republic Holdings, the parent company of existing Republic European banks and newly established offices, was a more traditional private bank focused on the European market, which Edmond had been working in since the 1940s. By the end of 1989, just twenty-one months after formally opening, Safra Republic's banks had $3.2 billion in assets. Because he spent much more time in Geneva and Europe than he did in the US, and because he had a formal operational role at Safra Republic, Edmond was a greater presence at the smaller, more intimate new bank than he was at Republic in New York. On December 19, 1989, he presided over the RNB Geneva traditional year-end cocktail reception at the Hotel Le Richemond, which more than 150 employees attended. To a large degree, he was consciously re-creating the family feel of TDB. "I have known some of you for many years, and I am looking forward to getting to know all of you better," Edmond wrote in the first issue of the Safra Republic newsletter, in June 1990, next to a picture of him smiling broadly, glasses in hand. "Do help us become an even closer family."[430]

From his teens, Edmond had always looked older than his age, and in his late fifties he presented an image of a paterfamilias of the Safra clan, of thousands of employees, of tens of thousands of depositors (whose savings he personally guaranteed), and of hundreds of thousands of Sephardic Jews around the world. Since the time he had provided refrigerating equipment to the Alliance Israélite Universelle in Paris in 1948 at age sixteen, Edmond had tended to the needs of Sephardic communities throughout the world, whether they were struggling in their historical homes, such as Aleppo and Beirut, or trying to carve out new lives in Europe, South America, the United States, or Israel. Now he was able to do so not just by writing checks but by working through his connections. By the late 1980s, only a handful of Jews remained in the Arab world outside Israel, which made it all the more important to protect their fragile legacy. In 1989, the Egyptian government was planning to build a road that would run through the Bassatine cemetery. Tracing its origins to the 900s, Bassatine was believed to be the oldest continuously operating Jewish cemetery in the world. Needing assistance in the US Senate to put pressure on Egypt, Clement Soffer, an Egyptian native whose synagogue in Brooklyn Edmond had supported years before, asked for help. Edmond invited Soffer to the Republic reception at the IMF meeting in Washington in September 1989. "Come stand next to me and you will see a parade of senators," Edmond told him. At the reception, he introduced Soffer to New Jersey Senator Frank Lautenberg with a slight exaggeration: "Frank, please help my cousin Clement Soffer." The Egyptian government ultimately got funds to build a bridge over the cemetery, and the World Sephardic Federation raised funds to build a protective wall around Bassatine.[431]

While he worked to protect the dignity of others, Edmond was still enduring the effects of what he regarded as the greatest assault on his own dignity. The lies and innuendo that American Express's agents had disseminated still circulated freely in the global stream of information and media. Much of the reporting of the Geneva newspaper *L'Hebdo*, published in May 1989, found its way into a book about money laundering by Jean Ziegler, a member of the Swiss parliament, titled *La Suisse Lave Plus Blanc*, which was published in February 1990. (The title translates to *Switzerland Washes Whiter*.) Once again, George Kiejman sued on behalf of Edmond. In April 1990, the Tribunal de Grande Instance in Paris entered a judgment finding that the book defamed Edmond, awarding a 150,000 French franc (about $30,000) judgment and a promise to remove those details from the book. And as press reports occasionally surfaced connecting Republic to money laundering, the lawyers had to remain vigilant. Jean Hoss, the bank's Luxembourg-based attorney, wrote to Pierre Jaans, director-general of the Luxembourg banking regulator, in the fall of 1990: "It is clear that the effects of the American Express defamation campaign continue to this day to spread like a disease which cannot be halted." As for *L'Hebdo*, the litigation remained open. [432]

But by the summer of 1990, a year after American Express's dramatic apology, Edmond and Lily were largely free to enjoy their busy life. Although they traveled a great deal, moving between their apartments in Geneva, Monaco, Paris, London, and New York, it was La Léopolda, which had become a base of operations and a haven during the American Express affair, that came to feel like a family home. Edmond spent most of the summer at the idyllic mansion in the hills above the Mediterranean, visited by friends and colleagues, and housing an expanding number of rambunctious grandchildren. By 1990, Lily's daughter, Adriana, and her husband, Michel Elia, had four young children: Samuel (born in 1981), David (born in 1982), Lily (born in 1985), and Ariel (born in 1987). The Elias would also welcome their nephew Gabriel Cohen (Claudio's son, born in 1987) into their family, after his mother's passing in 1992.

From his office overlooking the sea, or equipped with his telephone at the side of the pool, Edmond could monitor events around the world while enjoying time with his family and friends. In the meantime, the world could come to him. In the summer of 1990, Elie Wiesel came to stay from August 17 to August 24. When ISEF, the scholarship program for Sephardic students in Israel that Edmond and others had founded, held its "Bar Mitzvah" thirteenth anniversary fundraiser, the couple served as honorary co-chairs. At the end of August, Edmond and Lily made a quick trip to Norway. By September 11, the summer season over, they were back in Geneva, hosting a dinner for twenty at their apartment on Rue de Moillebeau. [433]

With rare exceptions, the attacks of the year before had not sundered the personal relationships Edmond and his family had built up over the years. And as his circle of contacts continued to expand, adding customers and clients around the world, Edmond took pains to bolster his banks' defenses. The flip side of discretion and privacy, so much a part of traditional banking culture, was that there was a certain amount that banks would not—and could not—know about their customers. And around the world, money from drug trafficking and other illicit activities coursed through the legitimate banking system. So Republic redoubled its efforts to install know-your-customer and anti–money laundering programs throughout the banks.

In September 1990, Anne Vitale, a former US attorney who specialized in prosecuting money laundering, joined Republic as managing director and deputy general counsel. Edmond told her, "I am so happy that you have joined us; you have a very important job." She made her first trip to Geneva to help the US Drug Enforcement Agency make a case against a suspect who had been using a safe-deposit box. In Switzerland, Republic held internal training seminars and sponsored a conference at the Swiss National Bank on combating money-laundering. In 1991, Republic also brought in money-laundering expert Charles Morley, a former Treasury agent and expert, who was immediately impressed with how the banks were run. "I found [Republic's] procedures to be far more effective and extensive than any I had ever heard of," Morley told Bryan Burrough.[434]

Edmond invested a great deal in rebuilding his reputation and image in Switzerland. Typically press shy, he could nonetheless turn on the charm when it suited him. In September 1990, he sat down for an interview with Anne M. Hegge-Lederman, editor of the Zurich-based financial newspaper *Finanz und Wirtschaft*, as part of a campaign to raise new capital for Safra Republic. He spun the oft-told tales of going to clients when he was seven or eight, repeated the philosophy he had imbibed on the streets of Beirut from his father, and proclaimed Jacob's motto: "If you choose to sail upon the seas of banking, build your bank as you would your boat, with the strength to sail safely through any storm." Maintaining his good standing in Switzerland mattered a great deal. "Geneva has been the center of my banking activities for almost my entire life. In almost every way, Geneva is the best environment that I know for banking," he said.[435]

His assets were certainly concentrated there. Safra Republic Holdings, of which he directly owned 20 percent, was growing rapidly, and in Edmond's own image. "The traditional assets of a bank are not loans, securities, or premises, but rather persons wishing to shelter their savings against the unpredictable tide of the times," he wrote in Safra Republic's 1990 annual report. "Similar to the basic laws in effect in 2000 BC, when credit was only granted to those who acknowledge full responsibility of their debt, conservatism dictates that prudent banks do not indulge in over-lending." Indeed, commercial loans were just 15 percent of the bank's assets, and nonperforming loans represented less than 1 percent of total loans in 1990. And whereas most European and US banks had a 60 percent ratio of loans to deposits, Safra Republic's was only 19 percent.

By June 30, 1990, Safra Republic had 500 employees and $6 billion in deposits, with a goal of reaching $10 billion. For its part, the Republic New York 1990 annual report—its landmark twenty-fifth— echoed a similar theme: "A tradition of safety." Reporting record net income of $201 million, the bank presented itself as an entity that, despite its size—$15 billion in deposits and $22.8 billion in assets— remained at its core a family operation. It included a picture of Hersel Mehani, the Egypt-born lending executive "who has been with us since 1968," and who was joined at the bank by his father and two brothers. "Collectively, the Mehanis now represent 71 years of Republic experience."[436]

Despite the fealty to tradition, the Safra banks were in fact evolving from their set ways of doing business. The convulsions that had spurred so many people in Edmond's orbit to flee from Iran, Iraq, Syria, Lebanon, Egypt, and Morocco had largely ended. The Sephardic diaspora had settled down; people were building new lives on more solid footing throughout Europe, the US, and South America. The traditional customers, not to mention the legions of new customers, were no longer interested in simply shielding flight capital and preserving assets. Like other well-heeled people, they wanted investment advice, the potential for growth, and exposure to stock markets. One clear area in which private banks were branching out was asset management, setting up mutual funds or other vehicles in which clients could invest.

Edmond had never particularly cottoned to the idea, in part because he still didn't like being in the position of recommending risky investments to clients. Of course, there was one stock he recommended heartily: Republic's. Between 1966 and June 1990, Republic's stock rose a stunning thirty-four-fold, compared with a fivefold increase in the S&P 500 bank index. At the end of 1989, Edmond owned 32.4 percent of the corporation's common stock.

Beyond shares of the institutions he and his family controlled, Edmond preferred the solidity of real estate. An accounting of his net worth in late 1989 showed the stakes in Republic and Safra Republic, BCN in Beirut (worth 4.9 million Lebanese pounds, or about 13,690 Swiss francs), plus the small Safra banks he had founded in Los Angeles and Miami. He also owned most of the large apartment block on Rue de Moillebeau in Geneva in which he and Lily lived. For his personal account, Edmond had been amassing office and residential buildings along Geneva's waterfront promenade, including the prestigious Quai du Mont Blanc.[437] And of course, there was art and furniture.

But Edmond understood that his clients had different prerogatives and needs for their personal investments than he did, and that his banks had to evolve in some way to meet their changing investing preferences. And so he went about offering investment funds in a typical way for him: by partnering with another member of the Sephardic financial network.

Gilbert de Botton, born in Alexandria in 1935 and the descendant of a well-known Sephardic Talmudist, had moved to Zurich in 1968 to work for the Rothschilds. In 1983, backed in part by Jacob Rothschild, he set up Global Asset Management (GAM), which placed high-net-worth investors' funds in vehicles around the world. "In September we are starting a joint venture with one of the leading European money managers, Mr. Gilbert de Botton, in a new equity fund whose shares we will offer our clients: Republic GAM," Edmond proudly told *Finanz und Wirtschaft* in September 1990. In effect, GAM agreed to set aside a portion of its portfolio for Republic clients. This was really one of the first times Edmond had agreed to commit his customers' funds to entities he didn't control and could not guarantee, and that didn't formally reside on his banks' balance sheet.[438]

In 1990, Safra began exploring a territory for his banking investments that was both new and, in some ways, deeply familiar. While he had long supported Israeli religious and social institutions, and had started to visit regularly in the 1980s, Edmond had generally kept his commercial ties anonymous, in part because he didn't want to complicate life for the dwindling Jewish community in Lebanon. In 1986 Jacques Nasser, a cousin of Dr. Rahmo Nasser, Edmond's sister Eveline's husband, purchased a controlling stake in FIBI (First International Bank of Israel) from the bankrupt Danot Investments for $21 million. The Safras never commented on the media reports that repeatedly hypothesized that Nasser was in fact representing Edmond—which was true. (Nasser never played an active role in the bank's affairs.)[439] Yehuda Levi, a fellow Beiruti who worked at Republic, suggested that Edmond and his brothers invest in the bank. Before the purchase, Levi went with Tzadik Bino, the Iraqi-born CEO of FIBI, to Paris to make a presentation to Edmond, Joseph, and Moïse in Edmond's apartment—and earned a gentle reprimand for putting a presentation board on one of Lily's Louis XIV chairs.[440]

But by 1990, the last of the Jews of Beirut had fled. Wadi Abu Jamil lay in ruins, and the Magen Avraham synagogue hadn't been used in several years. Edmond still owned BCN, but it was barely functioning. With the civil war finally drawing to a close but Syria continuing to exercise its dominance over Lebanon, there could be no return to Aley, Al-Ajami, and the St. George Hotel. But just to the south, Israel's economy was growing and reforming. And the Safras were increasingly interested in taking a more active and visible role in the country's financial sector. In late 1990, Moïse and Joseph Safra formally decided to step out in public as the owners of FIBI: that November, they had bought the controlling interest in the bank from Jacques Nasser. But, as with all the family's banks, regardless of who actually owned the shares, this investment was clearly a family endeavor. "*Alf Mabrook* [congratulations] for the acquisition," Yehuda Levi wrote to Edmond on November 16, 1990.[441]

Israel emerged as a new node in the network. Edmond would frequently call FIBI's CEO, Shlomo Piotrkowski, on Friday, to say "Shabbat Shalom" and to talk about the bank and the economy. And now Edmond could freely circulate in an area where the climate, food, and language evoked his native Beirut. Edmond and Lily would land at Ben Gurion Airport, the old Lod airfield from which Edmond and Jacques Tawil had departed in 1947, and make their way to the King David Hotel in Jerusalem, where an executive ensured there would always be a platter of baklava and pistachios. A stream of visitors would come through—rabbis seeking donations, ministers of finance, friends from Beirut, and new associates. On May 14, 1991, Edmond, Moïse, and Joseph met in Israel and held a reception at the Dan Tel Aviv Hotel in honor of the FIBI acquisition. Their first official public appearance in Israel was both a reunion and a formal, highly visible statement that the Safras were investing in the country.[442]

While he sat atop an ever-larger enterprise, whose global activities sprawled and expanded, Edmond continued to wade into the details of his operations. Shlomo Piotrkowski remembered being in Edmond's office while he was on the phone with a dealer in Hong Kong who had racked up a trading loss. "Why are you such a *hamor*?" (Arabic for a stupid person, literally *donkey*), Edmond yelled at him. Recalled Piotrkowski, "He took it like he had lost all his fortune."[443]

The attention to detail carried over into the continuing efforts to clear his name. In 1991, even as the banks had largely put the American Express affair behind them and were looking to the future, Edmond was still devoting significant time and resources to the ongoing legal campaign. The remaining outstanding litigation was against the Geneva publication *L'Hebdo*. The road map for the case had been laid out in the prior legal efforts. But Anne Vitale came over from New York in the summer of 1991 to help lead the charge. She traveled to Italy, and with the manager of the Milan office, Claudio Grego, tracked down the records relating to the 1957 mistaken identity memo and got a judge to sign an order giving Edmond and Republic a clean record in August 1991. When she took over a boardroom at Place du Lac to prepare for the trial, which was poised to start in the fall,

Edmond looked on approvingly: "Anne, this is wonderful; it looks like you are getting ready for war."[444]

That war was continuing because, two years after the scandal had been exposed, Edmond's lawyers still couldn't get a full accounting from American Express about the depth of their campaign. Tony Greco was arrested in Spain in June 1991, but he wasn't interested in speaking. (Several months later, when Walter Weiner and Bryan Burrough approached him separately, Greco demanded $1 million in exchange for telling his story.) Edmond refused to let it go. An active participant in his defense, he wrote his old nemesis Jim Robinson on August 1, 1991, asking for help in gathering information about Greco and Cantor's activities to be used in the *L'Hebdo* trial. "I regret to tell you that, two years later, I must continue to deal with the widespread consequences of that defamation campaign."[445]

The trial at Geneva's courthouse in November 1991 ultimately provided a measure of catharsis and closure. The Safra legal team was armed with the truth, and with voluminous evidence of the fraud that had been perpetrated. Edmond showed up every day and watched as his attorneys systematically knocked down the allegations in the reporting. When *L'Hebdo* defended itself by citing information from other published sources, attorney Marc Bonnant thoroughly dismantled them. Ultimately, editor Jean-Claude Buffle acknowledged that he had relied on the three fake dispatches from Peru that were published on January 17, 1989. Three times, Bonnant dramatically noted: "It is . . . a fake." Edmond's lawyers called Andrew Tartaglino, the American narcotics agent who wrote the 1957 memo, as well as money-laundering expert Charles Morley. But it was the final witness who provided the most powerful testimony. Late on a Friday afternoon, with the sun having already set over the mountains, Elie Wiesel took the stand as a character witness for Edmond. "I should have respected the Sabbath," Wiesel told the courtroom. "But to save the life of a man, it is permitted to transgress. And the honor of Edmond Safra, that is his life." He recounted how they had first met at a ceremony in Auschwitz, and spoke of the toll that the false campaign took on Edmond. "I saw him suffering. After all, what remains of a man after his death? Not his money. It is his name, his reputation, his honor."[446]

The court ultimately ruled for Edmond on December 17, putting to rest the legal efforts aimed at clearing his name. But even then, Edmond wasn't quite finished. On December 2, 1991, he wrote to Robinson, copying the board of directors of American Express, suggesting that the internal investigation the company had conducted was a cover-up. "Your withholding of information [for the *L'Hebdo* trial] is an unforgivable manifestation of a continuing effort to cause harm to me, my family, and my banks. It is clear by what is going on that the despicable effects of the American Express campaign have not been stopped. You say the matter is closed. Closed? For whom? Certainly not for us. And if not for us, it cannot be closed for American Express."

Robinson responded quickly, calling the allegations preposterous.[447] But when Bryan Burrough published *Vendetta* in June 1992, it backed up Edmond's claims. By December 1992, Robinson was out.

In his speech, whether he was talking about moves in the market or a development in his personal life, Edmond would routinely drop Hebrew and Arabic phrases such as *"Baruch Hashem"* ("Thank God," expressing gratitude for God's blessing), *"Inshallah"* ("God willing"), *"Has veshalom"* ("God forbid"), *"Salli ala Moshe"* ("Pray to Moses"), *"Hashem yishmor"* ("God protect us"), and *"Allah yilhimna al kheir"* ("May God inspire us to do well"). When Marc Bonnant asked Edmond if he really believed in an intervening deity looking on his daily endeavors and worrying about the price of the dollar, Edmond would smile wryly. "[His explanation] was more that God had accorded him his protection and benevolence in his everyday life, and that as a result he had a duty to continually thank and give back," Bonnant recalled.[448] That same duty carried over to the need to be ever vigilant in protecting his good name. For in the world that Edmond occupied, even though the Federal Deposit Insurance Corporation might stand behind Republic, it was ultimately the Safra name that stood behind the network's vast deposits, savings, and financial obligations. Edmond could not imagine a situation in which one of his banks might turn to the government for assistance, support, or a bailout—as the savings and loan industry was doing in the United States. And so any effort to undermine his name threatened the viability of a multigenerational family enterprise. As 1992 dawned, and his sixtieth birthday approached, Edmond felt that he had come through a quasi-biblical period of testing and trials.

Further trials awaited.

15

A Traditional Banker
in a Time of Change

(1992–1994)

By 1992, the Sephardic diaspora in the Middle East had essentially dissipated. The world of the Alliance was no more, save the depleted community in Iran and the remnants of the original and most enduring presence in the Middle East. In Aleppo and Damascus, a few thousand Jews were held prisoner by dictator Hafez el-Assad, unable to travel freely or leave, subject to arrest and torture by the secret police.

For decades, Edmond Safra had personally supported the remaining community trapped in Aleppo and Damascus, sending money and providing moral support. Finally, ferment in the region connected to the Gulf War, and the sudden prospects of peace between Israel and its neighbors, created an opportunity for change. Members of the Syrian diaspora, prosperous and firmly rooted in Brooklyn, now had the political clout to make their relatives' plight a consistent point on the US political agenda. Here, again, Edmond Safra's long-standing relationships came in handy. The Council for the Rescue of Syrian Jews enlisted Edmond, and together they worked with contacts in Congress to get a resolution passed in the US House of Representatives directing the George H. W. Bush administration to raise the issue with the Assad regime. President Bush did so directly with Assad in their groundbreaking meeting in Geneva in November 1990, and Secretary of State James Baker repeatedly pressed the point with Assad in Damascus. Syria's participation in Desert Storm, the US-led operation launched in January 1991 to eject Saddam Hussein from Kuwait, and Syria's significant financial needs, provided new points of contact and leverage. As advocates testified before Congress, Edmond personally lobbied the IMF to reject Syria's request for an $850 million loan. At the Madrid Peace Conference in October 1991, leaders from Israel, Syria, Jordan, and other countries met for the first time.

The breakthrough finally came on April 28, 1992, when Assad told the US he would let the remaining 4,500 Syrian Jews leave the country—although they wouldn't be permitted to go to Israel. As the Council for the Rescue of Syrian Jews, the Jewish Agency, and the Jewish National Fund swung into action, Edmond was intimately involved. Assad wanted those leaving to purchase round-trip tickets, giving the illusion to his own people that they might return. When Clement Soffer, representing the Council for the Rescue of Syrian Jews, told Edmond they needed $3 million for plane tickets, Edmond called his travel agency. "Please do me a favor: issue tickets, round-trip tickets, for 4,000 people."[449]

It was a bittersweet moment, as the last of the native-born Halabis packed their bags and bid farewell to Aram Tzova—likely for the last time. Next, the Syrian community in the US turned to the United Jewish Appeal (UJA), the powerful umbrella establishment group, for funds to help the new immigrants resettle. When Edmond learned that the UJA was not prepared to give the $21 million requested, he reminded a senior UJA official that he had just made a $10 million donation. Upset at what he perceived as yet another slight by institutional Jewish groups against his fellow Sephardic Jews, Edmond suggested he might ask for his donation back and said that in the future, "I will be sure to focus my funding on the needs of the Sephardic community and their institutions." Soon after, Edmond told Clement Soffer that the UJA would have a $21 million check for him. Next, Edmond instructed Hillel Davis, head of human resources at Republic, "400 Syrian Jews are coming to New York. Hire five of them to start." A dentist was put to work in the gold vault, and another new arrival was taught enough English to become a messenger.[450]

The cold entente with Syria was a manifestation of a larger trend. The world was opening in new ways in the early 1990s, as trade and travel barriers crumbled. The fall of the Soviet Union brought down borders in Eastern Europe. China was beginning to join the global economy. (On July 13, 1992, Republic opened a representative office in Beijing.) The passage of NAFTA was set to create a vast new free-trade zone between Mexico, Canada, and the US. Even Brazil's long-sheltered economy began to open up. The unmistakable trend was toward greater financial and commercial integration.

These were all positives for the global economy, the trading system, and the financial world. And yet the greater harmonization and lowering of barriers would also reduce the opportunities for arbitrage. Since his teens, Edmond Safra had thrived on his intuitive ability to work the seams of fraying empires and spheres of influence, to figure out how to trade between closed and open areas, and to lubricate the world's financial engine. With the savings and loan crisis behind them, and the memory of the Great Depression receding further, regulators in the US, the world's largest financial services market, were now proving more willing to sanction the idea of banks expanding rapidly into adjacent areas. The Glass-Steagall Act, the Depression-era law that had separated investment and commercial banks for two generations, was slowly eroding. Paradoxically, this world of lower interest rates and relative stability would bring new challenges to Edmond Safra's financial empire.

The environment was simply different from what it had been 20 years earlier, when Edmond and his colleagues had gone from door to door as part of their successful effort to buy Kings Lafayette. "We had described ourselves as traditional bankers in times of change," Jeff Keil said of Republic at the time. "But the change has accelerated so much that we cannot be totally traditional anymore." Republic and Safra Republic had first started to offer consumers investment products with the launch of the fund business in 1990. The next logical step for a New York–based institution like Republic was to move into other aspects of the securities business.[451]

Of course, Edmond knew this area quite well; he had been inter-
acting with investment banks since his twenties. But he had always
been leery of this world, with its high salaries and greater acceptance
of risk. Still, encouraged by Peter Cohen, he signed off on a strategy
to play with the larger establishments on their turf. The brash young
executive, who had left Shearson in January 1990, sold Edmond on
the idea of building up a securities operation—one that would provide
brokerage, research, and additional services to hedge funds and other
institutions. In November 1991, Louis Lloyd, who had worked with
Cohen at Shearson, was hired as president and chief executive of the
new unit, Republic New York Securities, which started with forty-five
employees and $100 million in capital. Cohen was named vice chair-
man and a director.

On October 9, 1992, the Federal Reserve approved Republic's
application to engage in securities-related activities. The unit would
engage in prime brokerage, securities borrowing and lending, margin
lending, third-party research, and vendor services for institutions and
wealthy individuals. It would also, Cohen thought, provide synergies
with Republic's asset management unit. "There is a crying need within
the Republic organization to come up with investment management
capability and products to service high-net-worth clients and the
800,000 retail accounts that are in our branch system," Cohen said.[452]

This approach marked a major departure for Republic. Those
clients who wished to assume greater risks would be linked up with a
rapidly growing constellation of money managers, investment bankers,
and hedge funds. A similar evolution was taking place at Safra
Republic, which continued to grow; by the end of 1992 it had $10.4
billion in assets and employed 540 people, including 350 in Geneva
and an increasing number in the rising private banking center of
Monaco. By the middle of 1993, Safra Republic and its partner Global
Asset Management were running seventeen funds with a total of $4.3
billion in off-balance-sheet client funds. At the end of 1993, it was
preparing to launch two new funds, the Republic Salomon Fixed
Income Strategies Fund (an open-ended fund) and Republic Long
Term Capital Holdings. The latter was a vehicle set up to hold shares

in a hedge fund backed by numbers whiz John Meriwether, which was promoted by Merrill Lynch. The fund, which used proprietary data and algorithms to make huge bets on the direction of markets, had a $10 million requirement for institutions or individuals; Republic clients, however, could invest as little as $1 million, provided they were willing to lock up the investment for three years.

By any measure, the banks were thriving. By the fall of 1993, the *Financial Times* listed Safra Republic Holdings as one of the 500 largest companies in Europe, at #361. For its part, Republic New York's market capitalization had risen from $11 million in 1966 to $2.68 billion in 1993, representing a remarkable annualized growth of 22.6 percent over 27 years. One analyst noted in 1993, "Mr. Safra and his team know how to build liability-driven banking institutions." The question now was whether that approach would be as effective in the coming five years as it had been in the previous five years.[453]

In the same way that he had been skeptical of American Express's efforts to pitch platinum cards and magazine subscriptions to his valued customers, Edmond didn't wholeheartedly embrace the new direction. The concept of off-balance-sheet funds—meaning the bank wasn't ultimately liable for what happened to them—was alien to Edmond. Whether he was operating in Beirut, Geneva, or New York, he always considered himself responsible for his clients if something went wrong, even if it was in the markets. When one Republic fund dropped in value by about 20 percent a few weeks after launching, Edmond, against the advice of his colleagues, determined that the clients who invested should be made whole with $20 million of the bank's money.

In 1993, Republic bought Mercadian Capital, a municipal and corporate derivatives boutique that was charged with helping hedge funds and private banking customers create contracts with counterparties in order to speculate on market movements. Derivatives represented a calculated bet that a counterparty would honor a contract if certain conditions were met. But investors never really knew who precisely was on the other side of the contract. Edmond could discount a note, or extend credit, based on his knowledge of the person or the family—and price the loan accordingly. "He knew everybody he owed money to, and he knew everybody who owed money to him," said Kenneth Cooper. But Edmond recognized that derivatives were different. "You will bring me people who understand both mathematics and risk at the highest possible level," he told Dov Schlein, "because I need to communicate with them and talk to them and understand." Still, the prospect of customers taking on risk remained deeply unsettling to Edmond. When Peter Cohen's team traveled to Brazil to meet with Banco Safra clients, Edmond fretted that it would embarrass his brothers if clients were to lose money. So he sent Sandy Koifman from Safra Republic Holdings to pitch more conservative Safra funds in tandem.[454]

His heart was never in these new businesses, in part because he believed their standard compensation structure, which differed so much from traditional banking, would lead these new employees to take bigger and bigger short-term risks in exchange for huge bonuses. In contrast, when in 1993 Republic hired Harvard Business School professor Michael Porter to advise on strategy, Edmond enthusiastically seized on his main recommendation: expand the private banking business for US clients. Republic hired Leslie Bains from Citibank that October and charged her with building up a unit from scratch that would serve people with $10 million or more to deposit. This was a business Edmond was willing to commit to and invest in. "I do not expect it to be profitable for five years," he told Bains.[455]

Meanwhile, Republic continued to invest in the core, traditional Safra businesses. In 1993, Republic folded in Safrabank California, the three-branch bank Edmond had established, renaming it Republic Bank California, and bought Citibank's banknote shipping service.[456] And Edmond still viewed New York's neighborhoods as fertile ground for collecting deposits. Greenpoint Savings Bank, the nation's largest independent savings bank, had some $6.5 billion in assets in branches dotted in blue-collar neighborhoods in Brooklyn and Queens. When it announced its plans to demutualize and ultimately go public, Edmond asked the board if it instead wanted to sell to Republic. After being turned down, Edmond offered incentives to depositors if they would agree to support a merger with Republic. Ultimately, in a rare setback, the transaction was shot down by regulators and shareholders, and Republic withdrew the bid in the fall of 1993.

In ways large and small, Edmond was keenly aware of the passage of time. Back in 1949, the decision by his older brother Elie to strike out on his own had fully cleared the way for Edmond to emerge as Jacob's heir. Over the decades, rejecting Edmond's entreaties, Elie had never formally worked in the family institutions, despite living close to Edmond and Lily in Geneva and occasionally working out of one of Edmond's offices. (Elie's son, Jacqui, had significant positions with the Safra banks as a currency trader and later produced films for Woody Allen.) In December 1993, Elie Safra died—the first of the Safra siblings who survived to adulthood to pass away. He was buried on the Mount of Olives in Jerusalem (from where, according to Jewish tradition, the Messianic resurrection of the dead will begin), and the family assembled at the King David Hotel to sit shiva.[457]

By now, the Safras were regular visitors to Israel. The Jewish community in Beirut was gone, and thanks to the emerging thaw in relations between Israel and the Arab world, the Safras no longer had to hide their commercial presence in the country and were comfortable becoming involved in projects beyond charity and religion. Edmond and Lily's circle of friends expanded to include Israeli Prime Minister Yitzhak Rabin and his wife, Leah, who visited La Léopolda, and Jerusalem Mayor Teddy Kollek. In 1992, Edmond traveled to Israel for the Bar Mitzvah of a nephew. In the winter of 1993, he took Lily, her daughter Adriana and son-in-law Michel, and the grandchildren to Eilat, where they engaged in classic tourist activities like riding camels and swimming with dolphins. That same year, the municipality of Jerusalem inaugurated its city hall and municipal complex in a vast new square that Edmond had donated. Appropriately enough, Safra Square, named after Jacob and Esther, sits at a point where Jaffa Road approaches the Old City—the West meeting the East, a symbolic point of connection between Jewish and Arab neighborhoods.[458]

The early 1990s were a rare period in Edmond Safra's life when things were actually looking up in the Middle East. To be sure, conditions were nothing like the integrated era of the Ottoman Empire in which Safra Frères thrived, or the period of relative calm and free movement during the British and French mandate eras in which Edmond had been born. Edmond always stayed out of partisan politics in Israel, yet he was keenly and personally invested in Israel's future and its relationships with its Arab neighbors. And although anyone who grew up in Beirut had to be cautious about the prospects for peace in the region, there was reason for hope. On September 13, 1993, when Prime Minister Rabin and PLO Chairman Yasser Arafat warily shook hands at the Clinton White House, Edmond called FIBI Chairman Yigal Arnon and told him it was the happiest day of his life.[459]

By the spring of 1994, Edmond and his colleagues had grown dissatisfied with the way the securities business was developing. He replaced Louis Lloyd with longtime confidant Vito Portera. On April 22, 1994, Peter Cohen wrote Edmond suggesting a revised business plan, urging greater investment in the unit. Edmond typically avoided direct conflict, but evidently didn't provide Cohen with the response he wanted. In the second quarter of 1994, Republic laid off 12 percent of the unit's employees and halted plans to set up an arbitrage operation for its own account, taking a $17 million charge in the process. "RNY has taken a series of steps to scale back and retrench trading for own account and instead doing more for customers," analyst Mark Alpert noted.

Aide Sol Gindi recalled: "Edmond was never comfortable with the foray into the securities business. He was much more comfortable with what he knew—the simple deposit investing business."[460]

Indeed, while Republic was pulling back from businesses that Edmond disdained, Republic wasn't sitting idle. Edmond's long-running campaign to become more international and more deeply entrenched in key businesses continued. In the first quarter of 1994, Republic agreed to acquire a branch in Brazil from Banco Exterior de España SA and was making plans to open a representative office in Copenhagen. Republic had maintained a representative office in Mexico City since 1972. Now, the Mexican Ministry of Finance and

Public Credit granted it a license to open a full banking subsidiary with an initial capitalization of $100 million. [461]

And then there was gold. For Edmond and Republic, the global trade wasn't a nostalgic business; it was one that provided low-risk and consistent profits, even in an age of supercharged global finance. In September 1919, the five main gold bullion traders and refiners had begun to meet at the London offices of N.M. Rothschild & Sons in St. Swithin's Lane to fix the daily price of gold. Among them were Jewish firms that generations of Safras had worked with, including Mocatta & Goldsmid, and Samuel Montagu & Co. When Westpac, the Australian bank that had acquired one of the fixing seats, put it up for sale, Edmond pounced. On December 31, 1993, Republic acquired Mase Westpac Limited and changed the name to Republic Mase Bank Limited, with units in Australia and Hong Kong. "For Edmond to have that seat was the crowning jewel," Fred Bogart recalled, noting that he uncharacteristically was willing to bid more than it was worth. Having started as a teenager scouring the capitals of Europe seeking gold he could ship to Beirut and Hong Kong, Edmond was now literally in the room where the price of gold was set. [462]

Gold, banknotes, and trade finance were the original businesses Edmond had learned from Jacob at BCN in Beirut. By 1994, the city of Edmond's birth was occupied and essentially controlled by Syria, and it remained so dangerous that neither Edmond nor many of his colleagues could visit. Edmond was sufficiently practical to no longer lament the fact that he couldn't visit the Ajami restaurant or the St. George Hotel. But he stubbornly clung to his father's bank, and to the notion that it played an important role in Lebanon's financial system. And he was effectively running it from Geneva, while striving to bring executives to Switzerland for meetings. This involved Republic soliciting the Swiss consulate in Damascus in the fall of 1994 to obtain visas for BCN directors such as Fadi Anis Daouk and Maurice Antoniades, as well as for Mohamad Naffi, a director of Lebanon's central bank, so they could travel to Switzerland. The idea of a Jewish Halabi reaching out to the Assad regime for assistance might have seemed daft. But there was a thaw in the air—even in Syria—that was furthered by the sealing of the Israel-Jordan peace treaty on October 24, 1994.[463]

Since Assad's announcement in 1992 that Jews could leave Syria, thousands had trickled out—to the United States and to Israel, in defiance of Assad's prohibition. In fact, about one-third of the 3,670 Jews who had left by the fall of 1994 had made their way to Israel under strict secrecy, worried that if they were discovered, it would cause Assad to slam the door. Rabbi Avraham Hamra, who would be the last chief rabbi of Damascus, stayed on to serve the handful who chose to remain. But in October 1994, Hamra departed for New York, and then publicly made Aliyah to Israel. The *Washington Post* noted, "The presence of Rabbi Avraham Hamra marked the virtual end of Jewish life in Syria."[464] Left behind were a few hundred elderly and other holdouts, along with precious community possessions. Over the years, Edmond had paid to rescue Torah scrolls from Lebanon and Syria and find homes for them in synagogues elsewhere. In 1993, he helped finance and coordinate an effort to bring all the remaining Torah scrolls from Lebanon. Community members split the scrolls into sections, hid them in bags of coffee beans, and sent them to Republic's vault in New York.[465]

Arranging for humanitarian relief and helping to smuggle Torahs while overseeing an expanding global banking empire were all in a day's work for Edmond. His once-hectic travel schedule had become somewhat less so, however. He alit in New York in the spring and fall, where he loved to hold court in his large, elegant private offices on the twenty-ninth floor. He and Lily traveled to London, Paris, and Monaco, where they had homes, and for vacations throughout Europe. But he spent most of his time in Geneva or at La Léopolda, which he would occupy for about one-third of the year.

Edmond relished keeping tabs on his vast network and empire through the long arm of Betty Loglisci, his legendary telephone operator, who was known for being able to locate anyone he wanted, anywhere in the world, at any time, sometimes calling every office or apartment in a Manhattan building if a taxi company had told her that a driver had dropped someone there, or ringing every pay phone on successive blocks if the doorman had told her someone had left the building and walked in a certain direction. One New Year's Eve, Republic executive Ken Cooper was at a resort in the Alps after having met with Edmond in Geneva. The phone rang in the kitchen of the small hotel. It was Betty. "I have Mr. Safra on the line. He wants to speak with you." Alarmed, Cooper waited.

"Oh," Edmond said, "I just wanted to wish you a happy New Year, and tell you how much I appreciated that you were here."[466]

Edmond would frequently call Sandy Koifman at Safra Republic to ask a specific question about the markets: "What is the euro dollar and deutsche mark exchange rate?" Koifman would look at his Reuters screen and give him the quote, knowing that Edmond had the same screen up on his desk and just wanted to make sure he was paying attention.[467]

It was important to pay attention, because there were constant threats. The crisis in emerging market debt in the early 1980s was one of the factors that had pushed Edmond to sell TDB to American Express. And because it operated extensively in Latin American markets, Republic always had to keep a careful watch on conditions there. In December 1994, Mexico was wracked by the "Tequila Crisis," when it sharply devalued the peso against the dollar. As the prices of Mexico's sovereign debt began to drift downward, Edmond insisted that the banks sell their positions quickly, even if meant taking a small loss.[468]

Edmond was certainly not slowing down, but he was perhaps settling in. At La Léopolda, he managed to re-create the close-knit and large family into which he had been born. He would make sure to fly down from Geneva on Fridays so he could be at La Léopolda for Shabbat. Whether it was Shabbat or any of the holidays, there was a very specific seating order at the table: Edmond at the head and Samuel, the oldest grandson, to his right. In addition, there was the constant stream of visitors who would make their way up the hillside overlooking Villefranche-sur-Mer: composer and pianist Marvin Hamlisch, Elie and Marion Wiesel, social friends from London and Paris and New York, Henry Kissinger, Margaret Thatcher, and business colleagues from around the globe.[469]

As the grandchildren grew older, the grounds were transformed into a kind of summer camp, with ponies, swimming, and tennis. Edmond loved to indulge the grandchildren. In 1995, he built a tree house for Lily Elia's tenth birthday, and gift-wrapped it. He made a ritual of snack time, with a trolley for homemade ice cream and a popcorn machine. Edmond embraced the chaos. He would putter around the property, talking on the phone as kids whizzed by on rollerblades or fired Nerf guns at one another. At Lily's prodding, Edmond made it a point to curse only in Arabic so they wouldn't understand. (The grandchildren quickly figured out the meaning of the word *sharmouta*.)

Edmond had been spending time in this part of the world since the 1950s, when he would summer in Golfe-Juan. Over the many seasons he had been repairing to the Mediterranean, change had been a constant. In those decades, Edmond had always been seeking new frontiers and territories to conquer. Although he still sought expansion and new campaigns, as he entered his early sixties, a different set of concerns began to weigh on his mind while he was walking the grounds of La Léopolda or watching his grandchildren swimming in the pool: the long-term prospects of Republic and his own health.

The two subjects had always been intertwined, of course. Edmond had never been in great shape physically. He didn't play tennis or golf, and he enjoyed his wine and whiskey and the occasional secret ciga-rette. The company had doctors on its payroll, and colleagues noted that he would seek advice for even minor issues in all the cities in which he lived and did business. He also joked mordantly about his health. Edmond told Roger Junod that he had given 500,000 francs to the intensive care unit at the Hôpital Cantonal in Geneva, and, departing from his usual practice, asked to have his name put on a plaque. "That way," he laughed, "if I have an emergency when I'm in Geneva, they'll know where to take me. And when I get there, they might even treat me well!"[470]

In 1993 and 1994, Edmond's assistants, close colleagues, and family began to notice subtle changes. He moved more slowly, and with greater difficulty. His speech began to slow down. People could see occasional shakings or tremors in his hands. When doctors were consulted, they confirmed that this was the onset of Parkinson's disease, a devastating degenerative neurological affliction.[471]

Unsurprisingly, the diagnosis troubled him. Edmond was now sixty-two. At this age, his father, Jacob, had essentially ceased being an active banker and was becoming increasingly incapacitated by his own medical issues, some of them neurological. Elie, Edmond's older brother, had died the previous year. Succession, or what might happen if Edmond were not able to keep running the banks, was not a topic that was discussed openly at Republic or Safra Republic. To be sure, there was a vague sense of how things would go. In theory, Edmond's banks, like Joseph and Moïse's bank, were family businesses. In a trust created in 1982, the banks were regarded essentially as communal property. The idea was that the Safra family members—or at least the family members of Jacob Safra's sons—were heirs to both the collective financial resources and the actual operating businesses.

But these were generally unstated assumptions, not ironclad agreements, and they didn't take into account all the complexities of the situations and personalities involved. Edmond didn't have his own children, so he would have no sons to work in the business or carry on ownership beyond his own life. Joseph and Moïse, who were busy running Banco Safra and other operations in Brazil, would slowly bring their own children into those businesses, but had no role in the operation of Republic or Safra Republic. And there really was no precedent for how to handle a succession of any kind. Safra Frères had dissolved long before Jacob Safra set up his own bank, and Jacob Safra had no brothers himself.

At the same time, Edmond had to think about how to protect Republic in the short term. The bank he had started had grown into the eleventh-largest in the US, and had $29 billion in deposits. But it still stood in the long shadows cast by its very large neighbors, such as J.P. Morgan and Citibank. Edmond's approach of marrying cheap deposits to low-risk assets abroad and carving out space in niche areas including trade finance, gold, and banknotes had brought the company a long way. But to keep growing, Republic would have to keep investing in new lines of business—not the securities business, perhaps, but asset management, consumer lending, private banking, and geographic expansion. It was much more complicated than offering televisions for new accounts and placing cheap deposits in IMF-backed loans. Meanwhile, the larger Republic grew, the more costs rose—for technology, compliance, systems, and processes. All this undermined the vaunted efficiency of the bank's operations. As costs rose amid increasingly challenging competition, Edmond found that the conversations with colleagues were less about where to expand and grab new opportunities, and more about how to control costs. "Everybody is looking to me for the solutions to make their business good enough to cover their costs and to deliver a profit," he told Thomas Robards, a Republic vice president.[472]

These challenges—how to manage his own health, guarantee a future for his banks, and figure out where the businesses fit in relation to his brothers—would come to occupy more of his time and thoughts, even as he continued to conduct business and seek opportunities to expand.

16

Transitions

(1995-1998)

Ever since he had founded Republic, Edmond Safra had regarded
the United States banking market as a land of opportunity;
America's wide-open skies and welcoming environment were the best
place in the world to grow a consumer-oriented bank. But by 1995,
the perspective was changing, due to a combination of forces in the
market, Republic's unique operating and business model, and a small
but noticeable decline in Edmond's health. Republic had built a record
of spectacular growth on the scaffolding of long-standing business
principles and powerful niches, many of which traced their origins to
Aleppo and Beirut. Even as Republic grew into one of the country's
largest financial institutions, Edmond, who spent only a couple of
months each year in New York, continued to run it through concentric
circles of trusted executives. By the mid-1990s, however, this modus
operandi had begun to be something of a drawback. An increasing
amount of his time was devoted to Safra Republic, whose growth was
now rivaling Republic's (By 1996, Safra Republic would count $25
billion in client assets.)

Over the years, Republic National Bank of New York had grown,
adding businesses and people, rarely stopping to assess the business.
"We had not done, in a long time, a very detailed review," said
Republic board member Jim Morice. Doing so in a dispassionate and
comprehensive way simply wasn't part of the culture. In 1995, when

Republic first undertook a review of operations with an eye to cutting costs, one senior executive likened it to a Jewish community fundraiser. John Tamberlane recalled, "Edmond called his senior managers to Geneva and said, 'We have to cut expenses.' People then raised their hands. 'I'll give 10 percent. I'll give 5 percent.'"[473]

To approach cost reduction in a more systematic manner, Republic turned to an outsider. Chandrika Tandon, the first Indian-American woman to be elected partner at McKinsey & Company, in 1992 started her own firm, Tandon Capital Associates, which specialized in taking a sharp scalpel to banks' operating costs. When Republic hired Tandon as a consultant in early 1995, her team took over offices on the twenty-eighth floor, and they put Republic through its first true American-style restructuring. The goal of the exercise wasn't growth, but rather improving the efficiency ratio—the ratio of total operating expenses to net interest and other income. Cutting the ratio, which stood at 57, by a single basis point would yield about $12 million a year in cost savings. Units were asked to consider how they might reduce costs by 30 percent. Consultants distributed knick-knacks that made the sound of a cow, to indicate that there would be no sacred cows. Walter Weiner came up with the name "Project Excellence Plus," or "PEP."[474]

On May 5, 1995, in a public filing, Republic announced it would start to implement PEP, using language that might have been seen at IBM: process redesign, vendor management, automation. The jargon cloaked the reality that the lion's share of the savings would come from reducing the bank's rising payroll. "We called it 'People Executing People,'" recalled Republic executive Joseph De Paolo. PEP turned out to be a grueling exercise for everyone at the bank. Republic was a family business, a haven to which hundreds of people had fled, where employees felt they had jobs for life. Trust and relationships often mattered as much as competence. Family businesses didn't simply fire hundreds of people for the sake of a few basis points in operating margins.

This type of exercise called for a dispassionate approach, one that Edmond was constitutionally incapable of taking—especially when the conversation turned to eliminating the positions of veterans. He was intimately involved in all the personnel decisions. When management suggested firing Ernie Ginsberg, the longtime lawyer for Republic and TDB who had devised the vital Margaret Thatcher clause in the American Express deal, Edmond was apoplectic: "Never in my life. *I will leave the bank before he leaves the bank.*" When they recommended letting go 75-year-old Albert Hattena, the Cairo-born banker whose brothers also worked at Republic, Edmond refused, telling Fred Bogart: "Fred, anybody that helped me build the bank, they will not be fired." In other instances, people who had been let go appealed to senior executives and were spared. Ultimately, in the second quarter of 1995, Republic took a $120 million pretax charge, 80 percent of which was to fund severance for 850 of the bank's 5,550 employees. The exercise sapped morale, and many veterans noted that the atmosphere inside in the bank changed, becoming more defensive.[475]

Through the tumult, Republic was intent on expanding, working to add to its $40 billion in assets. Crossland Federal Savings Bank, a hardy New York neighborhood bank that catered to middle-class customers, had been seized by the FDIC in 1992 and was working its way out from under a pile of bad real estate loans. On September 23, 1995, Republic agreed to buy Crossland for about $530 million in cash, bringing $3.7 billion in deposits, 385,000 customer accounts, and thirty-three New York branches into Republic's fold. In a sign of just how rapidly things were changing, this transaction—one of the largest Republic had ever made—was struck just after two local giants, Chemical and Chase, merged in a massive deal, creating a global financial supermarket with $297 billion in assets. As others grew by quantum leaps, Republic continued to grow incrementally. In 1995 and the first quarter of 1996, Republic agreed to acquire six Bank Leumi and three First Nationwide Bank branches, with another $600 million in deposits between them.[476]

Meanwhile, Edmond continued to utilize his network to find opportunities to put money to work. Paul Reichmann, an Orthodox Jewish businessman born in Vienna, had turned the family business in Toronto into a global real estate powerhouse. The Reichmanns' company, Olympia & York, borrowed a great deal of money in the 1980s to build Canary Wharf, a new financial complex to the east of the City of London. But the complex neared completion just as the economy plunged into recession, and in 1992, Olympia & York filed for bankruptcy. In 1995, with the economy recovering, Reichmann sought to purchase the complex back from its creditors. Only someone with Edmond Safra's network and history of operating across borders and cultures could have put together the syndicate that formed: the Orthodox Canada-based Reichmanns; the Tisch family, stalwarts of New York's Jewish community; Michael Price, who ran the Mutual Series funds; and Prince Alwaleed of Saudi Arabia. Together, the consortium paid 800 million British pounds ($1.3 billion) for control of the complex. Republic and Safra Republic Holdings each took 6 percent of the deal, while Edmond took 6 percent for his own account, and distributed 2 percent to clients.

As always, Edmond continued to pounce on opportunistic ventures in frontier markets. In 1995, when interest rates in Turkey were remarkably high, he calculated there was an arbitrage opportunity available—even if the country were to devalue its currency. So he dispatched an assistant to Istanbul, the seat of the Ottoman Empire that once housed a branch of Safra Frères, to put capital to work. And increasingly, Edmond's attention was drawn to another dissolving empire in the East: Russia. Edmond and his colleagues had conducted business behind the Iron Curtain since the 1950s, arranging gold, currency, and merchandise trades. After the collapse of the Soviet Union, Russia remained a troubled economy, albeit one with vast natural resources and connections to global trade. As such, Russia presented opportunities for financial intermediaries who were comfortable with risk and international arbitrage. [477]

Republic established a representative office in Moscow in 1994. The following year, Edmond received a visit from investment manager Bill Browder. In a neat historical irony, Browder was the grandson of Earl Browder, the longtime head of the US Communist party. Edmond agreed to invest $25 million in Browder's new Russian-focused investment vehicle, dubbed the Hermitage Fund, and become a joint venture partner. Wanting to get a closer look, in August 1996 Edmond traveled with Lily and their grandchildren to Moscow and St. Petersburg. In the former imperial capital, Lily, having been struck by the magnificent Grand Choral Synagogue, decided to make a significant donation toward its restoration in memory of her son Claudio.[478]

Given Russia's "Wild West" environment, Edmond found that the prospect of lending to companies or consumers there wasn't particularly appealing. But Russia had a nearly insatiable need for hard currency—especially dollars. And although the Federal Reserve and US Treasury were eager to supply Russia with bills, they didn't ship currency themselves. So it was natural for Republic to expand its already massive banknotes business to Russia.

By 1995, Republic New York was sending $30 million to $40 million in $100 bills on a daily Delta flight to Moscow. From there, Republic's subsidiary would distribute it to local banks. It was all done under the supervision of compliance officer Richard Annicharico, a former FBI agent, and with the express approval of the federal government. And yet, as had often been the case, the media tried to find nefarious motives at work. *New York* magazine in January 1996 ran a cover story about the banknotes business, "The Money Plane," in which it all but accused Republic of money laundering and cited some of the innuendo of the American Express episode. When Henry Kravis, the founder of buyout firm KKR, which owned *New York*'s parent company Primedia, heard about the article, he called the company's CEO and asked them not to run it, because he believed the accusations were baseless. After the publication, Kravis traveled to Geneva to apologize to Edmond in person.[479]

And of course, there was always gold. Republic accepted gold deposits from Russian government entities into its New York vaults, paid interest on them, and then consigned the gold to the jewelry market. When a delegation from Russia came to make a deposit, Republic executive Dov Schlein made a presentation about the bank's safety. The chairman of the delegation cut him off: "I know you are a safe bank. You are the Republic National Bank of New York."

(Coming from a country in which the state controlled most enterprises, he believed Republic had the backing of the State of New York.)[480]

Beyond the gold trade, the first businesses Edmond had known continued to occupy his interest. In November 1996, he was still tending to the affairs of BCN (formerly Banque Jacob E. Safra) in Beirut, writing to the Swiss Consulate in Damascus to ask that Antoine Gholam, the bank's accountant, be granted a visa to travel to Geneva. Nearly fifty years after he left Beirut, the city and its community remained a touchstone for Edmond. When Sol Gindi interviewed with him in 1996 to be one of his assistants, he had the right credentials: a BA and MBA from New York University, and a few years of experience at Republic. But when Edmond learned that Gindi's grandfather was Selim Shehebar, who had worked in Jacob Safra's bank in Beirut until 1972 and landed in Republic's loan department, the tenor of the conversation changed. "He's a good man," Edmond said. "OK, you're qualified. Come on the plane Monday."[481]

To a large degree, the rhythm of Edmond's life in the mid-1990s remained unchanged. He was always on the plane, traveling between the poles of Geneva, New York, Paris, and London, with the occasional visit to Brazil. The summer was spent at La Léopolda; the IMF meetings in the fall were a major event. The days were spent in an endless scroll—calls to Asia in the morning, Europe during the day, New York in the evening; dinners and meetings, juggling philanthropy, business, and his personal interest in collecting. And yet this rhythm was being disrupted by health issues. Although the Parkinson's diagnosis was not generally known to the public, the changes in his health were evident to those close to him. Edmond went to fewer meetings, and would occasionally leave if symptoms flared up. Assistants in the offices were aware of the intricate regimen of medications, and more time had to be freed up on his schedule to seek medical advice and attention. He was not eager to discuss it publicly, but Edmond Safra in 1996 began to confront the transitions that would be necessary to cope with a degenerative disease.[482]

One of the solutions was to arrange living space closer to the office where he was now spending more of his time. Safra Republic was aggressively building up its presence in Monaco, an important private banking center, and with its walking access to shops, restaurants, and healthcare, the principality had become a preferred base of operations for Edmond. As was typical, the bank took office space on the ground floor of a high-end, centrally located building, La Belle Epoque on Avenue d'Ostende. Replicating the situation from the Knox Building in the 1960s, Edmond and Lily purchased a majestic 17,500-square-foot apartment on the top two floors of the building. *Architectural Digest* would later write of the apartment: "Wherever you stand on its many balconies and terraces, there are plunging views onto the sparkling sea or the mountainous Riviera behind." Edmond and Lily filled the new apartment with paintings, objets d'art, and magnificent furniture. In December 1996, a slew of acquisitions from Sotheby's in Monaco included five drawings of historical dresses worn by the Queen of Belgium and an 1838 collection of works by Racine. Edmond's interest in collecting remained strong. Earlier that year, while on the phone from his dentist's office waiting room, he bought at auction the 1912 manuscript of Einstein's Special Theory of Relativity and donated it to the Israel Museum. "The gift is one of the most important we have received in Jerusalem, a gift which simply cannot be measured by any financial value," Jerusalem mayor Teddy Kollek wrote.[483]

The past had always been a powerful presence in Edmond's life, informing his relationships, business strategy, and behavior. By the mid-1990s, he couldn't help but look back with more perspective—and satisfaction. When Alberto Muchnick, a Republic executive in South America, came to La Belle Epoque for dinner, Edmond gestured to the bay. "You know, when I was a kid, I was working here and I saw these boats and I said, 'One day I will have a boat or an apartment here in this area.' And today I have the apartment, and I feel very proud that I can see the boats from this side of the bay."[484]

Approaching his sixty-fifth birthday, Edmond had been working for fifty years. Because he was the controlling shareholder and animating personality of both Republic and Safra Republic, it was difficult for anyone—inside or outside the banks—to imagine a future without Edmond Safra at the helm. In fact, the types of questions that would normally be asked at a large, publicly held company about the future generally weren't raised at Republic.

From a young age, Edmond had fretted over how to maintain stability for his family and clients. In 1982, he had sold TDB precisely because he believed American Express would provide a safe haven for his depositors in turbulent times. Throughout the Safra universe, there were a host of unstated assumptions. It was assumed that Edmond would run the banks until he could do so no longer, and that if something were to happen to Edmond, the bank would remain as an institution within the control of the Safra family, and that Joseph Safra would step in. These arrangements, however, weren't written down. Through the decades, the word *secretive* had often been applied to Edmond's business practices. The irony, of course, is that both Republic and Safra Republic were publicly held firms, which reported precisely how they made money, what lines of business they were in, and who owned controlling shares with complete transparency. Yet what wasn't clear to the public was the exact relationship between the Safra brothers—Edmond, Joseph, and Moïse. "The succession, which was never articulated or discussed at the board level, in spite of many polite inquiries by the board, was understood to include his brothers," said Peter Kimmelman, a longtime Republic board member.[485]

In fact, as is the case in all families, the relationships were complicated. There was love, respect, connection, and obligation, but also undercurrents of resentment and misunderstanding and occasional conflict. Banco Safra, now a major force in its own right in Brazil, was 100 percent owned by Moïse and Joseph. Under Joseph's initiative, it was expanding around the world—to New York, Luxembourg, and elsewhere. In theory, the brothers held the shares of the banks they owned and controlled, but on behalf of the family, not themselves. Joseph and Moïse plowed the profits into property and other assets in Brazil, such as real estate, and began to take advantage of the country's integration into the global economy. They teamed up with Bell South to invest in a cellular operator in São Paulo, for example.

Having served as a surrogate father for his younger brothers since the early 1950s, Edmond loved Joseph like a son. "Edmond regarded Joseph as his pupil," Rodney Leach said. "He taught him how to be a banker." They were in constant communication, speaking two or three times a day. If someone approached Edmond with an idea for a transaction in Brazil, he would send it to Joseph—with instructions that Joseph's decisions be followed. In 1996, when Republic opened a trading desk in Brazil, Edmond instructed Dov Schlein: "Be very mindful of Joseph. In fact, consult with him. Because if you make a mistake, it will embarrass Joseph. They don't distinguish between Safras."[486]

Edmond embraced the role of paterfamilias—at his companies, and in his family life. He was most in his element at La Léopolda, with grandchildren, nieces, and nephews visiting. He relished hosting large crowds on the holidays, leading a slow walk down the hillside to a restaurant, arranging family trips, or captaining yachting expeditions on the Mediterranean. Conflict among family members defied his idealistic vision for how families were supposed to operate. His grandchildren recall that one of the few times he lost his temper was when they were fighting, and one of them cursed at the other: "I hate you, I hate you! I don't love you as a brother!"

Edmond snapped: "Stop it, stop it!"[487]

But for all Edmond's emphasis on family, the Safra banks had never really been a complex, multigenerational family business. Jacob Safra had been the sole owner of BCN, having had no siblings. His active career ended when he left Beirut in 1953, and he left the bank he owned to Edmond. In the Sephardic tradition, only sons came to work in the business (not daughters or sons-in-law), and typically only males inherited major property. But Edmond didn't have his own children. He took a particular interest in the education and career prospects of his nephews, taking pains to ensure that they attended the finest schools. In the 1990s, Moïse's three sons, Jacob (Harvard '92, Harvard MBA '95), Ezra (Wharton '94), and Edmond (a student at Harvard), were just embarking on their professional careers; none of Joseph's three sons was yet of working age.

So Edmond Safra faced a complex and intricate puzzle—how to position the banks for the future, how to provide for Lily and their family, and how to adhere to tradition while designing a successful governing structure. One particular event made the prospect of such a transition even more real. In April 1997, his beloved older sister, Eveline, died at the age of seventy-two, leaving Edmond as the oldest surviving child of Jacob and Esther Safra.

In the fall of 1997, the market's faith in the future of his banks seemed virtually limitless. Earlier in the year, when Republic was raising $100 million in bonds, Edmond asked what the difference in interest would be between a thirty-year bond and a 100-year bond. Two investment banks responded with a quote, and Republic moved quickly. On July 22, Republic Bank took the rare step of issuing a 100-year bond. In an age of rapid change, very few leaders bothered to think beyond the next five or ten years, much less presume that their organization would be functioning a century later. But this was perfectly in keeping with Edmond's vision of Republic as a multigenerational, perpetual enterprise. Of course, the move also had salutary financial aspects: treated as debt for tax and accounting purposes, such long-term bonds were a way to raise capital on a quasi-permanent basis without having to dilute Edmond's substantial controlling ownership in Republic. If anything, Edmond was continually seeking to add incrementally to his 29 percent stake in the bank.

Once the sale was completed, it was suggested they go even further, to pursue a 1,000-year bond for Safra Republic Holdings. Edmond loved the concept, which the market would certainly regard as a novelty. "In a thousand years, people would probably be aliens on Earth. I cannot believe that somebody is going to buy this," he said. But Lehman Brothers agreed to back the deal, and in October 1997 underwrote an offering of $250 million in 1,000-year bonds. "Will Republic National Bank still be around in 2997?" asked *New York Times* columnist Floyd Norris on October 8. Bearing an interest rate of 7.125 percent, the bonds had a feature that let the bank buy them back at any time. In effect, they functioned like preferred stock—again without diluting Edmond's personal 21 percent stake in Safra

Republic. "This is the cheapest capital I will ever have. I never have to repay it, and it costs me 7 percent per annum," said Edmond.[488]

The fall of 1997 was a time for marking significant milestones. Edmond turned sixty-five in August. And although the traditional retirement age had no particular meaning for him, Lily was quietly planning an elaborate surprise party for November 9, 1997, fifty years since he and Jacques Tawil left Lod airfield for Italy. In the days leading up to the event, workers from Philip Baloun Designs took over the grand former headquarters of Greenwich Savings Bank at 36th Street and Broadway, an imposing Beaux Arts edifice that was a Crossland Savings branch, installing Masonite panels over the main banking floor. As was typical for a Safra fete, guests (family, friends, colleagues, and clients) came from every part of the world.

That day, as on many other Sundays, Edmond didn't shave, despite Lily's repeated entreaties. And so, at about 6:00 p.m., an unshaven and completely astonished Edmond Safra arrived to what he thought was going to be a small family dinner to find hundreds of people gathered to wish him well. When he figured out what was going on, he turned to Lily and said, smiling broadly: "Why didn't you tell me to shave?"[489]

Tables were arranged in a horseshoe, with Edmond, Lily, and family members, including his brothers, at the head table. Lou Dobbs, the CNN anchor who served as master of ceremonies, introduced a video that traced Edmond's career. Lily offered a toast in the film: "May our six wonderful grandchildren achieve in their lives the values and ideals that you, a deeply religious man, have bequeathed upon all of us: to be grateful for what we have; to be content with what we are; and above all, to walk humbly, mindful of the spiritual wisdom of Judaism. Throughout the ages philosophers have asked: What is a man? My answer is personal—someone who is wise, kind, considerate, decent, good-hearted, without vanity—and this is you, Edmond. I thank you for the privilege of having shared all these years with me, your wife." The evening touched on the many poles of Edmond's life: Beirut, Brazil, Switzerland, the United States, and France. Bette

Midler sang two songs, with personalized lyrics. After the main course, a belly dancer coaxed Edmond onto the dance floor, wrapping her shawl around him. Sergio Mendes and his orchestra, who had flown in from Brazil, were fronted by Bob Azzam, the Lebanese-Egyptian singer who had a nightclub in Geneva and who had been part of Edmond's circle since the 1950s. [490]

It was a bittersweet moment, in part because of Edmond's declining health. As the Parkinson's disease advanced, Edmond was somewhat unsteady on his feet and had limited energy for socializing. Regardless of his vision for a bank that would last 100 or 1,000 years, in November 1997, Edmond Safra faced a daily challenge of dealing with a degenerative disease for which there was no cure. The Parkinson's treatment was in the hands of a large international cast of doctors and nurses.

The disease had progressed beyond well-known symptoms such as slowness and tremors and was starting to affect his overall movement, speech, and, most importantly, his spirit. Although there had been no public announcement of his diagnosis, more and more people within the bank were aware of it. Beyond medication, Edmond required regular physical therapy, including exercises with rubber balls to relieve stiffness in his hands and massages to relieve the muscle cramps in his legs. The drugs aimed at treating Parkinson's had significant side effects and weren't always effective, particularly with regard to the non-motor symptoms of the disease. Mood swings, emotional outbursts, and episodes of generally feeling "off" began to become more common. Edmond hated the fact that people might look at him differently, or pity him. He told Lily more than once, "Please, *chérie*, never let me lose my dignity." At La Léopolda, a room was set up, out of view of guests and the grandchildren, where he could receive treatment. [491]

The banks, by and large, continued to prosper, albeit without engaging in major expansion efforts or acquisitions. Republic's stock rallied through 1997, from about $44 in March to above $57 at the end of the year. At year's end, Republic had total assets of $50.2 billion, total deposits of $33.5 billion, and stockholders' equity of $3.3 billion. It was immensely profitable, with net income at a record $449 million. Conservatism continued to rule the day. Loans totaled just $13.6 billion, about a quarter of total assets. Nonaccrual loans were a mere $94 million, just 0.76 percent of total loans outstanding. At Safra Republic, which reported assets of $20.4 billion, and total deposits of $15.4 billion, earnings in 1997 were a record $125 million.[492]

In the spring of 1998, the Safra brothers gathered again to honor Edmond—this time in Jerusalem, where, in recognition of his achievements in the world of finance, Edmond was to be granted an honorary doctorate from the Hebrew University in Jerusalem. It was another moment of pride, as Edmond, who had been an indifferent student at the Alliance and St. Joseph's, sat on the dais with Israel's academic elite and the chief justice of its Supreme Court.

The morning after the ceremony, Edmond's condition deteriorated significantly. The family quickly left, traveling first to the South of France, and then to the University hospital in Grenoble, which was known for expertise in Parkinson's, where doctors reduced Safra's medications significantly and put him on a new experimental regimen. He spent the rest of the summer at La Léopolda, frequently suffering from debilitating symptoms of the disease and side effects of medications.[493]

At this point, Edmond could no longer keep his condition from the public. So in early July, Republic issued an extraordinary statement. The press release announced the creation of the "Edmond J. Safra Research Foundation with funding from the Safra family of $50 million to support research in Parkinson's disease."[494]

Edmond tried to reassure his shareholders and customers. "Parkinson's is not life threatening. Since I was diagnosed several years ago, I manage my Parkinson's through a combination of medication, diet and daily exercise. I expect my participation and involvement with the senior management of the banks I control, including my roles as Chairman of Safra Republic Holdings SA and Republic National Bank of New York, to continue for many years to come."

But he indicated that others would join him. "I have frequently shared information and consulted closely with my brothers, Joseph and Moïse, on the affairs of our banks and other businesses. In light of my illness, I, along with members of our senior management teams, are drawing on Joseph's counsel and long experience more frequently, and I expect this to continue. Sharing of advisory roles and information is part of our family's tradition. . . . In fact, Joseph has reorganized his schedule to be able to devote still more of his time to join me in advising the senior managements of Republic New York Corporation and Safra Republic with respect to major policy decisions and other significant matters."

The statement seemed to imply that Joseph would be taking a more hands-on role, setting him up to be Edmond's successor. "The press release was very carefully drafted," Dov Schlein recalled.[495]

But the experiment proved short-lived. Busy with Banco Safra and other investments, Joseph was never particularly eager to take on the responsibility, in part because he felt the people at Republic didn't regard him as having authority. Joseph laid out a condition: nobody should get hired or get a raise without his approval. Within weeks, however, CEO Walter Weiner granted a raise to Kurt Anderson, a Republic executive in Hong Kong. This was far from an isolated incident. Within a matter of weeks, Joseph told Edmond he couldn't go forward: "I can't do it, not with people making decisions that I don't approve."[496]

Despite the announcement in early July, it quickly became clear that Joseph Safra would not succeed his older brother—although Edmond seemed to cling to the prospect. "Edmond had an ideal vision of the family," attorney Marc Bonnant remembered, "and voicing his disappointment would be giving [in to] reality."[497]

At that very moment, the need for a clear succession was made painfully apparent. After stabilizing in France, Edmond went to New York in August 1998, where a team of doctors at Columbia-Presbyterian worked to further refine his treatment program. In the late summer he moved to a leading Parkinson's clinic in Toronto, to seek further treatment. Anthony Brittan, a South African who had just graduated from Brandeis and had signed on as one of Edmond's assistants, was sent to the Four Seasons Hotel in Toronto to set up a temporary headquarters.[498]

All of this was going on at a time when firm and sober leadership were in high demand. In the 1990s, emerging markets crises had been a quasi-regular feature of the global financial landscape. In the summer of 1997, markets were roiled when several Southeast Asian markets were hit by currency devaluation and capital flight. Around the world, hot money retreated from risky markets. And in the summer of 1998, things started to go south in Russia. The Russian government borrowed on a short-term basis to finance its debt and operations, and paid remarkably high rates—25 or 30 percent annual rates on three-month debt instruments. Republic built up a large position in Russian debt. The strategy was to buy the bonds, collect the interest, and gain appreciation in value if interest rates fell. In the meantime, they would hedge the currency risk by covering the positions forward in dollars with government-backed banks like Sberbank.[499]

Such trades work fantastically, until the minute they don't. When Russia went out to renew its short-term bonds in the spring of 1998, there were few buyers. In August 1998, in a move that shocked global markets, the Russian government essentially defaulted on its bonds and devalued the currency. Overnight, Republic's $1.1 billion portfolio of Russian securities fell sharply in value. To aggravate matters, the Russian banks said they wouldn't honor the hedging contracts.

There were more troubles in Russia. In August 1998, Republic's reports of dubious transfers involving a company called Benex Worldwide Ltd. led the FBI and British authorities to uncover an arrangement between employees of the Bank of New York and Russian officials and executives, including Konstantin Kagalovsky, Russia's former representative to the International Monetary Fund, to siphon off billions of dollars of IMF payments.[500]

At Safra Republic, executives took the unilateral action of selling off chunks of the emerging market debt the bank held in August 1998. But at Republic New York, executives hesitated to act without explicit orders from Edmond, especially since he had been personally involved with building up the Russian positions. (When he found out they had waited, he was furious.) This was just one manifestation of a larger problem in the Safra banking empire: paralysis amid a fast-paced world. Edmond had once compared running a bank to "running a kindergarten." Although that was an exaggeration, it was true that the bank's executive team was so used to having immediate input and guidance from Edmond that they had difficulty moving quickly in its absence. Amid the carnage in the Russian markets, Republic's stock suffered, falling from $66 in March 1998 to $39.50 in the third quarter, a decline of more than 40 percent.[501]

As Edmond's health improved in October, he began to reconnect. He moved back to Geneva, and then to Monaco. There, he could fulfill his doctors' orders to exercise by walking up and down the Boulevard du Moulin, popping into the shops near the Hermitage Hotel, and stopping for ice cream. But Edmond was still having difficulty functioning at his customary high level. While on the phone, his assistants sometimes couldn't hear him clearly because his arm was shaking so much it would cause the phone to jerk around. His speech was hampered by a stutter, and he had difficulty conversing easily.[502]

More frequently, he found himself having to withdraw. At La Léopolda and in Monaco, he began sleeping in a separate bedroom, because he would wake up frequently in the middle of the night and didn't want to disturb Lily. When "off" episodes arose, he would suddenly excuse himself, in part because he didn't want his grandchildren or colleagues to see him suffering or in a weakened state. There were also, thankfully, periods when he would be better because the cocktails of medications were more effective.[503]

Amid these struggles, Edmond began to collect himself and chart a tentative path for the future. If his brother was not going to take over leading the bank, some changes would have to be made. Walter Weiner, the CEO at Republic, was approaching retirement age. In November 1998, Edmond summoned several of his top lieutenants to Geneva to discuss a succession plan for Republic. And on December 16, Republic formally announced the plan. After the annual meeting on April 21, 1999, Walter Weiner would step down. Dov Schlein would become the new chief executive officer and chairman of the board, Elias Saal would be named chairman of the executive committee, and Stephen Saali named president.

There was no mention of Joseph Safra or any role of the Safra family in the bank's management. At the same time, Republic signaled it was going to engage in another round of cost cutting. Weiner noted that "ongoing profitability review is absolutely vital to the strong competitive position of Republic as we approach the increasingly global and competitive marketplace of the 21st century."

Edmond affirmed, "I am confident that the new management team will ensure that the organization will thrive in the next century."[504]

Walter Weiner's impending departure represented the end of an era. But behind the announcement were indications that a greater epoch might in fact be ending. Republic's (and, by implication, Edmond's) façade of invincibility had been dented. The bank's earnings fell to $248 million in 1998, from $449 million in 1997, largely because of the $165.4 million loss on Russian investments and related hedges. "Such losses stemmed from management's decision to write down all of the Corporation's Russian investment securities to net realizable value," Republic reported.[505]

In Monaco, Edmond continued to soldier on, taking walks, stopping by a café run by an elderly Italian couple that reminded him of Milan, and plotting his next move. He had never been prone to existential angst and self-pity. His life had been a series of successful, energetic campaigns aimed at building institutions. But now he felt that he had reached an impasse, due in large measure to his declining health and the failure to hand over the business to Joseph. "Life as it is, is a *chaddah* [shit]," he lamented to an old Lebanese friend, in Arabic. "What can I do [with the business] if I am by myself?"[506]

In late 1998, the answer to this rhetorical question began to crystallize. Increasingly, as he looked ahead to the dawning of the twenty-first century, the subject of conversations with friends, colleagues, and employees on his walks, and on his phone calls, turned to what emerged as the only logical and intelligent solution: selling the banks.

"I've Sold My Babies"

(DECEMBER 1998–DECEMBER 1999)

In 1982, the only time Edmond Safra had sold a bank he had founded—TDB—he had agonized over a $500 million transaction. The combined price for Republic and Safra Republic would likely be twenty times that. More significantly, it would impact the careers of thousands of employees and the savings of hundreds of thousands of clients.

Edmond loved bidding in public auctions for artwork or fine wine. Even when his health restricted him from consuming rare vintages, he continued to add to his collection. "I can't drink anymore, but I still buy Petrus at auction," he told his lawyer, Jean-Pierre Jacquemoud.[507] But the thought of putting his life's work up for public auction, to be sold to anybody willing to pay, was inconceivable. He was as concerned with placing the banks in the right hands as he was with realizing a return. And this decision was his alone to make. He owned 28.8 percent of Republic's stock through his investment vehicle, Saban. Republic, in turn, owned about half of Safra Republic's shares. And Edmond himself directly owned a further 20.8 percent of Safra Republic.

In December 1998 and January 1999, whether he was on his regular walks in Monaco or holding court at La Léopolda, Edmond began to air the prospect of a sale with aides and colleagues, straining to find peace with the idea. "What do you think if I were to sell the bank?" he asked Sem Almaleh, who had been working with Edmond since the 1950s.[508]

The motives for the sale were personal rather than commercial. Neither bank was a case of what people in management consulting would call a "burning platform." Both were still quite profitable and boasted pristine balance sheets. Some of the Russian losses were ultimately partially reversed, after the markets recovered. Republic earned $248 million in 1998; Safra Republic's earnings rose 6 percent in 1998 to $132.7 million. But it was clear that changes were still needed. Just a few years after the PEP exercise, Republic was engaged in another round of painful restructuring and cost cutting. After reviewing the lines of business, Republic's new management, with Edmond's encouragement, doubled down on its core private banking and niche businesses. In an effort to save $67 million in annual operating costs, the bank moved to consolidate branches, outsource data processing operations, and exit some activities. In the first quarter of 1999, Republic took a $97 million pretax restructuring charge, largely to pay the severance for letting go of some 450 employees.[509]

Ultimately, it was Edmond's pessimism about his health that led to the sale. Parkinson's disease continued to take a relentless toll—physically and psychologically. Marc Bonnant, his attorney, recalls sitting with Edmond one evening when the Parkinson's symptoms were weighing on him. Bonnant, echoing the well-known poem *Inventaire* by Jacques Prevert, listed the many items on the asset side of Edmond's balance sheet. "Of course, you're shaking a bit, you're not gamboling about very much. But you're loved by an exceptional woman; you have friends who are loyal; you're the greatest banker of your generation." At which point Edmond shook his head. Bonnant countered: "Who are the others?"

And Edmond responded, "You know, I don't know them all."[510]

Edmond was making his peace with the fact that the Safra family banks likely wouldn't continue beyond the current generation. "Maybe my brothers are wrong. Maybe they're right. Their prerogatives are different than mine," he told a close friend.[511] Despite the tensions of the previous year, Edmond was still in regular contact with Joseph and Moïse. In February 1999, as the financial crisis spread to Brazil, Edmond and Joseph spoke frequently about how Republic should deal with its exposure to Brazilian bonds. "He is still my brother," Edmond said. "If I can help him I will help him."[512]

But without a successor he truly trusted, Edmond decided he needed to get his substantial and complicated estate in order. After all, if he were to succumb to his illness, Lily would have to sort out the future of two massive institutions. So in January 1999, the machinery for a sale was kicked into motion. Jeff Keil, the former Republic executive who served on the board of Safra Republic, began discreetly discussing the prospect with Wall Street contacts. Bear Stearns, the US investment bank, was one of the parties that was interested. Other confidants began to sound out potential suitors.

Although there were thousands of banks and financial institutions in the world, only a handful would make appropriate partners for Republic and Safra Republic. For starters, the transaction would have to be an all-cash deal. After the American Express debacle, Edmond had no interest in taking stock and having the value of his life's work depend on somebody else's management. And he was intent on selling both banks, which, given their huge assets ($50.4 billion for Republic and $21 billion for Safra Republic), would command a substantial price, at least $10 billion.

Among the small pool of potential buyers, one emerged as a front-runner: HSBC. The history of the Hongkong and Shanghai Banking Corporation resonated with Edmond. It was founded in 1865 in a commercial outpost of one of the era's great empires. One of its original directors was Arthur Sassoon, a member of the Iraqi Jewish banking dynasty that played a key role in the development of Hong Kong. HSBC had its feet firmly planted in established markets such as the UK and Hong Kong, as well as in emerging markets throughout Asia and Latin America. It had an ambitious private banking unit and a significant consumer-focused business in the US. It was, of course, much larger than Republic, with 5,000 offices in seventy-nine countries (compared with thirty-eight for Republic), and $483 billion in total assets. In other words, it possessed the scale and assets not only to absorb Republic and Safra Republic but to augment their efforts. [513]

HSBC CEO John Bond, whom Edmond had never met, was not the type of British banker with whom Edmond had been dealing for decades. Bond, who, like Edmond, never attended college, got into banking as a teenager in Hong Kong far from his birthplace, and spent many years in Asia before running the firm's US consumer operations. Having become CEO in 1993, he was seeking to build up the firm's US consumer and global private banking operations. So Bond was intrigued when he received a call from Rodney Leach, the former TDB banker who had gone on to a career at the Hong Kong–based conglomerate Jardine Matheson. "Would you be interested in Republic National Bank of New York?" Leach asked. Edmond was ready to sell and wished to avoid an auction. "He wants it to go to safe hands, and he thinks HSBC would be the best fit." Bond certainly knew of Edmond and his banks by reputation. As part of his due diligence, he read Bryan Burrough's *Vendetta*, and he called sources at the Federal Reserve.[514]

The approach made sense. But it would have to go in stages in order not to spook people or the markets. In April, Edmond and Lily came to New York, where Republic was holding a farewell party for Walter Weiner, who was finally stepping down as CEO, on April 21. A board meeting was scheduled for about the same time. After the meeting, Edmond summoned Dov Schlein, the newly installed chief executive officer, to his apartment on Fifth Avenue, and broke the news. Edmond had decided to sell the bank to HSBC, but they had yet to agree on the price. "I could see it was like parting with a child; it was an extremely difficult and very emotional decision," Schlein recalled.[515]

For the next two weeks, Republic's top executives would go as usual to their offices at 452 Fifth Avenue during the workday, and then leave at night to meet in hotel rooms with a team of senior executives of HSBC. One of the main points they discussed was price. Republic's stock had fallen to about $39 in late 1998 amid the Russia crisis, but by the spring, with earnings on the rise again, had rallied to the high $50s. Both Republic and Safra Republic were publicly held, which meant investors were continually informed as to precisely how the banks made money. But because of their unique business model, and because of the lingering image of Edmond and his family as secretive Lebanese-Brazilian-Swiss bankers, the value had to be patiently explained to HSBC. With its comparatively small securities and investment banking businesses, Republic remained an outlier among the financial supermarkets on Wall Street. But it had a vast retail bank and a series of highly profitable niche businesses in which Edmond had long excelled: precious metals, gold, currency, banknotes, factoring, private banking. At first, HSBC offered a per-share price in the low $60s. But Edmond was adamant that his team press for a more substantial premium. He had settled on a price of $72 per share, which would give the two banks a valuation of more than $10 billion. All those involved realized that the number seventy-two, being four times eighteen (the numerical value of the Hebrew word "*chai*," or "life"), held a special meaning for Edmond. Ultimately, HSBC, which saw an opportunity to double its private banking business and increase its presence in the vibrant New York market, while strengthening its already large balance sheet, agreed. [516]

Once the deal was struck at the end of April, Bond, who was at the Asian Development Bank meetings in Manila, rushed to New York, going directly from the Concorde flight to Edmond's apartment. There, upon meeting for the first time, they shook hands on the deal. [517] Edmond typically liked to announce deals on a Tuesday, or on the eighteenth of the month. But there was no time to wait for auspicious timing. On Monday, May 10, the transaction was presented as a fait accompli to the markets and to employees. The transaction had two components. First, HSBC would buy every share of Republic for $72 in cash, giving it control over about half of Safra Republic. At the same time, it would issue a tender offer for all the Safra Republic shares not owned by Republic at the same price. Saban, Edmond's investment vehicle, announced it would vote its 29 percent holding in Republic and accept the tender offer with respect to its 20.8 percent stockholding in Safra Republic Holdings. The transaction was expected to close in the fourth quarter of 1999. [518]

This landmark deal represented the highest amount of cash ever paid for a bank in the US, as well as the largest foreign purchase of a US bank. Ordinarily, the news of yet another swashbuckling trading coup by Edmond would trigger an international outpouring of mabruks, mazel tovs, and hearty congratulations. But there was a certain amount of restraint in the offices in Geneva, London, New York, and elsewhere. Part of it was personal concern. The *New York Times* noted, "The deal would likely result in layoffs at Republic's New York operations to eliminate duplication with HSBC Bank USA." Although it had been publicly held for decades, and mergers were quite common in the banking world, Republic had always been an acquirer. Despite Edmond's health issues and the awareness that Joseph Safra would not be taking over, few people at Republic had contemplated such a drastic change. "When the news came out that he agreed to sell the bank to HSBC, there was a stunned silence," noted Republic executive Trevor Robinson.[519]

Edmond, too, felt ambivalent. The transaction was a recognition of not only what he had gained over the years, but what he was losing. When Joseph called to offer his congratulations—"I heard you were selling the bank and I wanted to wish you good luck"—it highlighted the strained familial ties.[520] While many in his immediate circle jumped to congratulate him, they also empathized with the pain he was feeling.

"Yes," Edmond said, "it's like selling my baby. It's very tough. It's a very tough decision." Soon after the announcement, Anita Smaga, one of Edmond and Lily's closest friends, came from Geneva to New York to visit. When they embraced and she congratulated him for a remarkable achievement, he was glum: "You see? I've sold my babies."[521]

In a letter to employees released the day of the sale, Edmond made it clear that he undertook this move reluctantly. "I never could even have considered it except for the fact that my health simply will not allow me to participate in the operation of the banks in the only way I know—deeply and fully, with attention to daily details," he wrote. And for those with the memory of the American Express affair in mind, the sale surely would have prompted more concern. But Edmond assured employees that HSBC shared Republic's values and that John Bond was a man of honor.[522]

The announcement set into motion two processes that would occupy Edmond for the rest of the year: preparing for the merger, which was slated to be consummated in October 1999, and plotting his next campaign. In the summer, as usual, he and Lily repaired to La Léopolda. Perhaps for the last season, executives from throughout the far-flung Safra empire made their way to the magnificent estate nestled in the hills above Villefranche-sur-Mer. Although Edmond didn't plan to have a formal role at the company after the merger, he understood that he had a vital role to play in the remaining months of his banks' independence. HSBC was paying for Republic's financial assets, of course. But without the human assets behind them, especially those who worked in private banking, they weren't worth quite as much. All summer long, Republic private bankers sat with Edmond amid the cypresses to negotiate their future. John Bond came to visit as well, and he found a man who was in no way looking forward to retiring. Edmond was continually on the phone with people in the markets: "What's happening in gold? What's happening in the New York Exchange?"[523]

Maintaining these efforts was a struggle as Parkinson's continued to affect his ability to function at the nonstop pace he'd previously maintained. Given his increased difficulty in speaking fluidly, Edmond would often appear to be withdrawn and quiet. But his mind was continually engaged, and when the conversation struck the right chord he would become energized. Christie's auctioneer François Curiel recalls visiting on July 31, 1999, and enjoying a quiet dinner when they saw a yacht in the bay, "Look, the *Phocéa*, Muña Ayoub's boat," Edmond said. It sparked a twenty-minute conversation about the crew, the management of yachts, the complications of owning compared with renting. When friend Ted Serure came to visit in August, he was warned that Edmond was tired and he should expect to spend only a short time there. "But when he began talking about the past, it was like he was illuminated," said Serure.[524] Edmond's cousin Joseph

Safra, who lived nearby, came to celebrate Edmond's birthday in August. "He was very happy, very joyous. . . . He was very content having sold the bank."

As for the Parkinson's itself, managing the illness became a full-time affair involving a cast of professionals. The pairs of young assistants who always accompanied him were augmented by a large, diverse group of nurses; a spreadsheet showed the rotation, senior people on with junior people. Among them were head nurse Sonia Casiano; an American woman, Vivian Torrente; and a recent addition: Ted Maher, a US Army Special Forces veteran who had worked at Columbia-Presbyterian Hospital, and had been referred by friends of the family, who started in August.

Of course, Lily Safra was the chief and full-time caregiver. And as Edmond began to rely on Lily more and more, observers noted that their mutual affection grew. The progression of the disease had triggered a series of shifts in Edmond Safra—professional, physical, and emotional. In a way, Edmond regarded the struggle with Parkinson's as another one of his campaigns, a challenge to be attacked and surmounted with ingenuity, energy, and optimism. But unlike his campaign to start a new bank, or enroll new customers, this was a campaign Edmond and Lily Safra embarked on together. Dr. Alessandro Di Rocco, an Italian Parkinson's expert who treated Edmond and became a friend, said the couple were "fighting hand-in-hand against the horrible disease that had descended on them." As Edmond's autonomy declined, Lily embraced a role that went beyond organizing their social, charitable, and familial responsibilities, to managing his care and their increasingly complicated daily routines. "Lily was with him every single day, endlessly present, with all her energy and wit, rearranging and reaffirming his and their lives, reassuring with fierce determination that nothing, certainly not Parkinson's, would take away his health, dignity, beauty, purpose," Di Rocco noted. She organized the care and doggedly pursued treatments—accepting the irreversibility of the disease but never accepting the status quo. "When the limits of treatment became obvious, she just went on to the next step: there must be a better way, and we will do anything to find it," Di Rocco recalled. "There was not one day in Edmond's life with Parkinson's that Lily did not fight alongside him, with her strength and vast determination, and with boundless love."[525]

If the summers at La Léopolda were restorative, the routines of the fall were invigorating, always providing Edmond with a renewed sense of purpose. First came the Jewish High Holidays, which in 1999 fell in mid-September. Typically, the week before Yom Kippur, Edmond would dispatch his longtime employee, Abboud Abadi, to contact all the main Sephardic synagogues in Brooklyn and arrange for him to be the highest bidder for the dedication of the Kol Nidre Torah scroll, a particularly special honor, in memory of his parents. Edmond would badger his staff around the world to make sure all the usual donations to synagogues and Jewish community institutions had been made. Even as his illness grew more pronounced, Edmond insisted on fasting on Yom Kippur and standing through the long afternoon service, much to Lily's consternation. At one point, a group of rabbis intervened and effectively ordered Edmond to stop fasting, instructing him to take his pills and drink water on Yom Kippur.[526]

Immediately after the High Holidays, Edmond and Lily traveled to Washington, D.C., where the IMF annual meetings were held from September 25 to September 30. Republic threw one of its parties at the National Gallery. Edmond insisted on going, traveling with two doctors and three nurses. At the event, which attracted its typical large crowd of boldface names, a table was set aside in a quiet area where friends could visit with him. Anne Vitale, the Republic lawyer, had testified in Congress that day about the bank's exemplary anti-money-laundering protocols, and lawmakers had favorably mentioned Edmond and Republic's efforts. Edmond was effusive. "During the course of the meal at the table I would catch his eye, and that bright brilliant smile would be there," Vitale said. In October, Edmond returned to Monaco.[527]

In what should have been a triumphant moment, Edmond had to grapple with an episode that threatened to upset his plans—but that was resolved in typical fashion. On September 30, the US attorney for the Southern District of New York handed down an indictment of a prominent investor. Between 1995 and 1999, Martin Armstrong, an adviser who oversaw a firm called Princeton Global Management, was accused of defrauding Japanese investors. The indictment alleged that he sold $3 billion worth of notes to investors and plowed the cash into currency and commodities. When his trades blew up and notched more than $1 billion in losses, rather than come clean, the government charged, he lied again to investors. Armstrong maintained accounts in Republic New York Securities Corporation's Philadelphia office. With the cooperation of a corrupt employee there, it was alleged, he had issued statements on Republic's letterhead that contained inflated balances—thus helping to conceal losses from internal auditors, clients, and investigators in Japan.[528]

Investigators in Japan had started looking into Armstrong's activities, and in August the Japanese Financial Supervisory Agency forwarded a letter to the Federal Reserve and Republic about its inspection of Armstrong's Tokyo office. Republic took swift action. On September 1, a month before the indictment, it announced the reception of the letter, advised the relevant US regulatory and law enforcement authorities, fired several employees, and then quickly moved to replace the head of the futures division and suspended the chief executive officer of Republic New York Securities.

The timing was problematic. HSBC had scheduled a shareholder meeting on September 9, just a week after this disclosure, to vote to approve the Republic transaction. On September 3, two days after Republic disclosed the investigation, HSBC announced it would push the vote back to October 12. On September 30, when Armstrong was indicted, HSBC announced it would push the vote back again, this time to October 29. Given the fact that employees of a Republic subsidiary were accused of abetting Armstrong's actions, it was clear there would likely be financial consequences—lawsuits, settlements, and demands for restitution—for Republic. And since they were unlikely to be resolved quickly, these costs would likely be assigned to HSBC if it were to proceed with the acquisition. In fact, within weeks after Armstrong's indictment, two class-action investor lawsuits were filed, one on October 7, 1999, and a second on October 15, 1999. Now the $10.3 billion merger hung in the balance. It thus fell on Republic to reassure HSBC that it wouldn't be charged in the matter, and to shield it from potential liability. John Bond wasn't particularly concerned. "Either Edmond covers us, or we will use the force majeure clause" to get out of the deal, he said. He told colleagues at HSBC: "My judgment of Edmond is that he is the fellow who will fix this."[529]

This was a painful moment for Edmond, for whom nothing had ever been more important than his banks' reputation for integrity. Here was a series of actions by employees of a subsidiary that threatened that reputation. In effect, Edmond decided to personally salvage the merger. Over the years, he had always seen himself as standing behind the obligations of his banks. Now, rather than let the investors who owned most of the shares of Republic take a haircut on their price, which would have been the usual practice in such circumstances, Edmond suggested that it all come out of his personal holdings. On November 9, Edmond announced that he had agreed to accept $450 million less for his shares in Republic than he was originally entitled to—and up to $180 million less on top of that, depending on final liability. All the other shareholders would still receive $72 for each of their shares. "I am taking this action because I believe that a swift completion of the transaction will be to the benefit of Republic's clients, shareholders and employees to whom my life's work has been devoted," he wrote. "Both Republic and HSBC have always acted to maintain the highest reputations for their institutions. This is just one more example of the character of both organizations."

The statement also confirmed his support for the coming integration of the two banks. "Not only will I become a major client of HSBC, but I also intend to take an active role in ensuring a smooth transition for all our existing clients," he wrote. Bond's response was both relieved and gracious: "We have the greatest admiration for Edmond Safra taking personal action which embodies the spirit and integrity of Edmond and the franchise he has built. The strategic reasons for the acquisitions going ahead remain compelling."[530]

While it was all being ironed out, HSBC wanted to delay the payment for the merger into the new year—in part to minimize anticipated risks associated with Y2K. In effect, now, the books were closing on the independent lives of Republic and Safra Republic, two remarkably successful startup banks. In October, Republic released its final quarterly report as an independent entity. For the first nine months of the year, the bank had earned $316 million in net income, including a $45 million gain on its investment in Canary Wharf.

With the $72 share price assured, it was clear that long-term investors would make out quite well. At Safra Republic, those who had invested in the October 1988 initial public offering stood to realize a compounded annual return of about 20 percent. Even after ceding $450 million, Edmond would still be walking away with about $3 billion—on top of all the other assets he owned, which still included Banque de Crédit National in Beirut.

More than a quarter century after his last visit to Beirut, selling BCN, his father's bank, was still off the table. The ravaged city, and the troubled country in which it lay, still stood at the core of his identity. When Edmond was formally naturalized as a citizen of Monaco in July 1999, he faced a decision. It was a hard policy that Monégasques had to give up their prior nationalities. Edmond held Brazilian and Lebanese citizenship. He was resigned to giving up the Brazilian passport, much as he loved the country that had been a haven for him and his family. But Lebanon was another story. "I'm sorry, wait a second. Lebanon, I can't," he said. In the end, the Monaco authorities made an exception and allowed Edmond to keep dual citizenship—even though ever visiting Beirut again was out of the question.

Edmond's career presiding over a sprawling international bank was coming to an end. Seeking to avoid a repeat of the American Express debacle, he carved out a path forward. He agreed not to compete with HSBC for seven years, but he was allowed to hire several associates and could manage his funds and those of a certain number of clients—a family office with a maximum of $5 billion in initial funds and 100 clients. Over the summer and fall, he began to plot the creation of a "société financière." The trusted employees who were to join him, among them Ezra Marcos, Ariel Arazi, David Joory, Marcos Zalta, and Sol Gindi, dubbed the plan "Bedrock," after the Flintstones cartoon—in their world, Edmond was Fred and Lily was Wilma. The main office would be in Monaco, and they leased 10,000 square feet at the GM building on Madison Avenue and 59th Street in Manhattan. Bedrock would formally commence operations in January, once it received the funds from the sale.[531]

Despite his health issues, Edmond Safra maintained his continuous scroll throughout November. Based largely in his apartment in La Belle Epoque in Monaco, he was constantly on the phone, tending to issues, negotiating transactions, looking after charitable interests. He was looking forward to being honored by the French government as a *Chévalier de la Légion d'Honneur*, which was due to be declared on December 31. And he continued to receive visitors. Among them was John Bond, who came to Monaco to thank Edmond personally. On Tuesday, November 30, Bond and his wife, Liz, had lunch with Edmond and Lily in Monaco.[532]

With only a month until the handover, Safra was constantly on the phone to New York and Geneva going over various issues. And he was relentlessly looking ahead, even reflecting on some of the upsides of no longer being the chairman of a bank, but merely the owner of a finance company. From a very young age, Edmond had always taken pains not to be seen in a casino. But in the first week of December, his friend Victor Smaga was in the hospital, recovering from an operation. On Thursday night, December 2, Edmond called. "Well, Victor, now I am a free man." Smaga had always loved slot machines. "I promise you, if you get well soon, we will go together to the casino for the first time in my life."[533]

That Thursday had been a normal busy day. Edmond went to the office late in the morning. He met with the Bedrock team, as they were set to decide on the name of the new company. After a lifetime of naming institutions after his father, he was finally going to name one after himself: "Edmond J. Safra Asset Management." He called New York to speak to Republic CEO Dov Schlein, who told him he had just received the final approval necessary for the sale, from the

New York City Banking Department. "How wonderful," Edmond said. "Mazel tov." Amid the meetings, he took a phone call from Rabbi Ovadia Yosef, the revered Sephardic chief rabbi of Israel, who asked him to help pay for the emergency medical expenses of a poor family in need—Edmond agreed to send $50,000. He discussed the relocation of a component of his art collection with an assistant who had come from Milan. Edmond and Lily, who had just returned from London, where she attended the reopening of the Royal Opera House, dined alone together that evening.[534] It was a quiet end to a typically whirlwind day.

A Tragedy in Monaco

(DECEMBER 1999)

The circumstances of Edmond Safra's death, like those of his life, were the subject of a great deal of rumor and innuendo. But the facts surrounding it, as testified to by many witnesses and established in a court of law, were straightforward: Edmond Safra died at around 7:00 a.m. on Friday, December 3, 1999, of smoke inhalation after one of his nurses, in a misguided and criminally negligent scheme to prove his loyalty, intentionally set a fire in the Safras' apartment in Monaco. These actions; a series of mistakes and poor decisions by the responding authorities; and Edmond's understandable reaction to a visible threat to his personal security resulted in the tragic deaths of two people—and the sudden end of a remarkable life and career.

The prospect of someone being able to harm Edmond and Lily in their penthouse apartment on the fifth and sixth floors of La Belle Epoque seemed far-fetched. In the summer of 1999, an extensive integrated security system had been completed, which included reinforced doors, shutters that closed electronically, bulletproof glass windows, and a sophisticated alarm system (which included video cameras, motion detectors, and panic buttons in each room). These systems were linked to a security desk and in turn connected to Monaco Sécurité, a private security company. Given Edmond's need for around-the-clock medical care and the household staff, the systems were designed to replace a substantial physical presence of guards—the "SAS," in Lily's term. As security chief Shmulik Cohen later testified, "The idea for security was to build a sort of hermetic bubble and to put one of my guys inside." Lily felt no need to have a full security staff at La Belle Epoque. "What can happen to us here?" she asked Cohen in September. A more visible presence of guards, many of whom were former Israeli military, was deemed necessary only at La Léopolda, with its vast grounds and many points of access.[535]

The conspiracy that resulted in Edmond Safra's death began and ended with a single person inside the hermetic bubble, an unstable man with an increasingly tenuous grip on reality. Ted Maher, the nurse who had joined the staff in August 1999, was proficient and apparently reliable. But the former Green Beret was isolated and far from his family, who remained in the United States. Placed on a full-time status on November 20, Maher was insecure about his position and somewhat unmoored. He lived at a hotel alone, spoke no French, and was grappling with legal bills from a long-running custody battle with an ex-wife.[536] He fretted that other members of the staff had it out for him, and claimed that the head nurse, Sonia Casiano, purposely gave him difficult work schedules. His behavior, including asking questions about how the window shutters worked, and standing on a chair to lift up a ceiling tile in the nursing station to examine what was above, struck some as off. In early November, he had walked from Monaco to San Remo, a forty-kilometer journey, leading one staff member to privately compare him to the movie character Forrest Gump.

After fellow nurse Vivian Torrente told him that she had overheard someone repeat the Forrest Gump comment to Casiano, Maher grew upset and apparently snapped. As Maher told investigators a few days after the attack, he took several of Edmond's Clozaril pills and then took action that, he believed, would bolster his standing in the household. He would stage and report an attack, and then claim to have personally fended it off—at great apparent physical harm. He later told investigators, "I wanted to make the ultimate sacrifice in order to prove that I was worthy of being trusted."[537] And so, in the early hours of the morning, while the household was asleep, Maher began to act. Just after 4:30 a.m., he cracked open a window in the gym, on the sixth floor, adjacent to the nursing station and Edmond's bedroom. (Edmond was still insisting that Lily sleep in a separate room on the sixth floor.) This was to be the site of an alleged forcible entry. In the nursing station area, he scraped his face and stomach with sandpaper he had brought with him, to give the impression of having been wounded in a fight. Then he jabbed himself with a knife he had purchased on his trek to San Remo, creating superficial stab wounds on his leg and stomach.[538]

A visibly bleeding Maher then woke Edmond at about 4:45 a.m. and delivered the alarming news: an intruder was in the apartment. Together with Vivian Torrente, the other nurse on duty, Maher maneuvered Edmond out of his bed, with the assistance of a mechanical hoist, ushered them into Edmond's dressing room, gave them his cell phone and instructed them to lock the door. Edmond, believing Maher, immediately called Lily. He told her that there were intruders in the apartment and that she should stay in her room and lock the door. Lily called the guards at La Léopolda, as well as Shmulik Cohen, the head of security.[539]

Maher cleaned his wounds with alcohol, and tossed the bottle and bandages he had used into a waste bin. Then, in the act that turned an attempt at currying favor into a crime, Maher lit a fire in the small garbage can and positioned it under a smoke detector, which set off a fire alarm at about ten minutes to 5:00 a.m. A few minutes later, Maher shut the door to the nursing station and took the elevator down to the lobby. Upon seeing Maher bleeding, the doorman called an ambulance.[540]

Suddenly, on an otherwise calm morning in Monaco, there were twin crises on Avenue d'Ostende—a report of armed and dangerous intruders and a fire. The alerts set off a series of reactions that, far from mitigating the threat, aggravated it.

The police station and fire station were no more than a few minutes away from La Belle Epoque. And between 5:00 and 5:15 a.m., police officers and teams of firefighters, equipped with vehicles and ladders, arrived. Despite the presence of many high-profile individuals,

Monaco authorities weren't accustomed to dealing with violent criminals. Moreover, they were unfamiliar with the specific security situation in the apartment. So when they showed up to the lobby, and saw a bleeding Maher, who told them of the attackers, their instinct was to move cautiously and slowly. Rather than simply take the elevator to the fifth floor, breach the apartment by whatever means available, and evacuate the residents quickly, they proceeded methodically—securing one floor at a time. As the police tended to Maher's wounds, residents in the area began to alert the fire department to the smoke and flames visible at the top of the building.

Also arriving on the scene, at about 5:20, having sped down the hills from La Léopolda, was Shmulik Cohen. Knowing what he knew of the security system, he was skeptical that there had been an intruder. But although Cohen was intimately familiar with the apartment's layout, and knew precisely where Edmond and Lily were, the police wouldn't let him past the lobby. And when Cohen eluded them and hopped on an elevator to the fifth floor, the police, not knowing who he was, detained and handcuffed him.[541]

Almost from the moment they entered the dressing room, Edmond and Vivian Torrente were using the cell phone Maher had left them. Among those they called were Sonia Casiano, the staff at La Léopolda, building security at La Belle Epoque, and the Monaco police. The message they delivered was clear and consistent: they were locked in the apartment and someone with a knife was in the building.

Police finally allowed Shmulik Cohen to access a terrace on the sixth floor, where he and police forced open the electric shutters of the sixth-floor window to the bedroom Lily had been sleeping in. At 6:00 a.m., they helped Lily, still in a nightgown, crawl through an opening onto the fire escape, and brought her down to the street, where a small crowd had formed, including several members of the Monaco bank's staff. Spurred by an accelerant (the bottle of alcohol Maher had tossed in the waste bin) and plenty of flammable material, the fire had developed into a lethal conflagration. With the windows and shutters closed tight for the evening, the air conditioning systems began distributing smoke throughout the sprawling apartment. In the meantime, firefighters were attempting to attack the conflagration from the outside of the building.[542]

Like the first responders, Edmond Safra was, in some ways, ill-equipped to deal with the situation. The Parkinson's impaired him seriously enough that he normally needed assistance to move in the hours before his first dose of medication given at 9:00 a.m. The disease may also have affected his ability to think clearly in a moment of crisis. Personal insecurity had been a feature of his life, as he had grown up in a world where his community and family were routinely targeted for violence: in Aleppo, where riots in the 1940s caused family members to flee; in Beirut, where his school had been bombed and the family's apartment was ransacked; in Brazil and Argentina, where colleagues and family members had been targeted for kidnapping and ransom schemes. The American Express saga had further hammered home to Edmond that there were plenty of ruthless people who would not hesitate to cause him harm. But he may never have expected a betrayal from within.

Years earlier, in the 1970s, Edmond and Lily were at the headquarters of Ponto Frio in Rio de Janeiro, when thieves broke in. They hid in an office, taking care to escape detection, until the robbers left. Now, in what seemed to be a similar situation, Edmond's instinct was to shelter in place until the threat departed. So when the police spoke with him on the phone and urged him to open the door and try to make his way through the apartment to an exit or access point, he refused, believing Maher's warnings about assailants waiting outside.[543]

As the minutes went by, after 6:00 a.m., the supposed intruders weren't the most obvious problem; the fire was. Having spread through air handling ducts, smoke was coming from the roof and flames were shooting from a sixth-floor window. Here, again, the security measures aggravated the situation. Firefighters attacking the fire from the sixth floor managed to reach Safra's window via the aerial ladder but could not raise the shutters, in part because the fire had shut off the electric circuitry that controlled their operation. And as a result, they couldn't break the glass to create an opening for people or oxygen.

When Cohen was able to unlock the doors to the fifth floor on the opposite side from the dressing room, the smoke and heat were sufficiently powerful that rescuers couldn't go in without breathing apparatuses, which they didn't have.[544]

At about 6:30 a.m., smoke began to penetrate the dressing room. When Casiano called Torrente and told her to place wet towels at the base of the door and get on the floor, she could hear Edmond coughing. The call ended abruptly. Their lungs overwhelmed by smoke, both Edmond and Vivian Torrente lost consciousness. It wasn't until an hour after that last phone call that firefighters finally reached the dressing room. What should have taken a matter of minutes—securing the premises; finding Edmond, Lily, and the household employees; bringing them to safety; and extinguishing a fire—wound up taking nearly three hours. Edmond Safra and Vivian Torrente were dead.[545]

The shocking news, relayed from the first responders to family and associates on the ground in Monaco, spread quickly through the Safra network. Trevor Robinson, the head of London operations, received a phone call from his deputy: "Edmond Safra is dead." Michel Elia, Edmond and Lily's son-in-law, woke up Sol Gindi, Edmond's assistant, at 3:00 a.m. in New York, and told him to come to the South of France immediately.[546]

The news swiftly migrated into the electronic communication networks that were the circulatory systems for the global financial network, through cell phones and texts, through internal messaging systems and wire services. At about 4:00 a.m. New York time (9:00 a.m. GST), headlines began to cross the tapes on the Dow Jones, Bloomberg, and Reuters terminals. The small cadre of traders who worked the night shift at Republic's headquarters on the tenth floor at 452 Fifth Avenue were shocked to see incomprehensible news flash across their screens: "Edmond Safra believed dead." Throughout the morning, shell-shocked employees trickled into the offices, many congregating on the street outside, trying to make sense of the headlines.[547]

The reaction was a mix of shock, disbelief, and grief—and swift action. In the Jewish tradition, the machinery of mourning and burial kicks in immediately after the moment of death. Before people even understood what had happened, or began to process the loss and its implications, plans had to be made. For Jews, the mandate is to bury the deceased within twenty-four hours—accounting for the break of Shabbat, and, in the modern world, the need for travel arrangements. Thus, upon hearing the news of a death, burial societies immediately shift into gear, laying plans for funerals, sending people to sit with the body and read psalms, and making other arrangements.

Edmond Safra was at home in so many different places that the question of where he would be laid to rest was a complex one. There wasn't really a single family plot. His mother, Esther, was buried in the Jewish cemetery in Beirut, about a mile from the family's erstwhile home on Rue Georges Picot. His father, Jacob, was interred in the Butanta cemetery in São Paulo. Elie, his older brother, had been laid to rest in 1993 on the Mount of Olives, overlooking the Old City of Jerusalem. Edmond had long ago purchased a plot there, too. But in the moment, the decision was made to bury him in the place that he had called home for the longest time: Geneva.

Once again, as they had when invited to the sumptuous party at La Léopolda in 1988, or for the celebration of Edmond's fifty years in banking in New York in 1997, the constituents of the vast Safra diaspora began to gather—only this time, in deep sorrow. They came by private plane, by train, and by car, from Brazil and Brooklyn, from France and Israel and Italy. Rabbis, associates, employees, family, and friends jammed planes to Geneva. In a makeshift crisis room at Safra Republic, a host of plans were made for the funeral, to be held at Hekhal Haness, the Sephardic synagogue he frequented in Geneva. It was planned for Monday, December 6.[548]

In parallel, the fog of uncertainty enshrouding the events of Friday, December 3, began to disperse. For the first twenty-four hours after Edmond's death, the circumstances remained a mystery. There were, of course, no assailants to be apprehended. At first, Maher, recovering in Princess Grace Hospital, seemed a hero in the episode, and Edmond's staff arranged to fly his wife to Monaco to visit. But a different story quickly came out, even as hundreds of people began to make their way into Hekhal Haness. On Saturday, as they began a careful investigation, the Monaco police realized something was amiss in Maher's tale. On examination, the closed-circuit television cameras found no video footage of the alleged intruders. None of the other household staff noted an intruder. The physical evidence was also confounding. Maher was wounded, he said, by stabs of a knife—but there were no tears in his clothes. When he got into the ambulance, he had two knives in his possession. His story was inconsistent—with the facts, and with his own stories. At first, he told the police there were two masked intruders, one of whom hit him on the head while the other stabbed him. Then he said there was a single assailant, who was unmasked. On Monday, December 6, Maher confessed that he had cut himself and set the fire. "I was alone," Maher would write in his confession; "there was never any attack. I cut and mutilated myself, I started the fire, and I left in order to create the impression of an attack."[549]

None of this was known to the 700 people who gathered at Hekhal Haness on the morning of December 6. The audience, filled with people who had a personal, commercial, and communal connection to Edmond Safra, was stunning in its diversity and range. There were titans of finance, bankers, rabbis who hailed from Beirut and Aleppo, Muslim leaders, childhood friends from the Alliance, bank employees, and Israeli government officials. John Bond came in from Hong Kong. Only an event for Edmond Safra would attract Elie Wiesel and fashion designer Hubert de Givenchy, Prince Sadruddin Aga Khan and David Levy, Israel's former foreign minister.[550]

In the wake of Edmond's death, encomia had poured in from the powerful, the famous, and the wealthy. Henry Kissinger praised Safra's "warmth and humor, his wisdom and integrity." Margaret Thatcher lauded his "high intelligence and unquenchable energy," which "made him one of the outstanding bankers of the postwar era."

But the funeral itself was largely an occasion for humble and timeless Jewish traditions. As was fitting for a man who relished his connections to synagogues around the world, four rabbis were participating: Rabbi Joseph Sitruk, the Tunisian-born chief rabbi of

France, beloved by Sephardic Jews worldwide; Rabbi Mordechai Eliyahu, the revered former Sephardic chief rabbi of Israel and the founder of Jerusalem's Hechal Yaakov (a synagogue dedicated by Edmond and his brothers in memory of their father, Jacob); Rabbi Alexandre Safran, the widely admired eighty-nine-year-old Romanian-born chief rabbi of Geneva; and Geneva's Chabad rabbi, Rabbi Mendel Pevzner. The packed sanctuary echoed with the poignant tones of the psalms, sung in the ancient Sephardic intonations that had reverberated for centuries in the Great Synagogue in Aleppo; at his ruined childhood synagogue, Magen Avraham, in Beirut; and in humble street-front shuls in Brooklyn. Rabbi Sitruk gave brief remarks, touching on Edmond's philanthropy. Elie Wiesel and John Bond also spoke.[551]

The hearse led a slow procession on a three-mile route along winding roads away from the placid lakefront, across the gently flowing Avre River, up the Route du Pas de l'Echelle, and down a narrow side street that funneled the crowd past a modest farm at the foot of Mont Salève to the Jewish cemetery in Veyrier, which straddles the French border.

There is a finality and humility to Jewish funeral rites. At the gravesite, a cantor chants the haunting melody of the "El Maleh Rachamim" memorial prayer, and the mourners recite the Kaddish. After their loved one is lowered in the ground, as a final act of kindness and obligation, family and friends perform the mitzvah of shoveling dirt onto the coffin. In this manner, in this unmistakably European and Alpine setting, the son of Wadi Abu Jamil was laid to rest. The crowds dissipated to receptions, for the family to sit shiva and mourn for the week.

At noon, on December 31, 1999, just twenty-five days later, as the shloshim period—the traditional thirty days of mourning—was nearing its end, Edmond Safra's final banking coup came to fruition. In the weeks after Edmond's death, the long and complex acquisition process for Republic and Safra Republic continued. On December 29, 36.25 million shares of Safra Republic Holdings were tendered to HSBC, which, combined with the shares already owned by

Republic, represented 99.4 percent of Safra Republic's shares. At 12:15 p.m. on the last day of the twentieth century, the final milestones were achieved, and HSBC completed its acquisition of Republic. Henceforth, Republic would operate under the banner of HSBC USA, and the units of Safra Republic became HSBC Republic Bank. All shareholders received the $72 per share that had been promised, for a combined enterprise value of more than $10 billion—save for Edmond, who had agreed to take a reduced amount to account for the costs associated with the Armstrong affair. The shares were delisted from the stock exchanges on which they traded (New York and London for Republic, Luxembourg and Switzerland for SRH) and the process of integration began. "While we are extremely sad to be moving forward without Edmond Safra, merging our organizations and maintaining the highest standards of integrity and customer service will be the best way of honoring his memory," John Bond said.[552]

Edmond's life, filled with so many successful campaigns and triumphs, had also been touched by tragedy and difficulties, from the early death of his mother to the forced exile from Beirut, from the American Express smear campaign to painful familial rifts. And here, too, in the finality of these transactions, was an element of the bittersweet. The sale represented a triumph and a capstone to a life and career, although not necessarily the one he might have foreseen. At some level, there was disappointment that there would be no Safra family of banks going forward. But the events of December had proven precisely why the sale was the right decision. In Edmond's absence, the banks, their customers, and the customers' deposits were delivered into the safe hands of HSBC, to which it would fall to carry on Edmond's commercial legacy and tradition. Of equal import, the proceeds from the sale would provide the means to carry on his legacy and philanthropic vision in perpetuity.

In the weeks after Edmond's death, a host of impromptu memorial services took place at synagogues and schools in the US, Europe, and South America. Friends and associates of Edmond Safra spoke, now including "*alav hashalom*," ["peace be upon him"] with every mention of his name; videos about his life were shown; friends and colleagues shared recollections; and psalms were sung in Sephardic-inflected Hebrew. On the thirtieth day after Safra's burial, January 9, 2000, a memorial service in New York's Spanish and Portuguese synagogue attracted a large number of colleagues and family members. Lily Safra read to the audience a letter from their granddaughter, Lily. Zubin Mehta conducted members of the Israel Philharmonic. Among those who spoke were Shimon Peres, former Harvard University president Neil Rudenstine, former World Bank president James Wolfensohn, and Javier Perez de Cuellar, the former secretary-general of the United Nations. The same day, in the cemetery in Geneva, Edmond's gravestone was unveiled. Rabbi Yaakov Attie of Aleppo, Beirut, and, now, Bat Yam, chose two brief verses for the inscription: *Imru tzadik ki tov, ki pri m'alaleihem yochelu* ("Praise the righteous man for he is good, for the fruit of their deeds they shall eat" [Isaiah 3:10]) and *Tzadik b'emunato yichyeh* ("The pious man lives by his faith"), from Habakkuk.

These ceremonies and gatherings provided cathartic communal occasions to recognize and declare what Edmond Safra had accomplished in his sixty-seven years, to acknowledge what he meant to people, to grapple with his loss and absence, and to memorialize the great distances he had traveled in nearly seven decades of constant motion. After the shloshim ends, life is supposed to return to normal, even as people carve out time, energy, and emotion for remembrance. And so, in the first few days of a new century, and a new millennium, the books were closed on Edmond's life, on a business career that was like no other in the final half of the twentieth century, and on the two banks he had built from the ground up into vast global enterprises. While marking a sharp and definite conclusion to an era, the shloshim and these transactions also signified the beginning of an enduring legacy.

---

1 9

An Enduring Legacy

T hat image of the final moments of Edmond Safra's life, a physically diminished man trapped in perilous circumstances, could
not have been more distant from the realities of his sixty-seven-year
life. This was a person utterly unconstrained by the historical circumstances of his birth, by the vast geopolitical shifts that remade the
world, by sudden turns in the market that upended institutions, or by
campaigns orchestrated by those who wished to tarnish his business
and his name. For more than fifty years, Edmond Safra had been an
instigator, a founder, a creator who shaped history and influenced
thousands of lives by building banks—with an unrivaled record of
success. One would be hard-pressed to think of a more successful
banker in the second half of the twentieth century.

Edmond Safra's sixty-seven years contained enough travel, relationships, and accomplishments to last for several lifetimes. It was
a remarkable journey that touched every continent and involved
doing business with an extraordinary range of customers and clients,
from central banks to sheep farmers, from blue-chip companies to
small merchants. As Edmond founded and built immense institutions from scratch, he created his own atmosphere—there was a
distinctive manner in the way Safra banks acted, spoke, and worked.
Although there was no cure for the degenerative disease from which
Edmond suffered, the end of his life was nevertheless remarkably

abrupt. The funeral, the weeklong shiva, and the shloshim period passed quickly. The sense of tragedy was compounded by the fact that Edmond had felt that his life as a banker was part of a multigenerational calling. "What was intended to be a thousand-year story turned out to be a thirty-three-year story," said Jeff Keil, at least as it pertained to Republic New York.

After his death, there were no Edmond Safra banks. There would be no Edmond J. Safra Asset Management company to sign up new clients. In the years after Edmond's death, both Joseph and Moïse would continue their remarkable success with Banco Safra in Brazil, and would bring their own sons into their business. But their careers would also be plagued by intrafamilial conflicts and divisions. Both having also suffered from Parkinson's disease, Moïse died in 2014 at the age of eighty and Joseph in 2021, at the age of eighty-two.

The events of December 3, 1999, brought an end to a life of campaigns and obligations cheerfully assumed. Despite shouldering immense weights, Edmond Safra had a lightness and ease in the way he carried himself. A host of daunting tasks and concepts came easily to him, whether it was striding into new arenas, engaging with clients, or negotiating choppy markets. When he departed the scene, so too did the characteristic Safra style of banking—courtly and Old World; based on trust, reputation, and personal guarantees; fueled by a keen assessment and avoidance of risk, sharp trading insights, and ambition. The banker, as Edmond Safra conceived him, was supposed to be a guardian of assets and a careful lender. He was to keep to commitments even in the absence of formal written agreements, and to stand by his company's actions, deposits, and other obligations. He could make money—a lot of it—without using too much leverage or making reckless loans. Although many of those who worked with Edmond internalized his messages and carried them forward, those qualities have been in short supply in the global banking system since his death. His unique approach was thrown into sharp relief amid the 2008 financial crisis, when bankers, after an orgy of irresponsible lending, failed en masse and took huge bailouts from the government in order to avoid having their shares be worthless—only to pay

themselves massive bonuses. Amid an industry-wide lack of responsibility and care, journalist Gary Weiss asked rhetorically: "Where
have you gone, Edmond Safra?"

Edmond Safra believed that where you come from should be a
guide rather than a hindrance; that heritage and tradition are a source
of support, strength, and identity. And while they influence and direct
the way you carry yourself, they don't constrict your path. In fact, as
he showed time and again, the limits to human capacity are in imagination, work, intelligence, relationships—not the circumstances or
place in which you were born. Edmond didn't have to consult management books or professionals to decide what course of action was
the right one to take. Some of his judgment had been drilled into him
by his father, a great deal of it came to him by instinct, and more was
acquired: he continually learned from his experiences and applied
the lessons to his own life.

In a globalized world, Edmond Safra embodied the attributes
that management thinkers identify as agility and resilience. He was
comfortable with his multifaceted identity, at home in Brazil and
Switzerland, Beirut and New York. He could be at ease in the cor-
ridors of power or in a small Sephardic shul. A man who himself
left school at fifteen, he was a passionate believer in the transformative power of university education. The patron of mystics such as
Rabbi Meir Baal HaNess and Rabbi Shimon Bar Yohai was also a
major supporter of medical science. A devotee of traditions and
ritual, he continually embraced novel technologies and new ways of
doing business. The constant traveler who found himself at home
in so many different places was intent on creating safe and dignified
spaces for Jewish people to pray and gather in places where they
had long been—or in places where they wound up. Having lived
the Jewish diaspora experience, he was intent on making Jewish life
more comfortable.

Edmond Safra lived on a grand scale and undeniably was interested
in the accumulation of wealth, art, property, and fine objects. A happy
warrior for his clients and protector of his employees, he willingly
sought out and assumed more and more obligations because he could,

because he was expected to, and because it brought him great joy and satisfaction to do so. *Credit* comes from the Latin root meaning *belief.* And Edmond believed—in himself, in his family, in his God, in his employees, in his community, in the potential for the future.

What, then, is Edmond Safra's legacy? It's a complicated question, made more complicated by the traditions from which he came and to which he adhered. Unlike other multigenerational family businesses, his didn't leave behind an operating company. As important as his commercial success was, it was only one dimension of his work. The lessons from his life are manifold—to be learned, but also to be lived and experienced. In fact, a substantial portion of his work did continue after his death. His legacy is not merely the assets he left behind, which support a foundation. Rather, they are a mindset; a set of ideas; and an ethos of how bankers should conduct themselves, how people should treat each other, and how Jews should relate to their communities.

In his life Edmond Safra demonstrated this idea of responsibility to others in concentric circles: family, the local Jewish community, Sephardim around the world, Israel, and, ultimately, the world at large. In his later years, Edmond had occasionally expressed frustration about the fate of his banking empire: "I built this all, and for whom?" He was also prone to quoting Ecclesiastes, the poetic biblical passages that speak to the futility and evanescence of man's toil. But Edmond Safra built his wealth for a lasting purpose, and for the benefit of the world. When the sale to HSBC closed at the end of December 1999, his shares were turned into cash, which formed the lion's share of his estate. The value was estimated at about $3 billion, even after he agreed to take less than he was entitled to, in order to resolve the Armstrong litigation.

But there was much more. Edmond owned several highly valuable commercial buildings along the lakefront in Geneva. There were the homes he and Lily had in Geneva, London, and Monaco. And, of course, La Léopolda—one of the most valuable freestanding homes in the world. These homes were themselves filled with the remarkable collection of paintings and sculpture, furniture, watches, books, and other objects he and Lily had assiduously collected over the years. One of the smallest of his holdings may have held the most import. At his death, Edmond still owned Banque de Crédit National in Beirut, the bank his father had founded as Banque Jacob E. Safra on Rue Allenby several decades before—and where Edmond had absorbed his first lessons in the trade.

Edmond's will made provisions for Lily and her children, Adriana Elia and Eduardo Cohen; for Adriana's children; and for his surviving sisters Arlette, Huguette, and Gaby. The rest went to the Edmond J. Safra Philanthropic Foundation, instantly creating yet another institution that would invest for the future. Chaired by Lily, the foundation had a mandate to carry on Edmond's charitable work in an institutionalized manner, giving even more structure and purpose to his giving, which had started as early as the 1940s, when he provided refrigerating equipment to the Alliance in Paris.

The foundation took some time to get up and running. And in the months after his death, there was still some unfinished business for his loved ones to cope with. It would fall to Edmond's heirs and associates to continue to defend his honor and dispel mistruths, rumors, and innuendos—the kind that had always surrounded him simply by virtue of his background, those that had been actively fomented by American Express's agents, and those that were routinely aired by people seeking to make mischief or simply attract attention.

The months after Edmond's death were a difficult time for Lily and the Safra family, as they waited patiently for the machinery of justice to kick into gear. The circumstances of his demise inevitably led the prurient and the malicious to start rumors. Within days of Edmond's death, Ted Maher had confessed: there were never any intruders; he acted entirely alone.[557] But the wheels of justice turn slowly, and Maher didn't stand trial in Monaco until the fall of 2002, nearly three years later. That created something of a vacuum. Surely, many people wondered, there was more to the story than Maher's misbegotten plan and the unfortunate series of events in the early morning of December 3. The mix of money, tragedy, and fame proved irresistible to journalists and storytellers seeking attention.

Dominick Dunne, the *Vanity Fair* writer who specialized in the scandals of the well-known and well-born, undertook his own "investigation." In "Death in Monaco," which appeared in the December 2000 issue of *Vanity Fair,* Dunne, often unbound by journalistic conventions, freely aired anonymous sources making spurious suggestions without evidence, posing them as questions. Were there really two bullets in Edmond's body? Was it the work of the Russian mob? Was Edmond killed because he helped people launder money? Or, alternatively, because he had blown the whistle on Russian money launderers? Or it could have been Palestinian terrorists. Making himself a protagonist in the story, Dunne made a large meal out of the fact that Lily Safra obviously wasn't interested in engaging with his musings. In a sign that the American Express campaign continued to pollute the information stream fifteen years later, Dunne also recycled the discredited allegations that Edmond had dealt with Colombian drug cartels, and that his plane was used in the Iran-Contra scandal. These were twice- and thrice-told tales, no truer for the repetition. The difference was that this time Edmond wasn't there to defend himself.

It is worth repeating—again—that there was no evidence for either the grand conspiracy theories or the gossip columnist–manufactured "controversies," such as that all the security videotapes had been destroyed (they hadn't); that the Safras' security guards had been "mysteriously absent" that night (in fact, after the installation of the security system there were never any guards at the apartment in Monaco, only at the large La Léopolda property); or that Maher was obliged to sign a confession in French without an English translation, without understanding what was written (minutes of the interrogations and trial, during which he was provided simultaneous translation, prove this to be false). At several moments on the morning of December 3, events could have turned out differently. But the fundamental truth, as the courts would find, remained that Maher alone took the actions that led to the deaths.

As the state sought punishment for the deaths of Edmond and Vivian Torrente, the survivors of those killed sought symbolic damages of one euro each—Lily, Joseph and Moïse, Edmond's sisters, and his nephew Jackie, as well as Torrente's family. The defense, two distinguished Monégasque attorneys, Georges Blot and Donald Manasse, as well as an American, Michael Griffith, had little to work with, given the evidence and the fact that Maher had confessed. Nor did Maher's lawyers contest the basic facts—that Maher had created the scenario and intentionally set the fire. But they did try to deflect blame and muddy the waters. The defense argued that Edmond's death was the fault of the rescuers. Had they arrived more quickly, Maher and his attorneys argued, the two would have lived; thus Maher shouldn't be held responsible. A second line of defense tried to make something of the medical examiners' report of Vivian Torrente. There was blood in her thyroid gland, and bruises on her neck, which, the defense argued, were signs that she had been choked. The defense suggested that Edmond had physically stopped his nurse from leaving, as he feared she might give away their location. Consequently, Maher could be held responsible only for the death of Edmond Safra.[554]

The court found that this argument didn't stand up to the physical evidence, or the facts found at trial. Edmond's Parkinson's made even basic movements almost impossible. Medical examiners found the hematomas resulted from Torrente choking due to asphyxiation. They established carbon monoxide poisoning as the sole cause of death for both Torrente and Edmond. Furthermore, in none of the many phone calls that morning, including the last one just before 6:30 a.m., had Torrente given any indication of a disagreement or struggle of any kind. Maher was convicted on December 2, 2002, ordered to pay the symbolic damages, and sentenced to ten years in prison. As was his right, Maher filed an appeal, which was heard in 2003 and rejected.[555]

Although the sentence didn't lessen the grief and the loss, it did provide the measure of justice that was available. And it cleared the way to focus on the future—and what the foundation could do to honor Edmond's life and wishes. Edmond never kept a diary, wrote a memoir, or gave long lectures on his philosophy of life. But through his example, the foundation had a strong and clear road map.

This was to be the legacy: a professionally managed entity aimed at preserving and growing the fortune he had built while deploying it strategically in ways that were consistent with his principles and life's work. And Lily Safra would see to it that Edmond Safra would be explicitly associated with the foundation's work. In his lifetime, Edmond had hesitated to associate his own name with charitable donations, per tradition. As the head of his family, he took the responsibility to make donations in memory of Jacob and Esther Safra. This imprimatur could be seen in countless, diverse places around the world: on prayer books and commemorative plaques in synagogues and seminaries throughout Europe and the Americas, in the names of Jewish community schools from Manhattan to Nice, on endowed chairs at Harvard University and the University of Pennsylvania's Wharton School of Business, or on the street signs marking Safra Square, the new Jerusalem municipal complex Edmond had helped fund.

But now it was up to others to ensure that Edmond's name would be so honored. "In its decisions the Foundation Council shall take its inspiration from the concerns, values, and ideals held by Edmond J. Safra during his lifetime," the foundation's statutes proclaimed. The focus would be on three main areas.

Religion: "The maintenance of Jewish religious organizations, the construction and renovation of synagogues and the support of Jewish moral and religious authorities."

Medicine: "The creation of hospitals and clinics, the renovation of existing medical institutions, contributions to their operation, [and] contributions to research."

Education: "The benefit of education and training in the larger sense, including the creation of universities, chairs, scholarships, and the renovation of existing educational institutions and contributions to their operation (with Judaic studies and Judaic institutions to receive preference.)"[556]

In keeping with Edmond's life and career, the foundation's efforts have been geographically diverse. In fact, it is possible to retrace the arc of Edmond's life by looking at the foundation's work. It has not backed any initiatives in Aleppo, which has been utterly destroyed, or in Beirut, where the Jewish community is no longer extant. But in Milan, where Edmond truly started his career, the plaza outside the central station, which houses the city's Holocaust Museum, is Piazza Edmond J. Safra. On 63rd Street and Fifth Avenue, just a few doors from his New York apartment, the Edmond J. Safra Synagogue, designed by Thierry Despont, was inaugurated in 2003—the first Levantine synagogue to be built in Manhattan. In Aventura, Florida, the resort town north of Miami, where Syrian Jews congregate for the winter, the Edmond J. Safra Synagogue was established in 2001.

One of Edmond's legacies was that the example he set spurred those who worked with him, or who came into contact with him, to devote even more of their time and resources to charitable projects. In Deal, New Jersey, the summer enclave of the Syrian-American Jewish community, his friend Joe Cayre established the Edmond J. Safra Synagogue, noting: "This synagogue is named after my dear friend Edmond Safra, who was my mentor and who taught me how to give charity."

In the realm of healthcare and medical research, the foundation has devoted significant resources to Parkinson's disease research and patient care, including at some of the facilities where Edmond was treated: Toronto Western Hospital, University College London's Institute of Neurology, and the university and medical center in Grenoble. A theme running through these and other investments is the idea of supporting the quality of life of those who are afflicted, echoing Edmond's entreaty to Lily that she not let the disease rob him of his dignity. As well as funding research addressing these quality-of-life concerns through its longtime partnership with the Michael J. Fox Foundation, the Edmond J. Safra Foundation has funded an initiative that provides Parkinson's patients with a kit of resources aimed at helping them ensure they will get proper care if they are hospitalized; a service that brings a Parkinson's care team to the homes of advanced-stage patients; innovative programs to teach Parkinson's patient care to nursing school students and to nursing home care staff; community treatment and support efforts in underserved locations; and direct support needy patients can use to purchase medications, walkers, shower bars, and other essentials. The foundation also aims to help family caregivers secure the support they need. The Edmond J. Safra Family Lodge at the National Institutes of Health outside Washington, D.C., for example, offers guest rooms and accommodations for families accompanying participants in clinical trials.

The interests in religion, medicine, and education converge in Israel. Founded in 2002, the Edmond and Lily Safra Children's Hospital at the Sheba Medical Center in Tel Hashomer treats patients from across the Middle East. At the Hebrew University of Jerusalem, whose science campus is named for Edmond, the foundation created the Edmond and Lily Safra Center for Brain Sciences. The foundation continues to support ISEF, which by 2021 had granted over 16,000 scholarships to postsecondary students in Israel, including more than 1,000 who have sought advanced degrees. And, of course, there are synagogues. In his lifetime, among the many he supported in memory of his father, Edmond spent several years overseeing the minute details of a synagogue and school he built for the Lebanese Jewish community in Bat Yam, led by his rabbi from Beirut, Rabbi Yaakov Attie. The foundation, working with local communities throughout Israel, has built twenty-one synagogues in cities around the country in memory of Edmond. It has also renovated the tombs of Rabbi Meir Baal HaNess and Rabbi Shimon Bar Yochai, holy pilgrimage sites that held such deep importance for him.

Other projects backed by the foundation resonate with the triumphs, tragedies, and lodestars of his life. At the National Gallery of Art, where he hosted so many of the glittering Republic receptions at the World Bank/IMF meetings, the foundation created the Edmond J. Safra Visiting Professorship at the Center for Advanced Study in the Visual Arts. At Harvard, where Edmond endowed professorships in memory of his father and Robert F. Kennedy, the foundation endowed the Edmond J. Safra Center for Ethics, which seeks to advance teaching and research on ethical issues in public life.

The Alliance in Beirut was an important formative experience for young Edmond, and the network of the pan–Middle Eastern Francophone educational organization played an important role in his life and career. Many of the communities that the Alliance and its network of schools were constructed to serve no longer exist. But France's Jewish community, fortified by waves of immigration from North Africa and the Middle East, is now Europe's largest. And the Alliance's work is focused there. The Ecole Normale Israélite Orientale, the organization's educational hub and traditional home in Paris, has been renovated and expanded, and is now known as the Centre Alliance Edmond J. Safra. It includes a primary school and an institute for Jewish education and historical research. Recognizing the continuing vitality of the Francophone Jewish world, the foundation has funded a modern French translation of the Hebrew Bible (including a digital edition)—the *Houmach Edmond J. Safra*—and a comprehensive French translation of the Talmud— *L'Edition Edmond J. Safra du Talmud Bavli*—both with the distinguished ArtScroll-Mesorah publishing house.

These efforts are not fueled by a sense of nostalgia or a desire for historical preservation. In keeping with Edmond's spirit, these are investments in long-standing traditions that continue to evolve for the modern world. In some ways, the Middle East in which Edmond grew up, in which a Jewish banker in Beirut could freely travel and conduct business in Egypt, Saudi Arabia, Syria, and Kuwait, in which commerce and language functioned as binding ties, no longer exists. There is literally nothing left of the two millennia of Jewish presence in Aram Tzova, which housed the Safra family for generations. Rue Georges Picot, named after one of the French architects of the post-Ottoman Levantine order, is now Rue Omar Daouk. Alcy, Magen Avraham, and the other landmarks of Jewish Beirut live on only in the memory of older people and in Facebook groups. But one Beirut component of the Safra legacy remains. BCN, the bank that Jacob Safra founded in the 1920s, the bank whose charter and place as number thirty-six on Lebanon's liste des banques was such a source of pride, the one bank Edmond could never bring himself to sell, is a small but still functioning three-branch institution in Beirut. Its current ownership proudly notes on its website that it was founded by Jacob Safra.

As the years and decades roll on, there are fewer people alive who knew Edmond Safra personally, or who worked for him, or who banked with him. But every day, thanks to his life's work, thousands of people all over the world will show up to work, seek and receive medical treatment, delve into scientific mysteries, carry on ancient traditions, go to school, worship, or simply find succor in the comfort of others. As much as the remarkable path he carved through the world of twentieth-century banking, Edmond Safra's good work will constitute a remarkable and enduring legacy.

AUTHOR'S NOTE

"You were born to write this book." That's what my wife said when I first described this project to her. And in some ways, maybe I was. I'm a trained historian. I have spent my adult life studying and writing about business history and global finance, covering the way money moves around the world. And I'm a Syrian Jew. Gross is, of course, an Ashkenazi name. But my father is an only child whose parents died several years before I was born. The only family I knew growing up was my mother's—a large clan of Dweks and Nasars in Brooklyn, New York, and Deal, New Jersey. My great-grandparents were born and raised in Aleppo in the late-nineteenth century. My grandfather's family was from Damascus and sojourned in Jerusalem in the 1910s before settling permanently in New York.

What I knew from growing up is that our people were subjects not of the Habsburgs or the Tzars but of the Ottomans. The curses and terms of endearment I heard were in Arabic, not Yiddish. We ate rice on Passover and hummus long before it was a health food. I had a *sitto*, not a *bubbe*. And she made us *kibbe*, not matzo ball soup. The stories told at the Seder table, the melodies of prayers, our first and last names—all of them could be traced back to Aleppo (Halab) and Damascus (al-Sham). The Syrians have a strong sense of solidarity, community, and of being different. To outsiders, and to the dominant Ashkenazi American-Jewish culture, these people and practices seemed strange and insular, the "other." To me, they were normal. And why not? Jews were in Aleppo long before they were in Eastern Europe.

So when a colleague asked several years ago if I knew who Edmond Safra was, the answer was: well, of course I did. I knew he was a hero and icon in the Syrian Jewish community—a sort of Warren Buffett, Rothschild, and Schindler wrapped into one person. And from my years as a journalist, I knew *something* of his career. I knew he was a successful banker. I knew specifically how he was attacked by American Express (as shown in Bryan Burrough's 1992 book *Vendetta,* which I read at the time). I knew something of how he died, from the extensive media coverage. I knew there were several synagogues and Jewish institutions in the New York area named after him, as well as a center and several professorships at Harvard University, where I attended graduate school.

But as I began looking into it, I realized I had no idea who Edmond Safra was. And neither did anybody else. Because of his wealth, social circle, and charitable activities, he was certainly a public figure. But he was very much a private banker, and a private man—wary of publicity and in no way part of the financial-media industrial complex I inhabited. Covering the financial world and the intersection of finance and politics for decades, I had interviewed a half-dozen Treasury Secretaries and central bankers, and most of the era's leading financiers: the CEOs of JP Morgan Chase, Citigroup, Merrill Lynch, and Goldman Sachs; the heads of Blackstone and KKR; hedge fund titans like George Soros and Ray Dalio, and a handful of real estate billionaires. But I had never come across Edmond Safra in my journalistic work. He was not the type to show up at Davos (even though his Geneva bank was a sponsor of that conference in its early years), or in the green room at CNBC, or to keynote an industry fundraising dinner in New York.

Typically, if you mention Edmond Safra's name to somebody, he or she will share with you an anecdote, a story, or an opinion—that is almost certainly inaccurate or, in many instances, simply wrong— which isn't surprising. Because for an interested observer, there was not much of a way in. Republic, TDB, and Safra Republic were publicly held. And the SEC filings and annual reports tell the story of the institutions. But there is virtually no video or tape recording of Edmond Safra. He never wrote a memoir and rarely sat for long interviews. And because he had such a unique view of banking, and how it should work, even the most experienced banking professionals are at something of a loss to account for his banks' combinations of remarkable profits and low risk.

Yet it turns out that the resources for reconstructing his life exist. Edmond Safra was a meticulous record keeper. He accrued and maintained a vast archive of personal papers—letters and telexes, airplane tickets and documents, personal calendars and itineraries, and financial reports. Personal and professional, mundane and profound, they are in Arabic and Hebrew, Portuguese, Italian, French, German, Spanish, and English. There's even the odd document in Hungarian or Polish. What's more, these documents are supplemented by plenty of secondary material—newspaper and magazine articles, memoirs, analyst reports—that can aid in the reconstruction of the life of his institutions and the communities in which he lived.

I soon learned there was an invaluable trove of other sources. After his death in 1999, the Edmond J. Safra Foundation spurred two comprehensive efforts to compile interviews with hundreds of people who knew Edmond Safra at every stage in his life—from an elementary school student in Beirut to a titan of global finance. These were friends, family members, teachers, colleagues, rivals, associates, clients, intimates, and people he only met a few times. The first effort was led by Yossi Chetrit, a professor of linguistics at Haifa University, a few years after Edmond's death. A decade later, John Seaman and Isabelle Lescent-Giles, historians from the Winthrop Group, conducted scores of interviews. The transcripts of these interviews—carried out in French, Hebrew, Portuguese, and English—are a remarkably rich trove. In their investigations, the historians from the Winthrop Group also digitized the archive, tracked down primary and secondary sources, and framed portions of the story—in particular on Edmond Safra's early activities in Brazil. I was also given access to photos and documents provided by some family members and friends.

And so when Lily Safra asked if I had the skills to mine this material to construct a story that was simultaneously human and institutional, a story of banks, a banker, a man, a community—I thought I could. As I read through the archives at night, sitting in front of my computer in Fairfield County, Connecticut, I was transported to worlds that were both strange and familiar: Beirut in the 1940s, Rio and São Paolo in the 1950s, New York in the 1960s, the South of France in the 1980s. The past popped in front of me in vivid colors. I could hear the timbre and tone of my relatives.

The exuberance and optimism of the Syrian-Jewish diaspora, the nostalgia and sense of loss. The savvy business sense, the importance of family, tradition, and ritual. The experiences of a group of people who acculturate but don't assimilate, often embattled and misunderstood, but proud and resilient. The insistence on an identity connected to a world that no longer existed. All this was familiar to me. Here was correspondence with the leaders of the synagogues my grandparents attended, or a great uncle's name popping up in charitable donations. My own great-grandparents were contemporaries of Edmond's father, Jacob Safra, in Aleppo. I knew we had relatives who had made their way to Cuba, Brazil, and Colombia. In 1980, when my family was living in Israel for the year, we met distant cousins who had just managed to escape from Syria and arrived in Tel Aviv.

Also familiar to me was the story of the growth of global finance in the postwar decades that emerges in the life and career of Edmond Safra. It is easy to stereotype Safra—and people did for much of his life. The secretive banker with multiple identities. But his personality and life were much more complex. It is true that lots of people could have reconstructed the story of how Republic Bank grew from a start-up to the eleventh biggest bank in the US. But not as many, I suspect, would have understood why, when sending the family's possessions to Brazil, Edmond Safra included a kilogram of *za'atar*. Or why there were no synagogues named after him in his lifetime. Or what *ka'ak* were, and why he was always sending them to friends.

A large amount of the story is reconstructed from the interviews and the primary sources. The digitized records of the Aleppo Jewish community charting Brit Milah and marriages, can be accessed at Jewishgen.org.

There are several other vital secondary sources to which I am indebted. Any historian stands on the shoulders of those who have plowed similar ground. While an archive-based historical volume is always a solitary effort, several other people played vital roles—during and before my work. For the early chapters, Kristen Schultze, *The Jews of Lebanon: Between Co-existence and Conflict* (Sussex Academic Press, 2001) was an important source. Joseph Sutton is the historian of the Syrian Jewish diaspora. His books, *Magic Carpet: Aleppo-in-Flatbush* (Thayer-Jacoby, 1979) and *Aleppo Chronicle* (Thayer-Jacoby, 1988), were in my home. For the sections on the 1980s, I leaned heavily on *Vendetta: American Express and the Smearing of Edmond Safra*, by Bryan Burrough (HarperCollins, 1992). Among the many articles about Edmond, one is particularly useful: "The Secret World of Edmond Safra" (*Institutional Investor*, May 1979), by Cary Reich, himself a fine financial historian, the author of biographies of Andre Meyer and Nelson Rockefeller. And as mentioned earlier, historians at the Winthrop Group conducted interviews, gathered material, and dug into archives around the world.

It was Prosper Assouline, a publisher of great refinement, who first suggested that this might be a book I would want to write. He was an extremely helpful adviser throughout the process, helping to move it forward at several key moments. Max Coslov of the Edmond J. Safra Foundation was an immense source of help and constant prodding, continually feeding me documents, transcripts, data points, and connecting me to sources. Others who read the manuscript, or who commented and provided helpful feedback included: Jeff Keil, Marc Bonnant, Anita Smaga, Ezra Marcos, Neil Rudenstine, John Bond, Ronald Wilson, Stephen Gardner, Dov Schlein, Peter Cohen, Jean Hoss, William "Rusty" Park, and Anne Vitale.

Most of all I'd like to thank Lily Safra, Edmond's widow and partner—and the chief guardian of his legacy—without whom this book would not have been possible. Madame Safra, who chairs the Edmond J. Safra Foundation, gave me free range to rummage through the archives, sat for interviews, and provided valuable perspective.

This manuscript has benefitted from the attention and work of several editorial professionals. Geoff Shandler did a careful line edit of the manuscript. Victoria Beliveau copyedited the document—no small challenge given the amount of transliteration and multiple languages. Laura Stempel created the index. At Radius Book Group, Scott Waxman, Mark Fretz, Evan Phail, and the whole team, worked diligently to bring this to fruition. Alan J. Kaufman, Esq., publishing attorney in the US and Simon Heilbron provided careful readings and helpful advice. As she has done for every book I've written, Candice Savin read every word and provided constant encouragement. It has been her lot to share a life with a writer who is constantly on deadline, and I'm grateful for her enduring patience and love. My children Aliza Gross and Ethan Gross were, as they always have been, a source of support and inspiration.

A great deal of mystery and misinformation attaches to Edmond Safra's name, because of the life he led and because of where he was from. So it's natural that there is likely to be conflict about his life story. I don't regard this book as an effort to set the record straight. Rather, I see it as an attempt to place his life in context, to set down what is known, and what can be proven. Edmond Safra's journey is sufficiently fascinating and impressive that it doesn't require embellishment or speculation. And I acknowledge that the act of cobbling together a life story is as much an act of omission as it is an act of commission. There is a 494-page book about just one year of Edmond Safra's life. I have tried to stick to events, facts, and figures that were recorded and documented contemporaneously, or that were testified to by multiple sources. So much of Edmond Safra's world, of course, is lost and literally destroyed. But I did my best to document wherever possible, and to leave things out that were matters of speculation—whether prurient or idle.

In the notes, I frequently cite the interviews conducted as well as documents from the archive. A handful of the interviewees wished to remain anonymous. Unless otherwise specified, letters, documents, and interviews reside in the collection of the Edmond J. Safra Foundation archives. This is a biography, yes. But it is also a history of the institutions he founded, a window into how banking works, and a history of the Syrian-Lebanese diaspora, as seen through the remarkable journey of one of its members.

Many people feel like Edmond Safra "belongs" to them—the people who worked for him at his banks, the Syrian diaspora, the Lebanese diaspora, Sephardic Jews in general, and his large network of friends and colleagues. His life is the story of a family, a community—several communities, actually—and a large chunk of the Jewish people in the twentieth century. But ultimately, Edmond Safra's story is his alone.

ENDNOTES

1. James Wolfensohn remarks at Edmond J. Safra memorial, New York, January 9, 2000.

2. John Bond interview.

3. Maurice Levy interview.

4. Edmond J. Safra fiftieth Anniversary Video, October, 1997.

5. Steven Mufson, "American Express Offers $4 million and Apology," *Washington Post*, July 29, 1989.

6. Marc Bonnant interview.

7. Albert Hourani, *Minorities in the Arab World* (Oxford: Oxford University Press, 1947), 15–32; Sarina Roffé, *Branching Out from Sepharad* (Brooklyn, NY: Sephardic History Project, 2010). The Aleppo Brit Milah database 1848–1945 and Aleppo marriage database 1847–1934 can be accessed at JewishGen.org. The originals are held at the Jewish National and University Library, Institute of Microfilmed Hebrew Manuscripts, Jerusalem.

8. Lee I. Levine, *A History of Caesarea under Roman Rule* (New York: Columbia University Press, 1970), 55; Ronald L. Eisenberg, *Essential Figures in the Talmud* (Lanham, MD: Jason Aronson, 2013), 211; Catherine Hezser, *Jewish Travel in Antiquity*, Texts and Studies in Ancient Judaism (Tübingen: Mohr Siebeck, 2011), 144.

9. Walter P. Zenner, *A Global Community: The Jews of Aleppo, Syria* (Detroit: Wayne State University Press, 2000), 155; Joseph A. D. Sutton, *Magic Carpet: Aleppo-in-Flatbush: The Story of a Unique Ethnic Jewish Community* (New York: Thayer-Jacoby, 1979), 33–35; Matti Friedman, *Aleppo Codex: In Pursuit of One of the World's Most Coveted, Sacred and Mysterious Books* (New York: Algonquin, 2013).

10. Bernard Lewis, *The Jews of Islam* (Princeton, NJ: Princeton University Press, 1984); Howard N. Lupovitch, *Jews and Judaism in World History* (London: Routledge, 2009), 63–65; Bruce Masters, *Christians and Jews in the Ottoman Arab World: The Roots of Sectarianism* (Cambridge: Cambridge University Press, 2004).

11. Stanford Shaw, *The Jews of the Ottoman Empire and Turkish Republic* (New York: Palgrave Macmillan, 1991), 143.

12. Charles Issawi, *The Fertile Crescent, 1800–1914: A Documentary Economic History* (Oxford: Oxford University Press, 1988), 28.

13. Philip Mansel, *Levant: Splendour and Catastrophe on the Mediterranean* (New Haven, CT: Yale University Press, 2011), chap. 7; Issawi, *Fertile Crescent*.

14. Zenner, *Global Community*, 64–65.

15. For discussions of Aleppo and minority status in the Ottoman Empire, see Edhem Eldem, Daniel Goffman, and Bruce Masters, *The Ottoman City Between East and West: Aleppo, Izmir, and Istanbul* (Cambridge: Cambridge University Press, 2015); David Abulafia, *The Great Sea: A Human History of the Mediterranean* (Oxford: Oxford University Press, 2013); Zenner, *Global Community*.

16. Archives de l'Alliance Israélite Universelle, Paris: Paris and Kaspi, 2010.

17. Shaw, *Jews of the Ottoman Empire*, 165.

18. Aleppo birth, marriage, and *brit milah* records at JewishGen.org.

19. Joseph Masry interview.

20. Edmond Safra, personal diary, 1999.

21. Joseph Masry interview.

22. Sutton, *Magic Carpet*.

23. Georges Corm, *Le Liban contemporain: Histoire et société* (Paris: Poche/Essais, 2005), 86n13.

24. Mansel, *Levant*, chap. 15; Kais M. Firro, *Inventing Lebanon: Nationalism and the State under the Mandate* (London: Bloomsbury, 2003), 18–25.

25. Bruce Masters, *Christians and Jews in the Ottoman Arab World* (Cambridge: Cambridge University Press, 2004), 182–85.

26. Kirsten E. Schultze, *The Jews of Lebanon: Between Coexistence and Conflict* (East Sussex, UK: Sussex Academic Press, 2001).

27. Edmond Safra, personal diary, 1999; Ezra Zilkha interview; Elie Krayem interview; Joseph Masry interview.

28. Ezra Zilkha interview; Elie Krayem interview; Joseph Masry interview; Emile Saadia interview.

29. Isaac Obersi interview.

30. Joint Distribution Committee, "Report on Jewish Communities in Damascus, Beirut and Sidon, 13 February 1919," JDC archives.

31. Schultze, *Jews of Lebanon*.

32. Isaac Obersi interview; Safra Foundation, historical database of charitable gifts; Archives de l'Alliance Israélite Universelle, Paris: Paris and Kaspi, 2010.

33. Rabbi Yaakov Attie interview; Zenner, *Global Community*, 43–45. Isaac Obersi interview. Testimony of Mme Srour, from Beirut's Jewish community, on YouTube (private video) (http://www.youtube.com/watch?v=f0Qi8sdgGPg).

34. Brazil immigration cards, available through familysearch.org. Paulette's tombstone in Beirut's Jewish cemetery is inscribed with her date of death (1937).

35. Nagi Georges Zeidan, oral history of the Lebanese Jews: http://www.farhi.org/Documents/La%20communaute_juive_du_liban.htm; Ezra Zilkha interview.

36. Maury Mann interview; Emile Saadia interview.

37. Schultze, *Jews of Lebanon*, 7–8.

38. Schultze, *Jews of Lebanon*, 46.

39. Archives de l'Alliance Israélite Universelle, Paris: Paris and Kaspi, 2010.

40. Maurizio Dwek interview; Raimundo Shayo interview; Emile Saadia interview; Albert Zeitoune interview.

41. Simon Alouan interview.

42. Ernest Sasson interview.

43. David Braka interview.

44. Bryan Burrough, *Vendetta: American Express and the Smearing of Edmond Safra* (New York: HarperCollins, 1992), 33; Albert Nasser interview.

45. Ernest Sasson interview; Nagi Georges Zeidan, "The Jews from Aley," https://www.discoverlebanon.com/en/forum/viewtopic_t_283.html.

46. Rachel Mizrahi Bromberg, *Imigrantes Judeus Do Oriente Medio: São Paulo e Rio de Janeiro* (Cotia, Brasil: Ateliê Editorial, 2003); "The Mystery Man of Finance," *Business Week*, March 6, 1994.

47. Mansel, *Levant*, iv; Etre levantin, c'est vivre dans deux mondes à la fois, sans vraiment appartenir à aucun d'eux." quoted in Gabrielle Elia, *Les Funambulistes: Chronique des Juifs du Liban*, de 1925 à 1975 (privately published, 2010), 175.

48. Albert Zeitoune interview; Meir Ashkenazi interview.

49. Adriana Elia interview.

50. Jacques Nasser interview; Michelle Nasser interview.

51. Albert Zeitoune interview; Jimmy Hallac interview; Yehuda Levi interview; Maury Mann interview; Maurizio Dwek interview; Albert Zeitoune interview.

52. Emile Saadia interview.

53. Emile Saadia interview; Albert Zeitoune interview; Maury Mann interview; Michelle Nasser interview.

54. For a comprehensive overview of nationhood perspectives see Firro, *Inventing Lebanon;* Michelle U. Campos, *Ottoman Brothers: Muslims, Christians and Jews in Early Twentieth-Century Palestine* (Stanford, CA: Stanford University Press, 2011), 232–44.

55. For a discussion of the 1924 immigration law and its impact on Jewish Syrian and Lebanese immigration, see Zenner, *Global Community*, chap. 8.

56. Alessandra Casella and Barry Eichengreen, "Halting inflation in Italy and France after World War II," *NBER Working Paper* no. 3852, September 1991; Youssef Cassis and Eric Bussière, eds., *London and Paris as International Financial Centres in the Twentieth Century* (Oxford: Oxford University Press, 2005); Charles Kindleberger, *The Formation of Financial Centers: A Study in Comparative Economic History* (Cambridge, MA: Working Paper, Department of Economics, MIT,

1973); John Lambertson Harper, *America and the Reconstruction of Italy, 1945–1948* (Cambridge, UK: Cambridge University Press, 1986).

57. Albert Buri Nasser interview; Maury Mann interview.

58. Albert Buri Nasser interview; Burrough, *Vendetta*, 34 (hereafter simply *Vendetta*).

59. Jacques Tawil interview; Minos Zombanakis interview; Albert Manila Nasser interview; Moïse Khafif interview.

60. Jacques Tawil interview.

61. Jacques Tawil interview; Jeff Keil interview; Emile Saadia interview; Minos Zombanakis interview.

62. Ezra Zilkha interview; Simon Alouan interview.

63. Jacques Tawil interview; Jeff Keil interview.

64. Moussi Douek interview; Moïse Khafif interview; Maurizio Dwek interview; Simon Alouan interview.

65. Safra Letter Book 1969, note from Treves on family history for the renewal of his Italian passport; La Repubblica Archives, "Addio Camillo, finanziere discreto e tenace," January 31, 1993.

66. Jacques Tawil interview.

67. Brendan Brown, *The Flight of International Capital: A Contemporary History* (London: Routledge, 1987).

68. Timothy Green, "Central Bank Gold Reserves: An Historical Perspective Since 1845," Research Study No. 23 (World Gold Council, November 1999).

69. Tony Judt, *Postwar*, chap. 3; Green, *World of Gold*, 121, 124; Jacques Tawil interview; Ezra Zhilka interview; Moïse Khafif interview; Maury Mann interview.

70. Simon Alouan interview.

71. Adrian Tschoegl, "Maria Theresa's Thaler: A Case of International Money," *Eastern Economic Journal* 27, no. 4 (2001): 443–62. See also Green, *World of Gold*, 123; Jacques Tawil interview.

72. Ezra Zilkha interview; Albert Buri Nasser interview; Eduoard Schouela interview; Catherine Schenk, "The Hong Kong Gold Market and the Southeast Asian Gold Trade in the 1950s," *Modern Asian Studies* 29 no. 2 (May 1995): 387–402; Green, *World of Gold*, 49–52, 167–200.

73. Edouard Schouela interview; Jacques Tawil interview; Ezra Zhilka interview; Maury Mann interview; Carolyn Gates, *Merchant Republic of Lebanon: Rise of an Open Economy* (Oxford: Centre of Lebanon Studies, 1998), 116; Raimundo Shayo interview.

74. Rahmo Nasser private notes, 2003; Reeva Spector Simon, Michael Laskier, Michael Menachem, and Sara Reguer, eds., *The Jews of the Middle East and North Africa in Modern Times* (New York: Columbia University Press, 2002); Camille and Rafael Kassin interviews.

75. Camille and Rafael Kassin interviews; Rahmo Nasser letter, 2003.

76. Jacques Nasser interview.

77. Edouard Schouela interview.

78. Jacques Tawil interview.

79. Maury Mann interview.

80. Isaac Obersi interview; Emile Saadia interview.

81. Maury Mann interview.

82. Maury Mann interview.

83. Jacques Tawil interview; Simon Alouan interview; Maury Mann interview.

84. Minos Zombanakis interview; Jacques Tawil interview; Sammy Cohn interview.

85. Elie Krayem interview.

86. Victor Smaga interview; Rahmo Sassoon interview; Albert Hattena interview; Victor Hattena interview.

87. Rahmo Nasser letter, 2003.

88. Albert Zeitoune interview.

89. Albert Manila Nasser interview.

90. Elie J. Safra letter, October 21, 1949; Edmond Safra to Michael Picini, US Embassy in Rome, June 20, 1966; Albert Buri Nasser interview; Albert Manila Nasser interview.

91. Letter, newspaper clippings and photographs in the archives of the Alliance Israélite Universelle, Paris; Schultze, *Jews of Lebanon*, 90–91.

92. Camille Kassin interview; Rahmo Nasser letter, 2003.

93. Elie Krayem interview; Moïse Khafif interview; Jacques Khafif interview; Albert Buri Nasser interview; Rahmo Nasser letter, 2003; Cary Reich, "The Secret World of Edmond Safra," *Institutional Investor*, May, 1979. Arlette Hazan's Brazilian immigration cards, N 004550584, image 138, Brazil, Immigration Cards, 1900–65, available online via FamilySearch.org.

94. Green, *World of Gold*, 120–25; Elie Krayem interview.

95. Hansard House of Commons, March 10, 1948, paragraphs 1371–73.

96. Raffaele Pinto to Leon Sassoon, February 17, 1955 and August 21, 1955; Errol Flynn to Edmond Safra, December 14, 1952.

97. Raymond Halat to Leon Sassoon c/o Edmond Safra, November 11, 1955; Edmond Safra to Raffaele Pinto, September 19, 1956 and November 3, 1960.

98. Rahmo Nasser letter, 2003.

99. Jacques Nasser interview.

100. Rolando Laniado interview.

101. For Jewish immigration from the Middle East to Brazil, see Jeff Lesser, *Welcoming the Undesirables: Brazil and the Jewish Question* (Berkeley, CA: University of

California Press, 1995), 79; Jeff Lesser, "From Pedlars to Proprietors: Lebanese, Syrian and Jewish Immigrants in Brazil," in *The Lebanese in the World: A Century of Emigration*, ed. Albert Hourani and Nadim Shehadi (London: I. B. Tauris; New York: St. Martin's Press, 1992), 393–410; Ignacio Klich and Jeff Lesser, eds., *Arab and Jewish Immigrants in Latin America: Images and Realities* (London: Routledge, 1998); and Zenner, *Global Community.*

102. Family immigration cards, familysearch.org.

103. *Diário Oficial da União*, September 30, 1955, March 21, 1957, April 10, 1957, and November 18, 1954; the subsidiary was named Brascoton Industria e Comércio de Algodão Limitada. Brascoton Account.

104. Bill stamped November 9, 1955, OTIM; letter from Milan to Moïse and Menaham Khafif, November 11, 1955; Leon Sassoon to Selim Hamoui, November 25, 1955.

105. Rolando Laniado interview; *Diário Oficial da União*, October 11, 1955, documentos de companhia N. 99.875; *Diário Oficial da União*, September 21, 1956. Banco Credito letter, December 12, 1956; Werner Baer, *The Brazilian Economy: Growth and Development*, 5th ed. (Westport, CT: Lynne Riener Publishers, 2001), 53–56.

106. Paulo Fontes, "'With a Cardboard Suitcase in My Hand and a Pannier on My Back': Workers and Northeastern Migrations in the 1950s in São Paulo, Brazil," *Social History* 36, no. 1 (February 2011): 1–21.

107. Leon Sassoon to Selim Hamoui, November 25, 1955; "Foundation of Sudafin in Switzerland," official publication October 9, 1956; Sudafin to Samuel Montagu, October 20, 1959; Sudafin, *Balance Sheet*, October 31, 1959.

108. *Diário Oficial da União*, September 21, 1956; Banco Credito letter, December 12, 1956. Umberto Treves to Edmond Safra, August 7, 1957; Edmond Safra to Moïse Safra, October 15, 1957; Edmond Safra to Philip Habbouba, November 8 and 30, 1957; Edmond Safra to Moïse Khafif, November 29, 1957; Philip Habbouba to Edmond Safra, November 8 and 30, 1957.

109. Rolando Laniado interview; Mark Pendergrast, *Uncommon Grounds: The History of Coffee* (New York: Basic Books, 2010).

110. Rolando Laniado interview.

111. Invoice from OTIM: Organization Trasporti Internazionali e Marittimi, 1956.

112. Edmond Safra to Dean of Admissions, the Wharton School of the University of Pennsylvania, October 9, 1957; Assistant Dean of Admissions, the Wharton School of the University of Pennsylvania, to Edmond Safra, October 21, 1957.

113. Letter "Concerning Elie."

114. Alberto Milkewitz, "The Jewish Community of São Paulo, Brazil," *Jerusalem Letter* 124 (December 1, 1991); Jacques Khafif interview; Albert Buri Nasser interview; Rahmo and Emily Shayo interview; Moïse Khafif interview.

115. Leon Sassoon to Murad Shayo, August 11, 1958; Rolando Laniado interview.

116. Payment from Edmond Safra to Union Bank of Israel, for account of Rabbi Meir Baal HaNess Tiberias May 3, 1956; Edmond Safra to Isaac Shalom, July 25, 1958; Isaac Shalom to Edmond Safra, July 30, 1958.

117. Moïse Safra to Leon Sassoon, September 13, 1957; *Diário Oficial do Estado de São Paulo (DOSP)*, February 6, 1956, 3839; *DOSP*, March 20, 1957, 6499–6501; International Directory of Company Histories, vol. 20 (Detroit: St. James Press, 1998). For a detailed account of Panamerica's plans for a paper mill in Mogi Guaçu, see *DOSP*, December 12, 1957, 27905–7; Jacques Khafif interview.

118. Joe Michaan to Edmond Safra, March 1, 1962; Marty Mertz interview, Albert Manila Nasser interview.

119. Accounts of ECSA published in *Diário Oficial da União*, April 30, 1955; *Diário Oficial do Estado de São Paulo*, February 20, 1958, 59; Moïse Khafif interview.

120. Jacques Nasser interview.

121. Rahmo Shayo interview; Edmond Safra to Isaac Shalom, September 13, 1959.

122. Doctor's report, radiography results for Jacob Safra, Clinica Columbus, October 28, 1954; Professor G. Melli, statement about Jacob Safra, May 20, 1958; Edmond Safra to Dr. Morris Bender, June 22, 1961; Moussi Dwek interview.

123. Raimundo Shayo interview.

124. Banque Jacob Safra balance sheet, April 22, 1958.

125. Schultze, *Jews of Lebanon*, 100–3.

126. Irene Genzier, *Notes from the Minefield: US Intervention in Lebanon, 1945–1958* (New York: Columbia University Press, 2006); Emile Saadia interview.

127. Jacques Douek to Edmond Safra, July 24, 1958; Edmond Safra to Jacques Douek, August 21, 1958.

128. Schultze, *Jews of Lebanon*, 100–6.

129. Eli Krayem interview.

130. Eli Krayem interview; Edmond Safra to Henry Krayem, June 9, 1959.

131. Letter on Banque Jacob Safra letterhead, August 6, 1959; Jacques Ades to Edmond Safra, August 8, 1959.

132. Edmond Safra, telex to Schwabach & Co., November 5, 1959.

133. Edmond Safra, to George Rabbath, May 1960.

134. Rolando Laniado interview; Moïse Khafif interview; Moïse Douek interview.

135. TDB, *Balance Sheet*, December 31, 1960; Edmond Safra to Leon Sassoon, February 10, 1961; Roger Junod interview.

136. Albert Manila Nasser interview; Edmond Safra to Cesar Safdiye, May 25, 1960; Edouard Douer interview.

137. Edmond Safra to TDB Geneva, March 17, 1961.

138. Raymond Maggar interview.

139. Emile Saadia interview; Alexis Gregory interview.

140. Edmond Safra to David Braka, November 9, 1961.

141. Sem Almaleh interview; Moussi Douek interview; Alberto Benadon Saporta, *Live* (Spain: Cultiva Communicationes, 2014).

142. Edmond Safra to Leon Btesh, January 28, 1961.

143. Raymond Maggar interview; Rolando Laniado interview.

144. Simon Alouan interview.

145. Roger Junod interview; EJS accounts, receipts for trips, 1961–62; Edmond Safra to Henry Krayem, March 16, 1962.

146. Raymond Maggar interview; Libanaise de Ski to Edmond Safra, March 22, 1962; Moussi Douek interview.

147. Simon Alouan interview.

148. Albert Coen interview; Roger Junod interview.

149. Edmond Safra to Lionel Citroen, Portland Finance Company, London, February 21, 1962; Edmond Safra to TDB, July 25, 1960, November 22, 1960, and December 1, 1960; Edmond Safra to Motores Cummins Diesel do Brasil Ltda, December 6, 1960; TDB to Edmond Safra, July 23, 27, 1960.

150. Roger Junod interview; Moïse Khafif interview; Edmond Safra to M. R. Lasser and Albert Marini, July 24, 1964—correspondence with firms of Lasser (decorator) and Marini (electricians).

151. Sem Almaleh interview; Edmond Safra to Joseph Safra, April 6, 1962.

152. Moussi Dwek interview; Roger Junod interview; Albert Manila Nasser interview.

153. Roger Junod interview; Simon Alouan interview; Jacques Khafif interview; Michelle Nasser interview; Rosette Mamieh interview.

154. Edmond Safra to Selim Chehebar, March 27, 1961.

155. Rabbi Yaakov Attie interview; Edouard Schouela interview; Edmond Safra to TDB, December 15, 1960; memo re: purchase of Golden Mile Shopping Center (Toronto), n.d. [1961].

156. Jacques Douek to Emmanuel Barouch, May 15, 1961; Edmond Safra to Emmanuel Sella, June 15, 1961.

157. Edmond Safra to Joe Dwek, February 11, 1963; Edmond Safra to William Feingold, July 10, 1961; Edmond Safra to Henry Krayem: March, 22, 1961; Louis Baz, president of Club de Naguers in Beirut, to Edmond Safra, January 5, 1962; Rosette Mamieh interview.

158. Elie Krayem interview; Ernest Sasson interview; Albert Buri Nasser interview; Jacques Khafif interview.

159. Edmond Safra to John Slade, July 20, 1961; Edmond Safra to C. M. Van Vlierden, Bank of America, July 20, 1962.

160. E. B. Williamson, Chase Manhattan, to Edmond Safra, March 15, 1963; R. C. Boreall, Chase Manhattan, to Edmond Safra; Edmond Safra to Umberto Treves, July 8, 1963; Edmond Safra to Joe Michaan, May 27, 1963.

161. TDB, *Balance Sheet*, Comptes internes, 1963; TDB, *Annual Reports*, 1960–65.

162. Moussi Douek interview; Maurizio Dwek interview; Edmond Safra to Isaac Shalom, May 21, 1960; Isaac Shalom to Edmond Safra, May 26, 1960.

163. São Paolo Congregacio e beneficiencia sefardi Paulista to Edmond Safra, December 11, 1961; Edmond Safra to Dr. Morris Bender, June 22, 1961; Edmond Safra to Rosette Mamieh, February 24, 1961; Moussi Douek interview.

164. Of Safra SA's 100 million cruzeiros in capital in 1960, Jacob Safra owned 5 percent, with Edmond, Moïse, and Joseph directly holding 4 percent, 1.5 percent, and 5 percent, respectively. Edmond controlled the rest through his stakes in Sudafin (62 percent), ECSA (24 percent), and Comersul (1 percent); *Diário Oficial da União*, August 19, 1960, reporting on the June 21, 1960 extraordinary meeting of shareholders. "Safra historico do grupo financeiro," Carouge Archives Box 3, Saban SA folder correspondance bilans; Joseph Safra to Edmond Safra, December 22, 1960.

165. Cyril Dwek to George Rabbath, June 15, 1963.

166. Rahmo Nasser to Edmond Safra, June 17, 1963.

167. Document: Beirut, June 13, 1963. Joseph Safra to Edmond Safra, September 27, 1963.

168. Edmond Safra to Rahmo Nasser, July 18, 1963.

169. Rahmo Nasser to Edmond Safra, July 29, 1963.

170. Edmond Safra to Edmund de Rothschild, March 2, 1964.

171. Donald Schnable to Edmond Safra, May 21, 1964.

172. Donald Schnable to Edmond Safra, May 21, 1964.

173. Ernest Ginsberg interview; *RNB News, 20th Anniversary Issue* (1986): 174.

174. George S. Kaufman to Edmond Safra, June 9, 1964.

175. Marty Mertz interview.

176. Letter from Republic to Federal Reserve, 1966.

177. Ernest Ginsberg interview, Marty Mertz interview.

178. Claudine Favre to William Baumann, August 13, 1965; Jacques Douek to Cyril Dwek, July 13, 1965; Edmond Safra to Henry Krayem, November 1, 1965; Marty Mertz interview.

179. Jeff Keil interview.

180. "Kheel a Backer of New Bank," *New York Times*, July 1, 1966.

181. Edmond Safra to Herman Cooper, July 5, 1965; Herman Cooper to Edmond Safra, July 6, 1965.

182. Edmond Safra to Henry Krayem, October 14, 1965; Edmond Safra to Joseph Safra, October 22, 1965.

183. *Report on Republic.*

184. Minutes of Republic Board of Directors Meeting, November 15, 1965.

185. "Kennedy Cuts Ribbon at a New Bank on 5th Ave," *New York Times*, January 25, 1966.

186. *New York Times*, January 25, 1966; Marty Mertz interview; *Report on Republic*; Republic Statement of Condition, *American Banker*, July 25, 1966.

187. Letter from Republic, June 30, 1966; Republic Bank, *Annual Report*, 1966.

188. Leon Gell to Edmond Safra, March 17, 1966; Moïse Khafif interview.

189. Edmond Safra to Michael Picini, June 20, 1966.

190. Marty Mertz interview.

191. Douglas Denby to Edmond Safra, April 29, 1966; Joseph Mouadeb to Edmond Safra, December 21, 1966.

192. Selim Kindy interview; Marwan Shakarchi interview; Edmond Safra to Mahmoud Shakarchi, November 22, 1968.

193. Edmond Safra to Fortunee Tarrab, December 1, 1966; telegram from Barcelona to Isaac Sutton in Beirut, June 25, 1966.

194. Joe Cayre interview; Charles André Junod interview; Rahmo Sassoon interview.

195. TDB, *Balance Sheet*, December 1967.

196. Claudine Favre to Moïse Safra, June 3, 1966.

197. Moïse Safra, naturalization document, January 28, 1966.

198. Joseph Safra to Jacques Douek, September 22, 1966.

199. Ezy Nasser interview.

200. Ezy Nasser interview; Ernest Sasson interview.

201. Fred Bogart interview.

202. Marty Mertz interview; Edmond Safra to Cyril Dwek, November 3, 1966.

203. Sem Almaleh interview; Jacques Tawil interview.

204. Clement Soffer interview; Raimundo Shayo interview.

205. Rolando Laniado interview; Maurice Benezra interview; Saleh Shohet interview.

206. Simon Alouan interview.

207. Henry Krayem to Jacques Douek, November 28, 1967 and December 16, 1967; Joseph Mouadeb to Edmond Safra, July 2, 1968.

208. Selim Chehebar to Edmond Safra, December 11, 1967; Selim Chehebar interview; Raimundo Shayo interview; Nathan Hasson interview.

209. Republic National Bank of New York, press release, n.d. [1966]; Greg Donald interview; Eli Krayem interview; Bill Segal interview.

210. George Wendler interview; Fred Bogart interview; Marty Mertz interview.

211. Ernest Ginsberg interview.

212. Hershel Mehani interview; Thomas Robards interview; Selim Chehebar interview; Republic, *Annual Report*, 1970.

213. Henry G. Jarecki to Edmond Safra, June 5, 1970; Dov Schlein interview; Fred Bogart interview; Victor Hattena interview; Albert Hattena interview.

214. "Japanese Business Activities in Brazil," Economic Commission for Latin America and the Caribbean, March 23, 1989.

215. Edmond Safra to Hiyo Hiyamo, Marubeni-Lida Co., May 25, 1969; Edmond Safra to Peter M. S. Yagi, July 17, 1969.

216. Andras Kalman to Edmond Safra, June 18, 1968.

217. Albert Buri Nasser interview; Edmond Safra to Robert Bonfil, May 22, 1968; Magen David Yeshiva to Edmond, January 22, 1968; Rabbi Abraham Hecht interview.

218. Jacques Tawil interview.

219. Lily Safra interview.

220. Simon Alouan interview.

221. Peter Cohen interview; Jeff Keil interview.

222. Jeff Keil interview.

223. Jeff Keil interview.

224. George Soros to Edmond Safra, 1972.

225. Rabbi Abraham Shreim to Albert Benezra, August 2, 1971.

226. Selim Kindy interview; Vicky Mamieh to Edmond Safra, December 28, 1971; Chahoud Chrem to Edmond Safra, August 31, 1971; Freddy Salem interview.

227. Ezy Nasser interview; Jo Romano interview.

228. Republic New York, *Year End Report*, December 31, 1972; Equity Research Associates, Inc., note.

229. "Where are the Gold Bugs' Yachts," *Forbes*, July 1975; Jeff Keil interview.

230. Jeff Keil interview, *Wall Street Journal*, September 27, 1972.

231. *New York Times*, November 24, 1971; FBI to John De Palma, February 23, 1972; *Wall Street Journal*, August 9, 1972.

232. "A foreign banker invades Brooklyn," *Business Week*, August 17, 1972; *New York Times*, September 27, 1972.

233. TDB Report from Chairman, 1972.

234. Roger Junod interview.

235. "Safra Comes to London," *The Economist*, September 30, 1972.

236. Minos Zombanakis interview; Jean Hoss interview.

237. TDB, press release, September 27, 1972; *Wall Street Journal*, September 27, 1972.

238. TDB, *Report from Chairman*, 1972; *The Guardian*, September 27, 1972.

239. "Collector of Banks is Going Public," *New York Times*, September 27, 1972.

240. Simon Alouan interview; *Exame*, November 1972.

241. Roberto Faldini interview.

242. Jeff Keil interview.

243. Mark Kelman to Eli Krayem, May 31, 1974.

244. Selim Kindy interview; "Banks Lend Philippines $50-Million," *New York Times*, February 27, 1973; Emile Saadia to Albert Benezra, July 20, 1973; First Washington International Corp. to Edmond Safra, March 12, 1974; Edmond Safra to Mahmoud Shakarchi; Mahmoud Shakarchi to Edmond Safra, December 18, 1973.

245. Sudafina Mexicana List of Notes, Sudafina Mexicana folder, April 1, 1974.

246. Albert Buri Nasser interview.

247. Rabbi Yaakov Attie interview; Yehuda Ades to Edmond Safra, May 7, 1974; Kol Yaakov Announcement, June 18, 1974.

248. Jacob Rothschild to Edmond Safra, September 9, 1974.

249. Raymond Maggar interview.

250. David Braka interview; Fred Bogart interview; telexes between Banque National de Hongrie and Edmond Safra, June 10, 1975; Hungarian Foreign Trade Bank to TDB, April 30, 1974.

251. Minos Zombanakis interview; Moïse Tawil interview.

252. *Finance*, January 1973.

253. Report from Chairman of TDB, 1972.

254. Bruce Littman interview; Edouard Schouela interview; Jeff Keil interview.

255. Edmond Safra to Harvard University admissions office, February 1, 1974.

256. TDB Communique to Personnel, July 3, 1974.

257. Organization of TDBH, July 11, 1974.

258. Rodney Leach to Edmond Safra, August 9, 1975; "Men and Matters," *Financial Times*, January 30, 1976.

259. Bill Segal interview; Mac II (design firm) to Edmond Safra, January 31, 1975.

260. Victor Hattena interview.

261. Marty Mertz interview.

262. Maury Mann to Edmond Safra, August 10, 1975; Claudine Favre to Maury Mann, September 1, 1975.

263. Memo to Edmond Safra, April 22, 1975.

264. "Where are the Gold Bugs' Yachts," *Forbes*, July 1975.

265. Ernest Ginsberg interview.

266. Lee Poole to Edmond Safra, December 11, 1975.

267. Mourad Mamieh to Edmond Safra, December 19, 1975.

268. Cesar Sassoon to Edmond Safra, February 17, 1976.

269. Simon Alouan interview.

270. Lily Safra interview.

271. Martin Mertz interview; Roger Junod interview.

272. Edmond Safra to Edmund de Rothschild, December 8, 1976.

273. Edmond Safra to Edmund de Rothschild, September 6, 1977.

274. Edmond Safra to Sir Siegmund G. Warburg, March 3, 1977.

275. David Rockefeller to Edmond Safra, June 24, 1977.

276. Rodney Leach to Albert Benezra, October 14, 1977; Lily Safra interview, David Mehani interview.

277. "A Conversation with Edmond Safra," *Finance*, May 12, 1977.

278. Minutes of TDBH executives coordination meeting, March 23, 1976; Rodney Leach to Roger Junod, August 15, 1977; Rodney Leach to TDB, June 22, 1977 and November 11, 1977.

279. Jeff Keil to Roger Junod, April 4, 1977; Bruce Littman interview.

280. Fred Bogart interview.

281. Cesar Sassoon to Edmond Safra, June 10, 1977.

282. Rodney Leach memo, November 15, 1977.

283. Masako Ohya to Lily Safra, October 26, 1977.

284. Isaac Obersi interview.

285. Oury Lugassy interview; Joseph Gross to Albert Benezra, November 15, 1978.

286. Fondation Terris, September 14, 1975; Elie Krayem to Shlomo Toussia-Cohen, May 24, 1976; Elie Krayem to Toussia-Cohen, October 13, 1976;

Memo: Meeting with Solel Boneh, December 11, 1976; Rabbi Yaakov Attie, telegram to Edmond Safra, March 25, 1977.

287. "ISEF: My Two Thousand Children," December 6, 1993.

288. Joe Cayre interview, Nina Weiner interview; Edmond Safra to Nessim Gaon, November 30, 1978.

289. Jacques Laoui interview.

290. Rabbi Ishac Hadid to Edmond Safra, September 15, 1977 and October 18, 1977; Selim Chaya, telex to Edmond Safra, May 11, 1977.

291. George Balamut to Edmond Safra, May 24, 1978; George Balamut to Henry Rosovsky, August 31, 1978; Henry Rosovsky to Edmond Safra, February 14, 1977; Daniel Patrick Moynihan to Edmond Safra, March 2, 1979, quoted in David N. Myers and Alexander Kaye, eds., *The Faith of Fallen Jews: Yosef Hayim Yerushalmi and the Writing of Jewish History* (Boston: Brandeis University Press, 2014), 141.

292. TDBH Annual Report, 1977; TDBH Report from Chairman, 1978.

293. Jeff Keil interview.

294. Jeff Keil interview; Keil quote in "The Secret World of Edmond Safra," *Institutional Investor*, 1979; *Fortune*, September 25, 1978.

295. Banco Safra to Bankers' Almanac; profits data from *Institutional Investor*, May 1979.

296. Michelle Nasser interview.

297. Edmond Safra to Rabbi Ovadia Yosef, May, 16, 1979.

298. Edmund Sonnenblick to Edmond Safra, September 19, 1978 and May 16, 1979.

299. "A Conversation with Edmond Safra," *Finance*, May 12, 1977.

300. "A Conversation with Edmond Safra," *Finance*, May 12, 1977; "The Secret World of Edmond Safra," *Institutional Investor*, May 1979.

301. Raymond Maggar interview; Walter Weiner interview.

302. Security protocols, June 23, 1978.

303. Memo from Laperrouza & CIE, May 11, 1979.

304. Rabbis of Aleppo to Edmond Safra, September 16, 1979 and October 17, 1979.

305. Menahem Yedid interview; Rabbi Yaakov Attie interview.

306. TDBH, *Annual Report*, 1979.

307. "Head Office of Hanover Bank Sold," *New York Times*, August 25, 1981.

308. "New Tower for Republic National Bank," *New York Times*, August 16, 1981.

309. Record of Edmond Safra's Travels in 1981.

310. Anthony Bliss to Edmond Safra, December 15, 1981; Edmond and Lily Safra to Don Regan, September 15 1981. For exhibit, see https://www.nga.gov/exhibitions/1981/ganz.html.

311. Eli Krayem interview.

312. Selim Zeitouni to Edmond Safra, May 20, 1981.

313. William Rosenblum interview.

314. Republic, *Report of Examination*, 1982; TDB Board Meeting, March 31, 1982.

315. TDBH Board Meeting, May 11, 1982.

316. Jeff Keil interview; Dov Schlein interview; Raymond Maggar interview.

317. Meeting of Council of Administration of TDB, May 4, 1982.

318. TDBH Bilan, September 30, 1982.

319. Republic, *Ratio of Foreign Loans to Total Assets*, 1982; Republic, *Annual Report*, 1982; Republic to New York Stock Exchange, January 18, 1983.

320. Robinson quoted in *Financial Times*, January 19, 1983, and in *Vendetta*, 94.

321. Cohen interview; Keil interview; *Financial Times*, January 19, 1983.

322. M. Wetztein to Walter Weiner, et. al., November 23, 1982.

323. William Ollard to Edmond Safra, November 17, 1982; Edmond Safra to William Ollard, November 22, 1982.

324. *Financial Times*, January 19, 1983; *Wall Street Journal*, January 21, 1983; *Vendetta*, 89.

325. *Wall Street Journal*, January 21, 1983; Peter Cohen interview; *Vendetta*, 90.

326. Suzan Pearce interview; Raymond Maggar interview; *Wall Street Journal*, January 21, 1983; Sandy Weill interview.

327. *Vendetta*, 91.

328. *Wall Street Journal*, January 21, 1983.

329. TDB, *Balance Sheet*, December 31, 1982; *Financial Times* "Lex" column, January 19, 1983; Minutes of TDBH board meeting, January 17, 1983.

330. Ernest Ginsberg interview; *Vendetta*, 93–94; *Financial Times*, January 19, 1983; *Wall Street Journal*, January 21, 1983.

331. Ernest Ginsberg interview; Peter Mansbach interview.

332. American Express, press release, January 18, 1983; telex TDB to Edmond Safra, January 20, 1983.

333. *Vendetta*, 98; Jeff Keil interview.

334. *Vendetta*, 95; Jacob Rothschild to Edmond Safra, March 1, 1983.

335. Eli Krayem interview; Isaac Obersi interview.

336. *Vendetta*, 71.

337. Raymond Maggar interview; Rodney Leach to James Robinson, April 15, 1983 and May 19, 1983.

338. Memo, January 28, 1983.

339. Organization Announcement, April 27, 1983.

340. Dov Schlein interview; Peter Cohen interview.

341. Jacques Laoui interview; Michel Cartillier interview; *Vendetta*, 101.

342. Michel Cartillier interview.

343. Edouard Schouela to Edmond Safra, November 28, 1982 and August 18, 1983.

344. James Robinson, memo, August 5, 1983; James Robinson to Lily and Edmond Safra, July 18, 1983; IMF Invitation List, 1983.

345. EF Hutton equity research, October 26, 1983; Sandy Weill interview; John Tamberlane interview.

346. *Vendetta*, 103.

347. James Robinson, memo to management committee, December 21, 1983; Edmond Safra to James Robinson, January 20, 1984.

348. American Express, press release, February 16, 1984; Amendment to American Express contract, February 17, 1984.

349. Charles Teicher to Edmond Safra, April 25, 1984; Edmond Safra to James Robinson, February 29, 1984; Stephen Halsey to Michel Cartillier, July 26, 1984.

350. Jeff Keil interview; Sem Almaleh interview; "AEB Adapts to Life Without Safra," *Euromoney*, May 1985.

351. Roger Junod to François Lugeon, Edmond Safra, and Albert Ben Ezra, June 21, 1984.

352. *Vendetta*, 108.

353. Maurice Antoniades to Edmond Safra, November 14, 1984; telex from Beirut to Ezra Marcos, January 18, 1984.

354. Safrabank, press release, May 4, 1984.

355. *Vendetta*, 107–9.

356. James Robinson, memo, October 23, 1984; *New York Times*, October 23, 1984; *Wall Street Journal*, October 24, 1984.

357. Memo, October 29, 1984.

358. Roger Junod to François Lugeon, December 3, 1984.

359. Roger Junod to Edmond Safra, November 9, 1984.

360. Draft discussion memorandum, July 16, 1987.

361. Edmond Safra to James Robinson, December 11, 1984.

362. "AEB Adapts to Life Without Safra," *Euromoney,* May 1985; Eli Krayem interview.

363. Walter Weiner to Robert Smith, May 29, 1985; *Vendetta,* 122; Ken Cooper interview; Dov Schlein interview; Minos Zombanakis interview.

364. *Los Angeles Times,* June 30, 1985.

365. Eli Krayem interview; "AEB Adapts to Life Without Safra," *Euromoney,* May 1985; *Wall Street Journal,* August 26, 1985.

366. J. Safra Sarasin, *Annual Report,* 2015.

367. Keil quoted in *New York Times,* April 17, 1986.

368. *Wall Street Journal,* August 26, 1985.

369. *The Banker,* April 1985.

370. Memo from Leon Weyer on Republic Luxembourg, October 1, 1986.

371. Memo to Edmond and Lily Safra, unsigned, reference: Summer personnel, Vallauris, 1986.

372. "40 Millions pour une Villa," *Tribune de Genève,* February 28, 1986; *Vendetta,* 4–5.

373. Peter Mansbach interview; Ariel Elia interview; Lily Elia interview.

374. In 1979, Edmond bought his first two Rothkos, "Purple and Black" and "dark red, white, light red on red" at a Sotheby's auction. Letter from Sotheby's Parke Bernet, New York, November 8, 1979; Eduardo Cohen interview; Michel Elia interview; Charles Cator interview; document: "Art collection inventory, Paris apartment, August 11, 1983"; Safra collection listing, 1999.

375. Charles Cator interview; Kenneth Cooper interview.

376. Walter Weiner interview, *New York Times,* August 16, 1981; Greg Donald interview..

377. ISEF Statement of income, 1986; ISEF Newsletter, Spring 1987.

378. Memo from Vincent Funke to file, October 6, 1986; Republic internal publication, January 1987.

379. Republic New York, portfolio risk elements, September 30, 1986.

380. Leigh Robertson interview.

381. Senior Operations Committee, January 22, 1987; Republic, press release, April 30, 1987.

382. Jorge Kiminsberg to Dov Schlein, December 22, 1986.

383. Ezra Zilkha interview.

384. *Crain's New York Business,* January 12, 1987; Jeff Keil to George Ulich, November 11, 1986; "Republic in Brooklyn Bank Deal," *New York Times,* December 25, 1986; Republic, press release, December 31, 1986.

385. *Wall Street Journal,* February 27, 1986; document: Commission fédérale des Banques, 1987, «Chronologie des faits concernant la formation du groupe en

charge de la création de la future Banque RNB Suisse»; document: "TDB seeks to mislead and deceive the commission federal des banque," August 31, 1987.

386. TDB, document to Commission fédérale des banques, October 8, 1987; Memorandum Concernant la TDB à Genève, August 31, 1987.

387. "A Look Inside Republic," *RNB News*, September 1986.

388. Document: Employees Ex-TDB Amex Directly Hired by US; Comptroller of the Currency of the US to Kurt Hauri, Director of Swiss Federal Banking Commission, December 30, 1987; list of assets, August 13, 1987.

389. Ernest Ginsberg to Mark Ewald, July 2, 1986; press release, June 16, 1987.

390. Draft Discussion Memorandum, July 16, 1987; document to Commission fédérale des banques, July 1987; *Vendetta*, 141.

391. Press release, June 16, 1987.

392. Press release, June 16, 1987; "Concerning the Memorandum of Trade Development Bank," August 31, 1987.

393. SA Senior operations committee, July 23, 1987; Republic, press release, November 10, 1987; Senior operations committee, November 19, 1987.

394. Ted Serure interview.

395. Safra Schedule Occupancy Records.

396. Michel Cartillier interview; RNYC Swiss Bank Presentation, 1987.

397. Isaac Obersi interview.

398. *Financial Times*, September 20, 1988.

399. Republic, *Annual Report*, 1988; François Curiel interview; Judah Elmaleh interview; Consolidated Statement, Safra Republic Holdings, November 30, 1988.

400. Albert Manila Nasser interview; Stanley Cayre interview; Peter Cohen interview; Marwan Shakarchi interview.

401. Peter Cohen interview; Ezra Zilkha interview.

402. Peter Mansbach interview; Peter Cohen interview.

403. Walter Weiner interview.

404. "Edmond Safra Targets Geneva," *Institutional Investor*, March 1988.

405. *Vendetta*, 146.

406. *Vendetta*, 155.

407. *Vendetta*, 157–58; Rabb quote, xii.

408. *Vendetta*, 159–74.

409. Walter Weiner interview; George Kiejman interview; Marc Bonnant interview; *Vendetta*, 164–66.

410. Ezy Nasser interview.

411. Peter Mansbach interview; *Vendetta*, 171–72.

412. *Vendetta*, 182–83.

413. *Vendetta*, 188–93.

414. *Vendetta*, 198.

415. Boaz Ben Moshe interview; William Rosenblum interview; Dov Schlein interview.

416. *Vendetta*, 198–99.

417. *Vendetta*, 202–20.

418. Judah Elmaleh interview.

419. *Vendetta*, 251–52.

420. *Vendetta*, 260–68.

421. *Vendetta*, 404.

422. *Vendetta*, 432–36.

423. Republic to Philippe Mottaz, June 30, 1989.

424. Walter Weiner interview; Roger Junod interview; *Vendetta*, 441–42.

425. *Vendetta*, 445.

426. James Robinson to Edmond Safra, July 24, 1989.

427. *Vendetta*, 308, 423–24.

428. Fred Bogart interview; Dov Schlein interview.

429. Republic, *Annual Report*, 1989; "Manhattan Savings Bank, Williamsburgh Announce Merger Plan," *United Press International*, December 18, 1989; "Republic Sets Purchase of Manhattan Savings," *International Herald Tribune*, December 20, 1989.

430. Safra Republic Holdings, *Balance Sheet*, September 30, 1989; Safra Republic Holdings, Newsletter, June 1990.

431. "Dispute over Jewish Cemetery Rages amid Jewish Decline in Egypt," *Los Angeles Times*, February 29, 1990; Clement Soffer interview.

432. Jean Hoss to Pierre Jaans, September 11, 1990.

433. Nina Weiner to Lily and Edmond Safra, August 14, 1990.

434. William Park to Marc Bonnant, August 14, 1991; Anne Vitale interview; *Vendetta*, xi.

435. Edmond Safra interview with *Finanz und Wirtschaft*, September 10, 1990.

436. Republic, *Annual Report*, 1990; Safra Republic Holdings, press release, September 11, 1990.

437. Roger Junod to US Controller of the Currency, November 30, 1989.

438. Edmond Safra interview with Anne M. Hegge-Lederman, editor of *Finanz und Wirtschaft*, September 10, 1990.

439. *Jerusalem Post*, September 1990.

440. Yehuda Levi interview.

441. Yehuda Levi to Edmond Safra, November 16, 1990; *Israel Commercial Economic Newsletter,* November 23, 1990.

442. Shlomo Piotrkowski interview; Yehuda Levi interview; FIBI, press release, May 14, 1991.

443. Shlomo Piotrkowski interview.

444. Anne Vitale interview.

445. *Vendetta,* 463.

446. *Vendetta,* 465–67.

447. *Vendetta,* 468.

448. Marc Bonnant interview.

449. *New York Times,* April 28, 1992; Elie Elalouf interview.

450. Clement Soffer interview; Marcos Zalta interview; Hillel Davis interview.

451. Jeff Keil interview.

452. *Investment Dealer's Digest,* November 23, 1992; *Wall Street Journal,* November 12, 1992; Peter Cohen interview.

453. Presentation to Banks, Counterparties, and Analysts, June 1993.

454. Ken Cooper interview; Dov Schlein interview; Sandy Koifman interview.

455. Leslie Bains interview.

456. Republic, *Proxy,* March 16, 1994.

457. Bill Segal interview; Moshe Nissim interview.

458. Lily Elia interview.

459. Yigal Arnon interview.

460. Peter Cohen to Edmond Safra, April, 22, 1994; report by Mark Alpert, CFA, May 5, 1994; Republic 10-Q, second quarter, 1994; Sol Gindi interview.

461. Republic, news release, April 20, 1994; Republic, *Proxy,* March 16, 1994.

462. Republic 10-K, 1993; Fred Bogart interview.

463. BCN Beirut, telex to Ezra Marcos, October 19, 1994; Republic to Swiss Consulate in Damascus, January 12, 1995.

464. "Syrian Rabbi Reaches Israel via N.Y.," *Washington Post,* October 19, 1994.

465. Clement Soffer interview.

466. Ken Cooper interview.

467. Sandy Koifman interview.

468. David Joory/Ariel Arazi interview.

469. Ariel Elia interview; Samuel Elia interview; Lily Safra interview.

470. Roger Junod interview.

471. Eli Krayem interview.

472. Thomas Robards interview.

473. John Tamberlane interview; Jim Morice interview.

474. Vivette Ancona interview; Phil Burgess interview.

475. Joseph De Paolo interview; Fred Bogart interview; Shlomo Piotrkowski interview; Republic, 1999, 10-K.

476. Republic, Third Quarter 1995, 10-Q; Republic, 1996, 10-K.

477. David Joory/Ariel Arazi interview.

478. Bill Browder interview.

479. "The Money Plane," *New York*, January 22, 1996; Henry Kravis interview.

480. Dov Schlein interview.

481. Ezra Marcos to BCN, November 25, 1996; Sol Gindi interview.

482. Sol Gindi interview; Andrew Pucher interview.

483. "Nick and Christian Candy Renovate a Penthouse in Monte Carlo," *Architectural Digest*, June 19, 2017; Safra Collection Report, January 16, 1997; Teddy Kollek to Edmond Safra, May 13, 1996.

484. Alberto Muchnick interview.

485. Peter Kimmelman interview.

486. Rodney Leach interview; Dov Schlein interview; Alberto Muchnick interview.

487. David and Gabriel Elia interview; Ariel Elia interview.

488. Steve Saali interview; "Just in Time for the Millennium: An Issue of 1,000-Year Bonds," *New York Times*, October 8, 1997.

489. Adriana Elia interview; Ariel Elia interview.

490. Edmond Safra video script, November 3, 1997; Safra Event: Program for Evening, November 9, 1997; Sophie Nadell interview.

491. David and Gabriel Elia interview.

492. Republic, 1997, 10-K.

493. Marcos Zalta interview.

494. Republic, press release, July 2, 1998.

495. Dov Schlein interview.

496. Ernest Ginsberg interview.

497. Marc Bonnant interview.

498. Anthony Brittan interview.

499. Ron Wilson interview; Dov Schlein interview.

500. *New York Times*, December 3, 1999; Marc Bonnant to Etienne Leandri, January 6, 2000; *Times of London*, January 6, 2000.

501. Sandy Koifman interview.

502. Sol Gindi interview; Ariel Arazi interview.

503. Lily Elia interview; Ariel Elia interview.

504. Republic, press release, December 16, 1998.

505. Republic, *Annual Report*, 1998.

506. Simon Alouan interview.

507. Jean-Pierre Jacquemoud interview.

508. Marcos Zalta interview; Sem Almaleh interview.

509. Republic, First Quarter 1999, 10-Q.

510. Marc Bonnant interview.

511. Anonymous interview.

512. Anthony Brittan interview; Anne Vitale interview.

513. HSBC, *Annual Report*, 1998.

514. John Bond interview.

515. Dov Schlein interview, Kenneth Cooper interview.

516. Dov Schlein interview.

517. John Bond interview.

518. Republic, SEC filing, May 10, 1999, https://www.sec.gov/Archives
/edgar/data/83246/0000083246-99-000003.txt.

519. Trevor Robinson interview; "HSBC to Pay $10.3 Billion for Republic," *New
York Times*, May 11, 1999.

520. Jeff Keil interview.

521. Ariel Arazi interview; Anita Smaga interview.

522. Edmond Safra to Republic employees, May 10, 1999.

523. Anthony Brittan interview; John Bond interview.

524. Ted Serure interview; François Curiel interview; Joseph Safra interview.

525. Alessandro Di Rocco comments.

526. Rabbi Haim Pinto interview.

527. Phil Burgess interview; Anne Vitale interview.

528. "Fund Adviser Indicted in $3 Billion Fraud Case," *New York Times*, October
1, 1999; Republic New York, Third Quarter 1999, 10-Q.

529. John Bond interview.

530. HSBC, press release, November 9, 1999.

531. Sol Gindi interview; David Joory/Ariel Arazi interview.

532. George Kiejman interview; John Bond interview.

533. Michelle Nasser interview.

534. Lily Elia interview; Anthony Brittan interview; Dov Schlein interview; Adriana Elia interview; David Joory/Ariel Arazi interview.

535. Shmulik Cohen letter, January 22, 2001; Shmulik Cohen; Minutes of Witness Testimony, January 26, 2000.

536. The narrative in this section relies on several detailed court documents, testimonies, expert witness reports, Judgments, arguments, and rulings. Among the key documents are Minutes of Ted Maher's interview on December 6, 1999; Report of Olivier Jude, Chief Inspector (Police) for Monaco, July 5, 2000; "Minutes of Cross-Examination," July 25, 2001; Decision for an Indictment, Principality of Monaco Court of Appeal, June 18, 2002; Judgment of February 6, 2003," Court of Revision; and Detailed chronology, Procedure Penale, Part 1.

537. Decision for an Indictment, Principality of Monaco Court of Appeal, June 18, 2002; Henri Viellard, Expert Report, May 5, 2000; Ted Maher, Minutes 991206, Report of Olivier Jude, Chief Inspector (Police) for Monaco, July 5, 2000.

538. Ted Maher, Minutes, December 6, 1999.

539. Detailed chronology, Procedure Penale, Part 1; document, December 3, 1999: Les Heures Cles.

540. Detailed chronology, Procedure Penale, Part 1.

541. Testimony of Shmulik Cohen, December 3, 1999.

542. Testimonies of Shmulik Cohen, Mrs. Lily Safra, Police Officer Gilbert Garcia; Detailed chronology, Procedure Penale, Part 1; Shmulik Cohen, Minutes of Witness Testimony, February 21, 2000; Decision for an Indictment, Principality of Monaco Court of Appeal, June 18, 2002.

543. *Veja*, December 8, 1999; Testimonies of Police Officer Jean Marc Farca and Police Officer Serge Giet; Detailed chronology, Procedure Penale, Part 1; Decision for an Indictment, Principality of Monaco Court of Appeal, June 18, 2002.

544. Testimonies of Shmulik Cohen, Police Officer Alain Van Den Corput; Detailed chronology, Procedure Penale, Part 1.

545. Decision for an Indictment, Principality of Monaco Court of Appeal, June 18, 2002; Minutes 991203; Report of Gilbert Garcia, Divisional Inspector (Police) for Monaco; Testimony of Sonia Casiano; Detailed chronology, Procedure Penale, Part 2.

546. Trevor Robinson interview; Sol Gindi interview.

547. *New York Daily News*, December 5, 1999.

548. Marcos Zalta interview; Ariel Arazi interview.

549. Minutes, Oliver Jude interview with Ted Maher, December 6, 1999; Decision for an Indictment, Principality of Monaco Court of Appeal, June 18, 2002.

550. *Revue juive de Geneve*, December 24, 1999.

551. François Curiel interview.

552. SEC filing, January 10, 2000. https://www.sec.gov/Archives/edgar
/data/83246/000090342300000022/0000903423-00-000022.txt

553. Ted Maher, Minutes, December 6, 1999.

554. Principality of Monaco Criminal Tribunal, Judgment of December 2,
2002; Principality of Monaco Court of Revision, "Judgment of February 6,
2003."

555. Principality of Monaco Criminal Tribunal, Judgment of December 2,
2002; Principality of Monaco Court of Revision, "Judgment of February 6,
2003."

556. Statutes are found in document, "The concerns, values, and ideals held by
Edmond J. Safra during his lifetime". The list of projects the Foundation has
supported can be seen at its website: https://www.edmondjsafra.org/.

꒛ INDEX ꒜

Edmond J. Safra is the subject of this biography and references to him occur throughout. To make it easy to find references to Edmond J. Safra in the index, entries and subentries abbreviate his name as EJS. The book also frequently mentions Edmond's wife Lily Safra. In subentries, she is identified simply as Lily.